What You Should Know

About the

UNITED STATES CONSTITUTION

and the

BILL OF RIGHTS

DR. JOHN COLEMAN

Library of Congress Cataloging-in-Publication Data

Coleman, Dr. John, 1935-
What You Should Know About the
U.S. Constitution and The Bill of Rights

p. cm.
Includes bibliographical references

ISBN 1-893157-03-2

1. Constitutional law — United States — Popular works. 2. United
States Constitution 1st-10th Amendments — Popular works.
3. Conspiracies — United States. 4. Communism — United States.

I. Title.
KF4550.Z9C573 1999
342.73'02--dc21   98-46488
                                                                        CIP

Published by
BRIDGER HOUSE PUBLISHERS, INC
P.O. Box 2208, Carson City, NV 89702, 1-800-729-4131

Cover design by The Right Type
Printed in the United States of America
10 9 8 7 6 5 4 3 2 1

TABLE OF CONTENTS

FORWARD

Statement of Intent and Purpose:
Why The United States Needs a Constitution and Bill of Rights.

James Madison, "The Federalist, No. 51:"
"...In framing a government which is to be administered by men over men, the great difficulty lies in this: you must first enable the government to control the governed; and in the next place oblige it to control itself. A dependence on the people is, no doubt, the primary control on government; but experience has taught mankind the necessity of auxiliary precautions."

The Founding Fathers wrote the Constitution and the Bill of Rights for that exact purpose.

The neglect of the study of the U.S. Constitution and the Bill of Rights is one of the most appalling developments in education in the United States in the last one hundred years. That it is by deliberate design, is without question. Today, the Constitution is not taught in schools, it is not taught in a fitting manner in our colleges, universities, or in our law schools. Even the most prestigious law schools devote scant attention to this priceless national treasure. Quoting from a statement made by Dr. John Tiggert, United States Commissioner of Education, October 1924:

"I do not believe that there are more than a very limited number of persons, perhaps a 100, who really know what is in the Constitution of the United States."

Quoting from a report made to the Committee on American Citizenship on the occasion of a meeting of the American Bar Association (ABA) at Denver, Colorado, on July 14-16, 1926:

"Lawyers are being graduated from our law schools by the thousands who have little or no knowledge of the Constitution. When organizations seek a lawyer to instruct them on the Constitution they find it nearly impossible to secure one competent."

To which we may add that since 1926 the situation has worsened; today in 1997 one would be hard-put to find even one hundred out of hundreds of thousands of lawyers who know anything beyond their ability to recite the various clauses and amendments. The rest know very little of it, because they have not studied the fountainhead of knowledge of the Constitution; the Annals of Congress, the Congressional Globes and the Congressional Records.

Pages 100-103 Congressional Globe, May 20, 1870, the Hon. S.N. Arnell of Tennessee speaking:

"Education makes the man; that alone is the parent of every virtue, it is the most sacred, the most useful, and at the same time, the most neglected thing in every country." Arnell was quoting the works of Montesquieus, considered by many to be the father of the U.S. Constitution.

It is a national disaster that the Constitution, the knowledge of which is "most sacred, the parent of every virtue" is at the same time the most neglected in education in America. There has to be a national drive to restore the Constitution to its former preeminent position. For this we need to form a movement I suggest might be called, "Defenders of The Constitution" who will pledge themselves to stand up to and repel the appalling onslaught against the Constitution and the Bill of Rights.

If this nation is lost, as was the glory of Rome, it will be because of our neglect of the study of the Constitution and the Bill of Rights and our failure as a nation to restore its priceless truths to their rightful place of honor in the halls of learning, and once again, make it the supreme law of the land in the Congress, the White House and the Supreme Court.

It is our duty to make all men obey the Constitution, and if they will not, then it is our duty to depose them by constitutional means and to fight relentless battles to put in their places men who are dedicated to serving God and country, which means that such men must uphold the Constitution and the Bill of Rights and never, ever, deviate from them.

The United States must be allowed to fulfill the special destiny allotted to it; we must continue to stand unique among the nations of the world. We need to bring forth leaders in the mold of King Alfred and Oliver Cromwell; leaders who will brook no attacks on the Constitution and the Bill of Rights. When the plutocrats have gone too far in alienating and undermining the Constitution and the Bill of Rights, perverting our culture, our social patterns, and our religious principles, then they must be forced to retreat through our most ferocious acts of resistance. Then must the Defenders of the Constitution rise up and fight a relentless battle to end the designs of the oppressors, who hate the freedom bestowed upon the individual citizen by the Constitution and the Bill of Rights.

We must rout out the degenerate beast of "democracy" which is souring and soiling this nation. The United States of America is not a democracy, it is a Confederated Republic. Democracy did NOT spring from Christian social thinking, rather, democracy sprang from the French Revolution. The character of democracy is essentially totalitarian, bestial in character, a swindle of the people, which allows them the luxury of believing in equality where none exists, and that their voices are being heard, when they are not.

"What You Don't Know About The U.S. Constitution," would not be accepted by any of the establishment publishing houses for the simple reason that they are under the control of secret societies that control all books, newspapers and magazine published in the U.S. The secret governments of Britain and the U.S. operate principally through publishing houses, large and small. They are the guardians of Freemasonry who are steeped in the arts of control. Planting more than one story to create disinformation, is one of their most skilled arts, of which the Kennedy assassination is pretty typical; so many versions are put out in order to cast doubt on them all. The processing of humanity is their goal.

Against all of the techniques of our would-be slavemasters, we need no more than the U.S. Constitution and the Bill of Rights to preserve the integrity of the nation in order to defeat their complex web of deceit. Our people have been poisoned by "democracy;" by "tolerance;" by "brotherly love;" by "internationalism;" by "compromise" — all of which doctrines are straight out of the Communist Manifesto of 1848.

It is not the intention of this book to recite the sections, clauses and amendments to the Constitution and the Bill of Rights, mainly because what I call their "ABCs" are already known by many Americans. My intention is to concentrate on what is not known about the Constitution and the Bill of Rights, which comes only from diligent study of the Annals of Congress, the Congressional Globes and the Congressional Records. Nevertheless, I will include herein, something of the history of the Constitution and its various sections as a general guide.

My hope and my prayer is that "What You Don't Know About The Constitution" will help to turn this nation away from the evils mentioned above and toward a restoration of our traditional faith in God and our U.S. Constitution. We have no alternative but to seize the reins of power from the hands of the masters of the secret societies who are taking us on a pathway of steep decline toward a dictatorship of the One World Government — New World Order, so evil and barbaric, that we can never begin to even imagine what it will be like to live under such a system. Let this book be our guide to seizing the nettle and uprooting it, while there is yet time.

A short history of the background of the Constitution and the Bill of Rights.

It is generally recognized that the early settlers emigrated to the American continent with the purpose of escaping a strong state government. In the countries they left behind them, Mercantilism was related to totalitarianism — and in this regard — little has changed. The colonists threw off the yoke of a strong state; they rebelled against authority in the typical Irish tradition, whether in religious or economic realms. They did not like Mercantilism, which in their minds related closely to state power, and conditions of near-slavery, which the American Revolution eventually severed.

The England from whence many of the colonists came held no place for the landless, for the working class, was a society in turbulence trying to escape medievalism. Class was rigid. Harrison contended that "there are those born to rule" and those "to be ruled and not rule others." All men who worked with their hands, i.e. manual laborers, were strictly governed in their labors and their travel restricted by the Statute of Artificers. And if work failed, they were to be subjected to the rule of the parish overseers.

Those men not already artisans or apprentices, were subject to a life of agricultural labor on the demand of those who needed such labor and their wages, hours of work, and service conditions, subject to a fixed law, enforced by the landowners, backed by justices of the peace who were largely appointed by gentleman of class. If a laborer would not accept a job as an agricultural laborer, he was more than likely whipped or sent to prison. A laborer could not go where he pleased, because his movement was circumscribed by laws against vagrancy and restrictive laws as to where he might live. They were classed as "rabble" and "vagabonds," full of "tricks" and "dodges."

(The foregoing is taken from William Harrison's "An Historical Description of the Island of Britain, With a Brief Description of the Nature and Qualities of the People of England" published in 1586 and found in the British Museum, London. The spelling is as in the original document.)

On top of such injustices, it was the general belief among many in the Parliament that to be unemployed was a great social evil — this in the face of the manifested dreadful shortages of jobs: "To begin with, the laboring poor, they are indeed the Grievance of the Nation, and there seems an absolute Necessity to bring them by severe regulations, to some State of Immediate Subordination. The English laborer, in short, is incurably idle and wickedly improvident. He will work till he has a few shillings in his pocket, which he proceeds to squander at once in the ale house."

"The female part of the servant class carries an impudence even further than the male, for she not only demands exorbitant wages, but decks herself out in finery to the confusion of honest strangers. A Gentleman in a Visit lately at a House of Good Fashion, who being recommended to one of the Gentleman's Daughters, mistook the Chambermaid for her who was designed for his Mistress, and unhappily stepping up to her, saluted her first, which Misfortune cost him the loss of his Mistress." The poor were never allowed to forget that they were the servants and laws were recommended to keep the workman in his place who should no more be allowed to leave his place of work, than a soldier be allowed to desert in battle.

(Taken from papers found in the British Museum, London, written by Daniel Defoe, an avowed supporter of mercantilism and a condemner of the poor — the works, " The Giving of Alms No Charity" and "The Shortest Way with Dissenters." The spelling is exactly as it appears in these publications.)

If anything could characterize the England from which the "laboring class" sought to escape with its overcrowding, a woeful lack of jobs, brutally low wages, restrictive laws, etc., then Defoe's writings paint the best picture of the condition that I could find which precipitated emigration to America. On top of that, the laboring, landless, people — the unemployed — which Archbishop Laud called "the mob" — had to contend with the "Divine Right of Kings". William Laud was the Archbishop of Canterbury, and a King's Privy Counseller. Against the Puritans he turned this "right" into a sword, issuing a new prayer book and touring the country. In 1633, to enforce the right of the King as head of state, with powers from God, Laud demanded that for a Parliament to be loyal, it should never thwart the will of the King. Archbishop Laud also declared as official policy that any independence from the King was against the will of God, and those practitioners of it would suffer eternal damnation.

(The above information is taken from "Laud's Works Vol. I, Oxford 1847" found in the British Museum in London, one being a "Sermon On King James' Birthday, 1621" and "Sermon Before King Charles' Second Parliament, 1625." The Long Parliament eventually put an end to Laud by finding him guilty of treason.)

Thus it came to pass that having suffered under totalitarianism, the colonists wanted a system of government with strictly limited powers. They remained suspicious of all authority that was tied to government and for this reason they later chose a system that would severely limit government power. The colonists in the thick of the American Revolution held fast to this principle; they would not yield power unless it was accompanied by a Bill of Rights. We should realize from this that the Constitution was not written for government but for the people as a means of preserving their sovereign integrity.

Jefferson and Jackson led the fight in the federal arena and carried it into the states — virtually different, separate, individual, independent, countries. The French Revolution did nothing to break the power of the central government except to move it into the hands of even more ruthless tyrants. Only in the United States were the central and state governments compelled to recognize and respect the sovereign right vested in the people, in the individual citizen. This represented a shattering of privileges and a complete departure from the old ways of Europe.

One of the ways in which the sovereignty of the individual in the thirteen colonies was strengthened, was the division of government into three separate and distinct entities, each with its own responsibilities which were not to be transferred between them, nor be usurped one by the other. This stroke of genius was the work of Pelatiah Webster of Lebanon, Connecticut, a graduate from Yale, who moved to Philadelphia in 1755. In those days, Yale graduates were few and far between, so Webster's achievement in graduating was noteworthy. His dissertation about a congress divided into upper and lower houses was taken up by Alexander Hamilton, James Madison, and Charles Pinckney of South Carolina and out of this, the Constitution grew and the Bill of Rights was added.

The three entities were called the legislative, executive and judicial branches. Some will have it that these three divisions have equal powers, but that is a notion not borne out in the Annals of Congress, the Congressional Globes and the Congressional Records. The judiciary is not even co-equal with the Congress, which can, if it wishes, refuse to fund either the executive or the judiciary. Congress can overturn any acts of the judiciary, and the Constitution has made certain that the powers of the executive would not enable a president to "stand where kings stood."

The way in which the powers are separated has been an anathema to power-seeking individuals and they have chafed under its restrictions, ever seeking to circumvent the limits placed upon their power, which as Daniel Boone once said, must be bound with chains. The struggle goes on, with evil men fighting hard to whittle away at the Constitution and the Bill of Rights to give more power to government and rob the people of their sovereignty. Man has always sought to enslave and dominate his fellow men. The Constitution and the Bill of Rights were specifically designed to prevent such a calamity.

The colonists — a body of people in a fixed location — a colony in a foreign country — were determined not to allow any one man or government to have dominion over them. The original fixed location was Jamestown, Virginia, begun in 1607, and this was followed by twelve other colonies along the Eastern seaboard of the America. The original 13 colonies brought with them their own common law, consisting of the best of English common law. The men of the 13 colonies opted to keep their common law, which dated back to the common law of the very first Anglo-Saxon kings and up to the Norman invasion of England.

King Alfred was one of those who held common law in high esteem, yet today, his role in history has been relegated to the tale of a king who burned some cakes. But in reality, King Alfred was a staunch defender of common law. He translated Bede's "Historia Orosius" and Buthius' "Consollato" and it was he who set the basis of Anglo Saxon sovereignty upon which our Founding Fathers later drew:

"There is only one way to build any kingdom, and that is on the sure and certain foundation of Faith in Jesus Christ, and Jesus Christ crucified and it is on that foundation that I intend to build my kingdom," Alfred stated after battling the invasion of England by the Danes.

Who were the settlers? For the most part they came from England to escape the persecution of the Stuart kings. There were squires, countrymen, middle class Englishmen, but the bulk were those who were bound for life by English law to never being able to improve their lot. They settled in Massachusetts, Connecticut, Maryland, Virginia and the Carolinas, some 70,000 between 1607-1640, while 150,000 Scots-Irish and 75,000 Germans came between 1720-1770. Dutch colonists settled in New York, the Huguenots in the Carolinas while the English Quakers settled in Pennsylvania.

The Colonists were still tied to England with all of its restrictions on individual freedom and taxation. This led to stiff resistance by the colonists and eventually to a rebellion by the thirteen colonies against King George III. The thirteen colonies were united in this endeavor. By 1750 the spirit of rebellion was in the air, brought about in some instances by men like John Mayhew who said inter-alia that it was the duty of the colonist states to rebel.

By 1770 there were several large towns, with churches of only the Christian faith. There were no other religions in practice and the Anglican Church was established in Virginia, Maryland, New York, North Carolina, South Carolina and Georgia. The German Lutheran Church was also firmly established as were many other offshoots and sects of the Anglican Church, but the important point to remember is that they were all Christian churches. The fallacy of "Separation of Church and State" and "religious freedom" meaning freedom for all non-Christian religions to have equal place with Christianity, grew out of the judiciary trying to legislate. A look back at the period shows that far from erecting a "wall of separation" between church and state, the Founding Fathers were only making sure that no one branch of the CHRIST-IAN religion dominated the other, or, became the church of the state. All else is fantasy and the product of the vivid imaginations of those with no grounding in the Constitution and determined to undermine it.

Thus it came about that on September 5, 1774, representatives of the colonies met in the First Continental Congress at Philadelphia to adopt a Declaration of Rights and Grievances and submitted the declaration to the King. When scant notice was paid to the demands of the thirteen colonies by the King, a second Continental Congress was convened on May 10, 1775, which appointed John Hancock of Massachusetts as the president. The Congress voted to resist George III and to this end they raised an army and the Second Congress then called Colonel George Washington into service as the commander in chief of the armed forces on June 3, 1775.

On July 4, 1776, Congress moved to formally adopt the Declaration of Independence. When the Constitutional Convention met in Philadelphia in 1787, some of the best brains and most distinguished men in the country were assembled. These men were not the country yokels of liberal mythology and downright deception. In fact they were the exact opposite and at least 200 years ahead of their time. Unfortunately, 200 years later, we have not a single politician able to come anywhere near the stature of those delegates.

Their studies of the science of government left them masters of the subject; they were men of the highest ability and integrity beside which the members of the Clinton administration look exactly like what they are; garbage collectors and disseminators. They would never have tolerated a Clinton, Dodd, Kennedy, Glenn, or Ickes, among them. These builders of the Constitution were men of the highest integrity and honor. The sleazy conduct of the current Democrat White House would have nauseated them.

Twenty five of the delegates were college graduates, which may not mean as much today as it did then, but we have to bear in mind that colleges were few and far between, education expensive and it took tenacity of purpose to stay the course. More than half of the delegates had served in the military, many with distinguished service records. There were no slackers or dodgers among them. A substantial number of the delegates had served in the Continental Congress. Their professions varied from physicians, merchants, lawyers, financiers, planters, soldiers, judges and statesmen, a profession that has died off in these days of corruption, where swindlers spend their time seeking ways to circumvent the Constitution.

The delegates were men of great character, exceptional ability and natural strength, all attributes necessary to produce the second greatest written document in the world, second only to the Bible. The oldest was 81-years old Benjamin Franklin and the youngest, at 26 years, Jonathan Dayton. The average age of the delegates was 43 years. These truly great men met to discuss their differences and iron out a statement of intent which provided the greatest and longest-serving constitution in the world. Would to God that He would again raise up men of this caliber so that the fruits of their works may forever remain the highest law of the land.

Their tremendous devotion to duty, their great integrity, their courage, their honesty, should make us a proud nation when we consider that their work was done outside of the law of England which still pertained to them. Here they were, a group of rebels, busy transmuting themselves into an organ of government. In 1787 the great French writer, Robert Jacques Turgot, in a lengthy review of the American Revolution, wrote thusly:

"...It is impossible not to wish ardently that this people may attain to all the prosperity of which they are capable. They are the hope of the world. They may become a model to it. They may prove by fact that men can be free and yet tranquil; and that it is in their power to rescue themselves from the chains in which tyrants and knaves of all descriptions have presumed to bind them under the pretense of public good."

"They may exhibit an example of political liberty, of religious liberty, of commercial liberty and of industry. The asylum they open to the oppressed of nations should console the earth. The ease with which the injured may escape from oppressive governments will compel Princes to become just and cautious; and the rest of the world will gradually open their eyes to the empty illusions with which they have hitherto been cheated by politicians."

It is against this priceless heritage that the men of the One World Government — New World Order hurl themselves in their ceaseless quest to destroy it. In this I count the Democrat Party led by a man in the person of William Jefferson Clinton, seemingly dedicated to compromising, breaking down and tearing up the documents that guarantee what Turgot called, "political liberty, of religious liberty, of commercial liberty and of industry," but most of all, our personal freedoms and liberties which are now under such deadly attack.

In February, 1787 the Congress asked the states to send delegates to Philadelphia for the purpose of amending the Articles of Confederation. The framers of the Constitution did their work with skill that would floor most of the members of Congress, today. Their debating skills were wondrous to behold and from that Convention emerged a national union which became the prototype of the United States of America.

Space does not permit me to continue to expand on this brief history of what has gone before. I hope that what I have given will be sufficient to cause the dying embers of our national pride to once more burst into the flames of a new American Revolution against the sycophants of the One World Government — New World Order who daily, strive to stamp out those embers. In this regard, I refer once more to these leaders of the anti-Constitution, anti-American, Communist faction led by William Jefferson Clinton.

There is a tendency today for ministers of churches to exhort their congregations to obey government and to respect them. We often hear prayers for a wise government. That is all to the good, but today in 1999 we find a government so corrupt in certain areas, it is impossible to obey. The sermon delivered by Jonathon Mayhew in Boston in 1750 confirms this.

"It is blasphemy to call tyrants and oppressors, God's ministers, but such as are just, ruling in fear of God. When once magistrates act contrary to their office and the end of their institution; when they rob and ruin the public, instead of being guardians of its peace and welfare; they immediately cease to be the ordinance and ministers of God, and no more deserve that glorious character, than common pirates and highwaymen..."

How amazing that something written in 1750 be so perfect a reflection of the state of government in the United States as we near the end of the 20th century!

CHAPTER 1

THE RISE OF COMMUNISM IN THE UNITED STATES

A most deadly virus is threatening the United States and that virus is Socialism which the great Frederic Bastiat described as a branch of the tree of Communism. Hardly a day goes by in the life of the Clinton administration that does not confirm in indisputable terms Clinton's commitment to socializing America, which follows closely Franklin D. Roosevelt's Communist blueprint. The intent and purpose of this chapter is to shed light on the role played by the Democrat Party, and before that, the Radical Republicans who infiltrated Pres. Abraham Lincoln's cabinet.

Just how far down the road of the goal of a Socialist United States leading to a Communist United States this nation has already travelled is expressed. It leads to the conclusion that since 1912, the engine driving the nation down the tracks toward Communism is the Democrat Party.

For those who are familiar with the Bolshevik Revolution, it should come as no surprise that the USSR owed its founding and growth to the United States and Great Britain, and particularly, to British Intelligence MI6, backed by the U.S. State Department, President Wilson and President Roosevelt and bankrolled by Lord Alfred Milner and the Wall Street bankers. The cast of characters is as long as their bottomless deviousness; Milner gave Lenin £60 million in gold sovereigns and the U.S. gave Trotsky an open platform from which to preach his hatred for Christian Russia, and an American passport, to which he was absolutely not entitled. Jacob Schiff gave Lenin a gift of $20 million, and most Wall Street banks kicked in with large sums of money to get the revolution going in Russia.

What is not generally known by the American public is that the Bolshevik Revolution was to be the curtain raiser for the final act; the Communizing of the United States of America and supplanting the U.S. Constitution and the Bill of Rights with the Communist Manifesto of 1848. The sedition and treason committed against the United States by the State Department, Wilson and Roosevelt, was what ensured the success of the Bolshevik Revolution in Russia. And what ensured its success in the United States was the same key element; treason against the United States by the internal enemies of the Constitution and the Bill of Rights which treason continues today under the guidance of a Communist more subtle than either Wilson or Roosevelt, but far more dangerous, President William Jefferson Clinton.

Communism will triumph when its disguised version, the One World Government of the New World Order, overwhelms the United States. There are volumes of evidence to support the foregoing conclusion, but as this book is not about Communism per se, but rather about its effects upon the U.S. Constitution and the Bill of Rights, we must leave the subject of the Bolshevizing of the United States, which has taken the form of creeping Socialism, and pass on to its effects upon the legal system of this nation.

By now it is fairly common knowledge that creeping Socialism took root as the Federal Reserve Act; the Income Tax Act; the United Nations treaty/agreement(?), sending American troops to participate in wars outside of its national geographical boundaries; breaking down of morality and family values; opposition to Christianity; the introduction of homosexuality and lesbianism and their advent into the open public life of government; direct attacks on the U.S. Constitution and the Bill of Rights. These are but a few of scores of objectives already reached by the Socialist/Marxist/Communists in America.

There is no substitute for learning about the Bolshevik's determined efforts to overwhelm the United States. Since Bolshevism began in the United States, it is logical to suppose that it will not cease its activities unless and until the United States falls victim to it. While it will not be a "big bang" like the Bolshevik Revolution, its insidious slow poison is working inside our nation with even deadlier effect that if we were to be invaded by a Communist army. The tragedy of America is that our leaders do not read the Annals of Congress, the Congressional Globe and the Congressional Record, and with a few exceptions, have never done so. This great tragedy has resulted in an ongoing destruction of our Constitution and the Bill of Rights, which began slowly in the runup to the Civil War, the Civil War and post Civil War; Reconstruction era, from whence it was catapulted into government programs in the 1920s and 1930s.

Had members of the Federal judiciary, State, local judiciary and members of the Congress, been obliged to complete a minimum of five years of mandatory study of the Annals of Congress, Congressional Globes and Congressional Records, this disintegrating Bolshevik-inspired rot, could not have set in. Even a reading of the great debates of the "Golden Age" of the U.S. Constitution 1880-1900, if nothing else, would have been enough to turn back the Communist onslaught against our nation. Of course the Bolsheviks knew that, hence the reason why proper teaching of the U.S. Constitution and the Bill of Rights was efficiently scrubbed from our education syllabuses in schools and universities, and our law schools. Today few citizens know and understand it, even while they recite by rote its enormous benefits which their grandchildren will never be allowed to enjoy, unless and until a great revival whirlwind rushes over this land, even as it did with God's servant, Moody.

But the problem today, in 1999, is that we have no equivalent of Moody in the political ranks of the nation; there are no real leaders of our Christian heritage. No giant of political genius like George Washington has thus far come forward to stop the Communist rot and return our nation to the course and the character set for it by the Founding Fathers. Meanwhile our leaders of both political parties in the Congress are blown hither and thither and in every direction by the winds of change of the Communist Manifesto of 1848. Some examples are the Republican Party's monstrous violation of the Constitution in "granting" the President powers to which he is absolutely not entitled, and voting with the Socialists to strengthen the Communist Manifesto of 1848 planks of gun control, abortion, continuing membership of the U.N., and in voting for the long-planned destruction of our trade through NAFTA and GATT.

One can only be amazed and greatly alarmed at the behavior of Sen.

Trent Lott, the leader of the Republican Party in the Senate, who attacks his own Defense Department for enforcing its rules of conduct for its officers! Can he not see that by integrating women in the U.S. military, the Communists took a giant step forward toward their goal of destroying the morale of our armed forces? Is Senator Trent Lott, blind, deaf and dumb?

The 1997 government of Mr. Clinton has nothing to offer but complete spoliation and utter destruction of this nation, yet thus far, his game plan on behalf of his Communist masters, is not discernible to the American people! Mr. Clinton is busy binding the American people with the chains of despotism; and his administration will go down in history as the Communist group that bound the American people with chains of slavery! Yet, for all of this, historians will remark that the dictator remained popular with his captives right up to the very moment that he delivered them, like Samson, bound hand and foot to their tormentors and Slave Masters.

A lot of sophistry and cunning has gone into the Communizing of America, and the current tenant of the White House is well-versed in the arts of sophistry and deception and he is plying his trade with enough cunning and skill to ensure that he out-does Wilson and Roosevelt. He works night and day to turn the flank of the U.S. Constitution and the bill of Rights to the maximum advantage of his masters. Judicial usurpation, which has expanded under his administration is more dangerous than outright attacks on the law of the land. Our Republican Constitution was written to prevent the U.S. falling victim to the cunning of the "secret" Communists but as we near the end of the 20th century, we have no leaders like Washington, Jefferson, St. George Tucker who will fight to stem the foul tide of Communism sweeping away the fruits of the American Revolution. We are losing the battle against Communism because the vast majority of the American people simply do not want to recognize that the Communists are engaged in war to the finish with the United States.

One of the ways in which the Clinton administration is delivering telling blows against the Constitution and the Bill of Rights is by Congress not debating bills in the proper, constitutional manner. This has opened the door to dedicated Communists as well as plain and simple constitutional ignoramuses to introduce bills for consideration when such bills could never meet the test of constitutionality. The Republicans are not above criticism, in this regard, for only on rare occasions do they constitutionally debate their bills, and we need to remind ourselves that except for Republican support, such grotesque measures as "fast track," "line item veto," NAFTA and GATT — to name but a few constitutionally-deformed monstrosities — would not have passed into "law." In each case Republican votes turned the tide in favor of dishonoring and soiling the Constitution.

Being true to a Republican government, has been missing from both parties since the 1880s. The glaring difference between the new politics of the 1990s and those of the 1880s is that the current crop of legislators don't know the Constitution and this becomes obvious when one studies the debates in the Congress of the Golden Age, 1880-1900, and what passes for debate in the 1990s. It is this gap in our defense against the enemies of our nation, particularly the Communists in Washington, that has been widened until today, our enemies are pouring through the breach and flinging themselves against the Constitution and the Bill of Rights. With the departure of such constitutional stalwarts Goldwater and Ervin, who defended the crucial principle of full constitutional debate for all measures introduced in the House and Senate, the practice fell into total disuse.

This enabled Socialists/Marxists/Communists like Edward Kennedy, Moynihan, Waxman, Schumer, Boxer and Feinstein among at least one hundred others of their political credo, to circumvent the Constitution and introduce measures one hundred percent unconstitutional without a full debate as to their constitutionality, whose cumulative effect along with such measures passed since the 1920s, are collapsing the foundations of our Constitution and Bill of Rights to the point where this Constitutional Republic will crumble and fall by as early as 2005. By dumming-down the House and Senate, the Communist enemies — and I am referring to Communists INSIDE the U.S. — internal traitors with hearts filled with treason and treachery. They see their goal in reach. (When I use the word, "Communist," capitals are always intended.)

Such "laws" as abortion, gun control, civil rights, busing laws, affirmative action, welfare laws, putting U.S. military personnel under U.N. Command, laws giving additional powers to the FBI., treaties that grossly violate the Constitution, remind us of the demons addressed by Christ, whose response was: "We are legion." A whole legion of demonic "laws" have sprung up like tares between the wheat of the Constitution and the Bill of Rights, threatening the destruction of our Republican institutions, some of which have already disappeared. Without a Communist-penetrated Supreme Court, this could have been prevented.

Some will say, "well, the Senate confirms all justices appointed to the Supreme Court" and they are correct, but the real problem is that the bulk of our legislators don't know the Constitution, and lacking the necessary knowledge and confidence which comes with it, failed and or neglected to ask the nominees tough, penetrating questions, thus assuring easy passage of Socialist/Marxist/Communist justices Abe Fortass, Felix Frankfurter, Louis Brandeiss, Warren Burger, William O. Douglas, Arthur Goldberg, Earl Warren, Ruth Ginsburg, David Soutter and Stephen Bryer.

A Supreme Court packed with anti-Constitution and anti-Bill of Rights justices, inevitably wreaked havoc and confirmed measures passed by a Congress crawling with Communist termites, instead of throwing them out, neck and crop. Thus, using the legislative and judicial branches of government in the manner of Weishaupt, the founder of the Illuminati and his assault against the Catholic Church, the Supreme Court bored away at the Constitution, the Bill of Rights, States Constitutions and States rights, until today, the stout beams supporting our Republic, have been so eaten away by the Communist termites inside government, that they will soon be no more than hollow shells, able to support nothing.

Whether there is still time to call in the fumigation companies, is debatable. After all, it is no good calling in the fumigators when the timbers have already collapsed. But a step in the right direction, if it were to be taken in time, would be to fumigate the Republican Party and eliminate those Communist termites posing as conservatives working in its midst. The Republican Party is no longer the party of Lincoln and Jefferson. It has departed so radically from Republican principles and has sided so often with the Democrat (Communist) Party that it is no longer worthy of the name it used to bear so proudly. The regression of the Republican Party to where it stood just before the Civil War and during the post-Civil War-Reconstruction era, can only be properly chronicled in a separate book.

Some will say, "well, the secret Communist legislators were voted into office." And while this is true, the full account of *how* such traitors were voted into office is an amazing one, filled with chicanery, conniving, cheating, bribery and press support; largely made possible by the changes wrought by the 17th Amendment and making State elections under our Constitution become de facto "Federal elections."

The Democrats — latterly with the assistance of Republican Trojan Horses, are constantly trying to introduce new clauses into the Constitution, like centralized education, gun control "laws" "Federal election laws" like the unconstitutional "Motor Voter Law," abortion, line item veto powers — the list is endless and every one of them, flagrant violations of the Constitution.

The Communists try without ceasing to arbitrate the Constitution but the Constitution cannot be arbitrated. There is nothing in the Constitution which allows arbitrary power, but in the Clinton administration we have what the Communists have long sought to establish, a central government, a one hundred percent Communist plank, and they got it with the advent of a rapid advance toward a centralized Clinton administration. Already this centralized government has shown its fruits in the murders at Waco and Ruby Ridge, and there is no reason, other than the lack of will, why Clinton and Reno ought not to have been charged with crimes of murder.

The Constitution is common law in perfect balance and equilibrium. Much has been said and written about common law, but in truth common law can be boiled down to a few words and does not need to be explained in pretentious and tendentious terms.

This, the Communists hate, they do not respect common law and by inventing "abortion rights," gun control, line item veto power, the Communists are rapidly destroying the balance and equilibrium of the Constitution. No man sought more diligently or fought harder to destroy this rock-solid foundation of the Constitution, than the butcher of Hyde Park, Franklin Delano Roosevelt. If ever there was a wizard (male for witch) and a witch, it was Roosevelt and his lesbian Communist wife, Eleanor.

Roosevelt had studied the Supreme Court of the Civil War; the Reconstruction era; the actions of the Court in the 1920s. He was of the opinion that what he called "its lasses-fair" attitude would serve him very well. Roosevelt yearned for a Supreme Court like his much-beloved USSR's Supreme Court, an instrument of the State. In reviewing the cast of the Supreme Court of the 1920s, he is said to have resolved that it would have to be changed, and for that to happen, he would have to work diligently to oust Chief Justice William Taft, Edward Sanford, and what became known as "the Four Horsemen" — Pierce Butler, James McReynolds, George Sutherland, and William Van Deventer. Roosevelt knew that he would have to help the Communist dissenter Louis D. Brandeiss, and his liberal colleagues, Oliver Wendell Holmes and Harlan Fiske Stone by making Brandeiss the key to bringing about the changes the Communists demanded be made. Roosevelt forged ahead to revolutionize the Supreme Court.

Holmes had one fault, in the eyes of Roosevelt and his coterie of Socialist traitors — he respected judicial restraint and the 9th Amendment and at times his decisions went with the "Four Horseman" who had enraged Roosevelt by striking down all of his regulatory pronouncements as unconstitutional. Roosevelt saw his regulatory "laws" ripped to shreds by Butler, McReynolds, Sutherland and Van Deventer, often aided by Justice Owen Roberts. Roosevelt had successfully bamboozled the country by making his infamous "radio chats" putting forward Socialism as the remedy for depression ills. It was an ideal climate in which to advance Fabian Socialist ideas imparted to him by his Communist partner, Florence Kelly.

Roosevelt thought he had the country solidly behind him when he legisled raw Socialist agenda regulations he hoped would sweep Communism into being in the U.S. His plan to unseat the "Four Horsemen" and replace them with Brandeiss fellow-travellers, was to pack the Court with Marxist/Communist judges. It became known as the "court packing plan" which would have him appoint new justices for every member of the Court over the age of seventy. It went without saying that the new justices would be dyed-in-the-wool, ardent Socialists, Marxists, Communists.

A Democrat (Communist) Party-dominated Congress appeared to assure a victory for Roosevelt but when Senate Majority Leader Joseph T. Robinson died right in the middle of proceedings and Justice Roberts threw his weight against the "court packing plan," Roosevelt's cause was lost, a loss which left him embittered (some said at the time that he was almost "distraught") at seeing his plan shattered. It proved to be one of the worst legislative defeats Roosevelt ever suffered, but as the Four Horsemen left the bench, one-by one, Roosevelt replaced them with the most flagrantly pro-Communist judges ever to be appointed to serve the United States. It also pointed up the failure of the Senate confirmation process. It has always been my contention that the voters of the States should put up their candidates, who could then be tested by the voters as to what they know about the Constitution so that the voters would be the ones to have the last say on the nominees. What with the enormous climate of bribery and corruption prevailing in Washington in the last ten years, and which has increased greatly since 1992, the Senate is no longer to be relied upon to fulfill its function of "advise and consent" entirely free of outside influences.

With Roosevelt's "Red Brigade" justices on the bench, a constitutional revolution got under way in 1937, one that upheld the Socialist New Deal regulations and "laws" which cursed our country. Two of the most unsuitable and unqualified justices ever to disgrace the bench of the Supreme Court were Justice Douglas, a secular humanist Communist, and Justice Hugo Black who did not have a law degree recognized by the bar and who was a member of the K.K.K. to boot.

The Communist-packed Supreme Court began to do the will of Roosevelt to such an extent that to a student of constitutional matters, it became clear that the Red Horsemen were galloping the United States toward the Communist goal of a central government with diminution of States rights. In almost every case before the new Revolutionary Court where conflict between States rights and the federal government was an issue, it was federal government precedence over States rights which prevailed. The Revolutionary Court went out of its way to ensure that Americans were drilled into believing that the States were required to submit to the federal government in each and every instance.

Commentators in 1937 expressed the fear that thanks to the Revolutionary Supreme Court, States rights were being steadily submerged under rule by the Federal Government. It found 26 State laws unconstitutional in four years after Roosevelt's 1937 action and virtually legislated on such matters as grants in aid sanctioned by the "New Deal." It widely enhanced the scope of matter which had not, hitherto, been in the purview of the Court, especially in the area of social legislation, while the constitutional safeguard of upholding property rights fell from being used fourteen times in four years of the pre-1937 Court, to four instances in the post 1937 Court. It became recognized that the purpose of packing the Supreme Court was to ensure that far-reaching changes in conformity with the Communist Manifesto of 1848 were advanced at the expense of the Constitution and the Bill of Rights and States rights.

The Revolutionary Supreme Court also showed a marked propensity for siding with regulatory commissions, and tried to widen the scope of the Interstate Commerce Clause to embrace firearms. From 1940-1946 these regulatory agencies and commissions won in 107 out of 143 cases; in many instances, allowing the regulatory agencies greater powers than their charters allowed. The new court also set about setting a precedent in dealing with civil liberties and so-called civil rights. In the period 1923 to 1937, State cases involving civil liberties were invalidated on only four occasions, but when the court got the bit between its teeth after Roosevelt's Communist agenda was established, twelve such State laws were invalidated.

By then, Socialists and Marxists were openly speaking of the "Constitutional Revolution of 1937." On March 29, 1937, distinguished Court historian Donald Gjerdingen wrote: "The mosaic shattered. The Court's judicial review and constitutional law have never been the same since." Before 1937 all of Roosevelt's New Deal statutes were rejected, but after 1937, every single "New Deal" statute was ruled constitutional. It is said that by 1937 Roosevelt had beaten back a strong American tradition of a thorough mistrust of the central government.

Benjamin Wright, a noted authority on the Supreme Court, wrote in 1942: "No event or series of events has ever produced so many changes in constitutional doctrine within so short a time. In the four subsequent terms of the Court the reversals and distinctions have been so numerous and so sweeping that today much of the constitutional law of 1936, appears to belong in a different constitution."

So far-reaching were the decisions handed down by Roosevelt's Supreme Court, that the Democrat (Communist) Party of America, began to publish reports claiming that the Court's history could now be divided into two distinctly different periods since its inception in 1790; the pre-1937 Court and post-1937 Court. "The year 1937 marks a major divide in the constitutional jurisprudence of the American nation and in the decisional philosophy of the Supreme Court" the report said. Precisely! After 1937 the "decisional philosophy of the Supreme Court" became TOTALLY in line with Roosevelt's intentions of supplanting the U.S. Constitution and the Bill of Rights with the Communist Manifesto of 1848.

This was adequately borne out through the fact that from 1937 to 1946, the Court reversed itself thirty two times and most of the reversals came at the expense of the Constitution and the Bill of Rights. Bruce

Ackerman held that the "Constitutional Revolution of 1937 fundamentally altered the character of the Court's business, the nature of its decisions and the alignment of its friends and foes." In other words, the stamp of Communist doctrine had already been firmly imprinted on all Supreme Court decisions.

With 1965 came a change of attitude toward the Revolutionary Court with the Roosevelt-rot — seemingly checked. Fred Graham once said, "Some things have been found in the Federal Constitution that were not previously known to be there." And this was a liberal speaking! Perhaps the most notorious of such "phantom clauses" in the U.S. Constitution came with the busing law, Brown vs. Board of Education, Topeka and later in the so-called "women's right to choose" abortion ruling, which thus far, has cost the lives of close to 30 million babies, and the slaughter continues!

The drive to "nationalize" children as part of State control over the family began in earnest in 1918 — which under the leadership of Mr. and Mrs. Clinton is being emulated in 1999. The first move was introduction of the "maternity bill" (H.R. 12634 — 65 Congress) by a Miss Larkin, field secretary of Florence Kelley's National Consumer League. Details of the profound move to communize children are found in the Congressional Records, House, 1926. Basically, Florence Kelly was gearing up to adopt the policies of the Bolsheviks in "caring for children." But the a national child labor law (Bailey v Drexel Furniture) was found unconstitutional by the Supreme Court in 1923, and immediately set up a clamor for changes in the law, led by Eleanor Roosevelt's Red friends, Grace Abbott and Florence Kelly, both well-known as far-left Marxists.

What the Communists were trying to do was to have the Court rule children as part of interstate commerce, hoping to use the clause to mean anything they chose it to mean. We see this tactic very much in evidence today in so-called "anti gun laws." The gathering together of children under the banner of Socialism was very much a core program of Karl Marx. The Clinton administration is striving to do the same thing today, going even further than Kelly and Roosevelt went, with their ongoing attempts to "standardize" education, which is one of the main planks of the Communist Manifesto of 1848.

Before Roosevelt and the Clintons there was Woodrow Wilson. This seemingly mild-mannered Princeton Professor was instrumental in bringing about sweeping, unconstitutional changes that were to drastically undermine the bulwarks of the Constitution and the Bill of Rights, including the removal of trade barriers which had been the basis of the commercial bedrock of the nation; the introduction of Marxist graduated income tax; the establishment of an illegal central bank and sending the State Militia to fight on the battlefields of Europe knowing full-well that his actions were the curtain raiser to the First World War. What followed was U.S. participation therein; the Bolshevik Revolution; the destruction of Christian Russia, International Socialism; the Second World War; the United Nations; the rapid spread of Communism; under which heading came the rise of Communism in the United States under Roosevelt and Clinton.

While Wilson was apparently an unwilling tool of the Communists, subjected to the threat of exposure of his extramarital affairs with several married women, especially through his passionate love-letters to the notorious Mrs. Peck, love-letters which surfaced in the hands of William Wiseman, chief of MI6 North American desk. These were held over Mr. Wilson's head by Mandel House and Bernard Baruch. Roosevelt and Clinton by contrast with Mr. Wilson, were "eager beavers" delighted to work tirelessly for their masters in London, the driving force behind world-Communism.

One of Mr. Wilson's first actions once in office, was to call for a joint session of the Congress, in which he attacked the trade barriers which had made this country, financially, the strongest, in the world, and to press vigorously for legislation to remove them. Wilson made possible that the blueprint for future Socialism in the United States was adopted under the guise of "reforms." To quote from my book, "One World Order: Socialist Dictatorship:"

"The Four Pillars of the House of Socialism" written by Sydney Webb (the founder of the Fabian Society) became the blueprint for future Socialist action, not only in Britain, but also in the United States. The plan called for the destruction of the "system of production of goods and services based on competition, unlimited taxation, massive state welfare, no private property rights, and a One World Government. These objectives did not differ all that much from the principles laid down by Karl Marx in the Communist Manifest of 1848. The differences lay in the method of application, style, rather than in substance."

That Mr. Wilson was completely under the control of British intelligence MI6 is evidenced in the remarks made by Mandel House, his day-to-day controller. Quote from "One World Order: Socialist Dictatorship:"

"It was a group of 'affable anarchists' who elected Wilson. As House (Colonel Mandel House) saw it, U.S. citizens were little better than dolts who could be deceived by appearances. So certain was House that the voters would not see the nomination of Wilson as a candidate 'Made in England,' House sailed for England on the day Wilson was nominated at the Democrat Convention in Baltimore in 1912. 'I feel no need to watch the proceedings' House told Walter Hines who had introduced him to Wilson the year before. On his arrival in England, House told a gathering of Fabian Socialists of the RIIA that the American people 'would accept Mr. Wilson without question.' And so it was... As House put it, 'Wilson was elected to carry out a Socialist agenda without alarming the people'".

A fictionalized account of the Socialist agenda referred to by Col. House came in the book, "Philip Dru, Administrator". In the chapter "One World Order: Socialist Dictatorship" Dru's plans are laid out:

"...It set the agenda for the Wilson presidency as clearly as if it had been presented by Wilson himself. 'Philip Dru (actually House) proposed that he become the ruler of America by a series of Executive Orders. Among the tasks Dru set himself, was establishing a panel of economists to work on the destruction of tariff laws which would eventually 'lead to the abolition of the theory of protection as government policy.' The panel would also work out a system of graduated income tax and institute new banking laws. (Note the sly use of the word 'theory.') Protective tariffs were no theory: Customs duties had earned the United States a living standard that was the envy of the world. Trade protection was an established doctrine set in place by George Washington, which had proved its worth for 125 years and was not mere theory. History shows that Mr. Wilson put every one of Dru's proposals into practice, even to recognizing the Kerensky government set up by the conspirators in Odessa."

Pres. Wilson did not follow common law and much of the history of the Democrat Party shows a lack of concern for common law. The original 13 colonies brought with them their own common law, probably different from the common law of the Bill of Rights. This a trait shared by all Communist governments and adds a further proof that the United States grew further away from its common law heritage with each succeeding Democrat President.

CHAPTER 2

WHAT WE DON'T KNOW ABOUT THE CONSTITUTION & THE BILL OF RIGHTS

CONSTITUTIONAL LAW, TREATIES, 2ND AMENDMENT,
OKLAHOMA BOMBING, ABORTION, INSTANT CITIZENSHIP,
WAR POWERS, COMMANDER IN CHIEF, FEDERAL RESERVE

There is an old saying to the effect that "ignorance is bliss" and there is a new one I have invented: "An educated people shall not easily be subjugated." In the case of the American people and their Constitution and the Bill of Rights, ignorance of it will eventually lead to the destruction of the nation on which they are founded. What is most remarkable is that anyone can run for office at any level of government without knowing the first thing about the Constitution and the Bill of Rights. Sports celebrities like former Senator Bradley can enter politics at the highest level — the U.S. Senate — solely because he is recognized as a sporting figure, yet blissfully in ignorance of the limitations of power placed on the central government, and dream up bills that do not come anywhere near meeting the test of constitutionality, because of total ignorance of the Constitution and the Bill of Rights!

In short, these Constitutional Ignoramuses go on churning out bills which should never have got past their introductory stage. How is it that we send people to the House and Senate who are absolutely unqualified to make the laws because they have no knowledge of the U.S. Constitution and the Bill of Rights? How can they swear an oath to uphold and defend the U.S. Constitution and the Bill of Rights when they are in ignorance of it? How can We, the People, be so dumb as to allow this to go on ad-infinitum?

The time has come to make a law which says that unless a person running for office has qualified for the job by having completed a thorough study of the Annals of Congress, the Congressional Globe and Congressional Record, they may not be accepted as candidates. At the time of Abraham Lincoln it was accepted that any candidate for the House or Senate had to have at least two years of study of the Constitution and the Bill of Rights under his belt, and it was always assumed that every candidate was thus qualified.

A plumber, carpenter, electrician, bricklayer, has to undergo a ten-year apprenticeship before he can qualify for his trade. If we want to drive a car, we have to have a license and pass a test to get it; if we want a degree in political science, we have to study for it and pass an exam. But when it comes to the HIGHEST law of the land, people can just breeze into Washington, totally unqualified to legislate, and think they can introduce legislation on whatever whim comes into their head. A good example of this type of individual is Senator Boxer and her wildly unconstitutional proposals, and Comrade Charles Schumer is another example of the same kind. The people of the United States must be educated in the Constitution and the Bill of Rights, to prevent such malpractice legislators being elected.

There is a general consensus of opinion that the U.S. Constitution and Bill of Rights has been and is being ignored by government at both State and Federal level. Daily, we witness assaults on our precious heritage which ought be vigorously denounced across the length and breadth of the land. That such assaults are not challenged, or, at best, only weakly protested, stems from the lack of in-depth knowledge among the people of what is in the Constitution and Bill of Rights, or as in some instances, a determination to openly flout it, or surreptitiously circumvent it, of which both political parties are guilty.

The first principle of constitutional law is being flouted and dragged through the mud every day Congress is in session, every day when every court in the land is in session; every day when State legislatures are in session, and every day when local boards, municipalities and town councils meet. The first principle being battered to pieces is that no bills may be proposed without a full debate as to their constitutionality, and that having passed the test, the law or ordnance must always be based upon something immutable, not subject to passion and prejudice. The second principle is that the Constitution cannot be compromised on this or that whim of the legislators. If the U.S. Constitution is constantly compromised, then it won't be long before it becomes just a blank piece of paper as Thomas Jefferson said.

CONSTITUTIONAL LAW

The first rule on constitutional law is that a law has to be clearly written, or it is not a law. There can be no ambiguity about it; there must be a clarity of purpose and the law must be clearly stated. An example of ambiguity is found in H.R. 2580, which is the most perfect example of how NOT to write criminal law. This monstrosity wanders all over the place and has armed and dangerous right wing patriots hiding under every bed in the country. H.R. 2580 is vague, inexact, imprecise, its language inaccurate and confused and based on malicious gossip, scare stories developed out of an incident which most patriots believe was contrived by government itself.

The second rule of law is that the U.S. Constitution and the Bill of Rights cannot be compromised by or through any proposed legislation. If this occurs on a regular basis, the Constitution and Bill of Rights will suffer the fate of the Magna Carta by falling into disuse and becoming of no effect. The U.S. Constitution is based upon wisdom that dates back for thousands of years to the Greek and Roman empires. If a law is passed in the U.S. which is not in consonance with this principle and is not already in the Constitution or expressly implied, it is no law at all and eventually, such laws will result in a state in anarchy.

We have seen in our history time and again the constitutional anarchists set as their goal the destruction of the highest law of the land, the U.S. Constitution and the Bill of Rights and that by so doing, they have perverted and continue to pervert the principle in law that only laws based on truth, will ensure a just and enduring government. Any government that tries to prevail on theft, grand larceny, injustices, bribery and corruption, is bound to fail in the long run. Organized injustice, held in place by perverted laws and force to back them up, will eventually lead to revolution. No one can go on living at the expense of others.

Such a "law" was passed, and I am referring to H.R. 2580, which thoroughly violates the 2nd, 4th, 5th, 9th, 10th, and 14th Amendments to the U.S. Constitution and unlawfully presumes to take powers not delegated to the federal government in Article 1, Sec. 8., Clauses 1-18. H.R. 2580 are an example of so-called legislation drawn up by a coterie of Communists of both parties, a most inept piece of supposed "criminal law" which totally rapes the U.S. Constitution and is in perfect harmony with the Communist Manifesto of 1848.

The third rule on constitutional law is the law governing treaties. Examples are the U.N., GATT, NATO, C.W.C., Panama Canal, are all "treaties" which were unlawfully entered into by the United States and which are nullities, one and all. The U.S. Constitution is superior to all treaties, which are like any other law and can be abrogated by a variety of means, whereas the Constitution cannot be abrogated.

Treaties cannot be used to annihilate the U.S. Constitution which is what the Socialists in this country are trying to do with the U.N. treaty. The Genocide treaty can never annihilate the U.S. Constitution, and neither can the CWC treaty, nor NAFTA nor GATT. A treaty by its very terms may be self-executing, that is, it does not require funding by the Congress. The crooked Carter administration tried to tell the American people that the Panama Canal treaty was self executing, but it wasn't because Congress had to fund it.

This proves that a treaty, far from being the law of the land as some will incorrectly have it, is almost always dependent upon the goodwill of the Congress which has the constitutional power to pass all laws deemed to be necessary and proper and carry them into execution. But the legislators are not compelled to do anything in terms of the treaty of which the Congress does not approve..."And again, the treaties before us require execution by Congress and the very first article of the Constitution declares: All legislative powers herein granted shall be vested in the Congress of the United States."

Note, it does not say "vested in treaty making powers" so how in the world can a treaty be "the law of the land" and superior to the U.S. Constitution? The very idea flies in the face of common sense and the U.S. Constitution is based on common sense. As Sen. Thurmond said in one of the debates of the Reconstruction period: "A treaty is only a law." It is a temporary law at best and is subject to being constitutional and if it is not in consonance with our Constitution, it has to be rejected by the Congress. In reality, all treaties are no more than games, confidence tricks, to gain the ascendancy in one way or another and the history of the U.S. proves that it has been fooled and taken in by more treaties than any other country in the world.

I said that the Panama Canal Treaty was bogus. One good reason why it is bogus is that ONLY the Congress through a constitutional amendment can alienate U.S. territories, and this never happened. Instead we had group of self-interest traitors acting for the Wall Street bankers, "negotiate" away the Panama Canal. Congress has the power to void the Panama Canal treaty and it ought to be one of the things the Republican Party should be doing, instead of frittering away its mandate on "balancing the budget." Talk about a con game — this balancing the budget game is just another huge confidence trick.

Another bogus treaty is the U.N. treaty. We say elsewhere in the chapter dealing with the U.N. it would have taken one or perhaps two constitutional amendments to make U.S. "membership" of the U.N. a reality. In the 1945 debate in the Senate, shockingly insufficient time to debate the constitutionality of the U.N. treaty/agreement was allocated; in fact only one day was set aside for debate out of the three days that the measure was before the Senate. I have referred to the U.N. document as a "treaty" from time to time for the sake of convenience, but it is not a treaty; rather it is an agreement and agreements are not found in the U.S. Constitution, so that on this point alone, the U.N. "treaty" is a treasonous fraud.

On a second point, it was physically impossible for the senators to have studied the U.N. AGREEMENT within the three days allowed in an intelligent manner, but under tremendous pressure from the Roosevelt-controlled press, a climate rampant with of emotion was created — the timing well chosen to present the agreement for ratification by the Senate. Let us not imagine that the timing to bring it up in the Senate in 1945 was just happenstance; nothing could be further from the truth. Whipsawed by the press, with a terrible war in Europe fresh in their minds, with the bombing of Japan, Roosevelt and the *Tavistock Institute* knew that the time was right for the American people to be duped and connived into believing that the U.N. agreement was a peace plan.

And thus it was that the senators failed to do their duty, and Roosevelt and the Communists in Washington D.C. triumphed. Compare the time spent by the senators on the U.N. agreement with the 3 months they spent debating the Panama Canal treason, and even then, they could not get to the bottom of the Carter-Rockefeller-Wall Street fraud. Likewise with NAFTA and GATT.

One thing a study of the history of Congress has taught me is that our Congressmen and Senators of the 1880-1900 period, were a great deal brighter and better-informed on the Constitution than those in the House and Senate, today. Of course there are always one or two exceptions, but they are few and far between. There is a mass of evidence on treaties in the Congressional Records, and it is impossible in the space of this book for me to write them all up. Please find some of them in the Bibliography Section.

Today, we are no longer operating under the Bible of the Constitution, Vattels "Law of Nations," when it comes to treaties in international law. We are operating under the BOGUS, Communist front United Nations Agreement, which has no standing whatsoever and is not binding upon the U.S. and the several States, no matter what the politicians may say to the contrary. What is needed is a massive legal challenge to be mounted against this treasonous fraud, so that it may be exposed for what it is — a Communist Trojan Horse, designed to destroy the U.S. Constitution and the Bill of Rights and the American nation.

If we cannot get the responsible authorities to do their duty in this regard, then there must be an assembly of true and tried patriots in each of the several States, who will through a State Representative, call for a grand jury investigation into our alleged membership of the U.N. The grand jury assembled in each State will be presented with the thousands of pages of evidence in my possession in the form of Congressional Records (see bibliography) and then bring a recall petition against those in the House and Senate who refuse to vote for a bill in the Congress ending our so-called "membership" of this illicit body. And if the president should attempt to veto such a bill, impeachment proceedings would be launched against him immediately. This is of course only an outline of the procedure, which can and will be detailed to all who are concerned about what the U.N. is doing to the security of the nation, which today, is a very serious threat indeed.

On treaties, Vattels "Law of Nations" says that any treaty (it does not talk about agreements which are not in the Constitution), which is pernicious to the United States can and must be held null and void, and it is quoted over and over again in the Congressional Records listed in the bibliography. By failing to do its duty, in voting for the U.N. treaty/agreement, the Senate was responsible for the loss of thousands upon thousands of servicemen in Korea and in Vietnam, and we should pause for a moment to think about the sorrow, and anguish suffered by the families of those servicemen. We should never forget how much the bogus, treasonous, U.N. treaty/agreement has cost our people in pain and suffering, not to mention huge financial losses.

The Chemical Weapons Convention treaty/agreement is no more the law of the land than is the "Fat Lady" the President of the United States. No wonder Barnum said of the American people that a sucker is born every minute. The greatest infamy visited upon the American people in recent times came with the ratification of the bogus CWC "treaty." I wish to challenge all of the senators who voted for this circus sideshow of a "treaty" to show the American people, where in the U.S. Constitution it says that U.N. inspectors have the right to come into the States and unlock factories and warehouses, looking for "chemical weapons" and ask the citizens of the States all manner of questions, to which the stock response should be, "go to hell and get out of here!" My letter to Sen. Trent Lott on the subject points up the illegality of the CWC treaty/agreement.

It is of no use to look to the Congress or the White House to end this bogus, fraudulent, treasonous "treaty" agreement. It is up to We, the People, as the sovereigns, to take this matter up on a State level and then at the national level and see it through to its final goal, that being to rid the U.S. of the evil presence of the United Nations and sever all ties to it for once and for all. That is our constitutional duty. Let us not fail to be up to the task.

There is another thing We, the People, can and must do. We must take constitutional measures to impeach those in the House and Senate who voted in favor of H.R. 2580, Bill 735 and H.R. 1710. These measures are intended to bring anarchy and mob rule by Democrats operating under a Napoleonic Code. These unconstitutional bills violate the Constitution and the Bill of Rights, trammeling and tramping underfoot, roiling and despoiling the Constitution and the Bill of Rights.

Nothing so destructive of the Constitution and the Bill of Rights has come along since the Civil War than the so-called "anti-terrorist" legislation and the cunningly deceptive Republican Form of Government Guarantee Act. People often ask me: "Is Communism dead?" to which I reply, "No, it is alive and kicking in the House, the Senate and the White House, the State Department et al."

The modern-day Trotskys, Lenins, Stalins and Benedict Arnolds and their supporters would like nothing better than to see the U.S. Constitution and the Bill of Rights ripped up and consigned to the trash can in their efforts to get the United States communized and under a One World Government. They will succeed, unless We, the People, stop them. How to do this? I have long advocated a plan of action in my booklet, "Restoring Government To We, The People." I believe the Black Muslims co-opted my idea for their million-man march on Washington "stealing a march" on us and we need to do the same — march on Washington in our millions. The Muslims had the courage of their convictions to action the plan. Now it is our turn!

Those who call themselves our representatives on the Hill; those representatives in the House and Senate who voted for Bill S 735, HR 1710, HR 2580, cast their votes AGAINST the U.S. Constitution. The above noted bills are nothing short of treachery and treason; swindling sophistry, conniving deception, and a lot worse. Remember that Hyde and Conyers made light of the massacre of the Davidians at Waco, thus virtually condoning the murder of 87 citizens done to death in a bill of attainder forbidden by the Constitution. Hyde and Schumer were very happy with the FBI being the judge, jury and executioner of these innocent people and they rejoiced in it. These wildly reckless people, Schumer, Conyers, Hyde, dredged up the provisions of their bills from the turgid cesspools of the Communist Manifesto of 1848, without the slightest regard to their constitutionality.

The constitutional anarchists who are responsible for these outrages violated their oath of office to uphold and defend the Constitution and the Bill of Rights. We must like Andrew Jackson threatening the shylock bankers with a big stick, constitutionally threaten these discredited legislators and shake the big stick of the Constitution at them, and like Jackson, we must say "By God, we will rout you out! With the power vested in We, the People by our Constitution." Then, we must unite to impeach them, one and all of both parties who have so vilely transgressed against the U.S. Constitution, and the Bill of Rights.

We, the People, are the only people on the face of the earth who have an absolute legal right to get rid of a government and its representatives who violate our rights. We have a document which says we can get rid of the violators of the Constitution in a peaceful manner, without resort to violent revolution. That document is the U.S. Constitution and the Bill of Rights, written to protect our sovereignty against the wolves who have sneaked in to devour us. It is up to We, the People, to exercise that right, or face losing it forever.

Aftermath of Oklahoma City. By A.M. Rosenthal, Columnist New York Times.

"Timothy McVeigh awaits execution. The jurors who convicted and sentenced him have done their duty. The rest of American society has not. Congress has not. The state governments and their law enforcement agencies have not. America's political parties have not. The president did in the early days after Oklahoma City but then faded back. The next victims of these failures have been selected by category. They are officials and employees of state and federal governments, judges, federal and local police and Americans who do not fight the gangs of armed racists who conceived and organized the crusade that inspired Timothy McVeigh to murder 168 human beings in the federal building on April 19, 1995.

Since that day nothing has been done that diminishes the vivid likelihood that these gangs will carry out or inspire other bombings in other cities. They call themselves militia and patriots. But they are exactly what the prosecutor said about Timothy McVeigh — traitors. They talk and think like sick paranoids, which they are. But they know what they are doing. They are trying to inject civil servants with terror, prevent state governments from functioning, and eat away at American confidence to protect the citizenry and itself.

Since that day, these gangs have been doing what they did before. Across the country there have been arrests of members of the patriot movement...In most states, officials supposed to enforce the law get no encouragement from governors. From the senators and representatives the people send to Washington come nothing with a few exceptions, like the Democratic Reps. Charles Schumer and Jerry Nadler of New York... President Clinton did do his duty just after the bombing. He said America was being befouled by hatred spread by militia types and their flacks and to remain silent was a sin. Immediately politicians, lobbyists and journalists who wanted him defeated in 1996 whined that he was a vote-hunting manipulator.

Since then there has been not much leadership from the president against armed racism and rebellion, no plan of action. It is not too late. Important steps can be taken, and in another column I will list some...The press failed to report what was not happening after

Oklahoma City. And the public did not raise a gigantic fuss about the country's collective refusal to do anything but shake its head and wipe its eye."

The foregoing is but one example of how daily compromising of the 2nd Amendment and the Bill of Rights goes on. It is but one example of how the Constitution is being shredded through devilish cunning and sophistry, through compromise, especially where the 2nd Amendment and personal right to keep and bear arms is concerned. Hysterical excitement, supercharged emotion and figments of imagination are brought into play as an expedient, and it is wearing down and compromising the 2nd Amendment, and with it, the entire Constitution, which cannot be separated from the rest of the Constitution and the Bill of Rights as the rascally Justice William O. Douglas always tried to do.

On Closer examination the U.S. Constitution is far more complex than it appears to be, and thus it follows that a period of intensive reading and study of it is mandatory. There is no better way to achieve a good, sound, grounding in the Constitution and the Bill of Rights than an intensive, protracted, study of the Annals of Congress, the Congressional Globe and the Congressional Record. A minimum of ten years of intensive study and reading of these documents will put one in the position of having a good grounding in the Constitution and Bill of Rights. Without having completed such a study, there is little chance that one will know the Constitution and Bill of Rights.

I have read hundreds of debates contained in the Annals of Congress, the Congressional Globe and Congressional Record. With regard to the latter, I found, over and over again, the unwarranted assumption that the 13th, 14th, and 15th Amendments were constitutionally ratified by the States, when this is entirely wrong. I also found proof in these records that these three amendments, the 13th, 14th and 15th, are fraudulent, as is the Reconstruction legislation that went with them. States rights and State sovereignty have all but been forgotten by the House and Senate since the 1930s.

Because the legislature, the judiciary, go on piling one law upon another, mere hypotheses based upon the 13th, 14th, and 15th Amendments to the U.S. Constitution and the Reconstruction laws that followed, a good part of the book is devoted to exposing the fraudulent nature of these amendments and the laws based upon them, so that it can be clearly established, for once and for all, that the 13th, 14th, and 15th

Amendments are NOT a part of the Constitution and that ALL laws based upon them and the fraudulent Reconstruction laws are mere hypotheses heaped upon hypotheses.

When I started to write this book, several well-meaning friends said nobody would read it. That brought to mind the ancient Athenians, who put people into two categories: Those who set great store by learning and who had inquiring minds, and those who were what they called, the "living dead," sidetracked by non-intellectual pursuits and pleasures, which includes readers of fiction. I was told that people were more interested in making money than caring about what is happening to the U.S. Constitution and the Bill of Rights. To those who are of this mindset, I would quote Thomas Jefferson:

"To preserve our independence we must not let our rulers load us with debt. We must take our choice between economy and liberty, or profusion and servitude." With the foregoing in mind, I give you the following information, extracted and compiled from the "Annals of Congress, "the Congressional Globes" and the "Congressional Records" following 26 years of diligent reading.

ABORTION: MURDER OF THE UNBORN CHILD

The two greatest threats to the maintenance and stability of our republican form of government and our rights guaranteed by the Bill of Rights, are abortion, and gun control. The Supreme Court justices acted like madmen when they attempted to stretch the 4th Amendment to supposedly make child-murder a part of it. In all of my years of study at the British Museum — which included a study of ancient nations and their cultures — I never found a nation among them that willingly allowed mass murder of its children. In fact the Egyptian and Babylonian priesthood did not allow mass murder; they murdered only selected child victims for ritual sacrificial purposes. The priesthood of these two nations were able to do this because of their power and wealth arising from their alleged "higher secret knowledge."

The people of Egypt did not dare to disobey the priest-rulers until the reign of Amenhotep the fourth, in the Eighteenth Dynasty, when the priests of Osiris were put down by the brave young Amenhotep the fourth, who adopted the religion of what was the forerunner of the Christian religion.

It is utterly without explanation why the American people are allowing the liberal "priest class" and the politicos they control along with the "priests" of the Supreme Court with their alleged "higher knowledge" to go on murdering children at the rate of 1.4 million a year, for reasons of inconvenience of having a child. The "free love" drug is permeating every corner of the feminine population, getting them hooked on abortion. While in this mentally-drugged liberal-induced state, women are murdering their own unborn infants in staggering numbers.

This state of affairs is unconscionable and must be halted, even if we have to fight a Second American Revolutionary War to put a stop to the savagery. As I hope to prove, abortion is unconstitutional and we must stand fast on the Constitution and wage relentless opposition by whatever means possible against those who are violating the Constitution and the Bill of Rights.

Abortion ranks as the top priority of the Communists in the U.S. government. Second, comes so-called gun control, and we shall deal with this later herein. In my white papers/monographs, abortion is the first issue we deal with, followed by many other constitutional issues, one by one. Let us get the matter in proper perspective: Abortion is a Communist doctrine brought to the United States by the notorious Madame Kollontay, a functionary in the Soviet government. Her rampages across the U.S. in the 1920s and early 1930s, did inestimable damage.

The thrust of abortion is to murder in the womb, white, Christian American unborn children, and statistics show this group comprises the bulk of the nearly 35 million helpless, defenseless children who have been murdered since the Supreme Court turned the Constitution and the Bill of Rights, upside down. Lesbianism and homosexuality, constantly thrust upon the youth of our land by Hollywood and a Marxist administration under President Clinton, are other methods promoted by the Bolshevik Socialists to drastically reduce the number of white Christian Americans as the dominant population group, while unrestricted immigration from non-Founding Fathers countries is the third tool being used to permanently change America.

Today's "Madame Kollontays" are Barbara Boxer, Dianne Feinstein and Patricia Schroeder who got themselves elected to the Senate and House of Representatives respectively, with the backing of liberals and their money power. Boxer could well be described as a female Trotsky. The avid pursuit of abortion by these three women degrades and disgraces the femininity of women everywhere.

Abortion was "legalized" when the Supreme Court decided to hear the case Roe vs. Wade. The solution to the abortion murder epidemic raging across the nation is to have the House and Senate overturn this ghastly unconstitutional "law" that purports to make abortion legal. Through Article III, Section 2, Part 2 of the U.S. Constitution, the House and the Senate has the power to reverse any U.S. Supreme Court decision on a simple majority vote of both Houses. The disinformation, that a two-thirds majority vote is needed, is without foundation. There is not a single reference in the Constitution, nor is it implied, which says that such a vote has to be a two-thirds vote.

Quoting from pages 3837-3847, Congressional Record, Feb. 27, 1923:

"...John Marshall our first chief justice in Elliots Debate, Vol. 3, page 560: Congress is empowered to make exceptions to the appellate jurisdiction as to the law and fact of the Supreme Court. These exceptions certainly go as far as the legislature may think for the interest and the liberty of the people."

The falsehood that abortion is a "constitutional right" comes from the fevered imaginings of the Madame Kollontays of our time, Abzug, Feinstein, Boxer, Schroeder, Ireland and Smeale; the unsexed women class, hard-core Communists, who have led thousands of young women astray, backed up by a few Supreme Court Justices who don't know the Constitution, and who read their predilections (what they would like the Constitution and the Bill of Rights to say) into it; in defiance of the 9th. Amendment. If any influential person — in or out of the legislature — wants to take this issue up, I will help them to challenge the Supreme Court claim that abortion is a "constitutional right." I am not a lawyer, but have come to know the Constitution through more than 26-years of study of the Annals of Congress, Congressional Globe and Congressional Record, although I will say that a lifetime of study is not enough time to learn the complexities of our Constitution.

Supreme Court decisions made since 1910 which have so grossly harmed "the interest and liberty of the people" — and especially those decisions made by the Constitutional Anarchist-packed courts of the Roosevelt administration — must be overturned. Instead of the Republican Party playing right into the hands of Constitutional Anarchist William Jefferson Clinton, it should leave the budget debate farce alone and apply its energies to appointing a commission for this purpose: To review and overturn by a simple majority vote of both Houses, every single one of the hundreds of unconstitutional decisions made by the Supreme Court and States Supreme Courts since 1910. And especially Roe vs. Wade.

Nowhere in the Constitution is the word, "abortion" mentioned or expressly implied. Of course Statutory Law is expressly implied. The Supreme Court had no jurisdiction to hear Roe vs. Wade. Had the justices studied the Dred Scott decision, they would have been aware that the court lacked jurisdiction to hear Roe vs. Wade, but the justices were ignorant and ignorance prevailed and the court committed a cardinal blunder. The justices violated their oaths of office and unpardonably compromised the U.S. Constitution. They tried to make unborn children a part of interstate commerce, or a Federal issue. Another unpardonable sin was purporting to divide the life of unborn child into three periods, one being the so-called "trimester" period.

This is in direct and flagrant violation of the 5th, 10th, 13th, 14th, and 15th Amendments which give equal protection of the laws of life, liberty to the born as well as the unborn. Roe vs. Wade tried to make a distinction between the rights of the born and unborn child and the rights of their citizen-parents, when there is no difference. Nowhere in the U.S. Constitution is it expressly implied that there is a power to break the life of unborn children into convenient periods for the purposes of allowing them to be murdered.

To interpret the Constitution correctly, we must always look for an existing power or a power expressly implied and if that power is not found, or is not expressly implied by another power already in the Constitution, it is a prohibition of that power. In plain language, the Roe vs. Wade decision in favor of abortion was a violation of the prohibition against abortion. To pretend that the Constitution allows for abortion is a total perversion and an example of judicial fiat, a form of tyranny.

Why so? Because like the legislative and executive branches, the judiciary has only limited powers. The Supreme Court does not have absolute powers. It is subject to the same narrow constraints placed on the legislative and executive branches of government by Article 1, Section 8, Clauses 1-18. In the Congressional Record of the 44 Congress, we find the compelling truth in a statement by the first Chief Justice of the Supreme Court, John Marshall:

"The U.S. Constitution is an instrument of grants and inhibitions (prohibitions) of power and not a definition of which there is but one, of treason in Article III, Section 3, Parts 1 and 2."

Roe vs. Wade should have been offered as a constitutional amendment. The Supreme Court did not have jurisdiction in the case and should have refused to hear it. Dred Scott vs. Hanford in the Supreme Court's December Term of 1856, proves that contention for once and for all. Roe vs. Wade allowed the fevered imaginations of the majority of the Supreme Court justices to run wild and give free rein to their predilections, forbidden by the 9th Amendment.

Roe vs. Wade turned the judicial branch into a legislative branch in violation of the separation of powers doctrine of the U.S. Constitution. The Supreme Court cannot make laws. That is the function of the legislature, yet this is exactly what it did with Roe vs. Wade and Brown vs. Board of Education, not to mention a host of decisions that either crossed the line, or, were borderline at the very least.

Congress makes all laws, not the Supreme Court. Congress has the final say, not the Supreme Court. The righteous aura that now surrounds the justices of that court was artificially created by the Constitutional Anarchist, Franklin D. Roosevelt. It is time that the sovereigns, We, the People, swept aside this supposed Elijah-mantle glorification of the Supreme Court. The House and Senate can overturn any Supreme Court decision by a simple majority and the Supreme Court justices are not infallible. They are not the last word in deciding what is Constitutional or not. The House and Senate, long burdened with an over-abundance of constitutional anarchists, has forgotten this important power it holds.

No one in his right-thinking mind can possibly believe that the Constitution supports wholesale murder of unborn children which came into being in the wake of the unconstitutional Roe vs. Wade decision. For the "moderate" (read SOCIALIST) members of the Republican Party to try and sweep abortion under the carpet under the guise of the right to choose whether to murder a child or not, is morally abhorrent. Abortion destroys the morality of the nation. Under any pretext, it is totally repugnant.

Read Madame Kollontay's book and see that abortion was stated by this evil Bolshevik women as the way to destroy the morality of the American nation. Of course the "moderate" wolves in sheep's clothing actually believe that the Supreme Court has the right to decide at what period of the pregnancy it is perfectly acceptable to murder the unborn child. The Constitution protects life and property, not just a part of life. The "trimester" period-idea is the reasoning of simpletons. No one can deny that a baby in the mother's womb is alive, and the Constitution and the Bill of Rights protect life.

Those justices who voted for Roe vs. Wade tried to clothe their death sentence on millions of unborn children by dreaming up another name for a baby and dividing the life of the child into time zones: "Oh, its o.k. to murder the child now because the child is a "fetus." The word "fetus" is an escape hatch, and because "fetus" is not mentioned in the Constitution, it is a prohibition of the term, and in any case, all life is under the protection of life and liberty in the Constitution, no matter what some may choose to call that life.

The justices of the Supreme Court think they have the right to rewrite the Constitution. Well, they don't. They need to go and learn the Constitution by intensive study of the Annals of Congress, the Congressional Globe and the Congressional Record. They must also be de-glorified! They could learn a great deal from the early justices of the Supreme Court who really knew the Constitution and who rode on horseback from State to State to judge cases. They did not sit in marble halls and secret ante-rooms in an aura of sacred grandeur. The justices of the Supreme Court do not have any special powers. They are sworn to obey the Constitution, just like the rest of us. Their powers are limited, not unlimited. The judiciary is not even co-equal with the legislative branch of government. The Supreme Court has no sovereignty over the legislature and the people.

Even their case law is subject to Congressional approval. Congress, as the legislative body, need not, should not and does not automatically, accept the verdict of the Supreme Court as law. It is supposed to examine each decision on a case-by-case basis and then decide if it is to be entered as law or not. This "holy" nonsense attitude toward the Supreme Court has got to be stopped. This attitude was instilled into the American people by Roosevelt liberals, Socialists and the press they controlled and still control.

The dreadful casualties sustained by both sides in the Civil War were surpassed IN ONE YEAR by the casualties among unborn children whose fate was decided by the Constitutional Anarchists and the predilections of the Supreme Court justices. It is utterly appalling that President Clinton and his wife didn't think this huge tragedy even worth a mention in the State of the Union address Clinton delivered in 1996. Sen. Dole is no better. He dismisses abortion as a "moral and social" issue when it is a constitutional issue.

The President hasn't even a minimum of education in the Constitution, nor does his lawyer wife, since the Constitution isn't given more than a smattering of attention by law schools. The 5th and 10th Amendments have always provided protection for the unborn, and additional safeguards for the rights of the unborn were added by the 13th, 14th and 15th Amendments to the U.S. Constitution, even though these amendments have still to be ratified. Protection of LIFE extends to all life and that includes the life of the unborn baby.

The befuddled justices of the Supreme Court (or were they following orders?) who wrote opinions allowing abortion as a "constitutional right" obviously did not know the constitutional definition of 'people' 'person' and 'citizen.' I recommend that they be obliged to write a thousand times:

"...the words 'people' of the United States, 'person' and 'citizens' are synonymous terms, and they mean the same thing. They describe the political body, who, according to our Republican institutions, form sovereignty, who hold the power and conduct the government through their representatives. They are what we familiarly call 'the sovereign people' and every citizen is one of the people and a constituent member of the sovereignty..." And that sovereignty extends to the unborn also, as they follow the rights of the parents. (Page 404 of the Dred Scott decision, Supreme Court, Summer Term, 1865.) At that period in our history we had truly learned justices in the court who absolutely obeyed the Constitution and did not follow their predilections.

There is no talk here about a one-third person, a half-person and a three-quarter person as dreamed up by the justices who wrote their opinion favoring abortion. From whence cometh this weird, contorted language? I can provide the answer to that question: It comes from Madame Kollontay and her band of Constitutional Anarchists and their descendants who infest the halls of Congress and whose intemperate opinions found great favor with their counterparts of the Supreme Court.

Roe vs. Wade is no more than a cheap, sordid, underhand trick to deny citizenship to the unborn person, by calling the person, a "fetus." Vattel's "Law of Nations" the "Bible" relied upon by the Founding Fathers in drafting the U.S. Constitution, puts the matter beyond question and forever smashes the Communist Manifesto of 1848-concepts followed by the Constitutional Anarchists. In this category is included President Clinton and his wife; Senator Dole and his Republican "moderates" (read Socialists) and those justices of the Supreme Court who wrote opinions favoring abortion and then called their predilections, "constitutional" in open rebellion against the 9th Amendment of the U.S. Constitution and the Bill of Rights. In my opinion Justice Brennan was one of the worst violators of the 9th Amendments ever to disgrace the Court.

Vattel's "Law of Nations" pages 478-479:

"The citizens are members of civil society bound to the society by certain duties and subject to its authority; they actually participate in its advantages... As a society cannot perpetuate itself otherwise than by children who naturally follow the condition of their parents, and succeed to all their rights."

"Freedom of choice" is a gruesome farce. I cannot walk up to a man and tell him. "I am exercising my freedom of choice-right to murder you." That man would have the right to say, "and I choose to defend myself and I am going to shoot you first." Yet, the right of the unborn child of the citizen is denied the right to protection of his or her life, inherited from the parents, and in the words of "Vattel's Law of Nations," "follow the condition of their parents and succeed to all their rights." How cowardly to destroy a helpless, unborn child!

If Roe vs. Wade is correctly understood, where does "freedom of choice" come from? Such is not found in the Constitution! Again, it comes from the Communist Manifesto of 1848 and our Founding Fathers would start a second American Revolution were they alive today, and put the constitutional anarchists who allow child murder on a terrifying scale, out of business. They would be tried for treason. Imagine any of those great men who drafted the Constitution favoring child murder!

There is not one single word in the Constitution and the Bill of Rights nor is it anywhere expressly implied that women have the "constitutional" right to abortion — i.e. murder of the child in the womb. The late, great constitutional scholar Senator Sam Ervin once said of abortion: "In Roe vs. Wade, the Supreme Court found something that is not in the Constitution." This was also stated by Professor Arthur Miller of the Harvard Law School:

"The Supreme Court found a right to abortion without pointing to any specific word in the Constitution." Justice Byron White who dissented strongly in Roe v .Wade stated: "I find nothing in the language of history of the Constitution to support the court's judgment. The court simply fashions a new constitutional right for pregnant mothers and with scarcely any reason or authority for its action invests the right without sufficient substance to override more State abortion statutes."

"The upshot is that the people of the legislatures of 50 States are constitutionally disentitled to weigh the relative importance of the fetus on one hand against a spectrum of possible impacts on the mother on the other hand. As an exercise of raw judicial power (judicial fiat like a Bolshevik court), the court perhaps has authority to do what it does today but in my view its judgment is an improvident and extravagant exercise of the power of judicial review which the constitution extends to the courts."

Although he was on the right track, Justice White erred in several areas; mainly in talking about a "fetus" and by saying that the court "perhaps has the authority to do what it does today." A reading of the Dred Scott case plus a study of Vattel's "Law of Nations" would convince Justice White that no such authority exists, nor has it ever existed. Nor does the term "judicial review" mean exercising predilections in violation of the 9th Amendment, for which any and every sitting judge ought to be impeached and removed from the bench, if guilty of such heinous behavior.

Congressional Record, House, July 3, 1926, page 12942:

"It (the Communist Manifesto of 1848) has expressly abolished, prohibited all rights of inheritance, either by law or by will...they have promulgated decrees relating to marriage and divorce which practically establishes a state of 'free love' (abortion.) Their effect has been to furnish a vehicle for the legalizing of prostitution by permitting annulment of the marriage bonds at the whim of the parties." Today in the U.S. we call this abomination "no fault divorce." Abortion is the most important issue in the history of the United States. Those who would stand aside from it, are committing a grave error and delivering a cowardly blow against the Republic and its institutions by which we will stand or fall. What is the solution? We must immediately petition Congress to overturn the Supreme Court case Roe vs.Wade.

THE IDIOCY OF "INSTANT" CITIZENSHIP

From abortion to matters of immigration is but a short step, although at first glance, they are seemingly unrelated. In reality the two are intertwined with each other, interfaced in violating the Constitution and the Bill of Rights. In both abortion and "instant citizenship" the law has been turned on its head and made to follow a course entirely prohibited to it by the Constitution and the Bill of Rights. Instead of standing firmly against the rape of the Constitution and the Bill of Rights, the "priests of Osiris" of the Supreme Court have allowed the horrible crime of abortion and they now promote the horrible crime of making the children of illegal aliens born on our soil, "instant citizens." Both these errors will lead to the death of the American nation.

It is the latter crime whose threat is immediate. We need to utterly reject this inanity, and take whatever steps we have to take in order to put an immediate end to this dangerous practice, even if it means fighting a Second Revolutionary War. Furthermore, a major review must be conducted by a competent non-political committee to rescind citizenship already granted to illegal aliens.

On the one hand the conspirators against Founding Fathers America murder babies in the womb, by the millions, and on the other, they grant instant citizenship to children of illegal aliens (mostly the poor from Mexico, Guatemala, and other Central and South American countries — but not limited to them) whose parents enter the U.S. illegally and then have children on our soil. But for a Liberal-Socialist polluted Supreme Court and a Congress filled with constitutional anarchists for the past fifty years or more, such "instant citizenship" idiocy could never have been established and then perpetuated.

The motive of the conspirators is obvious. It is the same as found in the revolutionary 1965 Immigration Act which has flooded the United States with millions of citizens of Far and Near East, Africa, and South American countries, while at the same time choking off immigration from Founding Father countries (Britain, Western Europe.) Their aim? Turn the United States into a hybrid nation, a so-called "multicultural society" (sometimes also called "multi-ethnic" or "racially diverse" nation) in which "democracy" is pushed to its outer limits, making of what was to be the greatest civilization on earth, another Brazil or Balkans, or both. In short, the 1965 Immigration was purposefully intended to destroy the United States of America as envisaged by the

Founding Fathers. In place of the Confederated Republic was instituted, slowly at first, mob rule, as Plato called it, under a democratic government whose laws are taken from the Napoleonic code.

What does the Constitution say about "instant citizenship" for the children of illegal aliens? As always, scholars and students have to search and diligently study what the Annals of Congress, the Congressional Globe and the Congressional Record say on the subject. It is not "racist" to state the historical fact that the fifty five men who met in Philadelphia were all of Anglo-Saxon nationality. Hence it follows that the United States Constitution was written in the light of their common nationality and hereditary background and culture, and became in the document they wrote and produced, the identity, heritage and culture for the new United States.

The peoples of Europe, particularly England, Ireland, Scotland, Germany, France, Norway, Sweden, Denmark — the Nordic-Alpine people, desired to emigrate to the "new country" and when this desire reached other non-European nations a century or more later, there was planted a seed which has grown to grave proportions in a manner never envisaged — nor intended — by the framers of the Constitution.

The Founding Fathers would never have given legal status to anything illegal, like illegal aliens crossing our borders, squatting on our land and then delivering their babies on our soil. Common sense tells us that the framers of the Constitution would not have given children of people unlawfully in the U.S., instant legal citizenship. Vattel's "Law of Nations" says it all: Children "follow the condition of their parents and succeed to all their rights." Thus, if the parents of the child or children have no rights as illegal aliens — which is exactly what their legal status is — then the children have no rights which means also that they have no right to citizenship. It is worth repeating that Vattel's "Law of Nations" was the source of much of what the Founding Fathers wrote into the Constitution and the Bill of Rights.

It is a preposterous presumption to make citizens of children of illegal aliens. I might add that this peculiarity does not exist in any other country. The word "person" as Judge Roger Brooke Taney stated, applies only to citizens and not to aliens, and especially not to people who are in the United States illegally. The liberal Socialists-Marxist-Communist constitutional anarchists try to rationalize their preposterous "instant citizen" doctrine by citing the 14th Amendment. Even though it was not ratified the 14th Amendment states as follows: "All persons born or naturalized in the United States and subject to the jurisdiction thereof are citizens of the United States and the States wherein they reside."

Apart from violating the 10th Amendment and attempting to take away the right of the States to decide whom they will admit, we need to look closely at the words, "subject to the jurisdiction thereof..." Illegal aliens are not subject to the laws of the United States as they reside in the States as outlaws, i.e. they are outside of the laws of the States wherein they are living and therefore "not subject to the jurisdiction thereof."

Their children's presence here cannot be made legal if the parents are outside of the law. The child cannot be a citizen because of the outlaw status of their parents; they are not citizens. Again, quoting from Vattel's "Law of Nations:"

"... I say to be of the country, it is necessary to be born of a person who is a citizen; for if he born there of a foreigner, it will only be the place of his birth and not his country. The inhabitants as distinguished from the citizens are foreigners who are permitted to settle and stay in the country...Being born under our Constitution and laws, no naturalization is required as one of foreign birth, to make him a citizen."

The point here is that children of illegal aliens are not born "under our Constitution and laws." By what twisted, fevered, unrestrained predilections can it be supposed that the children of illegal aliens can suddenly come "under our Constitution and laws?" Since when can one illegal action make a second illegal action lawful? Pages 4257-4259, Congressional Record, House, 1876:

"...That part of the bill which relates to minor children is wholly useless. The Constitution itself declares that a child born within the United States of parents who are not citizens and not subject to the jurisdiction of the United States is an alien."

The term, "subject to the jurisdiction" is the key to what the Founding Fathers meant and speaks volumes in the first section of the 14th Amendment. When a women from one of the South American countries or Mexico crosses our borders and enters the United States illegally, or a Chinese women is smuggled into the United States and then these women have a baby here, the baby is not a citizen but an alien. An alien, not a "illegal immigrant" because the term is oxymoron. How can you be an "immigrant" if you are illegally in the country? The child follows the status of its mother who is an alien. This basic exception law is followed by every country except the United States and makes of us the laughing stock of the world.

The U.S. Constitution in this instance has no jurisdiction over people who cross into the U.S. illegally, or are smuggled in by ship or plane from countries like India, China and Africa, because they are outside of our laws. Yet, we have this happening with great frequency and then these illegal aliens have the audacity to claim citizenship for their offspring. In California, where this happens with clockwork regularity, it is an added insult that the State is obliged to bear the medical costs involved in the birth of the alien child, because the Federal Government, in gross violation of the 10th Amendment, and in violation of the federal guarantee of a republican constitution for each state, orders the citizens of California to pay these costs and does not provide any relief thereof. The Dredd Scott decisions of the Supreme Court made it abundantly clear what the parameters of citizenship are, and clearly excludes children born in the U.S. of illegal alien parents.

WAR POWERS ACT SUSPENDS CONSTITUTION: FACT OR FICTION?

Thus far we have examined some violations of the Constitution and the Bill of Rights which the legislature and the judiciary maintain are legal, when even to the untrained mind it must be obvious they are not. In this chapter we shall be talking about an area in the Constitution about which much disinformation has been spread — some by design — and some out of ignorance. In writing this book I have been confronted with remarks that my work is futile, because the Constitution is dead — killed by the War Powers Act. This dangerous misrepresentation appears to be fooling even the very elect.

There is no power in the U.S. Constitution that gives to government powers other than those delegated to it in Sec. 8 Art. 1, Clauses 1-18 and nowhere is it given that the Congress or the President has any right to amend, alter or suspend the Constitution and the Bill of Rights. Congress can do nothing to diminish the power of the Constitution, nor give itself any new powers, or alter any existing powers. The same iron-clad rule holds good for the Judiciary.

Whether the War Powers Act could achieve the impossible, and whether the Congress or the President can suspend any part of the

Constitution and the Bill of Rights is challenged and quite properly rejected. A subscriber sent me a copy of an article written by Dr. Gene Schroeder which was published in the "Spotlight" of October 9, 1996. I am not a subscriber to the "Spotlight" and the article was sent to me along with a number of letters expressing great alarm that what I have been teaching about the subject for the past twenty years is wrong.

For the past twenty six years I have diligently read (in the sense that one "reads" a subject at a first-rate university) from my private collection of these documents, as well as Blackstone's Commentaries on the Constitution by St. George Tucker, Vattel's "Law of Nations," the works of Justice Roger Brooke Taney and other eminent authorities including "Twenty Years of Congress" by James B. Blaine and "Commentaries on the U.S. Constitution" by Justice Joseph Story.

I regret to say that I found Dr. Schroeder's positions about the War Powers Act unfounded, as I believe that the Constitution is the supreme law of the United States, and specifically, it is not subject to restrictive actions by the Congress, the Supreme Court and or the Executive. The so-called executive orders quoted by Dr. Schroeder are null and void and of no force in law and ultra vires, as they are really proclamations, which are forbidden by the Constitution. Only the monarchs of England can issue proclamations. An executive order, no matter how it is drawn up or who signs it, is of no effect and the citizens of the several States are not duty-bound to obey one jot of such an order.

President Lincoln was the first to violate the Constitution in this manner. He did it mainly as a sly attempt to encourage the slaves to revolt against their masters in the South. Lincoln had the power to issue a habeas corpus suspension order because of the war that was raging. However, with the death of Lincoln, the order lapsed and was no longer and is no longer of any force and effect. But let me make haste to add that even under habeas corpus, Lincoln was not possessed of any power to issue executive orders. Lincoln later admitted his power grab was unconstitutional. There is even less excuse for his successors to issue "executive orders;" at least Lincoln had the excuse of habeas corpus, but that died with him and was not transferable.

In my book, "One World Order: Socialist Dictatorship" I detail the rise of the traitor Woodrow Wilson and how he was at all times under the control of Mandel House and the British whom he served. Wilson, instructed by House on orders from London, was told to usurp the powers Lincoln had under habeas corpus, plus I believe, ten additional powers. Wilson got away with this because so many of our legislators and the public at large believed then, and still today believe, the President is automatically commander in chief of the armed forces, a fraudulent trick pulled by almost every president since Wilson. They point to Lincoln as allowing them this title, but Lincoln had already been called into service by the Congress and was thus the legitimate commander in chief of the armed forces, unlike George Bush and William Clinton. It is worth repeating: Don't forget, the power of habeas corpus ended with the death of Lincoln.

What disturbs me about the Schroeder article is the references to so called emergencies which allegedly arose during the tyrannical rule of Franklin D. Roosevelt, the "mad butcher" of Hyde Park. There was no emergency when Roosevelt falsely demanded war powers because WWII had not yet begun. The ridiculous "emergency" dreamed up by the secretary of the treasury and attorney general was Roosevelt's imaginary "war on poverty." This was tied to the unconstitutional closure of all banks for which Roosevelt should have been tried for sedition.

There are only two kinds of emergencies that will bear constitutional scrutiny. The first is when the House and Senate in joint session passes a declaration of war and specifies what KIND of a war it is to be. The other emergency is under habeas corpus under very narrow strictures. Roosevelt's ridiculous "emergency war on poverty" was no more than a bunko operation, a fraud and a scam and Roosevelt would never have got away with it, except for the fact that our legislators, then as now, by and large, are woefully ignorant of the Constitution.

I spent 26 years in studying treaty provisions as well as following a trail that led to the nullification of common law by some of the traitors who pass for judges in the courts. Sometime ago I had occasion to write a 19-page work decrying the notion that a treaty can override the Constitution. This was done in response to urgent appeals from subscribers to "World In Review" who had received a flyer from a man who claimed this was what the Constitution says. The author of the pamphlet is well-meaning leader, popular in Christian circles because of his gift of weaving Bible prophecy into historical facts. But it is not true and can never be true that a treaty/agreement can override the Constitution.

There was absolutely no way that Roosevelt could have "suspended" the Constitution. Nowhere in the Constitution is there provision for any such action. Congress cannot "suspend the Constitution" much less the President. And remember, it is the Congress that makes the laws, not the President. Congress created the executive and judicial branches, yet not even a vote by the Congress could suspend the Constitution. Such opinions as the one expressing support for the alleged "suspension" of the Constitution by Roosevelt are harmful, and should be dismissed as being without substance. From the Congressional Record, Senate, Page 9893.

Senator Schall: "...Beginning with Wilson, there was a constant fight to drag us down to the level of Europe...The same personnel as in Wilson's time; the same wrecking crew that took us into the war and ruined us, are now in command. The president's first 'noble experiment' when he came to office was to look around for some means by which he could find something he was not authorized to do; look for some secret way of slipping something over. His chance came when Florence Kelly presented him with the Fabian Socialist book, 'A New Deal.'"

"He did not have any war as did his predecessor, Wilson: So he invented a war and called it a war on depression — along the lines of war democracy, you know, where the results of the war for democracy (WWI) has rendered the world bereft of democracy and rampant with dictatorships. He needed some show of lawful authority to quiet the people while he usurped authority." (Exactly what Bush did in his Gulf War and Clinton did in full measure with sending troops to Bosnia — and it is what Clinton is still doing.) "So he instructed his Attorney General to find some pretense of authority and the Attorney General found a law passed during the war (WWI) 'to make the world safe for democracy' and upon its pretended authority closed every bank in the country, to make sure we reached the bottom of desperation. What little courage and confidence was left, was taken away."

That is the sum and substance of the fraud of the so-called War Powers Act of 1933. It was a disgraceful fraud then and it will remain a disgraceful fraud unless the Republican Party finds the courage to rescind it. Well meaning people like Dr. Schroeder do a great disservice by perpetuating the lie. Roosevelt brushed aside the Constitution; to him it didn't matter that he was trampling the Constitution underfoot; his goal was to put Socialism on a firm footing in the U.S.

Today, we see Roosevelt in action through Clinton and Dole; neither man caring a fig about the Constitution. Dole made an astounding statement on national television to the effect that while abortion is an important issue there are other important issues. He classified abortion as a "moral and social issue." Abortion is not only a moral and social issue, it is first and foremost, a constitutional issue of the greatest magnitude. But like Wilson, Roosevelt, Carter and Bush, Dole and Clinton brush aside the Constitution. What Roosevelt did was summed up rather well by a former Secretary State under Wilson, Bainbridge Coley, which is found on page 9836 Congressional Record:

"Vast Bureaucracy Fastened Upon Us: A prominent Democrat (Roosevelt) has been called into being; and fastened upon us without our realizing it. (A technique used by William Jefferson Clinton.) Gradually it has dawned on the country and it is now quite plain, that recovery was only partially the aim of the administration. A great part of its interest has been radical institutional overturn and new modeling of the state. The guarantees of the Constitution are dismissed lightly as if they were irrelevancies of the present day life of America (a tactic later adopted by Justice Brennan.) The basic principals of the Constitution, we are told, must be some how got around." For the record, Roosevelt did not pull America out of the post 1929 depression. Rather, he perpetuated it. As Henry Ford once said, "history is bunk."

The so-called War Powers Act of 1933 was part and parcel of Roosevelt's plan to get around the Constitution and take additional powers to which the executive branch was not entitled. His action was FRAUDULENT and the War Powers Act remains a ghastly fraud on the American people.

WAR POWERS OF THE PRESIDENT AND
TRUTH ABOUT COMMANDER IN CHIEF STATUS

As for the war powers of the President, there are none. The powers of the President are limited and among them are ribbon cutting and making radio and television speeches, and being a telephone jockey. The powers of the President are very skimpy although Clinton in true Socialist style, has usurped more powers than even Roosevelt took, and that is saying a lot, not to mention throwing coffee binges at the White House, making phone calls from his office to raise funds for the Democrat Party in violation of the law, stonewalling Senate investigations etc. The oft-repeated falsehood that the President automatically becomes the commander in chief of the armed forces as soon as he is elected to office is a willful misrepresentation of what the Constitution actually says. Also, he has no power to declare war as stated in the Congressional Record, House, Dec. 1945 which talks about the U.N.'s illegality:

"It (the U.N. treaty/agreement) provides that the power to declare war be taken away from the Congress and given to the President."

Mr. Clinton is already acting as if he has a right to declare war under the aegis of the UN.

Henry Clay that great constitutional authority, stated that Congress declares war and makes policy and objectives for the war, not the President. Clay would have declared Clinton guilty of violating the Constitution by placing our troops in Bosnia and in the Persian Gulf had he been alive today. The president is responsible for purely military duties AFTER being called into service by the Congress, and he has nothing to say about the declaration of war, or its purposes and intent. That belongs exclusively to the House and Senate as Clay forcefully stated. And the title of commander in chief is temporarily conferred upon him by Congress, lasting only until the MILITARY objectives are reached or the war ends, at which time the title is taken back by the Congress and that is the end of it. The President doesn't retain the title of commander in chief ad-infinitum. It is not a title that automatically comes with the job. The President is not a king. Congressional Record, Senate, July 21, 1922. pages 2916-2920:

"In their final and deliberate judgment one of the most important features of the covenant (the U.S. Constitution and the Bill of Rights) was that our country should be distinguished from other nations in its refusal to concentrate in one man exclusive power over foreign relations of the Government and especially over the issues of peace and war..."

In no way would the Founding Fathers have allowed the President to become a king and a tyrant by giving him war-making powers. That comes through loud and clear. Appendix to Blackstone's Commentaries With Notes to the Constitution of the United States and the Commonwealth of Virginia, particularly page 329 (restrictions on the President.):

"The first shall be commander in chief of the army, the navy of the United States and the militia of the several States (not to be confused with the unenlisted militia or the National Guard) when called into the service of the United States...As to the first, he cannot make rules for the regulation and government of the army and navy himself and must govern according to the regulations established by the Congress."

In other words, the President is not automatically the commander in chief. Until such times as the Congress confers the title upon him, and even when appointed to this position his powers are very much curtailed and he cannot choose where to send the army and navy, nor decide the purpose of their mission. Until the Congress calls the President into service and confers upon him the title of commander in chief, he does not hold this position. Conferring the title of commander in chief is a future action, not a past action. It would be a past action if the President were to automatically become the commander in chief when elected to office. Only the Congress can confer the title upon the President when it calls him into actual service, and this, only after a constitutional declaration of war.

Today, the members of the House and Senate have little knowledge what these words "when called into actual service" mean. If it were true — as some assert — that the President is automatically commander in chief upon being elected — he would then "stand where kings stood" to paraphrase Pres. Lincoln. Our Founding Fathers did not want the US to have a king, which is why they placed this restraint upon the powers of the President.

Also, few of our current members of the House know how to draw up a constitutional declaration of war, which is a deliberately complicated procedure; a secretive procedure designed to curb hothead presidents like Bush and Clinton from rushing the U.S. to war. It also deals with the KIND of war it intends declaring — and note it is the Congress that makes the decision. This information is spelled out in the Congressional Record, House, July 21, 1888, and explains the difference between limited wars and unlimited wars. Pomeroy, the great constitutionalist of that period wrote in his work, "Introduction to Constitutional Law:"

"The organic law nowhere proscribes or limits the causes for which hostilities may be waged against a foreign nation. The causes of war it leaves to the discretion and judgment of the legislature."

As an example of a proper declaration of war, consult the House of Representatives Report No.1, 65 Congress, 1 session, page 319, Congressional Record, House, April 5, 1917:

"Whereas The Imperial German Government has committed repeated acts of war between the Government and the people of the United States of America: Therefore, be it resolved by the Senate and the House of Representatives of the United States of America, in Congress assembled, that the state of war between the United States and the Imperial German Government which has thus been thrust upon the United States, is hereby formally declared: and that the President, be, and is hereby authorized and directed to employ the entire naval and military forces of the United States and the resources of this government to carry on war against the Imperial German Government; and to bring the conflict to a successful termination. All of the resources of the country are pledged by the Congress of the United States."

Please note this declaration of war was for a perfect war, that is to say, every man, women and child in the United States was at war with every man, women and child of the belligerent state and that all the branches of the armed services were to be employed to this end; and, furthermore, please note that it was the Congress who directed the President what to do to further the war, not the other way around. Mr. Bush and Mr. Clinton turned this around and Clinton is bent upon once again putting one over on the American people by trying to rush the nation into a second Gulf War in November 1997.

Former Pres. Bush twisted and squeezed this vital section of the Constitution to suit his purpose of dragging America into a war in the Persian Gulf which was strictly a war to protect the oil interests of British Petroleum and to neutralize Iraq, seen as a threat to Israel. Bush chose to by-pass the constitutionally mandated declaration of war — which he knew he could not get — and instead got a "Senate resolution" to go to war against Iraq. There is no such thing as a "Senate resolution" in the Constitution. The Republicans knew very well that Bush was breaking the law, to whit, the Constitution, which is the highest law we have, but almost to a man, they chose party loyalty over obeying their oath of office, a crime of treason for which every one of those who supported the Senate's charade should have been tried, and that includes George Bush, the constitutional scofflaw.

We issue a challenge to the Supreme Court, the American Bar Association (ABA), indeed any person in the law profession, any member of the legislature, any member of the executive branch, to show us where in the delegated powers of the central government is it stated that the President has any war power; or where it says that the President can wage war without a constitutional declaration of war. Article II, Sec. 3. Pt II, says that the President shall only have military duties when called into service and he has NO role in the planning or choosing of the type of war to be fought. Furthermore the President has NO role in planning the war and the purposes for which the troops are to be used.

And please note it does distinctly say that only the Congress can authorize dispatch of U.S. military forces to foreign wars. Clinton had no right to send our armed services to Bosnia, and less still did Pres. Bush have any right to send our armed services to the Persian Gulf. The worst offender of them was Pres. Woodrow Wilson, who violated the U.S. Constitution and the Bill of Rights all over the place in 1917 in sending our Militia to the battlefields of Europe, as I explain in the chapter about the Militia and the Dick Act. Moreover, not only did Bush and Clinton not have any right to send our armed forces abroad without a constitutional declaration of war, they also lacked the authority to decide on the mission of our armed forces. Thus, the President has NO war powers. Let the doubters show where in the Constitution it is stated to the contrary.

THE FEDERAL RESERVE ACT OF 1913

One of the cardinal errors that has crept in to pervert the law and turn it from its proper purposes, is the Federal Reserve Act, that cardinal sin of unbridled greed imposed upon a once-free people to bind them like slaves and rob them of the fruits of their labor. The Federal Reserve Act of which I am speaking presumes that individual rights to property, life and liberty can be legislated against, as though these gifts come not from God but from government.

On the contrary, these gifts do not exist because of the law, but because of God. And by what law does government presume to take them from us? The crooked, corrupt politicians connived us into believing that an entity called the "Federal Reserve banks" has the right to plunder the people, whereas the truth is that every man has the right to defend himself and his property, that being the oldest law known to mankind.

For as long as the U.S. is cursed with the Federal Reserve banking system, its citizens remain in slavery, with only marginal differences between the people and the slaves of the Pharaoh Thotmes the fourth. Just as the slaves were able to throw off the yoke of the Pharaohs, so the time will have to come when the U.S. will produce its own "Moses" to lead the nation back to financial freedom.

To those who contend that the Federal Reserve Board is a legal governmental entity, I say, "please open your eyes to what follows. The Federal Reserve Banking system is not a legal governmental agency; it is a private entity which has absorbed the wealth of the nation and abrogated it unto itself without ever earning one red cent of it. The Constitution was perverted by men of greed, men of hate for this republic, of hatred of its nationality. The secret stockholders of the Federal Reserve live in untold wealth at the expense of the people, whose money they consume without having lawful title to it."

Like the priests of Pharaoh's Court, the men behind the Federal Reserve bank performed a magic trick; they turned fresh air into money and they are bent upon keeping the real creators of wealth, the people, enslaved for as long as the people will allow it. Establishing a central bank in the face of a constitutional prohibition was another of their magic tricks, this one inspired by the Communist Manifesto of 1848.

The golden age of America — constitutionally speaking — was the period 1880-1900. It was a time of overwhelming patriotism in defense of the Constitution and the scoundrels who supported Communism were exposed by a few brave legislators; it was a period when some of the greatest debates in our history took place in the House and Senate. It was a period when members of the House and Senate knew the Constitution, and they never betrayed their oath of office by bringing a bill or a measure to a vote of the legislature without first thoroughly debating its constitutionality. They had a thorough understanding of the depth and profundity of the Constitution and the Bill of Rights, so totally absent among the members of the Congress, today.

In this period of our history, we find the most courageous senators and representatives who were not afraid to challenge the mendacity of the Warburgs, Rothschilds, Rockefellers and their international banker friends, swindlers one and all. One such person, Rep. Charles Lindbergh, tried to tear away the veil from the bankers who have been predators on this nation ever since 1913. In actual fact, the American people have been fighting a war against international banking for more than two hundred-years. For his patriotism Lindbergh suffered having his baby son kidnaped and murdered, a punishment plot that involved trying to discredit Germany. It was a time when the House and Senate perceived these evil leeches were out to destroy the Republic of the United States of America by ending the fiscal soundness of bimetallism and its balance of 16 ounces of silver to one ounce of gold. Bimetallism was the foundation, the solid rock upon which the financial integrity of the young nation was built, upon which it rested.

It was also the time of the finest judges this nation has ever produced, judges of the caliber and quality of Judge John Davis, a giant of a man with an intellect with no equal then and who does not have an equal today, and Justice Roger Taney, the "incorruptible" judge who knew the Constitution and fiercely defended it against domestic and foreign enemies alike. But in the latter part of 1901, the standard of constitutional ability in the House and Senate began its gradual decline to where it is today; where almost total ignorance of the complexities of the Constitution is displayed by the majority of the legislators and the judiciary. The golden age of the American Constitution gradually drew to a close with Communists, Marxists and anarchists pouring into the U.S. from Russia and other Eastern-European nations, on a flood tide of immigration released by Roosevelt.

The bulk of these Communists and their fellow-travelers congregated in New York and New Jersey. They knew the value of pushing their cause through political channels — the Bolsheviks had taught them that was the way to go if they lacked naked firepower. Of course I am not tarring all the immigrants from Eastern Europe with the same brush, but the Congressional Records of the period show that among their ranks were large groups of militant Socialist, Marxists and Communists, Anarchists and Nihilists, among them Emma Goldman and her militants, one of whom assassinated Pres. McKinley.

They injected themselves into the political arena and they were the ones who pushed for passage of the Federal Reserve Act of 1913. A study of the congressional documents I have so often referred to will prove the foregoing. At the same time the British Fabian Society sent its leadership cadre to the United States to Socialize our country. All this is explained in detail in my book, "Socialism: The Road To Slavery" and the Federal Reserve Act of 1913 was a significant marker on that road, as was the 17th Amendment.

Those senators who stayed in Washington to do their duty, instead of joining the rush home for Christmas that fateful year of 1913, had they but known the Constitution, would have recognized the Federal Reserve Act instantly for what it was, a quasi-legal device to rob the people of the power to create money and currency of the nation and to regulate it. They would have realized that the bill before them was not "in consonance with" nor "in pursuance of" nor was it expressly implied by a power already in the Constitution and could not, therefore, be brought up for debate, let alone be voted on. In short, the Federal Reserve Act which met NONE of the above criteria of constitutionality, should have been dropped as DEAD ON ARRIVAL the moment it was introduced. It was a gigantic fraud and remains so to this day.

As Rep. Louis T. McFadden told the House on Friday, June 10, 1932:

"Mr. Chairman, we have in this country one of the most corrupt institutions the world has ever known. I refer to the Federal Reserve Board and the Federal Reserve Banks. The Federal Reserve Board, a Government board, has cheated the Government of the United States and the people of the United States out of enough money to pay the national debt. The depredations and iniquities of the Federal Reserve Board and the Federal Reserve Banks acting together have cost this country enough money to pay the national debt several times over..."

"Some people think the Federal Reserve Banks are United States Government institutions. They are private credit monopolies which prey upon the people of the United States for the benefit of themselves and their foreign customers; foreign and domestic speculators and swindlers; and rich predatory money lenders...Those 12 private credit monopolies were deceitfully and disloyally foisted upon this nation by bankers who came from Europe and who repaid our hospitality by undermining our American institutions..."

"In 1912 the National Monetary Committee (note the cunning deception in the title — not one word about the bill being a bill to establish an unconstitutional central bank) under the chairmanship of the late Senator Nelson W. Aldrich made a report and presented a vicious bill, the National Reserve Association bill. (Again, note the gross deception in the title.) The bill is usually spoken of as the Aldrich bill. He was a tool, but not an accomplice of the European-born bankers who for nearly 20 years had been scheming to set up a central bank in this country and who in 1912 had spent and were continuing to spend vast sums of money to accomplish this purpose."

The National Monetary Commission was a group of mattoids, bootlickers for the Warburg-Rothschild swindlers. The Congressional Record, January 9, 1912, pages 744-752 lays out the scope and duties of this so-called Commission, but all that this mattoid group did once in Europe, was copy the tyrannical money systems of the Bank of England, the German Reichsbank, the French National Bank, and then when they came back to the U.S. they recommended that a carbon-copy banking tyranny be imposed on the American people. Of course, several senators whose strings were being jerked by the Warburgs and Rothschilds, were only too happy to accept the treasonous report of the National Monetary Committee.

This was the commencement of the unconstitutional "special powers" supposedly given by Congress to the Federal Reserve, which special powers are not in the delegated powers of Congress to give, and they mainly consisted of making "legal" U.S. funding of international banks and bank loans to all and sundry in Europe. This was Bill S 2472:

"The bill authorizes corporations be organized and managed under the supervision of the Federal Reserve Board, to deal with international banking."

It was the first step to drawing the U.S. into the coming world war that began the very next year. What Congress did was to act like a gigantic embezzler, supervising theft through fraud on a gigantic scale, the ultimate goal being the destruction of the U.S. Constitution and the Bill of Rights and dispossession of the middle class, reducing them to poverty and peonship. Such a people is easily controlled and will make no trouble nor raise any rebellion. There is no more evil and example of how the technique works than the way in which the middle class in South Africa, once stable and productive, was reduced to beggary, and this is what will happen to the American middle class unless as a distinct but fast-fading class, this group can somehow be aroused and made to see what is happening to them.

The cumulative damage done by the swindlers, plunderers, embezzlers, liars, thieves, and their monstrously unconstitutional Federal Reserve bill will be impossible to overcome for at least another 100 years, and then, only if it is immediately recognized as an illicit creation and its powers axed by the legislators within the next 12 months at the very latest. That these evil men were intent upon defrauding and swindling the nation is apparent when one reads how the Federal Reserve act was passed. Congressional Record, December 1913, pages 1441-1452:

"When the bill was reported to the House for passage, a rule was brought in from the Committee on Rules, *limiting the debate to four hours* on a bill that none but the Republican members of the banking and Currency had ever read, and it was an objection from the new chairman of the Banking and Currency Committee that brought a printed copy of that bill before the House *for the first time.* It came fresh from the printer, green, and wet, and was rushed through under the rule, (the rule limiting debate to four hours) practically without consideration and without amendment...The bill is now brought back to the House in a 58-page document in triple columns and a 30-page closely printed report, *which the house is to accept after a two hour discussion,* in order that the President (Wilson) and Members may go off on their holiday vacations..."

Surely, the miscreants, plunderers of the American people, treacherously, treasonously, sold us into bondage, from whence we have never emerged. Our lot is akin to the slaves of the Pharaoh. The backers of the Federal reserve act lied to the American people, blatantly and without any sense of shame. They violated their oath of office to uphold the U.S. Constitution, and for that, all who voted for this grand theft ought to have been tried for treason and sedition, and if found guilty, they should all have been hanged. Because this was not done, the Congress ceased to be independent once the Federal Reserve act became "law" and today we don't have anyone in Congress truly representing We, the People. Congress has become a chamber of cowards ruled by the brooding spirit of the illicit Federal Reserve, its members sycophants and flunkies, terrified, quaking beneath the boots of their banker-slavemaster. There are no McFaddens among them.

Since then, a whole generation of Congressmen have continuously vacillated and have failed to do their duty to close down the Federal Reserve banks, having been conditioned to accept their slavemaster's dictates with equanimity and with an eye to keeping their positions of power and privilege in the House and Senate, constantly, each and every year, violating their oath to uphold the Constitution and to defend it against all enemies, domestic and foreign.

There were a few Senators who saw through the ruse, that fateful year of 1913, and this was especially true later, when in the 1930s Roosevelt was grabbing powers to which he was not entitled, on a grand scale. Roosevelt, a former director of the International Banker's Association, prepared the ground for the 1921-1922 depression while Governor of New York. He sent millions of dollars to Europe under the guise of loans so that there was not enough money for domestic use. Of course without the Federal Reserve there would have been no such "loans" and no post Wall Street crash depression.

Roosevelt was able to go about his criminal business because of the Federal Reserve. Much of the criminal activity of the Roosevelt administration sheltered behind the revetments of the Federal Reserve. The bottom line is that there is no provision in the Constitution for a central bank and that is what the Federal Reserve Bank is. It was sold to the American people as the savior of our economy and the badly-connived American people accepted it as such, because their representatives had so miserably failed to do their constitutional duty.

So-called Federal Reserve notes are not legal tender because there has not been a constitutional amendment to make them legal tender "in obligation of contracts" as the Constitution says. In short, Federal Reserve notes are the equal of fiat money. The American people are not obligated to accept them but in the absence of anything else, they have accepted them, and also, because they have been lied to by the Federal government, the public is in ignorance of the true status of this gigantic fraud and rip-off.

To quote Rep. McFadden again:

"The Aldrich bill was condemned in the platform upon which Theodore Roosevelt was nominated in the year 1912, and in that same year, when Woodrow Wilson was nominated, the Democrat platform was adopted at the Biltmore convention, expressly stated: 'We are opposed to the Aldrich plan for a central bank.' This was plain language. The men who ruled the Democrat Party then promised the people that if they were returned to power there would be no central bank established here while they held the reins of government."

"Thirteen months later, that promise was broken and the Wilson administration, under the tutelage of those sinister Wall Street figures who stood behind Colonel House, established here in our free country the worm-eaten monarchical institution of the 'king's bank' to control from the top downward, and to shackle us from the cradle to the grave...The danger that the country was warned against came down upon us and is shown in the long train of horrors attendant upon the affairs of the traitorous and dishonest Federal Reserve Banks...."

McFadden knew what was going on. As Chairman of the House Banking Committee, he was in a position to know and he was not afraid to tell what he knew. Unhappily, today, we have no legislators of the stature of McFadden; what we have are legislators standing in mortal fear of the international banker's cabal, so much so that year after year, they go

on betraying their oath of office to uphold the Constitution, which makes
them unfit to hold office. It is hard to imagine Sen. Trent Lott and Rep.
Newt Gingrich standing up to the Federal Reserve banks as McFadden did
on every possible occasion. Imagine them challenging the current chairman, ex-musician Alan Greenspan: "Mr. Chairman, where is your mandate to exist found in the U.S. Constitution?" "A brave man dies once, but
a coward dies a thousand deaths" as someone once wrote.

McFadden went on to denounce the Democrats as the principal
architects of the Federal Reserve Board from the floor of the House:

"Not all the Democratic Members of the Sixty Third Congress voted
for this great deception. Some of them, remembering the teachings of
Jefferson and through the years, there have been no criticism of the
Federal Reserve Board and Federal Reserve Banks so honest, so out-
spoken and so unsparing as those which have been voiced by
Democrats..."

After 1913, the House and Senate voted on numerous occasions to
strengthen the python's grip upon the American people by sanctioning
such measures as the Monetary Control Act of 1980, signed into "law"
by Communist James Earl Carter, the truth about whose career as a life-
long Communist is just now beginning to emerge. This measure like
those before it, was deceptively titled. What the Monetary Control Act
actually was, was a device to keep the Federal Reserve charter from
lapsing, the fear being that Congress would one day awake from its tor-
por and cancel it. The Monetary Control Act of 1980 was foretold in the
Congressional Record, December 20, 1913, pages 1297-1302:

"To have succession for a period of 20 years from its organization
unless sooner dissolved by an act of Congress, or unless its franchise
becomes forfeited by some violation of the law..."

Long before 1913, in fact in 1898, an even more compelling predic-
tion and dire warning was made by Senator Allen about the coming of
this evil bank: Congressional Record, Senate, January 7, 1898, pages
418-424:

"Financial Policy: I regard it as a signal of danger that we have
entered on the money issuing-interest bearing obligations on every con-
ceivable occasion and pretext. The Founding Fathers of our country
warned us against being in perpetual human bondage, and those who are
obligated to pay it are slaves. They may assemble and resolve that they are
free, but they are bondslaves until the debt is paid, and the Government,

like a prudent individual, should get out of debt as speedily as possible and remain out. It would be useless to point out that the Government interest-bearing debt of less than $3,000,000,000 at the close of the war has cost the people in their labor and production over $7,000,000,000 thus far, and yet we have a thousand million left and the administration and Mr. Gage, the Sec. of the Treasury, would have us increase this interest-bearing debt to a thousand million more, the interest charge to the people in such circumstances being $60,000,000 annually."

The Rothschilds held the bonds for most of the Civil War debt, and they resolved to keep the American people in perpetual servitude. (The Civil War debt was finally paid of in 1932.) What can be done to rid ourselves of this yoke around our necks? Two things, 1) the Congress can pass a law which will close down the Federal Reserve, either directly or 2), indirectly, the latter could be if Congress passed a law that the Federal Reserve pay 95 percent of its ill-gotten gains in taxes, retroactive to 1914. This would tax them out of business and at the same time return to the nation's treasury, a small portion of the money the Fed. Reserve has stolen from We, the People.

What the robbers behind the Federal Reserve act wanted, was to ensure that if their sinister intentions were discovered, Congress could not shut down the Federal Reserve for a period of 20 years thereafter. Thus, it is clear that Congress knows it can dispose of the Federal Reserve, but its members lack the integrity and fortitude to put this evil empire out of business and free the American people from a state of eternal servitude.

To add to the injury done to the American people by the robbers and thieves of the Federal Reserve and their backers in Congress, Law 12, U.S.C., exempts the privately owned and controlled Federal Reserve bank from paying income tax. This punitive law was passed 10 months after the 15th Amendment was ratified. The source of this information is the Appendix to the Congressional Record, Nov. 6, 1969, pages 33558-33559. And there it remains.

CHAPTER 3

THE CONSTITUTION CANNOT BE TWISTED, SQUEEZED OR BENT

I n the preceding chapters we have seen a number of instances where constitutional anarchists have tried to twist, bend or squeeze the Constitution for their own ends and that corrupt judges often uphold such violations of the Constitution based upon their predilections which conduct is forbidden by the 9th Amendment. It would be foolish to think that such assaults on the Constitution and the Bill of Rights will just stop without judges and lawmakers being sharply reined in.

The Constitution of the United States and Bill of Rights is immutable and cannot be changed to suit "force of circumstances" nor any other expediency. Since the advent of Franklin D. Roosevelt and his Socialist Supreme Court, we have seen many attempts to bend the Constitution out of shape. The great Judge Cooley, Congressional Record, House, pages 2273-2279:

"The Constitution itself never yields to a treaty or enactment. It neither changes with time nor does it in theory bend to the force of circumstances."

We have a present stretching back over 200 years which is being destroyed and trampled upon by Socialist/Marxist members of the legislature, the executive and the judiciary, either out of total ignorance of its truths, or out of hatred of them. If we are to save the U.S. Constitution and the Bill of Rights from being obliterated, then every man, women and child in the United States needs to have a manual that will provide them with information they so sorely lack. I believe "What You Don't Know About The U.S. Constitution" will go some way toward meeting this great need. Some examples of how the Constitution has been twisted and bent to "yield to force of circumstances" are as follows:

THE 10TH AMENDMENT

This amendment is seldom expanded upon in a good number of books on the Constitution, indeed, some of the most important law library books do no more than mention it in passing, yet it is one of the most important safeguards against Central Government encroaching the rights of the States. It is was known in the 1880s as "the quarantine amendment." The State of Massachusetts would not join the Union until the 10th Amendment was accepted as part of the Constitution. The Congressional Record, House, March 28 1904, pages 3898-3906 contains an explanation of the 10th Amendment from Judge Cooley's book, "Constitutional Limitations" and it says on page 706 of this excellent constitutional reference, as follows:

"In the American Constitutional system, the power to establish the ordinary police regulations has been left with the individual States and it can not be taken from them, either wholly or in part, and exercised under legislation of Congress. Neither can the National Government through any of its departments and officers, assume any supervision of police regulations of the States."

What is meant by "police powers?" These State powers were health, education, welfare, family affairs and police protection. They were always collectively referred to as "the police powers of the States." Clearly these rights are States rights and cannot be infringed upon or interfered with the Central Government. Pomeroy the great constitutionalist said in his work, "Constitutional Law"...."These affairs which are local, which affect the individual citizen in his private capacity, abstracted from his relations to the whole political society, are managed by separate State Governments which were found in existence and left remaining by the same Constitution."

9 Wallace 41: "No power is conferred by the Constitution upon the Congress to establish mere police regulations within the States."

14 Howard 17: "The power to make municipal regulations for the restraint and punishment of crime, for the preservation of health and morals of her citizens has never been surrendered by the States or restrained by the Constitution of the United States..."

Clearly and unmistakably the Founding Fathers intended the States to be in full control of health, education, welfare and police protection and not subject to even a whiff of Federal Government interference. Under the clear and unmistakable language of the 10th Amendment it is simply that there is no such thing as a grant that would allow a "Federal" police force interfering with law enforcement in the States; no Federal Health Department, and no Education Department can operate in the States. These "police powers" belong with the States and were never relinquished to the Central Government.

The statement made by Sen. Calhoun on Feb. 15, 1833, showed that the 10th Amendment is a power for the several States. Congressional Globe, Jan. 31, 1866:

"But it is contended that the Constitution has conferred on the Supreme Court the right of judging between the States and the General Government. Those who make this objection overlook, I conceive, an important provision of the Constitution. By turning to the Tenth Amendment article it will be seen that the reservation of power to the States is not only against the powers delegated to Congress, but against the United States themselves, and extends, of course, as well to the judiciary as to the other departments of government. The 10th Amendment fixes the type of limitations upon organic law and makes the Federal Government one of delegated powers not original powers."

Again, we have the profound statement made by Rep. Denison in the Congressional Globe, Jan 31, 1866, pages 546-549:

"...So it was competent for the States when they created this government organization and called it the United States, by the Constitution to delegate therein certain powers *and the right to do certain things* and thus place the powers delegated under the control of the Federal majorities, and reserve certain powers to be controlled by the people of each State, and for the exercise and control of which they were not to be answerable *to any other power.* If the States did absolutely and unconditionally reserve these powers, then they cannot be taken away by two thirds of this House and three-quarters of the States anymore than the majority of stockholders of a bank, in which I might have stock, take over my horse or my farm for the use of the corporation, because the States never placed these reserved powers in the common fund of powers to be controlled by the Federal majorities."

"Their condition was the same as to these reserved powers after adoption of the Constitution as before. The people of each State constitute a sovereignty before the adoption of that instrument. They were equally sovereign over the reserved rights after its adoption, and they cannot be taken away, except by the will of each State,; unless there be something in the Constitution to authorize it; for a State, like an individual, cannot be bound further that it agrees to bind itself. Have the States parted with these rights by agreeing to amend the Constitution? If so, then these powers were not reserved absolutely, but only retained until the Federal majorities as represented by two-thirds of the House and three-fourths of the States my choose to transfer them against the will of the people of the State, or it may be one-fourth of the States, from the respective States to the Federal Government. This point ought to be settled by the Constitution and I think it is."

"The most important feature of the 10th Amendment is that it fixes limitations on the Federal Government which is one of delegated powers and not original powers. It makes it impossible for government to take any power by inference. The power to be taken, or exercised must be clearly expressed in the Constitution or it cannot be taken. In Article 5 there is the right to amend, but not to make new. It would not be an amendment to abolish the Constitution and adopt the Communist Manifesto of 1848, or the laws of France. An amendment has to be something germane to the instrument, it must be something already in the Constitution or it fails the test of an amendment. But making a new Constitution would only be binding on those States as agree to be bound by it and could not become a part of the Constitution until every State should adopt it."

What this means is that no one can alter the 10th Amendment nor twist it to suit their own purpose, whatever they might be and means also that the Federal Government can do nothing which is not in its delegated powers, Art. 1. Sec. 8, Clauses 1-18. The 10th Amendment puts such matters as police powers, health, education and welfare out of reach of the Central Government and gives these powers solely to the States. The rape of the 10th Amendment has been a highlight of the Clinton Administration.

EDUCATION IS RESERVED TO THE STATES AND LOCAL INSTITUTIONS UNDER THE 10TH AMENDMENT

It has always been the desire of the Communists and their fellow-travelers in America, especially in the 1920s and 1930s in the Roosevelt era, to "nationalize" or "standardize" education. In 1923, the Supreme Court served by justices who knew the Constitution and which was free of politicized Socialist justices, ruled in the case of Meyer vs. Nebraska that: "The State may not interfere in the right of the parents to control the education of their young."

This dealt a blow to the Communists who were rushing at breakneck speed to get bills passed that would negate the 10th Amendment and give control of education to the Federal Government. I have extracted from the Congressional Record, Senate, 1926 and particularly from page 12917, the following to bear out the truth of the foregoing:

"Miss Jane Addams said her wish for Mrs. Kelley was 'long life; that she might live to see no children in America unprotected by Congressional legislation...'" (Addams was one of the leading lights of the Communist "feminist" movement centered at Hull House and Mrs. Kelly was a dyed-in-the-wool Communists and close advisor to Eleanor and Franklin Roosevelt.) "Thus while all the pacifism, internationalism and social legislative schemes in America, together with the Women's International League, the national Women's Trade Union League...the United States Children's Bureau... cradled at Hull House, we find that Hull House was first taught to walk the socialist road by the ubiquitous Mrs. Florence Kelley..."

"...The point is that one of the fundamental designs of the communists is to capture and control not only the content of education but the teachers themselves as 'apparatus of power' and propaganda, and that Mrs. Kelley has been in key positions for years to spread communist propaganda in schools and colleges and among teachers as well... Nicolai Lenin saw the strategic importance of the education system as an apparatus of power: 'Hundreds of thousands of teachers constitute an apparatus that must push our work forward...The communists active in the field of popular education must learn and understand to conduct this mass, which runs into hundreds of thousands...It is important and necessary that he should be guiding masses of teachers...'"

If we substitute the names of William Jefferson Clinton and Mrs. Clinton for Florence Kelley and Lenin, I think it becomes very clear that the President and his wife are carrying on where Lenin, Mrs. Kelley, and Franklin Roosevelt left off. The White House has taken the place of Hull House when it comes to Communizing education and the "masses" of teachers who have charge of it.

The Communists regard children as the property of the State and many attempts were made in the 1920s and 1930s to force this alien idea into the laws of the United States in violation of the 10th Amendment. "Regulation of Child Labor" pages 9962-9977 of the Congressional Record, May 31, 1924 and "Maternity and Infancy Act," Congressional Record pages 12918-12951, shows how the Communists in the Democrat Party desperately wanted their plan to take education away from the States to succeed.

Some further references to the Communist plan to take over education in a centralized government department comes from other prominent people in the field of education:

"Education as a practical instrumentality for the creating of a New World Order...Education is a form of Social control comparable with armies etc..." Dr. William B. Owen, president of the National Education Association in a speech, June 23, 1923.

The words, "new world order" were commonly used in speeches by Socialist/Marxist/Communist leaders in the U.S. during the 1920s. In private the National Educators Association members were told, "it is a synonym for the Communist Manifesto of 1848."

"Citizenship today must be broader than nationalism. There must be an international conscientiousness; there must be an international heart; and a world mind. This world mind is largely an attitude of habit of thinking in the larger units of the world etc... The peoples of the earth must now live together, and we, the teachers of the world's children must prepare the world's children for these new relations... In order to change the ideals of the nations, we must begin with the child when he first becomes teachable; because the child is unprejudiced; and as we lead him up through the winding path of education and experience, we gradually instill into him his own prejudice...There was a day when a person was simply a citizen of his locality and possibly of his country...Today the citizen must be a citizen of the world...Therefore, children must receive the larger viewpoint and the larger understanding. That viewpoint, that understanding, must come through the teachers." Dr. Augustus Thomas, president of the World Federation of Educational Associations, July 21, 1935.

There we have it. What the Communists are after is domination in education through a centralized government which will push internationalism for all of its worth to the exclusion of nationalism and patriotism, which will submerge national entities and countries in a New

World Order. This is what Florence Kelley and the National Educators Association fought for; this is what Franklin and Eleanor Roosevelt fought for; this is what Mr. and Mrs. Clinton are fighting for. In education, we are in a struggle to the death, one which if we lose, will see the end of the United States in less than eighty-years.

In the following you see how the Communists in the U.S. tried to put their plans to communize schools under a centralized Communist Federal Education Department:

Congressional Record, May 24 1924, page 12928:

"Federal Department of Education Bill Pending was one such determined effort to gain control of education by the central government in the form of a U.S. Department of Education — not mentioned in the Constitution nor expressly implied and thus, a prohibition — but the Senators at that time were well aware of what was going on and they beat back the challenge." One thing I have learned about the despoilers of the Constitution and the Bill of Rights; they are very patient and never admit defeat. Rather, they bide their time until a more propitious moment, mostly created by a press which is largely under their control.

And so it was with education. In 1980, Communist James Earl Carter realized the dreams and schemes of Miss Addams; Miss Lathrop; Mrs. Kelley; Franklin and Eleanor Roosevelt and their fellow travelers: finally they got a bill enacted to establish an unconstitutional Department of Education in defilement of the U.S. Constitution and in flagrant abuse of the 10th Amendment, and Carter signed it. The Federal Department of Education is just one of a large number of government agencies operating outside of the Constitution which are not mandated by the Constitution. If we have any conservative members of the legislature of either party, they should resolves to close down all such scofflaw agencies, beginning with those which violate the 10th Amendment powers reserved to the States.

Congressional Globe Jan. 31, 1866, page 548:

"The 10th Amendment fixes the type of limitation upon organic law, and makes the Federal government one of delegated powers and not original powers."

Former Pres. Carter apparently felt quite happy when he violated this important restraint upon the Federal Government by signing into "law" the Federal Department of Education. There is nothing in the Constitution that would permit a Central Department of Education. To make the kind of bill which Carter signed into "law" 1980; and which Mr. Clinton and his wife are making in 1997, turns the Constitution into a blank piece of paper by construction, to paraphrase Thomas Jefferson. It would take at least two amendments agreed to by all of the States to make the Federal Department of Education a part of the Constitution and secondly, to allow it to override State education laws.

OUR REPUBLIC:
A GUARANTEE OF EQUAL RIGHTS OR ALL MEN ARE EQUAL?

Our Constitutions says that the United States is a Republic, and this has to do with the 10th Amendment. One of the more troubling aspects of the times is the almost continual reference to America as a "democracy." The United States is a Republic. Here follows the definition of a Republican form of Government. Congressional Globe, Feb. 18, 1896, page 903:

"That the United States will guarantee every state in the Union a Republican form of government and Congress is empowered to enforce this guarantee. The definition of a Republican government was solemnly announced by our fathers, first, in the great battle-cry of the Revolution 'taxation without representation is tyranny' and secondly in the Great Declaration at the birth of our Republic that all men are equal in rights and that the government stands on the consent of the governed. A Republic is where taxation and representation go hand in hand, where all are equal in rights and no man is excluded from participation of government."

Please note it did not say that "all men are equal." This is a Socialist — Marxist spin on what the Founding Fathers meant, namely, that "all men are equal in rights," a very different thing from "all men are equal." Yet, in spite of the clear language in which it is written, ever since the Reconstruction legislation and the Civil Rights Act of 1866, politicians have sought to twist and squeeze the meaning into "all men are equal" solely for political purposes.

WAS THE 10TH AMENDMENT TO THE CONSTITUTION TWISTED AND SQUEEZED TO CREATE A CENTRAL POLICE FORCE?

Perhaps one of the most serious of many serious violations of the Constitution and the Bill of Rights, came about through Pres. Teddy Roosevelt's twisting and squeezing the Constitution in defiance to the

10th Amendment, when the Federal Bureau of Investigation was established by an unconstitutional so-called "executive order." If we were a nation in obedience to the Constitution, then the FBI would have no standing in the States, other than to perhaps, guard federal property. The 10th Amendment rules out FBI activities in the States except in such places as Federal Government institutions, forts, magazines, etc. Chief Justice John Marshall so stated.

Since its inception, tiny at birth, the FBI has grown into a gargantuan monster, until today, in 1997, it is the most powerful secret police agency in the world, dwarfing in scope and size the Soviet MKVD and its successor, the K.G.B. The FBI today in 1997, is the greatest threat to the liberty of the citizen and its expansion over a broad spectrum of American life is positively dangerous, which if not curbed, will eventually prove fatal to the Confederated Republic and the Constitution and Bill of Rights.

Yet in the face of many demonstrable blatant abuses of power by the FBI, Congress has not had the political will and integrity to call the FBI to account for such wrongdoings as Waco, Ruby Ridge, the Atlantic Park bombing, characterized by the jackal press as "mistakes." The performance of the Senate and the House in the Ruby Ridge and Waco hearings can only be described as pathetic, the constitutionality of the FBI was never once raised by those charged with upholding the Constitution and the Bill of Rights against all enemies, internal and external. With the FBI being used as a political weapon, the FBI's power over the lives of citizens — and it seems, our legislators — is at its highest point in our entire history. It was former Attorney General Edward Levy who ordered the FBI to end its investigations of Communists and Socialists in the Communist Socialist Workers Party.

The FBI's intrusion into the affairs of the States in violation of the 10th Amendment should be of the gravest concern to all who hold States rights dear, is an ominous portent of what is to come from this agency. The FBI continues to expand its powers into the political arena in a most frightening manner. A large proportion of the FBI's methods of collecting information are not subject to public accountability, which is the very reason why the Founding Fathers decreed that there could be no central police apparatus and law enforcement was left up to the States under the 10th Amendment. In fact, most FBI-information collecting is totally unsupervised by the House and Senate.

For instance, the agency's SET (Surreptitious Entry Team) whose job is to break into private homes and private property as well as other localities where it has no legal right to intrude, does so with seeming impunity. The object is to leave behind secret hidden microphones and tiny cameras. I don't believe that this kind of conduct is sanctioned anywhere in the Constitution and the Bill of Rights and I cannot see how it can be allowed as it violates at least five or six clauses of the Constitution and the Bill of Rights. How can the House and Senate "authorize" such unlawful behavior?

Far from declaring the FBI's unconstitutionality and at least curbing its unlawful conduct — the Constitution being the highest law of the land, Congress has deliberately and steadily, vastly expanded the "right" of the FBI to encroach on civil liberties to an extent that is frightening, without regard to the fact that such "laws" do serious violation to the U.S. Constitution and the Bill of Rights. Where in the Constitution is the FBI mentioned or expressly implied? It is only in existence because Teddy Roosevelt twisted and squeezed the Constitution for his own political agenda.

Where in the Constitution does it say that Congress can grant powers to the FBI which are unconstitutional? Where does it say in the Constitution that the Congress can delegate powers to the FBI which Congress itself does not have in the delegated power of Sec. 8, Art. 1, Clauses 1-18? It is just not there! Thus what we have here is the desperately serious situation where Congress grossly violates the Constitution and the Bill of Rights and gives authority it does not have in the slightest degree, to a central, secret police agency expressly forbidden by the Constitution.

Another very alarming fact is that a 1979 secret federal court decision approved surveillance of thousands of people suspected of being a national security risk. The problem is that no one knows whether they are suspected of this or anything else, and there is no way to tell whether surveillance of innocent people is being conducted at multiple levels, innocent people, who have come under scrutiny because of their political persuasions.

But by far the most disturbing aspect of the way in which the FBI gathers information is the all-invasive use of equipment called "pen registers" and "trap and trace" which records all numbers dialed from a "suspect" phone and the numbers of the callers to that phone. These actions are supposed to be under a warrant, so it is known that in 1993 there were 3,423 such warrants issued. The courts also permit the FBI to subpoena telephone records by alleging that the records belong to the telephone company and not to the individual, and so in this manner the FBI avoids alerting the subscriber that he or she is under surveillance. Rep. Don Edwards said recently that federal investigators scan lists millions of long-distance calls each year, conveniently provided by AT&T computerized print-outs. The fact that this is all 100 percent unconstitutional and therefore illegal, does not phase the FBI one little bit, nor does it disturb our Congress which is charged with the responsibility of making sure that this kind of conduct is not tolerated.

About thirty years ago the business of "market surveys" began, where companies wanting to sell a particular product needed to know which areas to concentrate on. The marketing companies got their information from motor vehicle registration records, telephone records, household questionnaires they themselves sent out and which were obligingly filled in by the householders, telling everything from age, marital status, number of children, etc. Marketing companies were able to put together remarkably accurate profiles of over 130 million households across the U.S. arising out of these "confidential surveys."

Into this profitable source of information, the FBI, the DEA and the IRS regularly delve. The FBI now has a huge data base on hundreds of millions of Americans without their knowledge, which it continually updates: how much money they earn, what is the source of your income, who does your daughter date, what is his religion, what car do you own, what church you attend; the names and ages of your family members, and what school your children attend; are you a registered voter and do you vote Democrat or Republican. You may not want to believe this, but it is accurate and it is being collected all the time.

What does this do to your constitutional right to privacy, freedom of assembly, freedom of speech? It rips the constitutional guarantees to these fundamental protections to shreds, then stamp them into the mud of indifference. The FBI can do this and get away with it because it is its own boss. Forget about the Justice Department being in charge. It is not — at least from a practical, everyday standpoint. So who is left to monitor the unconstitutional FBI? Naturally, you would be expected to answer: "the lawmakers of course, the senators and representatives." But you would be dead wrong. Not since the days of Edgar Hoover has the Congress exercised any meaningful supervision of the FBI, and today, in

1997, such necessary and proper supervision has all but vanished as the legislators walk in seeming fear of the FBI.

WHY DO WE NEED A FEDERAL GOVERNMENT?

When we look at our political and economic situation as we live in the several States, we must sometimes ponder on the need of a federal Government. Why do We, the People need a Federal Government when most sovereign people spend their entire lives in the States? It has become a millstone around the necks of the American people and its expanded activities must be curtailed. The House and Senate should not be allowed to convene for more than three months each year, during which times their deliberations must be confined solely to defense of the realm. The bulk of the time Congress is in session is spent on whittling away at the rights of We, the People and the Bill of Rights, and States rights.

The people who reside in the States are the true sovereigns of the nation as the following shows: When a child is born he or she gets a State birth certificate, not a Federal Government birth certificate.

A child gets a grade school education from the State. Federal intervention in education is baneful and harmful and this unconstitutional Federal Government intrusion has turned schools into a large pool for Socialist, anti-Christian activity and to wipe out all knowledge of the Constitution. This will yet turn America into a totally Godless nation without morals and into a humanist Communist society as is already happening.

A student receives a high school diploma from the State.

A student receives a degree from a State college, not a Federal Government college.

People get married in the State and receive a State marriage license.

Teaching certificates, law degrees, doctor's degrees are all matters for the State and are not issued by a Federal Government.

With so many essential services taken care of on a State level, there cannot be a real need to allow a bloated Federal Government to continue in its present form, and there is a need for those who fear big government — as did all of our Founding Fathers — to put an end to this dangerous state of affairs.

Elsewhere herein, I explained how the Constitution and the Bill of Rights is being twisted and squeezed by a central government which includes the Executive, the Congress and the Legislature. Some of the more glaring examples of this dangerous situation which we have allowed to creep into our national life are found in the areas of treaty powers and immigration powers, which has given rise to such dangerous conditions as to pose a terrible threat to our Constitution and the Bill of Rights.

No treaty powers of the Federal Government can interfere with the powers reserved to the States. No State need obey GATT, NAFTA, the U.N. State legislators must assert themselves on these issues. The States have the right to exclude whomsoever they desire to exclude when it comes to immigration. This is enlarged upon to a considerable degree in the book as we proceed.

We come now to an area where no greater twisting and squeezing of the Constitution and the Bill of Rights has occurred, and that is in the area of religion. There has been and continues to be, all-out war waged against the constitutional validity of America being a Christian nation, so let us examine the question of whether or not America is constitutionally, a Christian nation.

After WWII, the Supreme Court began to depart from the Christian heritage of America as established by our Founding Fathers — and you can ignore the red herring of Masonry so often dragged across the trail solely to divert attention from the truth that we are a Christian country — and began its Socialist interpretations of "freedom of religion," instituting pagan ideas, usurping legislative powers to which it was not entitled, in order to bring about the Socialist changes desired by the Democrat_(Communist) Party and its Communist leader, Franklin D. Roosevelt.

The twisting and squeezing by justices of the courts to destroy the constitutionality of America being a Christian nation — a virtual rebellion against the Constitution and the Bill of Rights, took root in this period of intense twisting and squeezing in which Socialist/Marxist/Communist Justices Frankfurter, Douglas, Brennan, Fortass, Brandeiss, Burger and Warren became the standard bearers of the Communist revolution against the Constitution; their relentless twisting and squeezing of it will go down in the history of how to subdue a nation without resorting to force of arms. Is America a Christian Nation? Justice Brewer said so in 1905:

"This Republic is classified among the Christian nations of the world. It was so formally declared by the Supreme Court in the case of

Holy Trinity Church vs. United States 143-U.S. 471. That court, after mentioning various circumstances, added, 'these and many other matters which might be noticed, add a volume of unofficial declarations to the mass of organic utterances, that this is a Christian nation. We constantly speak of the nation as a Christian nation — in fact as the leading Christian nation of the world. This popular use of the term certainly has significance. It is not a mere creation of the imagination. It is not a term of derision but has a substantial basis — one which justifies its use.'"

The great constitutional scholar Justice Joseph Story in his "Commentaries on the United States Constitution" explained matters thusly:

"...and of the first amendment to it...the general if not universal sentiment in America was, that Christianity ought to receive encouragement from the state so far as it was not incompatible with the private right of conscience and the freedom of religious worship. An attempt to level all religions, and to make it a matter of state policy to hold all in utter indifference would have created universal disapprobation, if not universal indignation...the real object of the Amendment was not to countenance. Much less advance Muhammadanism, or Judaism or infidelity by prostrating Christianity, but to exclude rivalry among Christian sects, and to prevent a national ecclesiastical establishment which should give to a hierarchy the exclusive patronage of the national government."

There is no such thing as "Separation of Church and State" in the Constitution And The Bill of Rights. There is little doubt that the Founding Fathers always intended that the U.S. be known as a Christian nation, yet the Liberal-Napoleonic Code Courts with which we are saddled, consistently attempt to twist and squeeze the Constitution in contending against what is already established, and as the Prophet Isaiah said:

"...We have conceived lies in our hearts and repeated them in slanderous, treacherous words. Justice is rebuffed and flouted while righteousness stands aloof; truth stumbles in the market place and honesty is kept out of court, so truth is lost to sight, and whomever shuns evil is thought a madman." (Isaiah 59:13-15).

Liberalism in the courts is a heresy, as is twisting and squeezing the Constitution in attempting to alter it by what the Marxist, Zinoviev, called "the legislative route." Legislative action means judges acting as legislators, and it also means the Executive branch issuing unconstitutional proclamations a.k.a. "executive orders" on the premise that they will correct some imagined religious, political, moral and or economic wrong. In reality executive orders are steps to centralize government or destroy the proper functioning of the Constitution through the separation of powers.

Continuing with their program of twisting and squeezing the Constitution and the Bill of Rights, we hear the Socialist/ Marxist/Communist legislators talking about "Federal Courts." There is no such thing as "Federal Courts" Or "Federal Judges" mentioned in the Constitution, at least not as far as I could find, thus it would seem to me that such courts and judges are a prohibition, an inhibition of unconstitutional powers. There is absolutely *nothing* in the Constitution that would permit the "Federal courts" to have draconian powers they presently exercise. Politically appointed "Federal judges" who are not elected by We, the People, and their "courts" are instruments of tyranny, placing authority of government in their hands, which power they often misuse to alter the Constitution by twisting and squeezing, which was never intended by the Founding Fathers. Today, a single "Federal judge" can thwart the will of the legislature and We, the People. This is rule by judicial fiat by political "Federal" judges, tyranny worse than anything encountered in the former USSR. The current and growing abuse of the court system to impose tyranny upon We, the People was anticipated by the Founding Fathers.

Thomas Jefferson:

"The Constitution, on this hypothesis is a mere thing of wax in the hands of the judiciary, which they may twist and shape into any form."

The reason why the 9th Amendment was passed was to prevent this massive and growing twisting and squeezing of the Constitution and the Bill of Rights from happening. Courts today ignore this check on tyrannical conduct. The majority of "Federal judges" have become political activists whose rulings constitute new laws not passed by the legislature, most of which are non-Christian, unconstitutional, socialistic rulings. These judges interfere in matters reserved to the States under the 10th Amendment, often to ordering what type of persons must be employed by local boards, and what books school boards are allowed to include in curriculum and school libraries.

Perhaps the Founding Fathers anticipated this tyrannical twisting and squeezing of the Constitution by "Federal" courts might one day, and in their far-seeing wisdom, they provided for it.

The Congress, by a simple majority can overturn any ruling by the Supreme Court. It does not require a two-thirds majority. Article III Sec. 2 Part 2 of the U.S. Constitution. John Marshall, our first chief justice of the Supreme Court said in Eliotts Debates Vol 3, page 560: "Congress is empowered to make exceptions to the appellate jurisdiction as to law and fact of the Supreme Court. These exceptions go as far as the legislature may think proper for the interest and liberty of the people."

There we have it. The Supreme Court is not the final word on the Constitution. It is not even co-equal with the legislative and executive branches of government. Congress should be ordered by We, the People, to start using this long-forgotten power, and to declare a ten-year moratorium on Roe vs Wade, Brown vs Board of Education, the Immigration Reform Act of 1965, Brady Bill, Assault Weapons ban. etc. This would put a stop to unconstitutional twisted and squeezed Federal and State laws which would then be subject to review by a panel of constitutionalists who have made at least an in depth five-year study of the Annals of Congress, Congressional Globe and Congressional Record.

Never has there been a more blatant, openly contemptuous twisting and squeezing of the Constitution and the Bill of Rights than that which is occurring now under the direction of Socialist Pres. Clinton. Clinton has usurped powers he isn't entitled to take, twisted and squeezed other to suit his Socialist agenda, and nowhere is this more blatant, than in the area of education and not since the 1920s has the central government tried so hard to wrest control from the States, as Mr. and Mrs. Clinton are working diligently to do in 1997.

" In the case, Church of the Holy Trinity vs. the U.S. Justice David Brewer ruled, "...general Christianity is, and always has been, a part of the common law of Pennsylvania." In the case, People vs. Ruggles, Chancellor Kent, chief justice of the Supreme Court of New York State said "...we are a Christian people and the morality of the country is deeply ingrafted upon Christianity and not upon the worship of impostors." (Other religions).

Page 12931: Florence Kelly, confidant of Roosevelt and his wife Eleanor, pressed the issue of Socializing the United States.. After she returned from England and Germany where she was lauded by the Socialists and Marxists, Kelly received a letter from Karl Marx dated January 27, 1887, in which he instructed her how to Socialize education in America and how to introduce Socialism "into the flesh and blood of

Americans." These instructions became the blueprint of the Democrat Party in its plans to Socialize education, and have followed ever since and are now part and parcel of the Clinton Agenda for America.

The United States of America has one law, common law, which was retained by the States when they came into the Union, as is mentioned in Article VII of the Bill of Rights. Pres. Clinton, like Pres. Wilson and Pres. Roosevelt thinks he can act under implication but no law in the Constitution and Bill of Rights is by implication. Laws have to be *expressly implied* — a very different thing to "by implication" which is one of the ways the Constitution is twisted and squeezed. All federal government departments, including the FBI, the CIA, the BATF came into being by implication. None of these entities is *expressly implied* in the delegated powers of the Federal Government Article 1 Sec. 8, Clauses 1-18 and it is therefore an inhibition or prohibition of these entities. Chief Justice John Marshal said "when the Constitution is silent on a power it is a prohibition of that power."

The most consistent offender when it came to twisting and squeezing the Constitution and the Bill of Rights was Franklin Delano Roosevelt. One of his underhand, deceptive, efforts successfully destroyed the U.S. money system of bimetallism. Shown in this book is how Roosevelt unconstitutionally fixed the value of gold and sold the credit and labor of U.S. citizens to the international bankers, particularly the Rothschild gang who refused to take payments in silver. From Congressional Globes and Congressional Records, we learn that the Constitution says the credit and labor of an American citizen belongs to each citizen and NOT the state (the basis of Communism), not to the federal government, and shows Roosevelt was able to twist and squeeze and violate this vital principle and sell the American citizen, individually and collectively, into slavery and bondage to the international bankers. Indentured laborers truly had more freedom that today's citizen, because, eventually, they gained real financial freedom by paying off their debt to the bondholder. American citizens of this century can never do this.

Roosevelt and his wife, Eleanor, were surrounded by Marxists and Communists. His wife's closest friends included the well-known Marxists Florence Kelly, Jane Addams, Julia Lathrop, Grace Abbot and Dr. Anna Louise Strong. All were avowed admirers of Lenin. According to Dr. Strong:

Congressional Record, May 31, 1924, pages 9962-9977

"The greatest man of our times was Nicolai Lenin. No public man has been so increasingly loved by so many millions of people."

Thus it came about that what with the jackal press in his pocket, the courts under his control, Roosevelt was able to twist and squeeze this nation into one disaster after another, for which We, the People, are still paying dearly. The silent war to turn the United States into a nation other than the one desired and planned for by the Founding Fathers, is visible in the manner in which the Constitution and the Bill of Rights were twisted and squeezed to take on a Communist slant, is found in the area of immigration and citizenship. The granting of citizenship to all and sundry destroyed ancient Rome and is also destroying the United States of America.

In the year 212, Caracalla (properly Caracallas) passed the Edict of Caracalla which granted citizenship to all free men in the Roman Empire. His actions caused anger and dismay because, hitherto, citizenship had provided a distinction between Roman-born and foreigners, which was very much prized by the former class. With the extension of citizenship to all and sundry, a distinction which had been continuous through the history of the empire, was demolished and citizenship became cheapened to the point where it no longer meant anything. In other words, it was totally demeaned. This is reckoned among historians as one of the main reasons why Rome collapsed just as the United States is in the process of collapsing and perhaps for the same reason also. Commenting on citizenship, Vattel in his work "Law of Nations" the "Bible" upon which the Founding Fathers based the Constitution and Bill of Rights. Pages 474-479 says:

"The citizens are members of civil society bound to the society by certain duties and subject to its authority; they equally participate in its advantages. The natives or natural born are in the country of the parents who are citizens. As society cannot perpetuate itself otherwise than by children, they naturally follow the condition of their parents and succeed to all their rights. Again, I say that to be of the country it is necessary to be born of a person who is a citizen; for if he be born there of a foreigner, it will only be the place of his birth and not his country. The inhabitants as distinguished from citizens are foreigners who are permitted to settle and stay in the country."

(This is quoted also in the chapter on "instant Citizenship" as its importance can never be overestimated.)

Dred Scott vs. Hanford is perhaps the most famous or notorious case (depending upon one's viewpoint) used to prove Vattels description of citizenship. The U.S. Supreme Court in the summer of 1856 found in Howard 19, U.S. Reports, found the case was particularly correct in obeying the Constitution. In the Dred Scott case the justices quite constitutionally properly left it up to the States (under the 10th Amendment) to decide what do about the status of the Negro and only the State of Maine gave the Negro citizenship.

On page 404 of the Dred Scott decision: "...The words, people of the United States and citizens are synonymous terms and mean the same thing. They both describe the political body, who, according to our Republican institutions, form sovereignty, and who hold the power and conduct the government through their representatives. They are what we familiarly call, "the sovereign people" and every citizen is one of the people and a constituent member of the sovereignty, etc."

In the first place the Supreme Court did not have the slightest authority to grant citizenship to the Negro, even though its ruling was for a worthy cause. To grant such citizenship was the prerogative of the States and then, Congress and the 14th Amendment did this, but the 14th did not have one word about race in it. Congress started that process of citizenship for the Negro with the Civil Rights Act of 1876 which was 100 percent unconstitutional and the 14th Amendment remains unratified and not a part of the U.S. Constitution, of no effect whatsoever if the truth, as harsh and unpalatable as it be, is told. Of course the remedy is quite simple, Congress must revive the 14th Amendment, grant citizenship to the Negro and then submit the resolution to the States for proper ratification. It can and it should be undertaken at the very earliest opportunity.

CHAPTER 4

SEPARATION OF CHURCH AND STATE A MYTH
9TH AMENDMENT AND JUDGES
9TH AMENDMENT AND THE FEDERAL GOVERNMENT
TREATY POWERS, WARS,
TREATIES FURTHER THE ONE WORLD GOVERNMENT.

E nemies of the Constitution and the Bill of Rights have hidden behind the facade of democracy and worked without ceasing to pervert the Constitution and the Bill of Rights in specific areas, one of them being to further the cause of Communism under the pretext that their "religious rights" are violated. Such is the case with the so-called "separation of church and state" law, which is no law at all as it is not so stated in the Constitution and the Bill of Rights nor is such a clause pursuant to and in consonance with the Constitution and the Bill of Rights.

Over the years, I have consistently condemned the so-called doctrine of separation of church and state as 100 percent unconstitutional and repeatedly pointed out that the phrase "a wall of separation" does not exist in the Constitution and that the Supreme Court has led this nation away from its Christian heritage by means of fraudulent deception and deceitful terminology having its origin the Communist Manifesto of 1848. The brevity of the Constitution gave rise to the Earl Warren Secular Humanist Supreme Court abusing Article 1 of the Bill of Rights. This Amendment to the Bill of Rights came directly from the Virginia Constitution.

Where it is briefly stated in Article 1 of the Bill of Rights, the so-called "religious freedom" clause, even the most cursory examination reveals that it was lifted directly out from Virginia State Constitution at the time the Federal Constitution was written. The Supreme Court knew this, but went ahead and abused the clause to give it an entirely different meaning to the one intended by the Founding Fathers. The Supreme Court knew very well that the Virginia State Constitution made it plain that what the Founding Fathers did when they put this clause into the Bill of Rights was to secure the position that no one *Christian* sect would have dominance over another Christian sect, if it should become the State religion. It was never meant to eradicate Christianity from the life of the government.

The evil men seized upon the fears of religious groups with nothing in common with the Christian religion, telling them that prayers in school and the nativity scene on government property, "threaten your religious rights." These evil men saw a chance to create a schism and they seized it and exploited it for all it was worth, often creating intense strife and confusion where none existed before. The so-called "Wall of Separation" doctrine is one of the seven deadliest sins in our national life which has given way to a situation where hatred has supplanted reason.

In the case, Church of the Holy Trinity vs. United States, Mr. Justice David Brewer ruled: "...general Christianity is, and always has been, a part of the common law of Pennsylvania" and in the case of People vs. Ruggles, chancellor Kent, chief justice of the Supreme Court of New York State said: "...we are a Christian people and the morality of the country is deeply ingrafted upon Christianity and not upon the worship of impostors."

There were no other religions worthy of note in existence in the colonies at the time the Constitution was drafted. The Virginia State Constitution makes this perfectly clear; what the Founding Fathers were doing was securing the right of the people NOT to have the Church of England become the government church as it is in England. The crooked Communists among the Supreme Court justices saw an opportunity to twist and subvert the Bill of Rights by isolating this clause from the balance of the clauses and then admitted all manner of other religions into the protection of Article 1. The clauses of the Constitution can not be separated and isolated from the rest of the Constitution as such an action will inevitably destroy the perfect equipoise of the whole document.

This was fraudulent deception by the Court, and in the so-called "separation of church and state" interpretation by the deceitful Warren court, the Communist Manifesto of 1848 was followed to the letter.

I was therefore intrigued by a book, "To Build A Wall" by Gregg Ivers (University Press of Virginia) in which the author not only confirms my constitutional position but takes great delight in telling the entire story of how the deception was carefully worked out, and by whom. The author names the American Civil Liberties Union (ACLU) as one of the chief conspirators and quotes the great constitutional scholar, Sen Sam Ervin of North Carolina as complaining, "this ruling (by the Supreme Court) has made God unconstitutional."

In a review of the book, Stephen Whitfield says, "yet both the nation and the society were founded by Christians, especially Protestant Christians. The United States has always been a Christian society, but is no longer a Christian nation." Both the book and reviewer Whitfield spell out in great detail just who was responsible for such monumental, utterly destructive changes made by the secular human teachings of the Warren Court.

The reviewer says the forces trying to erect the so-called "wall" were a small minority who worked silently from behind the scenes for years "and convinced the Supreme Court to interpret the Establishment Clause of the First Amendment as erecting a very high wall of separation between church and state. They invested more resources in changing the minds of judges. Instead of appealing exclusively to the court of public opinion, these organizations appealed to the courts for relief from the obtuse, complacent and even hostile majorities that controlled legislatures." He does not say to whom they were "hostile."

The book names one individual, Leo Pfeffer, as being, "recalcitrant, single minded and domineering in helping to prevail for more of a third of a century to persuade the bench that the Establishment Clause mandates vigilance on behalf of religious minorities and the irreligious." It goes on to explain how this man enlisted support from even Christian churches (such as the apostate Unitarian Church), "school boards, legislatures were counteracted and how judges were addressed and persuaded."

"To Build A Wall" is rather disappointing in that it does not describe *how* the Supreme Court itself worked in analyzing the logic of the opinions from 'Everson vs. The Board of Education' that have cleaved church from state for half a century. Reviewer Whitfield concludes that the phrase, "wall of separation is missing from the Constitution" and concludes that the success of the forces opposed to Christian America "achieved a stunning victory." In short, there is no *Constitutional* grounds on which to base the so-called doctrine of "separation of church and state."

JUDGES, LEGISLATORS, MUST BE REINED IN: THE 9TH AND 10TH AMENDMENTS DEMAND OBEDIENCE.

We come now to one of the most dangerous developments of modern times; the presumption by the judiciary that they, somehow, along the way acquired the power to legislate, even though it is expressly forbidden to the judiciary to make laws, their only function being to interpret them. To prevent the judiciary from exceeding its powers under the Constitution the 9th Amendment was passed which forbids the thoughts of judges — called predilections — from being inserted between the lines of the Constitution and the Bill of Rights.

To pervert the law as so many political activist judges are doing today is to make for a pool of impotent rage as people see their collective wills expressed through a referendum, being thwarted by a single judge. This is happening so frequently today in 1997, that soon we are going to have millions of disaffected voters signing off from the system and taking the law into their own hands. This will result in estrangement of a long-lasting nature leading to anarchy.

The *first* rule on constitutional law is that the U.S. Constitution and the Bill of Rights cannot be compromised. All laws in our Republic must be based upon something immutable that cannot be altered to suit a particular whim, heated moments of great excitement, figments of imagination, cunning sophistry and temporary expediencies.

As we have said, the Constitution does not allow for a "federal" judge. Where a power sought is not mentioned in the Constitution then there is a prohibition against it. Where in the Constitution is the term "federal judge" written? It is just not there. Yet, we have these "federal judges" increasingly thwarting the will of the people of the sovereign States on a host of issues and grossly intervening in matters that are in the purview and sole prerogative of the States. A case in point was the ruling by a "federal" judge that California's anti "motor-voter" law is unconstitutional. An anti-motor voter law was overwhelmingly desired by the citizens of California to stop illegal aliens from voting. The Democrat (Socialist) party majority wanted anyone who applied for a driver license to register to vote on the same form. This greatly helped register people who have no right to vote, just what Roosevelt's Communist Party (the Democrat Party) wanted.

Then there was a case where a "federal" judge told the City of San Francisco to employ more minorities and women firefighters and this judge had the audacity to issue an "order" to this effect, which should have been ignored by the city administration, but which was not. A further example of blatant unconstitutional action by a "federal" judge concerns the case in Georgia where one of the colleges and the State attorney general sued to stop a group of homosexuals and lesbians from holding a "national homosexual convention" on college property. The people of the state didn't want this amoral crowd holding their meeting on college property and neither did the majority of students.

Along comes a federal judge and blatantly revokes the 10th Amendment rights of the State of Georgia and pokes his nose into what is essentiality state rights protected by the 10th Amendment. I hope that the attorney general of the State of Georgia petitions to have this obdurate judge impeached for violating his oath of office. If We, the People, do not take instant constitutional action to remove judges who are law breakers because they violate the Constitution, then we are going to see ourselves ruled by judicial fiat in ever increasing spirals.

Another federal judge in California ruled the State's gas chamber "cruel and unusual punishment" as though she had never even heard of the 10th Amendment. California's San Quenton gas chamber, used to execute murderers sentenced to death, had to be closed down and executions henceforth carried out by lethal injection while the judge's ruling was being appealed.

The 9th Amendment, particularly, is a restraint to prevent judges from reading their own views — predilections — into the Constitution. During the Roosevelt era, the Supreme Court was packed with constitutional anarchist justices, who got around the Constitution by reading their own thoughts into it. Brown vs. Board of Education was one of the more infamous instances of judicial predilections overriding the Constitution, and of course, the most horrifying of all was Roe vs. Wade, when the 4th Amendment was bent out of shape, stretched and twisted to mean what the constitutional anarchists wanted it to mean.

The 9th Amendment was written to prevent gross distortions of the Constitution by judges. Massachusetts would not join the Union until this amendment was adopted. The 9th Amendment is also a protection for We, the People, along with the 4th and 5th Amendments. It is poorly understood by judges and the legal profession in general. In order to fully comprehend the Constitution and its provisions we must take note of the federal government is a government of delegated powers and understand that the same restrictions apply to judges. The delegated powers are known as primary powers of Congress and are found in Article 1, Sec. 8, Clauses 1-18. Government has no power other than those enumerated here and which are the total powers given by We, the People, the sovereigns, to the federal government, of which the Supreme Court is one part.

The judiciary is not co-equal with the legislature. It is the legislature which makes the laws, not the judiciary, although the Supreme Court has a long and undistinguished record of purporting to have this right as we see in Brown. vs. Board of Education, Roe vs. Wade and so called "gun control laws" not to mention the scores of unconstitutional decisions reached by the Roosevelt Supreme Court. A newcomer, Justice Ruth Bader Ginsburg told the Senate that "occasionally, the Supreme Court has to legislate." Ginsberg's nomination, on the basis of her statement, should have been instantly rejected. The nomination should have been declared dead on arrival (DOA) and sent back to President Clinton.

Judges are constantly trying to isolate amendments and clauses of the Constitution, but every part of the Constitution has to be read and interpreted in the light of the whole. It cannot be fragmented, otherwise the perfect equipoise of the Constitution is lost. The Warren court in particular, used the 14th Amendment to mean anything the Warren Court — notorious for its predilections — wanted it to mean. Justice Brennan was another judge who made free with his predilections and history may show him to have been even worse than Warren when it came to violating the Constitution and the Bill of Rights. This man was supposed to be a Catholic, but he never displayed any of the symbols of Christianity on his person or in his surroundings, and even at his funeral, there was nothing to indicate his supposed Christianity.

Nefarious judicial conduct is rule by judicial fiat and it will destroy the United States if not checked as a matter of extreme urgency. When the Constitution is silent on a power and it is not incidental to another power, nor is it an expressly implied power, it is an inhibition (prohibition) of that power. This is a corollary to the 9th Amendment which was meant to apply chiefly to judges and to prevent them from going outside the boundaries of the U.S. Constitution and when they do this, their rulings and decisions have no force in law. In short they become law breakers.

AN EXAMPLE OF THE CORRUPTNESS
OF THE JUDICIARY RELATING TO TREATIES

Nowhere is the need to rein in the judiciary more explicitly demonstrated than in the area of treaties. Roosevelt, the mad butcher of Hyde Park in his secret dealings with Joseph Stalin translated his agreements into treaties/agreements with the Soviet butcher, a terrifying experience for the nation. Roosevelt blatantly violated the Constitution and got away with high crimes and misdemeanors, some of the worst on record and he did this without ever consulting the House and Senate; except in retrospect when his crimes were in danger of being exposed post facto. In these flagrant violations of the Constitution, a corrupt Supreme Court almost always rubber-stamped such treaties or laws passed to meet the needs of the situation.

THE 9TH AMENDMENT IS A
RESTRICTION ON THE FEDERAL GOVERNMENT:

"The enumeration in the Constitution of certain rights shall not be construed to deny or disparage others (or the other enumerated rights) retained by the people."

It follows that because certain rights are not enumerated in the Constitution and Bill of Rights, the government cannot destroy, subvert or usurp those rights not directly enumerated. Government cannot fill in between the lines that which it has not been given. The 9th Amendment does not grant the Supreme Court or the lower courts the right to insert into their rulings that which is not already in the Constitution and the Bill of Rights.

To properly understand the 9th Amendment, we must research the debates found in the Annals of Congress, Congressional Globes and Congressional Records. This is a tough and tedious job as these are well-hidden under misleading titles and it requires a certain tenacity of purpose to find them and those who undertake this task will find a lot of material in the Annals of Congress, June 1789.

Pages 2273-2297, Congressional Record, House, February 20, 1890:

"The 9th Amendment to the U.S. Constitution expressly states the existence of other rights which are retained by the people and that these rights shall not be denied or disparaged because certain express rights are enumerated in the Constitution or its amendments." As the great constitutionalist, Judge Story, put it when dealing with the 9th Amendment:

"The enumeration in the Constitution shall not be construed to deny or disparage others retained by the people. The maxim, rightly understood, is perfectly sound and safe, but it has often been forced from its natural meaning into support of the most dangerous political heresies." (A perfect description of the actions of the Roosevelt Supreme Court). "The amendment was undoubtedly suggested by the reasoning of the Federalists on the subject of a general bill of rights."

Perfect examples of the maxim "presumed to admit in them any recondite meaning" and "strangely forced from its natural meaning into the support of the most dangerous political heresies" are all so-called gun control laws, so-called "gay rights," abortion rights, Brown vs. Board of Education, etc. ad infinitum.

Although aimed expressly at the judiciary, all local, state and federal officials are also bound by the 9th Amendment and are forbidden, along with the justices of the Supreme Court and the judges of the several States from imposing recondite, esoteric, abstruse meanings, philosophical acuteness, elaborate shades of meaning, all manner of the products of uncontrollable figments of their predilection-riddled imaginations, upon We, the people in their judicial rulings. That is the purpose of the 9th Amendment.

We quote Thomas Jefferson's letter to Dr. Ritchie on the need to rein in justices and judges of the Supreme Court and the several States:

"The judiciary of the United States is a subtle corps of sappers and miners constantly working underground to undermine the foundations of our Confederate fabric. They are construing our Constitution from a coordination of a general and special government to general and supreme one alone. This will lay all things at their feet and they are too well versed in English law to forget the maxim 'Boni judicis est amplidire' jurisdiction. A judiciary independent of a king or executive is a good thing but independence of the will of the nation is a solecism at least in a republican government."

Note, Jefferson did not say a "Democratic Government" in the Clinton manner. The United States Constitution was written to protect the sovereign citizens of the sovereign States from tyranny. The 9th Amendment is the key amendment adopted for this purpose and it puts a permanent crimp and curb on the predilections of judges, who nonetheless, continue to violate it with seeming impunity.

TREATY MAKING POWERS:
NO TREATY IS SUPERIOR TO THE CONSTITUTION

Lately there has been a surge of articles in right wing publications telling us that the U.N. Charter is the law of the land. One of these appeared in a publication called the "National Educator." I do not subscribe to this paper but a friend of mine sent me a copy of an article in the "National Educator" which says that the U.N. Charter is the law of the land. Let me say unequivocally, the "National Educator" is 100 percent wrong and very disturbing to those who are really trying to understand treaty-making powers in relation to the Constitution.

The Congressional Record, May 25, 1892 pages 4656-4666:

Senator Gray:

"Why, Mr. President, a treaty made in pursuance of the Constitution of the United States, is no more than a law enacted by Congress." (And a law enacted by Congress can be repealed and so can a treaty.) Continuing, Sen. Gray said:

"Do you suppose the executive of the United States is any where clothed with authority, expressed or implied, to ignore our dual system of government? Do you suppose that its treaty making power, so often referred to in terms more or less vague and inexact, has been slumbering here all these years as Pandora's box, from which it can escape the enemies that are to destroy our institutions between local autonomy and imperial government?" The members of the Security Council of the U.N. other than the U.S. delegate are aliens, and the executive pretends to give these aliens special powers and privileges over U.S. citizens. To quote Sen. Gray again:

"No executive has the power to give peculiar privileges to an alien. No President of the United States has ever suggested, nor has the Senate ever assented, that a treaty should provide a that a citizen or subject of a foreign state should be clothed with a panoply of protection denied our own citizens? The utmost limit of a treaty-making power is to guarantee equality of right before the law with our own citizens..."

It is worth noting that the renegade Pres. Wilson granted a U.S. passport to the Bolshevik leader, Leon Trotsky, a peculiar privilege which was not his to give. This unconstitutional action by Wilson, led directly to the Bolshevik Revolution. In the same instance the U.S. "treaty" grants a panoply of protection" to the U.N. Secretary-General and gives him that which is denied to our own citizens.

Our position is the same as that expounded by the late Sen. Sam Ervin: "There is no way under the noonday sun that the U.S. could have joined the U.N." The enemies within our gates have manipulated the American people who by and large do not know the Constitution. Oh, they know the articles, and sections and clauses but they don't know the profundity and depth of meaning, the complexities of the Constitution, because they have not studied the Annals of Congress, Congressional Globe and Congressional Record and that is the only way one can get to know the Constitution and Bill of Rights.

All law in our Republic must be based upon the immutable Constitution and not on some flight of fancy or emotional, personal, reason such as the Panama Canal treaty. The Constitution cannot be used as part of a treaty as has happened so many times before under the misleading tenure of past Socialist presidents, not to mention the arch-Socialist in the White House in November of 1997. A treaty can only be law if it is properly in consonance with our Constitution. A treaty is not the law of the land. It is merely like an ordinary domestic law which can be amended or ended by the will of the Congress. In fact any domestic law passed by the Congress is superior to a treaty, and no treaty — which is only a temporary law anyway — can supplant, interfere with, or in any way change the provisions of the Constitution and the Bill of Rights.

That is why the Constitution says in Article VI Section 2: "The Constitution and the laws of the nation which shall be made in pursuance thereof." The reason "in pursuance of" was inserted to make certain that all bills, treaties, proposed laws, be subjected to rigorous constitutional scrutiny to ensure that they are "in pursuance of the Constitution." The U.N. treaty was no more debated as to its pursuance of the Constitution than was Stalin declared a peace maker, and it is no more "in pursuance of the Constitution" than Alice going through the looking-glass! Since the U.N. treaty is absolutely outside of the pale and the ken of the Constitution, if we have any men of courage in the political process today, they have the most solemn duty to abrogate it, forthwith.

The only treaty-making exception to this hard and fast rule is the American Indian treaty/treaties. All other treaties like the flim-flam GATT, NAFTA and U.N. treaties are null and void and of no substance. The U.N. treaty/agreement is a good example of an imprecisely-written document which is of no effect for this reason alone, but more so because the treaty/agreement tries to commingle the language of the Constitution with the wording of the U.N. treaty. The US Constitution's language is proscribed and forbidden to be written into any treaty. This deception was practiced with the U.N. treaty/agreement.

Congressional Record, Senate, Feb. 14, 1879, pages 1305-1306.

Senator Thurmond speaking:

"A treaty is a law according to the Constitution and its modifications or its abrogation belongs to the department that makes these laws." (Note the great constitutionalist says "laws" and does not say "treaties.") "There is no such thing as an indissoluble partnership; there is no such thing as an indissoluble treaty..."

Senator Thurmond was the greatest expert on the Constitution and the Bill of Rights of his time, and he has no equal today in the Congress, so this was not just any member of the Senate expounding his views.

Could anything be clearer than that? A treaty can not be, and is not, greater than the Constitution. Any legislator who believes and practices that a treaty supersedes the Constitution is committing an act of treason. A treaty has to be written up with great accuracy and precision in order to comply with the requirements of the delegated powers of the central government. If an amendment is proposed to accept a treaty — as should have been done with the U.N. treaty/agreement — then it is imperative that the wording of the proposed treaty be precisely related to something already in the Constitution. It cannot be about anything new and outside of the powers delegated to Congress.

Congress cannot, without violating the Constitution, confirm acceptance of a new treaty which does not comply with the Constitution. Certainly, the U.N. treaty/agreement does not comply with the Constitution in a whole maze of areas and because of this it is ultra-vires. Inasmuch as the Constitution does not mention the "United Nations" it is a prohibition of the U.N. Moreover, the Constitution does not recognize as sovereign powers, states, and or countries, any body or organization lacking in a sovereignty. No one can argue that the U.N. has sovereignty, or that it is a recognized country, but all are obliged by the facts to regard the U.N. as unqualified to make treaties. Failing in so many places, the U.N. treaty/agreement should have been rejected in 1945.

Franklin Roosevelt had no constitutional authority to invite the U.N. to come and roost in our national tree. In allowing this travesty of justice, Roosevelt violated his oath of office and should have been impeached and made to pay the penalty for treason, if found guilty. The U.S. is the only country in the world which does not enforce punishment for treason. A U.N. presence in our country without a constitutional amendment authorizing it, is a heinous crime against the Constitution, the Bill of Rights and the laws and government of the people. The framers of our Constitution contemplated and discussed and agreed that the States (the several States), their judiciary, their autonomy, were fully recognized by the Constitution and could not be interfered with or abrogated by any legislative, executive or judicial branch of government. The Constitution institutionalized these States rights for all time.

What is not understood by those who favor the U.N. is that in the diplomatic language of treaties, such treaties are subordinated to the municipal laws (the 10th Amendment) of the States. No country degrades its own institutions. You can look at the history of nations and you will not find it. Yet, along came Roosevelt and he degraded our institutions in the most heinous act of treason ever to have occurred up to that period of our history and subordinated them to the U.N. Is that not gross treason? The U.N. treaty was designed to destroy States rights above all else! The U.N. was programmed to remove the block complained of by Socialist Ramsey McDonald in 1895 after his visit to America. He told an assembly of Fabian Socialists that the U.S. could never be Socialized until the States and Federal Constitutions were destroyed. Now you know why Roosevelt can justly be branded as a traitor, guilty of treason.

People have written to me to say they are disappointed in the way the U.N., "a good organization, is performing." Well, the U.N. is performing exactly as programmed by the Communists who forced it upon the U.S. and is achieving its goals, one after the other. The U.N. is a Communist One World Government tool, unacceptable in the States of this nation. Was that not so stated during the World Federal Government Conference in Copenhagen, Denmark in 1953?

At the conference delegates (including those from the United States) recommended that a revision be made to the U.N. charter to make the U.N. the One World Government. Universal membership with no right to secede, disarmament of all nations enforced by U.N. inspectors — such as is going on now in Iraq — and note this, all individually-owned firearms to be surrendered to U.N. inspectors. International courts, world legislatures and executive councils with superior powers over national legislative bodies and courts and world citizenship the only citizenship to be recognized. Those who are blustering for the U.N. to destroy Iraq will change their tune when U.N. inspectors, BATF agents deputized as U.N. inspectors among them, go on a rampage across the U.S. looking for individually-owned arms and confiscating them. The worst part about it is that the U.S. taxpayers are funding the very instrument which is slowly but surely, enslaving them.

We can once again consult Vattel's "Law of Nations" for confirmation of the foregoing. It is only because of the power of the Rockefellers and the Wall Street banks, and its lackeys in the Congress that the U.N. vulture continues to roost on our soil, thanks to the Committee of 300. Their spokesmen made eloquent speeches about the peace keeping role of the U.N. but there have been more undeclared wars since the end of WWII than in our entire history because of the U.N. I say undeclared wars, because only a sovereign country can declare war and the U.N. has no sovereignty whatsoever.

Franklin Roosevelt butchered the Constitution to suit his internationalist friends and the One World Government, especially in the area of treaty-making where it concerned his relationship with the Soviet Union. In each case he was upheld by the corrupt Supreme Court. When Eisenhower became President, he believed quite incorrectly that it was constitutional for him to make treaties with foreign powers without resorting to the House and Senate, in whose orbit treaty-making powers rested.

Eisenhower marshaled the power and prestige of his office and threw it behind Senate Democrat leaders Lyndon Johnson to kill the Bricker amendment, sponsored by Sen. Bricker, the 1944 GOP nominee for Vice President. Arch-traitor John Foster Dulles backed by a large number of Republican Radical Trojan Horses voted with Johnson to kill Senate Joint Resolution 1, which would have limited the treaty-making aspirations of Eisenhower, powers which did not belong to the executive branch of government in the first place. This group of traitors was successful in defeating the amendment by a majority of one vote, the count being 63-33. This alone demonstrates why democracy is no more than mob rule under a Napoleonic code, which must be utterly rejected by the American people. Every democracy in history has gone down to perdition.

Treaty-like agreements which are neither fish nor fowl allegedly give the President the authority to bind the nation to another nation without the "advice and consent" of the Senate. As far as I was able to ascertain, since 1944 nearly 12,000 of these so-called treaty/agreements were called "the law of the land." No wonder that Davy Crockett said "the executive – like a lion, must be caged." Rampant Presidents Roosevelt, Johnson and Clinton have demonstrated that the Founding Fathers knew that an uncaged executive would attack every safeguard in the Constitution via "executive orders" and "treaty-like agreements," all unconstitutional and null and void.

In George Washington's Farewell Address, co-authored by Thomas Jefferson, Alexander Hamilton and Governor Robert Morris and which took five years to write, Washington set out what the foreign policy of the United States should be, for all times and when he urged the U.S. not to become entangled in foreign alliances, he was referring to making treaties and agreements with foreign powers:

"...Providence has not connected the permanent felicity of a nation within its virtue. The experiment at least, is recommended by every sentiment which enables human nature. Alas! it is rendered impossible by its vices. In the execution of such a plan, nothing is more essential than that permanent, investigate antipathies against particular nations and passionate attachments for others, should be excluded; and that in place of them, just and amicable feelings toward all, should be cultivated. The nation which indulges toward another an habitual hatred, or an habitual fondness is in some degree a slave. It is a slave to its animosity and affection, either of which is sufficient to lead it astray from its duties and its interests. Antipathy of one nation against another dispossess each more readily to offer insult and injury, to lay hold of slight causes of umbrage, and to be haughty and intractable when accident or trifling occasions of dispute occur."

"Hence, frequent collisions, obstinate, envenomed and bloody contests. The nation, prompted by ill will and resentment impels to war the government contrary to the best calculations of policy. The government sometimes participates in the national propensity and adopts enough passion what reason would reject; at other times, it makes the animosity of the nation subservient to projects of hostility instigated by pride, ambition and other sinister and pernicious motives. The peace, often sometimes the liberty of nations, has been the victim"

"So the passionate attachment of one nation for another produces a variety of ills. Sympathy for the favorite nation, facilitating the illusion of an imaginary common interest exists, and infusing into one enmities of the other, betrays the former into a participation in the quarrels and wars of the latter, without adequate inducements or justifications."

"It leads to concessions to the favorite nation of privileges denied to others which is apt doubly to injure the nation making the concessions, by unnecessary parting with what ought to have been retained, by exciting jealousy, ill-will, and disposition to retaliate to the parties from whom privileges are withheld; and it gives to ambitious, corrupt or deluded citizens who devote themselves to the favored nation facility to betray or sacrifice the interests of their own country, without odium, sometimes even with popularity, gilding with appearance of a virtuous sense of obligation, a commendable deference for public opinion, or laudable zeal, for public good, the base or foolish compliance of ambition, corruption, or infatuation...etc"

Washington then goes on to warn against getting entangled in foreign alliances, (treaty-making) which is just as applicable today as it was at the time when he was talking about France.

In pages 2273-2297 of the Congressional Record, House, Feb 26 1900, we find a lot of material which tells us that a treaty is "no big deal" to use the modern vernacular. A treaty is merely a law and like any other law it can be set aside. On page 2290 we find Justice Mclean saying:

"No powers can be exercised by Congress which are prohibited to the Constitution or which are contrary to its spirit." Certainly, placing the U.N. Charter above the Constitution is prohibited by the Constitution and is clearly "contrary to its spirit."

So how could Congress pass an agreement/treaty that supersedes the Constitution which the U.N. treaty/agreement does in so many ways? There could be no greater authority on the Constitution than Thomas Jefferson, and he said:

"To hold treaty-making powers boundless is to render the Constitution a blank piece of paper by Construction."

In the case of Cherokee Tobacco vs. United States, (11 Wall, page 616) we find the court said:

"...A treaty cannot change the Constitution, or be held valid if it be in violation of that instrument. This results from the nature of the fundamental principles of our government."

No one who reads the U.N. treaty/agreement will contest that in many key areas it violates the fundamental principles of the Constitution. An opinion handed down by chief Justice Waite in 1887 in the case Spies vs. Illinois (123 U.S. 166) includes the following:

"That the first ten articles of amendments were not intended to limit the powers of the State Governments in respect of their own people but to operate on the National Government alone, was decided more than a half-century ago and that decision has been adhered to ever since."

The several States were not consulted about the U.N. treaty/agreement and this is a profound reason why it has no validity. The senators representing the States abrogated their responsibilities; they did not read the document. They should have insisted on a full debate as to the agreement/treaty's constitutionality and not allow it to be rushed through in three days. Moreover, an agreement/treaty purporting to supplant the authority of the Constitution as the U.N. treaty/agreement holds, would first have to be submitted to all of the States in the form of a Constitutional Amendment for ratification, before it could come into effect.

Nowhere does the Constitution grant the Senate and the House any right to change anything in the Constitution without the assent of all of the States. In fact the Constitution expressly forbids the legislature to do anything that would add to or subtract from the Constitution without first being presented in the form of an amendment and submitted for ratification to the States. For Congress to make a treaty with any body, organization or country, and hold that such a treaty is superior to the Constitution, is an attempt to rewrite the Constitution without the permission of We, the People and is tantamount to treason.

Worth repeating is the remark made by Senator Ervin that there is "no way under the noonday sun that the U.S. could have joined the United Nations." It is a Constitutional impossibility! Congressional Record, House, Feb 26, 1945:

"The extent of legislative power of the Government of the United States can not legally and properly be construed and interpreted under international law. There is nothing in the law of nations to construe the Constitution of the United States to warrant the limitations of its powers under international law, nor any of its provisions. Neither is there anything in the Constitution of the United States to warrant the limitations of its power by international law. The operation of the Constitution of the United States upon its Government and the departments thereof can not be abrogated by any rule of law of any other nation or family of nations..."

The "National Educator" is 100 percent wrong when it says that the U.N. Charter is the law of the land. I say to them, IT IS NOT. Go and study the Congressional Records and find out. The people must not be mislead, even unintentionally, as is the case with the "National Educator" article. It is worthwhile to repeat what Sen. Thurmond said, which I have already quoted: Congressional Record, Senate, Feb. 14, 1879, pages 1305-1306:

"A treaty is a law according to the constitution and its modification or abrogation belongs to that department that makes the laws. There is no such thing as an indissoluble partnership; there is no such thing as an indissoluble treaty..."

How then, we might ask, can the U.N. treaty/agreement be superior to the Constitution? How could any member of Congress have voted for the CWC treaty, for example, without violating the Constitution? Can anything in the Constitution and the Bill of Rights be abrogated by an act of Congress? Of course not! Can anything in the Constitution and the Bill of Rights be altered by a mere vote to this effect in the House and Senate? Of course not! Can any provision in the Constitution be cut off by a refusal of the Congress to fund it? Of course not! Yet all of the fore-going restrictions apply to a treaty — especially the U.N. treaty/agreement — which means that a treaty does not even come close to being co-equal with our Constitution. Don't think for a moment that Alger Hiss and his fellow Communists didn't know the U.S. Constitution. They did! The U.N. agreement/treaty was their way of attempting to circumvent our Constitution, especially in the area of States rights.

It is enough that the American people are connived, intentionally misled, lied to, day after day, year after year without well-meaning people adding to the confusion. No nation has been lied to so malignantly and consistently as the American nation. In 1945 we had the spectacle of the late John Foster Dulles lying through his teeth to the Senators and using the Constitution to befuddle them into passing a piece of treachery, the U.N. treaty/agreement. Dulles was a master dazzler and deceiver and used his talents well to deceive the gullible Senators about the U.N. treaty/agreement before them.

The same methods used to stir-up passions that brought on the Civil

War were used to hoodwink the American people in 1945 that there was a pressing need for the U.S. to participate in a One World Government body — the correct description of the United Nations. Reading through the Congressional Records for July — September 1945 I was appalled to see confirmed the little time allowed to debate the measure. What came out from this study was that passion dominated the content of the speeches. Markedly absent were calls for calm reason. Instead, a climate of uncertainty that was just beginning to show up was cut short as soon as a few legislators began to ask some hard questions, which were never answered.

One of the things these enemies of We, the People do to confuse the majority, is to isolate the Constitution and interpret it one clause at a time. This is chicanery and they know it those *conspirators*. I am not afraid to use the forbidden word and they put this kind of treachery over on the people, all of the time.

The treaty-making powers of the Constitution cannot be read in a vacuum, isolated from the rest of the Constitution. It has to be interpreted in the light of the whole Constitution as to its constitutionality. In the 3-day wonder so called "debate" on the U.N. in 1945, this is what Dulles and his Treason Hill co-conspirators did — they isolated the treaty-making power clause of the Constitution and then passed off their bastard-child U.N. agreement as constitutional. In this Dulles and his gang committed treason for which they ought to have been indicted, found guilty and hanged — the penalty for treason and for violating the oath of office they had taken.

The Constitution cannot be stretched to fit international law, nor can international law be used to minimize the U.S. Constitution. The constitutionality of the U.N, treaty/agreement can only be decided by the Constitution itself as stated in Vattel's "Law of Nations." Congressional Record, May 25, 1892, pages 4653-4665:

"Now, without attempting to point out the precise clause in the Constitution which it violates, or rather points out the absence of any authority in this Constitution of the United States the powers that are claimed under it, we must seek and find the grant of the power under which proposed action is to be had and not rest upon the mere absence of an inhibition (prohibition) of a power."

Under our Constitution when the U.S. Constitution is silent on a power, it is a prohibition of that power. Where is the power for the U.N. mentioned or expressly implied in the U.S. Constitution? If it is also not

incidental to another power already in the Constitution, then it is a prohibition of the power, so where do these constitutional contortionists get
the notion that the U.N. treaty/agreement is the law of the land?
Congressional Record, House, October 2, 1893, pages 2027-2031:

"...Incidental means something occurring from the existence of a
principal fact or entity, and such occurrence depending upon the existence of the principal fact or entity. Implied means derived from and
included in some foregoing facts or entities."

How then does the U.N. treaty/agreement qualify as the law of the
land? The power sought, i.e., to establish the U.N. charter as superior to
the U.S. Constitution is just not there! Hence, the 1945 vote by the
Senate — a vote that supposedly, allegedly, made the United States a
member of the U.N. is ultra vires, of no effect, no law at all, and must
not, should not, be obeyed by anyone who does not wish to violate his
oath to uphold the Constitution of the United States against all enemies,
domestic and foreign, which enemies have joined in a conspiracy to
destroy the U.S. Constitution, by alleging it to be inferior to a mere
agreement!

All of the foregoing constitutional prohibitions should have been
brought up and debated in 1945, but it did not happen. Thus passage of
the U.N. agreement was an exercise of arbitrary power forbidden by the
Constitution. As far as my research shows, the paucity of what passed
for the U.N. debate by the Senate can be measured by the number of
pages — 100 in all — in which the record of the debate was contained.
Had the Senate done its job properly, the Congressional Record of the
debate would have run into at least 500 or more pages.

Note how well the traitors in Washington picked their time to push
for this so-called U.N. treaty. They were well-schooled by the Tavistock
Institute on how to manipulate the citizens of this country, tired of war,
and looking for new hope and new ways to prevent war in the future.
The U.N. was touted as that new hope for peace, when in fact, the U.N.
is a vehicle for war, not for peace. On the known longing of the people
for peace, this bogus treaty-agreement was brought up and rammed
through the Senate.

In 1945 the Senate sold the nation a false bill of damaged goods.
The Senate might as well have passed the Communist Manifesto of
1848, in 1945, for that is where the U.N. Charter had its origin. The U.N.
treaty/agreement is no more than a warmed-up version of the stale left-

overs of the League of Nations treaty, properly rejected by a more constitutionally alert Senate of the 1920s. The parody of the 1945 U.N.
debate proves once again what I have said many times before; we no
longer have a confederated Republic but an authoritarian government
run by an ultra-liberal-Socialist-Communist Democrat Party, operating
under mob rule and the Napoleonic Code, and its current leader in the
White House, is the best (or worst) example of the accuracy of my
views, a true tyrant if ever there was one.

The U.N. treaty/agreement opened the door to other unconstitutional treaties/agreements such as NAFTA, GATT, and the CWC treaty
which came into "law" thanks to the treachery of a large body of
Renegade Republicans who sold out and sided with Mr. Clinton's "free
trade" stance. As we learned earlier, Mr. Wilson was the first U.S.
President to denounce the protective trade barriers placed about our
domestic markets which Washington had so strongly recommended stay
in place.

The Constitution says our government can only make treaties with
nations demonstrating sovereignty. Where is the sovereignty of the
U.N., which runs on the principle of democratic mob rule as rejected by
Plato? The House did a better job of debating the U.N. treaty/agreement,
than the Senate. Congressional Record, House, December 18, 1945,
page 12284:

Rep Smith: "...If only the public really understood the meaning of
this grandiose scheme to establish a United Nations or organization and
to make the United States a member of it would never have been proposed in the first instance. A vote for this measure is a vote for permanent underwriting with the sweat and toil of our people for the
economies of other so-called member nations of this organization —
with the blood of our sons and daughters and for the preservation of
British imperialism."

"The nucleus of this international organization is a military alliance
between the United States and Great Britain, the rest being mainly win-
dow dressing. Also a vote for this proposal is to give approval to world
Communism. Why else would it have the full support of all shades of
Communism everywhere? This strikes at the very heart of the
Constitution. It provides that the power to declare war shall be taken
away from the Congress and given to the President."

"Here is the essence of dictatorship; the control over all else must inevitably follow. The president is to be given absolute power to at any time he elects, and upon any pretext whatsoever, snatch our sons and daughters away from their homes to fight in battle (Korea, Vietnam, Gulf War, Bosnia) not only for as long as he pleases but as may suit the majority of the members of the international organization..."

Rep. Smith knew what he was talking about. Since he made his speech in the House we have seen Truman lead us into Korea; Kennedy and Johnson lead us into Vietnam; Bush lead the nation into the Gulf War and the current Socialist dictator in the White House, setting up our forces under U.N. command in Bosnia as he readies for WWIII and going around calling other nations "rogue states" to please his masters in the petroleum cartel who covet all oil in the Middle East.

Is the U.N. document passed by the Senate a treaty or an agreement? The language of the document is neither fish nor fowl, a confused, unclear mixture of the language of agreements and of treaties, and they cannot be mixed, otherwise there is no legal clarity. All legal documents are governed by the law of clarity. The mixing of language occurred because both the State Dept, which comes under the executive branch, and the legislature, tried to write the wording and what they came up with was document so mixed-up as to be 100 percent unconstitutional. Congressional Record, Senate, July 25, 1945, page 8025:

"That provision must have contemplated some difference between the technical term, treaty, as used in the Constitution and the word "agreement" as used in the U.N. Charter."

If ever we need a perfect example of how the State Department tried to write provisions of the Communist Manifesto of 1848 into the Constitution, this U.N. treaty/agreement is it. This is what Vattel's "Law of Nations" the Bible upon which the Founding Fathers relied so heavily when drafting the U.S. Constitution, has to say:

"The compacts which have temporary matters for their objects are called agreements, conventions and pactions...Thus, they cannot be called a treaty."

Congressional Record, Senate, July 25, 1945, pages 8321:

"I understand the emphasis in article 43 (of the U.N. document) was placed on what is termed an agreement. *It does not have to be a treaty.* The language does not refer to a treaty but to an agreement and the Congress may agree to legislation as to where our armies and navies are sent. A treaty with another is not required in order that we may determine where and in what strength our armed forces must be sent for any purposes..."

Senator McClellan made that incredible statement. The poor man was utterly mixed up and deluded. No wonder I fault the Senate for allotting only 3 days of debate to the U.N. document. The State Department probably didn't know the meaning of the word, "paction" and was all at sea when it wrote the U.N. *agreement,* for it is not a treaty. In any case, most of the State Department consisted of hard-core Communists who were happy about the turn of events. The labeling alone of the U.N. *agreement* as a treaty, is enough to void it. Congressional Record, July 21, 1898, pages 6308-6312:

"Mr. President, when you come to construe any instrument, be it the Constitution, statute, or contract, you construe it with reference to the accepted meaning then existing of the term used in it. In determining in what sense the word "treaty" is used in the Constitution of the United States we must look to the meaning given it in international law (Vattel's "Law of Nations") and between civilized nations of the world at the time the Constitution was adopted."

"It is an instrument of that sort; it is impossible to go into detail as they were understood at the time when they are placed in such an instrument: A treaty is a compact between sovereign states just as a contract is a compact between individuals. It is so defined in all works on international law and by our statesmen." I quote from *Glenn's International Law,* Essentials of a Valid Treaty or contract between two or more independent states:

a) Capacity of the parties to contract.
b) Duly empowered agents to act on behalf of other states.
c) Freedom of consent.
d) The object of the contract to be in conformity to law (in this case the U.S. Constitution-JC)

The U.N. is not a sovereign nation and meets none of the criteria for a sovereign nation; it has no land, no borders, no laws to keep out illegal aliens, no stable government obtaining revenue from a stable population, no de jure government

The U.N. treaty/agreement fails most miserably under the foregoing rules for a constitutional treaty.

The House and Senate in a joint resolution, must obey the Constitution and rescind the 1945 U.N. document. If the House and

Senate fail to do their duty, the legislators will be violating the oath of office taken by each member. That is treason as the Founding Fathers understood it, and they considered treason through failure to uphold the oath of office so heinous an offense, that death was prescribed as the penalty for those who defiled their oath. Let us now examine the above-mentioned conditions necessary for a valid treaty to be concluded:

A) One party — the U.N. — was bereft of any capacity to contract.

This is because the U.N. document is 100 percent unconstitutional, and the legislative, executive or judicial departments of the US government has no authority to make a compact based on an unconstitutional document.

In any case, if the U.N. document were a treaty, then it would have required one or possibly two amendments to the U.S. Constitution which would have had to be submitted to the States for ratification. This was never done. It is most probably for this reason that the Communists in the State Department and the Senate wanted the document to be called an "agreement" and why they hesitated to call it a treaty.

Any treaty which involves war-making powers of the Congress being delegated to some other entity — in this case the U.N. — has to be ignored by the House and Senate. Our Constitution does not allow the State Department to declare war. This is very important to bear in mind, and the same holds good for any and all unelected officials in any federal government department. Only the House and Senate in joint session can declare war.

Had the Senate been constitutionally well-educated, the Vietnam War could not have got started, or come to a an abrupt halt. The Gulf of Tonkin Resolution was an unconstitutional declaration of war drawn up by the State Department, in a most flagrant violation of the separation of powers invested in the Constitution. Pres. Johnson knew he could not have the White House write it up, so slyly, he handed the job to the State Department. Those in the State Department who were responsible for this gross violation of the Constitution should have been charged with treason and when found guilty, they should have been hanged. I think only one or two senators at the time recognized that the Gulf of Tonkin Resolution was a declaration of war, or two of them believed it was.

The U.N. document should not even have been considered by Senate because the U.N. lacked sovereignty and the Constitution has no provision for dealing with foreign bodies or entities who lack full sovereignty. It provides ONLY that treaties be made with individual nations, and not a world body. The U.N. is totally lacking in sovereignty because it has no recognized sovereign territory, no recognized borders and it is not a nation and has no de jure government. Our Constitution says the U.S. can only conclude treaties with NATIONS, not with the world at large and what is the U.N. if not the world at large?

B) Capacity of the parties to contract.

I have already explained that the State Department and the White House lack capacity (authority) to negotiate a contract/agreement/treaty. More than that, the question of a violation of the oath of office has to be considered here, because by negotiating the U.N. document, the Constitution was violated and those who violate the Constitution are ruled incompetent and cannot be parties to a contract. They are either mentally ill or criminals, or both, who have a committed a crime and as far as I am aware, criminals cannot make a valid contract nor can a contract be valid where the intent is to subvert the law of the land, i.e., the United States Constitution.

C) Freedom Of Consent.

One party to a contract cannot sign it if he does not know and understand it. Clearly, ninety-eight of the senators did not know and understand what was in the U.N. document. It would have taken them at least one and a half-years to properly read it, not three days. They were lied to by John Foster Dulles, who misrepresented the terms of the contract. Misrepresentation in a contract by one party renders it null and void and Dulles, the master liar, did exactly that; he MISREPRESENTED the content of the U.N. document in the Senate. The real sovereigns of this nation are We, the People of the several independent States. We did not get the chance to examine the U.N. contract, because it was not submitted to the States in a form of an amendment to the Constitution as mandated by the Constitution. Instead, arbitrary power was used to ram it through the Senate and such an exercise of arbitrary power is forbidden by the Constitution. Exercising arbitrary power is unconstitutional, especially so when the object is to deceive.

D) The Object Of The Contract To Be In Conformity With The Law.

What law are we talking about here? Obviously, the law of the

United States Constitution for We, the People, the sovereigns are not bound to obey ANY other law. We also comply with the provisions contained in Vattel's "Law Of Nations" in matters of international law. Does the U.N. document conform to the U.S. Constitution? Does it comply with international law as stated in Vattel's "Law of Nations?" I have already explained that in key areas and lots of other areas which I did not have the space to include here, the U.N. contract grossly violates the U.S. Constitution.

Therefore, to talk about the U.N. treaty/agreement being the law of the land as maintained in the "National Educator," is absurd. No one who has studied the Annals of Congress, the Congressional Globes and Congressional Records even for the barest minimum of five years, would ever publish such a profound error. The Constitution is silent on the U.N. and where the Constitution is silent on a power it is a prohibition of that power as John Marshall, the first chief justice of the Supreme Court, explained. The Constitution does not allow membership of a world body. Moreover, inasmuch as the U.N. treaty/agreement is ultra vires, of no effect and not incumbent on U.S. citizens to obey its provisions, by what right does the Congress (House and Senate) continue to fund this monstrous organization? Such funding violates the authority over government vested in of We, the People.

The Congressional Record, House, Feb. 26, 1900 page 2290, Justice McLean:

"No powers can be exercised by the Congress which are prohibited by the Constitution or which are contrary to its spirit."

Placing the U.N. treaty/agreement above the Constitution is certainly pernicious to the Constitution and "contrary to its spirit." As Thomas Jefferson said, "To hold treaty making powers boundless is to render the Constitution a blank piece of paper by construction." In Cherokee Tobacco vs. The United States — 11 Wall page 616 — the court said:

"... A treaty cannot change the Constitution or be held valid if in violation of that instrument. This results from the nature of the fundamental principles of our government..."

The U.N. treaty/agreement violates every tenet of the Constitution and the Bill of Rights, on every single one of its pages, as well as egregariously violating international law expounded by Vattel's "Law Of Nations" which was the guiding light for our Founding Fathers when they framed the Constitution.

A very important piece of information in treaty-making powers is found in the Congressional Record, May 16, 1922, pages 7069 - 7079, and although it refers to the League of Nations, the principle remains exactly the same when we talk about the U.N., which in any case, drew much of its content from the old, defunct League. I cannot quote it here as it runs into many, many pages. But a shorter and equally-good reference on treaty making powers is found in the Congressional Record, July 21, 1919 pages 2916-2918:

"...In their final and deliberate judgment, one of the most important features of this covenant was that our country should be distinguished from other nations in its refusal to concentrate in one man exclusively power over foreign relations of the Government and especially over the issues of peace and war..."

The U.N. treaty/agreement violates Washington's Farewell Address and if we substitute U.N. for "League." In the following, we see just how wise were our Founding Fathers. Congressional Record, July 21, 1919. pages 2916 — 2919:

"...Article 10 of the League of Nations (U.N.)...The League of Nations (U.N.) even at its birth had announced itself impotent to fight Bolshevism..."

Since both the League and the U.N. sprang from the Communist Manifesto of 1848, this is not surprising. The League's (U.N.'s) peace objectives: "The dragons teeth see us in a half a dozen wars which have been sown by the peace conferences and if the harvest be averted, it will only be because of the frightful characters of modern armaments and the consequences of war... The League (U.N.) will not stop these wars, of which there are a number in progress...If experience counts for anything, these leagues dissolve in critical times like the soap bubble a child blows..."

As I have said before, the duty of every Representative and Senator is to immediately demand that the illegal treaty/agreement with the U.N. be rescinded and our so-called ambassador recalled immediately. Nothing less will do and anything less is a violation of the oath of office which each and every one of them took. Another aspect which we seldom hear mentioned is that the U.N. treaty/agreement violates States rights and it is my contention that the U.N. was set up to do just that. The important case of Patsome vs. Penn, commented upon by Justice McKenna says among other things:

"...In other words, as the ruling was given point by the special power of the State over the subject matter, then clearly rights claimed under a treaty against such power of the Senate are void and if void they are void because State power which collides with treaty power is superior to it." State laws annulling treaties are generally those of the police powers of the State; health, education and police protection. (The 10th Amendment.)

The U.N. "Year of the Child" is no more and no less than a ruse to get around States rights in the area of health, education, welfare and police protection and to internationalize our children as was attempted in the 1920s.

From where does the U.N. draw its power to intervene in the laws of sovereign countries? Who has given it these powers? Certainly not the Constitution and not Vattel's "Law of Nations" and none of the sovereign countries of Europe or Japan. "Wheat's International Law" does not confer such authority on the U.N.. The only source of empowerment for the U.N. comes directly from the Communist Manifesto of 1848. The U.N. agreement/treaty is an attack on States rights and the U.S. Constitution and the Bill of Rights and was designed specifically for this purpose.

On each and every occasion that the Congress funds the U.N., it is aiding and abetting the destruction of the Constitution and the Bill of Rights, and ultimately contributing to the Communizing of the U.S. under the dictatorship of a One World Government — New World Order. Every Congressman who votes funding for the U.N. is committing treason, and I hope and pray that in the immediate future, the penalty for treason will be enacted against this heinous crime.

TAKING AN OATH TO SERVE UNDER U.N. COMMAND

Forcing our armed services personnel to take an oath to serve under U.N. command is unconstitutional and part of the plan to destroy US sovereignty, the first reason why the U.N. was founded and sent to roost its vultures in the US. It would take two constitutional amendments before our soldiers could take an oath to serve the U.N. Until then, any American soldier who serves under a U.N. command is in violation of the Constitution. Calling our servicemen to serve under U.N. command cannot be enforced by the President, who is not the commander in chief until actually called into service by the Congress following a joint declaration of war by the House and the Senate. Even when so appointed, the president still may not do anything contrary to the Constitution and if he does, he is subject to impeachment proceedings. Neither President Clinton nor any future president can add to or subtract one comma from the Constitution and the Bill of Rights and neither can the House or Senate. For conformation of this statement, see the Congressional Record, April 23, 1884, Contested Elections Wood vs. Patterson.

THE SECOND AMENDMENT BROOKS NO EXCEPTIONS
AT ANY GOVERNMENT LEVEL

There are those like constitutional anarchists Feinstein, Schumer, Boxer, Kennedy and Lautenburg, to name a few of the comrades warring against the right to keep and bear arms, who would seek first to water-down and then eliminate altogether the tamper-proof right of We, the People, to keep and bear arms. The latest attacks equate guns, especially hand-guns, with crime, a theme constantly being promoted via T.V. "news" items and by the jackals of the press also. It is done by linking the word, "crime" to guns, but we should not be fooled by such knavery, as nowhere in the Constitution is "crime" associated with the 2nd Amendment.

Lautenburg and his fellow violators of the Constitution and the Bill of Rights got their idea of linking crime to guns from the British who lamely asserted that guns caused a depletion of wild game, and ergo, guns had to be taken away from their citizens. For crime to be linked to guns would take a constitutional amendment specifically stating that guns cause crime. Lautenburg and his fellow Communist scofflaws want the public to believe that crime will be "depleted" if guns are removed from private ownership; a bald-face lie.

The word, "crime" appears only ONCE in the Constitution and it is found in the Bill of Rights, Article 7, which has to do only with "suits in common law" and nothing to do with the 2nd Amendment and is not found anywhere in the 2nd Amendment. The constitutional anarchists would have us believe that crime is mentioned all over the Constitution, and in this they are succeeding, the problem being that the vast majority of the American people, don't know their Constitution, and are thus, ripe for subjugation. Today, we have justices and judges in the courts who are abysmally ignorant, giving vacuous, puerile, infantile interpretations of the Constitution and they are an ever-present danger to our freedom, because quite apart from being constitutional ignoramuses, they lack judicial restraint and are in awe of their own predilections. They constantly violate the 2nd Amendment when they rule in favor of gun control laws. The 2nd Amendment was won in heated debate by some of the greatest patriotic statesmen ever produced by the United States.

Samuel Evans: "...The Constitution shall never be construed to prevent the people of the United States from keeping their arms."

Note the definition of people, which is interchangeable with citizens as they mean one and the same thing. The Founding Fathers were highly educated men with a near-perfect command of the English language, avid readers of history and prolific writers and they were clear and explicit on the right of the people to keep and bear arms. Note also, that the right to keep and bear arms is a PERSONAL right and Evans confirmed it by saying "from keeping THEIR arms."

Patrick Henry: "Guard with jealous attention the public liberty. Suspect every man who approaches that jewel. Unfortunately nothing will preserve it but downright force. Whenever you give up that force, you are ruined...The great object is that every man be armed, everyone who is able may have a gun."

Thomas Jefferson: "No free man shall ever be debarred from the use of arms."

George Mason: "They (the militia) now consist of the whole people, except a few public officers."

Zachary Johnson: "The people are not to be disarmed of their weapons. They are left in full possession of them..."

James Madison: "...Besides the advantage of being armed, which the Americans possess over the people of almost every other nation, the existence of subordinate governments, to which the people are attached and by which militia officers are appointed, forms a barrier against the enterprise of ambition, more insurmountable than any which a simple government of any form can admit to."

No talk here of duck hunting or sporting rifles. The right to bear arms is a check upon tyrannical government, plain and simple. The Dick Act and the National Guard Act are aimed at the Democrat (Communist) Party's efforts to rob the people of their right to keep and bear arms and they thought that introducing language not in the Constitution, such as "assault rifles;" "junk guns;" "Saturday night specials" was a good way to promote a course of action that would rob the people of their right to keep and bear arms.

Fisher Ames: "The rights of conscience, of bearing arms, of changing government are declared to be inherent in the people."

Note the juxtaposition of "arms" and "changing government." The Founding Fathers, unlike Sen. Gramm and Pres. Clinton did not believe the primary purpose of their guns was to hunt ducks, but to keep government in line within the bounds of the Constitution. The Founding Fathers said that armed citizens are a bulwark against a tyrant in the White House. Now we have the Schumerzites and Boxer-Feinsteins, Lautenburgs and Livermore City Council and a Morton Grove judge telling us that the right to bear arms was confined to the militia.

St. George Tucker: "This may be considered the palladium of liberty — The right of self defense is the first law of nature: in most governments it had been the study of the rulers to keep this right within its narrowest limits possible. Wherever standing armies are kept, *the right of the people,* liberty, if not already annihilated is on the brink of destruction."

St. George Tucker also warned against expost facto laws and bill of attainder laws which would threaten the right of the people to keep and bear arms: "They (expost facto laws and bill of attainder laws) are state-engines of oppression in the last resort..."

Note the following also: "A well-regulated Militia being necessary for the security of a free state, the right of the people to keep and bear arms shall not be abridged." (See also chapter, "What You Don't Know About The Militia.") The very language of the 2nd Amendment speaks of the "right of the people" and the 1st Amendment and the 4th Amendment use the language, "the right of the people." In fact the entire Bill of Rights is addressed to the people-citizens of the States, not to the Federal Government and the 10th Amendment makes the distinction between the people and the Federal government even sharper: "The powers not delegated to the United States (singular) by the Constitution are reserved for the States (plural) respectively or to the people." And note that the term "well regulated" meant not to be regulated by government, but to be "well supplied."

Nor is it expressly implied or incidental to another power that the Federal Government, the Congress, the President, the States, local government, municipalities, town boards, can abolish, usurp, to in any way, shape or form, infringe upon, alter, amend, abridge the right of the people-citizens-freemen-militia to keep and bear arms as guaranteed by the 2nd Amendment.

It is gross impertinence for local boards, municipalities or any other bodies to pass ordinances that would limit the power and scope of the 2nd Amendment. Some time ago the Socialist in the White House ordered his Attorney General to come up with new ways of circumventing the 2nd Amendment. Of course neither Clinton nor Reno can do any such thing without violating the oath they took to uphold the Constitution. The 2nd Amendment is tamper-proof!

The type of ordinances, laws, which attempt to tamper with the 2nd Amendment guarantee is found in the Brady "waiting" Bill, the Lautenburg bill, the Livermore City Council ordinance banning "junk guns," and the California State legislature's ban on certain types of semi-automatic weapons. Gun control is the incubus of tyranny, an amalgam of treason, sedition, calumny, treachery, malfeasance and sophistry of which the term "assault rifles" is but one, and "junk guns" another. There is no such thing as "assault rifles," nor is there any mention of "cheap handguns" or "Saturday night specials," or "junk guns" in the Constitution. These are terms made up by those who are more ingenious in trying to circumvent the Constitution than they are about upholding it, and is typical of such circuitous language.

Constitutionally, legislators at every level, which includes town councils, State assemblies and the federal government, have no constitutional right to categorize guns in this manner, and even less still do they have any constitutional right to attempt to place guns under the Interstate Commerce clause, from which the Founding Fathers specifically exempted all firearms.

Trying to separate the rights of We, the People, from the right to keep and bear arms is nothing but venal, puerile, degrading ingenious mendacity, quackery, specious, sagacious, nefarious double-speak, practiced by the supporters of the Communist Manifesto of 1848, marauders, one and all. The Constitutional Anarchists try to isolate the 2nd Amendment from the rest of the Constitution which was the standard approach of Bolshevik judges of the caliber of Warren Burger, and his fellow constitutional miscreant, Brennan, both of whom should have been impeached a thousand times over for violating the 9th Amendment.

A more nefarious judicial fraud and constitutional miscreant lacking in judicial restraint than Warren Burger, whose assaults on the Constitution were legion, would be hard to find, but Brennan was a close second. It is the duty of every American citizen to read "The Right of the

American People to Keep and Bear Arms," pages 3578-3589 Congressional Record, May 28, 1978, where it is confirmed what was perfectly settled by the Constitution:

As late as 1809, John Randolph expressed in these words the same dread Washington had of a standing army:

"I believe that the people of the United States are not content and would never be content to see a standing army well equipped, armed and disciplined, while our Militia, our defense against internal enemies and external enemies (of the States) remained unarmed and defenseless...The people who will consent to remain unarmed while arms are put in the hands of a standing army governed by martial law, are ripe for a master."

And are We, the People, willing to see the servants of the people armed, while we are robbed of our arms and left nakedly defenseless? Why should the *servants* of the people be armed, and not their masters, the sovereign people of the sovereign States? It is worthy of note that Randolph made it perfectly clear that it is the right of the people to be armed. What the Federal Government, the courts, local government bodies try and do, is to insert clauses between the 1st and 10th Amendments and this cannot be done however well-disguised such attempts may be. This is particularly true of the vacuous, specious, nefarious ordinances passed by the Morton Grove and the Livermore City Council. The 9th Amendment is part of the Constitution adopted precisely to prevent such attempts to amend the Constitution and the Bill of Rights through unlawful predilections of officials and judges alike, including officials who serve on municipal boards, county councils, mayors and so forth. The Constitution cannot be twisted and squeezed to fit the wishes of 2nd Amendment haters, nor can the 2nd Amendment be isolated from the whole Constitution.

The great St. George Tucker makes this perfectly clear in his book, "Blackstone's Commentaries, Views of the Constitution" on page 315:

"The Congress of the United States possesses no power to regulate, or interfere with the domestic concerns of any State, it belongs to them (the States) to establish any rules respecting the rights of property, nor will the Constitution permit any prohibition of arms to the people. Or peaceful assemblies by them for whatever purpose, and in any number, whatsoever they may see occasion." And this applies with equal force to State legislators and local town councils etc.

The unratified 14th Amendment did not try to rob the States of property rights and other States rights, and note that its framers did not try to apply it to the right to keep and bear arms, as Congress in itself has no power to alter the Constitution: "The enumeration of certain rights shall not be construed to deny or disparage others retained by the people" said Chief Justice John Marshall, the third chief justice of the Supreme Court, a man who would turn in his grave over the likes of the Schumerzite Gun Grabbers Club, Sarah Brady, Feinstein, Lautenburg, the Livermore City Council in California and the California Assemblymen, whose fatuous bills invoking "gun control" were recently presented and sent to the California State Senate. The right place for such measures is the garbage can.

An attack on the 2nd Amendment is an attack on the whole Constitution. Supreme Court justices, Congressmen, town council members; this work puts you on notice that you may not make laws to suit your political liking. You've got to obey the Constitution and the Bill of Rights. There is no exception to this rule. The first rule of law in our Republic is worth stating again, and again: The U.S. Constitution and the Bill of Rights cannot be compromised nor can any clauses be separated out from the rest of the Constitution. This was made so as to thwart people control by a tyrannical government. The Oregon State Constitution in Art. 1, Section 27, says what the majority of State constitutions say:

"The people shall have the right to bear arms for the defense of themselves (note English spelling of "defense") and the State, but the Military shall be kept in strict subordination of civil power." That is why they instituted State militias, organized and unorganized.

Then, as now, the people have good reason to mistrust a standing army under federal government (centralized) control. The destruction of life and property at Waco (termed as a "mistake") is a grim reminder of what can and will happen. The 2nd Amendment is *immutable,* and cannot be compromised nor separated from the whole Constitution. "Gun control" seeks to halve or quarter the 2nd Amendment. It cannot be done. Trying to use extenuating circumstances such as "crime can be reduced if we ban Saturday night specials" just won't cut it. The liberals — and you will not fail to notice they always vote in a bloc for gun control, love to use this Marxist-type phraseology. A good example of the way their minds work is found in the following account:

Senator Lautenburg attached a gun control bill to a U.S. Postal Appropriations Bill which had nothing to do with guns, and was thus able to slip it through the Senate. This is one of the tactics often used by the Communist traitors in the House and Senate. Lautenburg's gun control bill is so deformed that it would take hundreds of pages to fully describe just how unconstitutional it is, but let us start with the more glaring examples of how a bill should not be drafted:

It violates Article 1, Section 9 Part 3: "No bill of attainder or expost facto law shall be passed. As mentioned above. St. George Tucker warned about this type of bill violating expost facto law and bill of attainder law, which he described as "State engines of oppression in the last resort." On this ground alone, the bill should have been declared dead on arrival. Congressional Globe, January 4, 1867, pages 279-283. Calder vs. Hall, Judge J.Chase discusses the question, what is an expost facto law?:

"Literally it is only that a law shall not be passed concerning an after the fact or things done or action committed...I will state what laws I consider expost facto within the words and intent of the prohibition:

1] Every law that makes an action done before the passing of the law, and which innocent when done, criminal, and punishes such action.

2] Every law that aggravated the crime, or making it greater when it as committed.

3] Every law that changes the punishment and inflicts greater punishment than the law annexed to the crime when committed.

4] Every law that alters the legal rules of evidence and receives a different testimony at the time than that the law required at the time of the commission of the offense (English spelling) in order to convict the offender."

What is a bill of attainder? Quoting from the Congressional Record, February 16, 1882, pages 1195-1200:

"If the punishment is less than death, the act is termed a bill of pains and penalties. Within the meaning of the Constitution, bills of attainder include bills of pains and penalties. In these cases the legislative body, in addition to its legitimate functions, exercises the power of office of judge; it assumes, in the language of the text books, judicial magistracy; it pronounces upon the guilt of the party without any forms of safeguards of trial; it determines the sufficiency of proofs produced, whether conformable to the rules of evidence or otherwise; fixes the degree of punishment in accordance with its own notions of the enormity of the offense."

A bill of attainder and expost facto law is *prohibited* by the Constitution and the Bill of Rights, *no matter what the force of circumstances may be.* Senator Frank Lautenburg's gun control "law" violates entirely the foregoing prohibition and on this ground alone, is null and void, ultra vires, no law at all and incumbent on none to obey. Lautenburg's bill is, in fact, an overt act of treason with which he should be charged.

* Lautenburg's unconstitutional bill violates expost facto prohibition because he comes up with the word "misdemeanor" which word is only used in the Constitution in reference to impeachment of judges and presidents and all civil officers — it absolutely cannot be applied to so-called violations of so-called gun control laws. Nor can "misdemeanor" be introduced as co-equal with the word "crime" because the two would overlap *without* being *precise* and *exact* as to meaning, and they do this in his bill. The Communists first introduced "misdemeanor" in the 1920s to apply to other crimes which is unconstitutional to this day: Article 11, Section 4: "removed from office on conviction of treason, bribery, or other high crimes or misdemeanors."

* Lautenburg's bill would force the courts to accept a bill of attainder and expost facto law.

* Pomeroy, in "Constitutional Law:"...Those affairs which are local affect the individual citizen in his private capacity (family rights, domestic matters not subject to Federal Government interference), abstracted from his relations to the whole political society, are managed by the Separate State governments which were found in existence and left remaining in existence by the same Constitution."

* Howard 17: "The power to make municipal (States) regulation for the restraint and punishment of crime, for the health and preservation of the health and morals of her citizens has never been surrendered by the States nor restrained by the Constitution of the United States."

* Lautenburg's bill purports to allow the Federal Government violate all of the foregoing constitutional safeguards against Central Government interference and to permit it to intervene in family affairs, thus violating the 10th Amendment as well as Article 1, Section 8. Nowhere does it say in the delegated powers of the Federal Government

that it can interfere in any way in family affairs. Family affairs rights come under personal rights in States constitutions. The 5th Amendment protection of life liberty and property reside in the States, where they have always been, and Lautenburg's bill has not one shred of Constitutional right to bar persons who have engaged in domestic violence from owning guns, or others from selling such persons a gun, and making it a "misdemeanor."

Congressional Record, House, March 28, 1904, pages 3898-3906, on Judge Cooley's "Constitutional Limitations" page 706:

"In the American constitutional system the power to establish the ordinary regulations of police (municipal) regulations has been left with the States and cannot be taken away from them, either wholly, or in part, and exercised under legislation of Congress. Neither can the national Government through any of its departments or officers, assume any supervision of the police regulations of the States."

* Lautenburg's bill *purports* that the 2nd Amendment could be overturned through a mere misdemeanor — a Constitutional impossibility. It also violates the 5th and 10th Amendments.

* Lautenburg's bill purports to give the Federal Government the power to retroactively punish a person guilty of a family assault, a most serious violation of the expost facto law — by making what was not a crime at the time of the offense — a crime retroactively, or after the fact.

Nor can due process be denied to any who have their gun seized.

* Lautenburg's bill violates the Militia Act of 1902 which Congress cannot alter without upsetting the basis of the draft which again, would be a violation of a bill of attainder and expost facto law.

On just these restriction, alone — and there are of course, more, Lautenburg's gun control bill falls flat on its unconstitutional backside and is declared null and void, no law, and incumbent upon none to obey. Of course the main constitutional violation indulged in by Lautenburg and his preposterous gun control bill is the 2nd Amendment, which forever bars all government at whatever level — town, county, State or Federal, from abridging the unfettered right of citizens to keep and bear arms. Senator Lautenburg should be tried for treason and if found guilty, he should be made to pay the penalty demanded by the Founding Fathers by reason of the fact that an attack on any one part of the Constitution is an attack on the whole Constitution.

Further information about anti-2nd Amendment Communist efforts to destroy the Constitution and the Bill of Rights, of which the 2nd Amendment is the first plank, can be found in the chapters, "Some Aspects of The Communist Doctrine of Gun Control And What Gun Control Laws Mean" and "What You Don't Know About The Militia."

WARS, TREATIES, AS A MEANS OF FURTHERING A ONE WORLD — NEW WORLD ORDER, FORMERLY KNOWN AS COMMUNISM

There is ample evidence that the First World War was a thought in the minds of two British politicians as a means of ending the trade superiority of Germany. Britain lives by exports and Germany was taking over many former British markets, and especially, it was becoming a threat to British oil supplies in the Middle East. The British knew that if they started getting the worst of it in the war they were contemplating, they could always call upon the United States to pull their chestnuts out of the fire. With this in mind, Woodrow Wilson, whose reputed German ancestry was thought to be an advantage to Britain, was selected and elected by the Royal Institute for International Affairs (RIIA) to become their man for the Oval Office.

We often get so bogged down in history that we lose sight of the main objectives of any war, which are a far cry from the stated causes. Just so with WWI and WWII, both instigated by Britain to further the cause of Communism (capitals always deliberately used throughout) which would lead to a One World Government — New World Order. So on November 5, 1913, Wilson was elected President of the United States. His first action was to call for a joint session of the Congress in which he strongly attacked U.S. Customs tariffs and trade policies, which Lincoln, Garfield and McKinley were assassinated for upholding, and he called for a new round of "free trade" to be imposed on an innocent, unsuspecting American people.

"Free trade" had long been a policy of Britain, a policy tied in with furthering a One World Government — New World Order. The next order on the RIIA's agenda was to get Wilson to steer the 16th Amendment through Congress — the Marxist doctrine of graduated income tax — and the Federal Reserve Act. Both were vital cogs in preparing the machinery for WWI, without which, the British would never have instigated that war. When we think of what progress our enemies have made with "free trade" then we can gauge how close we are to a One World Government — New World Order, (formerly

Communism) being ushered in. "NAFTA" and "GATT" actually began with the Wilson presidency, as my book, "One World Order: Socialist Dictatorship" establishes.

The U.N. "treaty"/agreement was not created in a vacuum, and should be seen in the context of the One World Government — New World Order (formerly Communism.) When we look at the U.N. in this context, the goals of the U.N. become crystal clear, and they are the same as the League of Nations, sponsored by The RIIA, supported by Walter Lippman, Woodrow Wilson under the control of Colonel House, and the delegates to the Paris Peace Conference; Socialists/Marxists/Communists, one and all. As I said about the U.N. treaty/agreement, the senators would have needed at least two years to properly study what was in the treaty and whether it was constitutional, but thanks to the lies and persuasions of John Foster Dulles, the senators passed this illegal agreement within three days!

My studies of the Congressional Records, etc., persuaded me that Dulles knew very little of substance about the U.S. Constitution, and he lied most of the time when explaining this "treaty" to the senators, who were themselves, insufficiently versed in the Constitution to know the difference between an agreement and a treaty. Today we have Madeline Albright as Secretary of State, who if anything, knows even less than Dulles. That Albright was appointed by the Senate speaks volumes about the lack of knowledge of the Constitution among the members of the Senate who confirmed this lady, a lady who didn't seem to know her ancestry until she discovered it after her appointment. Any test of Albright's knowledge of the Constitution and the Bill of Rights would quickly show it is zero.

Having failed in their objective to end German domination of Europe (through trade), the British hierarchy decided to have a second go around, and so in 1921 they tried to lay the foundation for the Second World War, through establishing the League of Nations, a Fabian Socialist concept upon which the U.N. treaty/agreement is founded. But unlike the 1945 senators who were outclassed by Dulles and the cast of Socialists under the direction of Roosevelt, plus pressures from the jackal press, the senators in 1919-1921 knew that the League "treaty" was pernicious to the interests of the U.S., and they refused to ratify it.

Thus it was left to Franklin Roosevelt to carry out the agenda of the international bankers, and as a former member of the International

Bankers Association, the RIIA's choice of Roosevelt as their man in ramming through the One World Government — New World Order, U.N. treaty/agreement was a particularly favorable choice. I hope that by now the American people realize that they do not elect their presidents; this is controlled by the Committee of 300 as the guiding light for a One World Government — New World Order and we get what these conspirators choose. Roosevelt and Clinton are two examples of this, although the principle applies to every president from Woodrow Wilson onwards.

The League of Nations was meant to lead the U.S. into WWII, but the traitors in the House and Senate were overruled by those who knew the Constitution and saw through the aims and objects of the League. But, as we know from our enemy, they never give up and will come back, year after year with the same proposal, sometimes thinly disguised — like the United Nations — meant to be the chosen instrument of the One World Government — New World Order (formerly the Communists) for small brush wars. It is out of these wars that the international bankers make billions of dollars on the backs of U.S. servicemen and the taxpayers of this nation.

Similarly, other treaties like NAFTA, GATT, CWC and the Club of Rome's NATO are guaranteed to lead eventually to bigger and better (for our controllers) wars and the U.N. is the prime vehicle which is a document guaranteeing future world conflicts to implement Socialism and Communism. The cunning timing of the U.N. treaty/agreement made it look as if the U.N. was established to stop future wars, when in fact, its goal is the exact opposite. If the American people are to save themselves, then they must demand of Congress that the U.N.treaty/agreement be abrogated, forthwith. A far cry from being "the law of the land" the U.N. and ALL treaties can be abrogated by Congress just like any other law. They are only ordinary laws.

The Second World War was at least ten years in the planning stage and one of the key part of the plan was that in the aftermath of the war, a supreme body would be set up that would control all nations, and particularly, the United States.

CHAPTER 5

WE THE SOVEREIGN PEOPLE: THE EFFECT OF THE 13TH, 14TH AND 15TH AMENDMENTS

WHY PRESIDENT JOHNSON SUFFERED AN IMPEACHMENT ATTEMPT.
REPUBLICANS GAVE US THE 13TH, 14TH, AND 15TH AMENDMENTS.

P ossibly the best definition of the sovereign citizen was given by Judge Roger Taney, whose knowledge of the Constitution and the Bill of Rights was always widely respected. Congressional Record, House, Feb 26, 1900:

"Speaking of sovereignty, the learned judge (Judge Taney) said: "The words, people of the United States, and citizens are synonymous terms and mean the same thing. They both describe the political body who according to our republican institutions (note, he never said "democratic" institutions — JC) form the sovereignty and who hold the power and conduct the sovereignty through their representatives (mainly in the House). They are what we familiarly call "the sovereign people" and every citizen is of these people and a constituent member of this sovereignty."

Thus, it is We, the People, who wield all power vested in us by the framers of the Constitution. We are the rulers of the United States, not the government. We demonstrated this truth at the time of the forming of the covenant when we delegated the narrowest of powers to the Federal Government (Sec. 8, Art. 1, Clauses 1-18) which government can neither subtract from or add anything to it. Most of the members of Congress have no idea just how much their powers are circumscribed and hedged about, and for this reason they get their legislative aides to write bills that are thoroughly unconstitutional and a real mess. Then, there are the Socialists, like Rep. Charles Schumer, Sen. Boxer and Sen. Feinstein who think they have the power to do away with the 2nd Amendment which they flagrantly violate through so-called "gun control laws." Should We, the People, lose our sovereignty, we would then lose our liberty also, as sovereignty would then reside with the Federal Government acting with the power of a king. In essence this is what has been happening, starting with Woodrow Wilson, vastly accelerating under Roosevelt and continuing with Pres. Clinton who is doing so much damage to the Constitution that it will take at least 50 years or more, to undo the harm he has wrought through unlawful "executive orders" and seizing powers to which he is not entitled.

A very important case about sovereignty is Yick Wo vs. Hopkins (118 U.S. 356, 369):

"When we consider the nature and theory of our institutions of government, the principles upon which they are supposed to rest, and to review the history of their development, we are constrained to conclude that they do not mean to leave room for the play and action of purely personal and arbitrary power. Sovereignty itself is, of course, not subject to law, for it is the author of the law and the source of law, but in our system, while sovereign powers are delegated to agencies of government, sovereignty itself remains with the people by whom and for whom all government exists and acts. And the law is the definition and limitation of power..."

Congressional Record, Senate, Dec. 19, 1898, page 288:

"As a nation the United States is sovereign. Sovereignty and nationality are correlative terms. There can be no nationality without sovereignty and there can be no sovereignty without nationality. As to every matter the United States as a nation possesses sovereign power, except where it has been reserved to the states and the people.

The Cumberland road debate found in the Congressional Record tells us a great deal more:

"...The history of the world affords no such example of two separate and independent governments each established over the same people, nor can it exist in governments not founded on the sovereignty of the people. In monarchies and other governments not representative there can be no such division of power. The government is inherent in the possessor, it is his and cannot be taken away from him without a revolution. In such governments alliances and leagues alone are practicable, but with us, individuals count for nothing (Roosevelt, Clinton et al) in the office they hold; that is why they have no right to them. They hold them as representatives by appointment from the people in which sovereignty is exclusively vested."

This clearly does not allow any President to issue "executive orders;" in reality, proclamations, for such proclamations take the power away from the people and place it with would-be tyrants as we have seen in the case of Roosevelt, Bush and Clinton. The U.S. flag is also part of sovereignty of the nation, which is much misunderstood, as the Flag Debate shows.

THE REPUBLICAN PARTY GAVE U.S. THE THIRTEENTH, FOURTEENTH AND FIFTEENTH AMENDMENTS TO THE U.S. CONSTITUTION: THE BIGGEST FRAUD OF THE 19TH CENTURY

Had the Republicans not replaced the leaders of the South and put puppets in their place in their State legislatures these amendments might have been properly ratified (except the 3rd section of the 14th would have had to be excised) and we would never had the fraud of these three amendments nor the fraud of Reconstruction, civil rights and voting rights upon which they are based. The 13th, 14th and 15th Amendments are mere scraps of waste-paper and equally worthless. The Reconstruction debates legislation would never have been passed but for blackmail by the Radical Republicans. Remember, the Civil war was a political war and Reconstruction legislation was taken solely from European history: Congressional Globe, May 17, 1870, pages 3509 — 3521:

"Enforcement of the 15th Amendment: What did Austria make of her pains and penalties and disabilities in Hungary? Nothing but smothered rebellion, nothing but outbreaking revolution..." It then goes on to say what happened with the British in Ireland.Even President Lincoln tried to distance himself from them. Congressional Globe Dec. 15, 1870, pages 131-142:

"President Lincoln notified Congress that his approval was not necessary to the resolution submitting to the States the articles of amendments and the 13th, 14th and 15th Amendments were not sent to the President for his approval..."

The basis of all civil rights is the 14th Amendment which has never been ratified and is thus, null and void, ultra vires, lawless, revolutionary and incumbent upon no one to obey, if the Constitution is to be upheld and enforced. The 13th, 14th and 15th Amendments are not part of the Constitution and are fakes, sophistry, mendacity, the biggest fraud of the 19th century. The Supreme Court keeps up this mockery by misrepresentation to We, the People, and our Representatives in both Houses of Congress cynically perpetuate the falsehood, instead of denouncing it.

After the Civil War the Republican-dominated Congress went to extraordinary lengths to seat puppets from the Confederate States, not only in State legislatures but also in the Congress to make it appear as though these three amendments were properly ratified. We know from the History of Congress that military force and intimidation was applied to the secessionist States, to get the amendments through. From this it follows that the Reconstruction legislation was also totally bogus, as it followed after the 13th, 14th and 15th Amendments..

One of the best constitutionalists of the 19th century was Sen. Thurmond of Ohio. His speech on the chicanery of the 14th Amendment is found in the Congressional Record, Feb. 26, 1792, pages 1795-1797:

"...There is not one word in this action of the 14th Amendment that has any relation to race, color or previous condition of servitude; but the senator goes out of his way to clear outside of that, and finding some evil as he supposes existing in the country, undertakes by the exhibition of evil to change the fundamental law of the land. If we were to argue that way, where would the Constitution of the U.S. be? Sir, there are other evils in this country besides those he depicts. There are other people who suffer besides the colored races..."

Sen. Thurmond was explaining that the 14th Amendment was supposed to make all persons "equal under the laws" but it seemed to him that the Negro was to receive preference. The 14th Amendment added nothing new to the Constitution even if had been properly ratified by the States. The privileges and immunities clause of U.S. citizens in the first section of the 14th was nothing new as it was already implied in the Constitution when citizens are outside the country, or serving in the armed forces.

The great St. George Tucker is clear about the purposes and intent of the three amendments, that being to wreck States rights and defeat what George Washington referred to as the Confederated Republics of the United States:

"...The Constitution of the United States, then being the instrument by which the federal government hath been created; its powers defined and limited and its duties, and functions of its departments prescribed; the government, thus established may be a confederated republic, composed of several independent, and sovereign democratic states, united for their common defense against foreign nations, and for the purpose of harmony, and mutual intercourse between each other; each state retaining an entire liberty of exercising as it thinks proper, all those parts of its sovereignty, which are not mentioned in the Constitution, or act of union as parts that ought to be exercised in common. It is the law of the land..."

It is this "law of the land" that the Radical Republicans sought to overturn with their 13th, 14th and 15th Amendments, and nowhere more so than with their so-called civil rights legislation.

One of the biggest fallacies abroad today — and I hear it so many times – is so-called "civil rights." Lawyers make the same mistake — not to mention the Supreme Court — almost to a man they say that the first section of the 14th Amendment gives "equal protection of the law" based on race. There is not one word about "race" in this section, which is indirect and this is generally true of other parts of the Constitution, which is an indirect instrument.

We must bear in mind that the 14th Amendment was drawn up in secret by a select group of radical Republicans from the House and Senate, which included Thaddeaus Stevens, whose input was carefully noted by the secret committee and it is well-demonstrated in the third section of this amendment, the most revolutionary of all of its sections and which alone prevents it from being constitutional.

Stevens was a bitter enemy of the Democrats of the eleven secessionist states. A man with a venomous tongue who knew the political superiority of the Democrats of the South, Stevens hated the fact that their sons were better educated than the sons of the Northern States, by virtue of having attended prestigious schools and universities in Europe. Stevens connected Southern superiority with the issue of slavery, saying slavery had made it financially possible for the sons of the South to have a better education than their Northern counterparts.

Not only did Stevens want the South to be humiliated, he wanted to make sure that the secessionist states were stripped of their States rights, which were retained by the States as a condition of joining the Union, alongside of the Federal Government's guarantee that each State was to have a Republican form of government. This is what Stevens wanted the 14th Amendment to mean as we find in his speech in the Congressional Record, House, January 25 1922 pages 1723-1729:

"The Constitution limits only the actions of Congress to correct unjust legislation of the States. This amendment (14th) supplied that defect and allows Congress to correct the unjust legislation of the States, so far that the law which operates upon man shall operate equally upon all. What ever law punishes the white man for a crime shall punish the black man in precisely the same way and to the same degree."

This was no less than a fraud, a deception, and Stevens knew it. The cunning and deception of the 14th Amendment did not always make fools of judges then, as it does most often today. In the Slaughterhouse cases, the Supreme Court justices poked fun at the 13th, 14th and 15th Amendments, and as we shall see, the Republicans who precipitated the Civil War with their violent and inflamed rhetoric, saw in these three amendments an opportunity to stay in power through the Negro vote, and by barring Confederate officers from holding public office. We shall also see that the strategy backfired on the Republican Party, and that today, the whole nation is paying a huge price for the deception they perpetrated.

Congressional Globe, Feb. 15, 1871, pages 114 - 117:

"The plea of political necessity (as used too often in the bogus gun control laws — JC) by the Senator, justified the adoption of the 15th Amendment, is always ready, and has become the law of the existence of the party which having forfeited the confidence of the people, is now compelled to retain power by fraud and force. Hence the bill to employ the army to enforce the 15th Amendment...This legislative trial is a bill of attainder prohibited by the Constitution of the United States. Congress has no power not given by that instrument: and when it inflicts punishment without its authority, it is no more than a mob..."

"In the case of Cummings vs. The State of Missouri the question involved was the right to pass an expost facto law of bill of attainder, disqualifying persons from the exercise of the right of suffrage and such attempt was pronounced by the Supreme Court to be unconstitutional, null and void. But after the Reconstruction acts were passed the

McCardle case arose under those acts, came up by appeal to the Supreme Court; and what was the conduct of the Republican Party?" (We know what happened, the Supreme Court ducked the case saying that it could not rule on acts of Congress or words to that effect.)

In Cummings vs. The State of Missouri, the Supreme Court ruled that refusal to hire former "rebels" in all forms of employment was a violation of a bill of attainder. Notwithstanding this crystal-clear precedent, the judiciary in all of its mendacity and sophistry has for scores of years gone on ruling that "affirmative action" (a bill of attainder violation) is legal, when they knew of a certainty that it was nothing of the kind. This ought to prove beyond the shadow of a doubt that the judicial system in the United States, having been infiltrated by Socialists, Marxists and Communists of every stripe, is probably one of the most corrupt in the world today, with the exception of openly Communists states like Cuba and China.

Of course the much-compromised judiciary tells us that they base the legality of "affirmative action" on the 13th, 14th and 15th Amendments, but they fail to bring to our notice that nowhere in these three amendments is "affirmative action" expressly implied; thus even if the 13th, 14th and 15th Amendments were a part of the Constitution — which they are not — never having been ratified, "affirmative action" could still not be predicated upon them.

In their haste to force the 14th Amendment through Congress, the secret committee clean forgot to give the Negroes the right to vote and so they had to go back and cobble together the 15th Amendment to correct their error, but the 15th Amendment — even more revolutionary and unconstitutional — was never ratified, so the radical Republicans only succeeded in compounding their error. There are other things wrong with the 15th Amendment and we shall be returning to them. Of interest here is the desire to punish the South arising out of hatred for the South expressed by radical Republicans, which distorted the Constitution and which has left constitutional questions of the most profound nature, unanswered.

Congressional Globe May 19, 1870, pages 3607-3615: Enforcement of the 15th Amendment:

"What we want" said Jeff Davis, "is not so much slavery, about which we care little, as national independence we will have, or we will have annihilation."

Then on page 3611: "There is no legislation that could reach a State to prevent it passing a law. It can only reach the individual citizens of the States in the enforcement of law. You have, therefore, in any appropriate legislation, to act on the citizen and not the State. If you pass an act by which you make it an indictable offense for an officer to execute any law of a State by which he trespasses upon any of these rights of the citizen it operates upon him as a citizen and not as an officer..." This is of course, incorrect as the 13th, 14th and 15th Amendments are addressed to the States and NOT to the individual, which nullifies completely the so-called Civil Rights Act of 1964, and the so-called Voting Rights Act of 1965.

The venomous hatred of the radical Republicans for the South is well-demonstrated on page 3615:

"For one, I propose to keep this nest of adders, who have given us so much trouble — I mean those who have hissed the loudest and were the most poisonous in their bite — away from my premises."

Not exactly charitable words of friendship and it so graphically illustrates the point that the truth about the South's position in the Civil War has never been fully told. History, as is its wont, is nearly always a much lop-sided account of events from the point of view of the victor and this is no less true of the accounts of the Civil War, and our history books are woefully lacking in this regard.

Perhaps the finest explanation of the unconstitutionality and utter fraud of the 15th Amendment is found in a speech by Senator Davis, Congressional Globe, May 20, 1870: "Enforcement of the 15th Amendment," pages 3660-3665.

"Now Mr. President, I will avert to one or two other important cardinal, essential principles of free speech and constitutional government which I will never sacrifice, and the destruction of which I will never give my consent to. The Congress of the United States claimed and has triumphaly and frequently exercised the power to propose amendments to the Constitution by excluding eight, ten, and eleven members of the Union from representation in both Houses of Congress. That was a revolution, in the language of the scholarly and able Senator from Missouri."

"The Constitution provides for its own amendment. It proscribes the particular mode in which it may be amended; and if that mode is honestly and faithfully administered, it is not a revolution, but is simply the execution of a principle of the Government, of the Constitution itself, for the alteration and amendment of the fundamental law. But when a dominant majority in times of civil war (note Sen. Davis correctly called it a war and not a rebellion) or of peace claim the power, and exercise it too, of excluding almost one-third of the States in both Houses of Congress, and then propose amendments to the Constitution by propositions passed by the remainder of the two Houses of Congress, when the Constitution itself says that such propositions shall not be passed, except by the vote of two-thirds of both Houses, I will insist to the extent that such a mode of amending the Constitution is lawless, revolutionary, destructive of our Constitution and one of its fundamental principles, and is entitled to no obedience and no respect from any quarter whatever."

"Sir, when it is contended that the dominant faction in Congress may of its own will upon the suggestion of its own lust for power, take Representatives and Senators by the throat and thrust them from the halls of Congress, and then claim a constitutional right to amend the fundamental law so as to subserve their own purposes of ambition, of acquisition or retention of power, I say that is *a lawless aspect of revolution,* which deserves the opposition and the sternest and most inflexible opposition of every enlightened American patriot..."

The 13th, 14th and 15th Amendments are the basis of the Civil Rights Act of 1866, the meaning and interpretations of which came later and shows up this act where the Negro was given his civil rights but not any social rights which are not in the above-mentioned three amendments. The 15th Amendment came later and does not nor has it ever applied to individual citizens, but only to the States, one of the things being that States cannot pass legislation depriving the Negro of the right to vote because of color; and likewise, the Congress is also forbidden to pass such legislation. In any event the 13th, 14th and 15th Amendments and the statutory law based on them, will take a thorough whipping if they are ever placed before an impartial judicial review panel. For instance, since the last slave died a long time ago, the 13th Amendment must have died with them. If not yet buried, then it is time to inter the 13th Amendment.

The 15th Amendment does not provide anything constitutional that would allow government to interfere with personal rights such as forcing a private club to admit people the club does not wish to accept as members. Personal rights embodied in the 10th Amendment are those rights not enumerated elsewhere and which express personal rights. It is worthy of note that in spite of their vindictiveness toward the South, the Republican makers of the three amendments did not try to interfere with personal rights of the Southerners. (They did not try to take away the personal right of owning and bearing arms from the South.)

Congressional Globe, May 16, 1870, pages 3479-3493:

"Enforcement of the 15th Amendment" In May of that year the Republicans tried to pass a so-called civil rights act in 1870, it being a bill of pains and penalties.

The fraud of the 15th Amendment comes out in the debates on the civil rights act of 1870, supposedly the enforcement legislation for the 15th Amendment. Much more fraud followed with the so-called voting rights act of 1965, allegedly based upon the civil rights act of 1870, this being no more and no less than a pyramid of fraud heaped upon fraud, and the judiciary has demonstrated time after time that it cannot be trusted by the American people, because they have gone on and on perpetuating this fraud, deceiving the American people into believing that all of these frauds on the Constitution and the Bill of Rights are actually the law!

Congressional Globe, May 16, 1870, pages 3470-3493, Senator Vickers:

"...But if, contrary to all the analogies and distinctions which existed in the respective forms of government, Congress shall arrogate the power to regulate State elections and electors, I contend that this so-called fifteenth amendment is not constitutional and legally a part of the Constitution of the United States:

FIRST: Because no amendment to the Constitution can be legitimately proposed and adopted unless all of the States shall at the time exercise the right to be represented in both Houses of Congress.

SECONDLY: That no amendment can be ratified unless all of the States ratifying them shall have a right to adopt or reject them without being subject to any condition but must be free and untrammeled.

THIRDLY: That no amendment can be valid unless all of the States that vote on it at the time of voting are equal in right, dignity, and honor.

FOURTHLY: That the fifteenth amendment received only 27 votes exclusive of New York and Indiana, 28 being necessary for ratification; New York having revoked her ratification and Indiana having ratified without a constitutional quorum of her legislature being present, and in open violation of her constitutional provision."

Congressional Globe Feb. 15 1871, pages 1250-1253.

On page 1250, fully spelled out, is found a joint resolution of the legislature of Indiana, withdrawing its assent to the 15th Amendment. "Three other States, Virginia, Mississippi and Texas voted to ratify under coercion, their admission on representation being made to depend on their affirmative vote; these three being deducted, leave only twenty-four States voting for ratification, *four less than 3/4 of the states.*" Later, Oregon sent notice that it was nullifying its vote for the 15th Amendment, leaving the number of States necessary to ratify far short of the required two-thirds of the States.

Congressional Globe, May 20, 1870, pages 420-423:

The Hon J. Fowler of Tennessee:

"I have said that the amendment is inadequate to protect the rights of citizens. It founds the right to vote on no principle. It asserts no positive grant of power (in other words it is not found in the delegated powers of the Federal Govt., Art. 1, Sec. 8 Clauses 1-18) it does not base the right to vote on manhood or its natural rights...It does not guard any of his interests as a member of society, or secure to him equal rights before the law...The amendment can do nothing for the citizen that the State could not do without it and do much better, and therefore, it was not demanded..."

What is worthy of note here, above the condemnation of the 15th Amendment as unconstitutional, is the correctness of Fowler's assertion about States being able to do a better job than the Federal Government in protecting the rights of its citizens. The reserve powers of the States not enumerated in the Constitution allows States more room than is the case with the Federal Constitution which has no reserve powers or unenumerated powers, but only the delegated powers in Art.1, Sec. 8, Clauses 1 — 18. of the U.S. Constitution.

It is a widely mistaken belief that only the Federal Government can give civil rights as to life, liberty and property, which the States never relinquished at the time they joined the Union. The State provides a birth certificate, a high school diploma, a marriage certificate, driver license and a death certificate, so why do citizens need the Federal Government to intrude in States rights? Of course the States don't need such interference and in any case, it is unconstitutional.

Could anything be more explicit than the foregoing as to why the 15th Amendment is unconstitutional, null and void, and revolutionary, apart from the fact that it has never been properly ratified and, therefore, not a part of the Constitution of the United States? The validity, the brilliance, the accuracy of the analyses by Sen. Davis and Sen. Vickers, among others, must forever lay to rest the question as to whether the 15th Amendment is constitutional or not. The Constitution cannot be used as an instrument of revenge and retribution; it is an instrument of law. Sec. 3 of the 14th Amendment, for example, is brazenly and openly vindictive and revengeful, aimed against the Democrats of the South and the people of the Southern States in general.

A study of the Congressional Globe of the period reveals that most of the members of the House and Senate knew that the amendments and the Civil Rights Act of 1870 were frauds and filled with deceptions. If one reads the Congressional Globes of the period this comes through very strongly.

Congressional Globe, May 20, 1870, pages 3667-3690

Sen. Thurmond, the greatest constitutionalist of his time:

"But now, sir, within thirty days of the adoption of the 15th Amendment, or the proclamation of its adoption, on the bill to enforce the 15th Amendment, this proposition which has no more relation to the 15th Amendment than it has to the solar system, is introduced here at the last hours of the night session..."

What Sen. Thurmond was objecting to was the number of matters thrown in for good measure, none of them related to the 15th Amendment. The Republicans tried to cram in all that they had overlooked in the 13th and 14th Amendments and the bill was a sorry, soggy, mess. What was left unsaid — and it was typical of the deceptive practices engaged in by the Republicans at the time — was that the so-called Civil Rights Act was aimed mainly at Chinese contract labor in Oregon and California.

To return to the powers of Congress and whether Congress can compel the sovereign States to do something to which they are opposed.

Congressional Globe, May 16, 1870, pages 3479-3493:

Enforcement of the 15th Amendment.

Senator Vickers: "Congress has no power to legislate and punish State officers, judges of election and registers of voters who are appointed by and are responsible for State laws. Individuals who may deem themselves aggrieved can appeal to the courts for relief. But, if contrary to all analogies and distinctions which existed in the respective forms of government, Congress shall arrogate the power to regulate State elections and electors, I contend that the 15th Amendment is not constitutionally and legally a part of the United States Constitution..."

This means that the so-called Brady bill is illegal because in addition to violating the 2nd Amendment, it purports to order State police officers to check for criminal backgrounds of would-be purchasers of handguns, in itself unconstitutional in view of what Senator Vickers said.

WHY PRESIDENT ANDREW JOHNSON SUFFERED IMPEACHMENT PROCEEDINGS

One of the most interesting chapters in the saga of the Republican-dominated Congress to force passage of the 15th Amendment deal was an attempt to impeach Pres. Andrew Johnson, an attempt that narrowly failed. At first the Republicans accused him of being a secret Democrat while pretending to be a Republican, but they began impeachment proceedings in earnest when it came out that Pres. Johnson was opposed to the 15th Amendment and had taken steps to throw a spanner in the works of the Republican majority vote in its favor. Congressional Globe Feb. 15 1871, pages 114-117:

"... We have seen this body not only denying representation to the people of eleven States, but foisting government upon those States and putting its own creatures into the Halls of Congress as Representatives of those States, merely to strengthen the hands of the dominant party. Thus reinforced, it was able to override the President's veto and to withdraw from the courts all the power to revive its action. (The McCardle case which the Supreme Court said it could not rule on.) Coercing the President to execute its behests by the fear of the impeachment power has been unlimited. In this way it carried out the Reconstruction acts and the constitutional amendments, and intends to perpetuate its power in defiance of the popular will. The dangers which now menace the liberties of the people could never have occurred if by refusing to execute its revolutionary program, the people could have been called to decide between Congress and the President..."

Congress threatened Pres. Johnson with impeachment and intimidated him, punishing him for carrying out the policies Lincoln would have instituted had he not been assassinated. In studying the history of the period it comes out strongly that Lincoln favored keeping the State governments of the eleven secessionist states in place, and seating their delegates in both Houses of Congress, and it comes over clearly that Lincoln would never have countenanced the fraud and chicanery of the Reconstruction legislation. What angered the Republicans was that Pres. Johnson had ordered his Secretary of State to find ways and means of scuttling the 13th, 14th and 15th Amendments, and of course it follows that Pres. Johnson did not agree with these amendments.

The way these things normally work is that following passage of any amendments to the U.S. Constitution passed by the House and Senate, the Secretary of State has the task of coordinating properly and correctly rules for ratification by the States, although this is not mentioned in a direct form in the Constitution. As I read this part of the record, it became apparent that Johnson, a secret Democrat, with the aid of Republicans secretly sharing his views and themselves against ratification of the amendments, and aided by the Secretary of State, also a secret Democrat, was bent upon scuttling them through non ratification or inaccurate ratification that would exclude them from becoming part of the U.S. Constitution. The Republicans could not put this in the articles of impeachment without tipping their hand, simply because they knew very well that the 13th and 14th Amendments were frauds and a type of chicanery against the people.

Thus it came about that the 13th and 14th Amendments and later the 15th Amendment, were null and void and no law at all, because they were either unratified or improperly ratified, or both, thus rendering ALL laws based upon them no more than shams, frauds, no laws at all, and incumbent on none to obey them.

In the tenure of Office of Act of 1867, the Senate Republicans felt they had the right to say who would sit in the Senate under the spoils of war system. However, this was not a foreign war but a civil war between the States and "spoils of war" did not apply. Lincoln would have left the "rebels" in power in States legislatures. The excuse for threatening impeachment proceedings given by the Republicans was that Johnson was secretly trying to put Democrats in power in public offices, but the real reason was that Johnson was doing his best to sabotage the 13th, 14th and 15th Amendments so that the could not be ratified by the States, and also his opposition to the fraudulent Reconstruction legislation. That is what is meant by the references to it contained in the Congressional Globe, February 15, 1871.

What the 1 Section of the 14th Amendment *does say*, is, "equal protection of the law, as to life, liberty and property," "as to due process of the law," meaning a jury trial. Remember, all other considerations aside, the 14th Amendment was never properly ratified and, therefore, remains null and void. My purpose is to expose how the 14th Amendment was created and manipulated to punish the South, and not to justify its bogus existence. But let us just suppose for a moment that it is a valid part of the U.S. Constitution, then, why weren't the parents of children bused against their will to conform with the bogus Brown vs. Board of Education Topeka ruling, given a jury trial?

The children were forced-bused because of their race. It is not a crime, nor has it ever been a crime, for races to express their wish to be segregated. Property rights are segregated rights. The word, "segregated" has been badly misused by the Communists to mean something evil and sinister; their doctrine of imputing inflexibility to certain words to suit their purposes. The Constitution does not forbid segregation. If as is so often averred by "civil rights leaders," that the Constitution forbids segregation, or the desire of one race to live separately from another, then I invite them to point out exactly where in the Constitution and the Bill of Rights it so states? They cannot, because it is just not there!

The word "segregate" was first used in a speech by Rep. Baker during the 39th Congress — incidentally, the first Congress to convene after the end of the Civil War: Congressional Globe, Jan. 27,1866 pages 461-470:

"...So the revolting states did not for a single moment succeed in segregating themselves as a sovereign power..."

Thomas Jefferson alluded to segregation as one of the inalienable rights of man, being natural, but did not enunciate it, more the pity. The right of races to segregate themselves is thousands of years old. In the same speech Baker talks about the "holocaust" of the Civil War and a bill of pains and punishment for the secessionist states and this hate legislation was the real reason why the Republicans wanted the 14th Amendment so badly. Congressional Globe, January 27, 1866, pages 461-470:

Finally, the suggested amendment excluding rebels forever from all high offices of honor or profit under the government of the United States, the value of such an amendment would be great. As I have suggested, it would furnish a large human and bloodless satisfaction to justice..."

Rep. Baker was a constitutional ignoramus, a twister and convoluter of the Constitution and his vengeful statement reflects these characteristics. As we read in the Congressional Globe on page 466; when asked what was the constitutional authority for his proposed 14th Amendment, Baker's lofty reply was that it was the right of eminent domain and the general welfare clause! Could anything more absolutely wrong have come from Baker's mouth? A bill of attainder, and pains and penalties ex post facto is what Baker was driving at, a violation strongly forbidden by the U.S. Constitution.

There we have it straight from the horses mouth, the real objective the Republicans were seeking to impose pains and penalties through the 14th Amendment was to keep the governments of the secessionist States from functioning again, and this gave rise to the desperately wicked "carpet baggers" plague of total injustice which fell upon the South. Baker knew very well that the "rebels" would not live forever, thus, by using language of this nature can be seen the passion of hatred for the South and the lack of objectivity is in the fact that his speech was composed in a passion of hatred for the South.

Congressional Globe, June 18, 1866 pages 3241-3250. In these pages we find the bankruptcy of the Reconstruction period with all of its speeches and debates. The Reconstruction legislation was the worst legislation ever to be passed by the Congress, except for the "New Deal" Communist legislation adopted by Franklin Roosevelt in the 1930s. Reconstruction legislation gave rise to the so-called desegregation actions of the Warren court and there is no basis for it in the U.S. Constitution and the Bill of Rights. The Reconstruction laws along with the 13th, 14th and 15th Amendments are frauds of the most glaring kind it is possible to find.

If, as the Supreme Court decision in Brown vs. Board of Education, Topeka implies, segregation is a CRIME, why didn't the parents of the children get "equal protection of the laws," as to "life, liberty and property" "as to due process of the law." In other words, a jury trial? Why were the parents denied a jury trial, if, as "civil rights" jurists aver, segregation is a crime? Here we have a clear case of "*Unequal* protection of the laws." So what we are left with is a bogus 14th Amendment under color of which, certain citizens were denied "equal protection of the laws."

The justices of the Warren court showed their total lack of schooling in the history of the Constitution and an abysmal ignorance of the history surrounding the 13th, 14th and 15th Amendments. Not only were the justices of this particular court ignorant of the background history of these amendments and the Reconstruction legislation which went with it, but the vast majority of judges today, are equally uneducated when it comes to the history of the period, especially the so-called "Federal" judges who are mere raw, political appointees, of which one of their number, Judge Thelton Henderson, is a particularly frightening example. Henderson is the judge who thwarted the will of the people in staying the execution of Proposition 209, the anti-affirmative action law passed by the voters of California.

The facts speak for themselves; judges are notoriously lacking in knowledge of the history of the Reconstruction period. If this were not the case, we would never have had the Supreme Court heaping hypotheses upon hypotheses and pyramiding so-called statutory laws, one atop the other in utter confusion, based on the 13th, 14th and 15th Amendments to the United States Constitution. Had the Federal judiciary (The Supreme Court and Federal judges) read history, they would have taken cognizance of the Slaughterhouse cases, and declared the 13th, 14th and 15th Amendments, null and void, not part of the U.S. Constitution. Instead, historically ignorant judges of our courts go on, year after year, acting as if these amendments and the Reconstruction laws that went with them are valid, and part of the Constitution and Bill of Rights.

Where is a Cromwell, an Horatio at the Bridge, a man like Rep. Raymond, a true genius, well schooled in the Constitution and a man who knew the history of the times? Rep. Raymond was a Republican from New York, who was at least 150 years ahead of his time. He was one of a few honest Republicans among the majority of Republicans who brought this country almost to the point of no return by their treachery in the House and Senate during the Civil War and post-Civil War period. Where indeed is there today, any one Senator or Representative who could compare with Sen. Thurmond or Rep. Baker?

What I have said about judges being ignoramuses (with a few exceptions) when it comes to the history of the nation, particularly the Civil War period and post-Civil War "Reconstruction" fraud period, applies with equal force to the members of the House and Senate, again, with a very few notable exceptions. Our representatives in the Congress are woefully and dreadfully ignorant of the history of the period in which the 13th, 14th and 15th Amendments were written.

Were this not true of congressmen and judges, we would never have had the farce, the fraud and the fairy tale of Brown vs. Board of Education, Topeka, Kansas. I will take it a step further and say, if we had but ONE brave representative in the Congress, he would have stood up and denounced the farce, like the boy who boldly declared, "the King has no clothes" while all around him the charade was played out. Yes, that is what the 13th, 14th and 15th Amendments are; a gigantic charade, a Constitutional nullity, yet, sadly, we lack that one *statesman* who will leap to his feet in the House or Senate and shout this truth in a loud voice. Rep. Raymond, was such a man, a genius who knew history and the Constitution. Congressional Globe, June 1866, Page 3242:

Rep. Raymond: "...But, sir, in my previous remarks from which I have already quoted, I insist that the States in voting upon these amendments (13th and 14th) should act freely, without coercion. I regard that, sir, as of vital importance. Amendments to the Constitution forced upon an unwilling people will never command the respect essential to their full validity. They will always be regarded as badges of injustice, as permanent and indelible marks of inferiority, and whatever acquiescence they may command will be reluctant and constrained, not the cheerful obedience which a free people will always yield to the Constitution and laws freely made."

"This bill violates that fundamental condition. It seeks to coerce the States lately in rebellion into the ratification of these amendments. It denies them representation unless they do ratify them...Now, if I am right in this, I ask any one here to point me to the clause of the Constitution which confers upon Congress the right to say that Representatives from any State shall not be received into Congress until that State shall perform certain acts, make certain laws, or do certain things which we may dictate. *Where is it in the Constitution?* Is it embodied in any article? Is it implied in any clause either directly or indirectly? I cannot find it!"

"On the contrary, I find an express declaration in the articles which empowers Congress to propose amendments of the Constitution, an explicit provision that 'no State shall be deprived of its equal suffrage in the Senate without its own consent, even by amendment of the Constitution. This bill proposes to deprive States of suffrage by a law. It proposes to do by enacting a law what Congress and the States together cannot do by amending the Constitution. I must maintain, until I am shown to the contrary, that we have no power under the Constitution of the United States to pass such a bill as this, or to enforce its provisions if it should become law."

"I hold that while it crushed the rebellion it did not impair, to any degree or extent, the validity, force or binding authority of the Constitution of the United States, or the rights, duties or obligations of the States under the Constitution of the United States. On the contrary it reaffirmed and reestablished the authority of the Constitution in all its fullness over the States and over every department of Government of the United States. The Constitution is today for us, for Congress, for the President, for every State and every Legislature and for every court in the State, the 'supreme law of the land.' We have crushed the rebellion which disputed its sovereign authority, but we thereby only confirmed and reestablished its supremacy. We have achieved no conquest over that, and no law of conquest touches that in a particular. We are bound by its provisions, we are restricted by its prohibitions..."

Could anything be clearer or more definitive? I would ask every justice of the Supreme Court, every judge of every State Court: Show proof where it says in the Constitution it is legal to coerce the States into ratifying any amendment to the Constitution; in the manner in which the South was coerced into ratifying the 13th, 14th and 15th amendments under threats that they would lose their suffrage if they did not? The 14th Amendment, the Civil Rights Act of 1870, the Civil Rights Act of 1964, the Voting Rights Act of 1965, are all constitutional nullities, ultra vires, of no effect and no laws at all, if for no other reason that force was used to get the three amendments, on which these fraudulent laws rest, ratified. They are chicanery, frauds, deceptions, flim-flammery, deceit, hypotheses heaped upon hypotheses, and every so-called "statutory law" predicated on these amendments and the Reconstruction laws, are unconstitutional and binding upon no one. Now can be seen the duplicity, the mendacity of Brown vs. Board of Education, Topeka; every affirmative action law, every equal employment law, every civil rights law and so on ad infinitum.

One further point about Reconstruction legislation being fraudulent: Rep. Raymond stated correctly that after the peace was signed between the secessionist States and the Union in 1865, the Constitution superseded all laws, including the Reconstruction laws which the radical Republicans had gone outside of the Constitution to secure, a

Constitution based on Vattel's "Law of Nations." The extremist Republicans tried to charge the South with treason, but the South believed it was within its rights based on the book, "A View of the Constitution" by William Rawles.

There is one point with which I am in disagreement, and that is the frequent use of "rebellion" to describe what was a Civil War. The Republicans who were largely responsible for the war getting started were forever calling it a "rebellion" when it was no such thing. It was done, I believe, to get past the fact that the Constitution is silent about what steps to take in a civil war. The radical Republicans believed they could pass the 13th, 14th and 15th Amendments and the Reconstruction legislation under color of the auxiliary Clause 18, found in Art. 1, Sec. 8, Clauses 1-18, but this is wrong. Sec. 8 begins with "To make all laws that shall be necessary and proper for carrying into execution the fore-going powers (i.e. 1-17) and all other powers vested by this Constitution in the government of the United States, or in any department or office thereof."

This demonstrates what I have often written about; the depth and layer upon layer of profundity found in the Constitution. What we must observe is that in their genius — and the Founding Fathers were two hundred years ahead of their time — they made two general clauses, 1 and 18 and in between Article 1, Sec. 8, the specific powers of 17 so that by no stretch of imagination could violating the Constitution as occurred with coercion of the States by Congress, could be called "necessary and proper."

The Congress did not respect the rights of the States and this was a major contribution to the war. We find reference to it in the Congressional Globe, Jan 31, 1866, pages 546 - 548:

"But this war (the Civil War) could not have taken place if the rights of each State had been respected by Congress and the people of every other State. (The extreme Republicans made sure that lack of respect for States rights did not become a cause-celebre.) We have heard much about the 'first gun' in the rebellion. That first gun was not fired by rebels at Fort Sumtner, or by old John Brown of Virginia, but it was fired by the American Congress when that body passed the Missouri compro-mise and usurped the right to regulate upon the subject of slavery, a mere domestic institution, resting with the people of each State..."

One other point which I believe to be very much overlooked. The eleven Southern States had the right to secede, but the North did not. Lincoln was a lawyer and he knew this to be true by virtue of the Northwest Territories Bill. Ohio was a part of the Northwest Territories and Lincoln was in Ohio. In 1797 Congress made the stipulation that the Northwest Territories were to remain in the Union in perpetuity, in other words, they could never secede from the Union by virtue of the Northwest Territories Bill. Lincoln was determined to keep the South in the United States in spite of knowing that he was acting unconstitutionally, and the radical Republicans backed him and incited him to make war on the South. The South badly underestimated Lincoln's tenacity of purpose and by the same token, in haughty disdain of the Union, they underestimated its military strength.

Historians are still debating whether Lincoln committed treason, (and he did with the suspension of habeas corpus) but there is no discussion necessary to confirm that the Democrat Party of the 20th century openly committed both treason and sedition. We shall list some of these acts of treason which began with Woodrow Wilson and is still ongoing with the Clinton presidency. Much of this is found in the thousands of pages of the Congressional Globe, 1850s — 1880s.

If the Republicans could be made to leave off their obsession with "balancing the budget" they could get on with passing by a simple majority a law that would overturn and make null and void, "Brown vs. Board of Education, Topeka." I repeat, the 14th Amendment is a sham, a fraud, chicanery, bogus, deceptive ruling, and all laws based upon it passed for the past 60 years are BOGUS LAWS incumbent upon none to obey. The same holds good for the 13th and 15th Amendments which are also totally fraudulent and all laws based upon them are a sham and a fraud.

The 13th, 14th and 15th Amendments are not the law of the land and have never been, although they purport to give the Negroes their practical rights, but definitely did not give them social rights. Again, these three amendments sprang directly from the Civil Rights Act of 1866. The Supreme Court can rule again and again to try and make them the law, but it will not succeed. The Fifteenth Amendment was hastily strung together in an attempt to put teeth into the Congressional flim flammery. The Republicans tried to enforce these rights through the 15th Amendment.

Congressional Globe, May 20, 1870, pages 3654-3658: "Enforcement of the 15th Amendment." The reasons for the 15th

Amendment are given here, and it is clear that it does not relate to INDI-VIDUALS but rather is a restriction on the State Legislatures and the Federal Government. Basically what it says is that neither the State Legislatures nor the Congress can make laws that would abridge or diminish or deny an individual the right to vote based on race or color.

These three amendments could never pass judicial scrutiny, yet the justices of the highest court in the nation, go on with the charade. Specifically, the 1964 Civil Rights Act and the 1965 Voting Rights Act are nothing but sophistry, chicanery and as worthless as if they were blank pieces of paper. If Congress actually wants to be honest for a change, then let it resubmit the three so-called amendments to the States for proper, constitutional ratification.

The courts go on piling hypotheses upon hypotheses in legal chi-canery of immense magnitude. The 14th Amendment is obsolete, even if it were to be ratified, the Civil War is over and with that the issue of slavery died and along with it, the 13th Amendment died also. The 13th, 14th and 15th Amendments are all dead as are all statutory laws based upon them, because:

1. The 13th, 14th and 15th Amendments were never properly ratified and are still not properly ratified.
2. The Reconstruction legislation that gave birth to these three amendments went far outside the pale and the ken of the U.S. Constitution.
3. The secession governments of the Southern States were entitled under the Constitution to remain in power and in control of State governments. The puppets forced upon the people of the seceded states did not represent the wishes of the sovereign people of those states who were thus disenfranchised.
4. Congress violated the United States Constitution, particularly Article IV, Section 4, Clause 1, which guarantees every one of the several States a Republican form of government. Congressional Globe, Jan 27, 1866, pages 461-470: In the case of Luther vs. Borden — one of several such cases, the Supreme Court decided in 1849 what a Republican form of government was in Article IV, Section 4 Clause 1 of the U.S. Constitution.

The secession States already had a Republican form of government and the Congress was not authorized anywhere in the Constitution to deprive these States of their Constitutional right to a Republican form of government. The carpetbagger form of government installed by the North was a violation of Article 1V, Section 4, Clause 1, to whit, the Federal Government guarantee that every state shall have a Republican form of government.

5. Congress tried to make out that the bootlicking carpetbaggers it had installed as the government of the secessionist states was legitimate, thus legally able to "ratify" the three amendments when is was plain that this was a fraud perpetrated upon the seceded states. Congress put in the 3 section in the 14th for the sole purpose of punishing the South in pursuit of grudges against the secessionist States which, even in 1900, were still strongly held. Congress had no authority for this and it is another reason why the 13th, 14th and 15th Amendments could not have been properly ratified and this is still the position today.

6. The sycophant States legislative government installed by the Congress were largely composed of Communists who had infiltrated the Civil War with the prime instruction from Marx and Lenin that they were to wreck the U.S. by "legislative action" ninety percent of which was bogus, a sham and a fraud. To those who say that even if the three amendments were bogus, what the amendments set out to do could have been done under the war powers of the president. This false line of reasoning is just that, utterly false as the president has no war powers worth discussing, and certainly nothing as broad as the bogus, guile, fraudulent 13th, 14th and 15th Amendments.

While the Democrats crowed about the darkly-stained pages in the history of the Republican Party, their own record in the 1920-1960s, including the spurious 1964 Civil Rights Act and the bogus 1965 Voting Rights Act, more than match the deception practiced by the Republican Party during the so-called Reconstruction period.

Without some of the strictest press control ever seen in the U.S., coupled with the two terms of Pres. Grant, the chicanery, flummery, mendacity of the 13th, 14th and 15th Amendments would have been exposed — and the bogus Civil Rights Act of 1870 along with it — long before the Supreme Court struck down the latter "law" in 1884. It was strict press control and Grant's two terms that kept the greatest hoax of the 19th century from being exposed.

Enforcement of the 15th Amendment, which was the beginning of
the so-called Civil Rights Act of 1870: The history is found in the
Congressional Record: "If we merely wish to pretend to do something
and not accomplish anything substantial or important, the House bill is
a perfect recipe for doing that." What this act did, and it is apparent
when a study is made of the speeches in the House, was to find a for-
mula to punish the South. Radical Republicans who were really responsible for the Civil War, were seeking ways to revenge the death of
250,000 of their sons and to perpetuate their Communist infiltrator's
agenda, which so confused Pres. Lincoln.

Appendix to the Congressional Record, "Fifteenth Amendment,
Feb. 15 1871, pages 114-117:

Speech by the Hon. F.P. Blair of Missouri:

"The plea of 'political necessity' by the Senator justified the adoption of the 15th Amendment., is always ready, and has become the law
of the existence of a party which having forfeited the confidence of the
people, is now compelled to retain power by fraud and force. Hence the
bill to employ the army to enforce the 15th Amendment..."(Already
mentioned elsewhere but worth repeating.)

The Civil Rights Act of 1870 was hate legislation of the worst kind
and all the act did was come up with a mishmash of ideas that would
humiliate and degrade Southern whites. The radical Republicans who so
confused Lincoln did not care how low they stooped to achieve their
hate law Civil Rights Act of 1870. Congressional Record, Senate, May
18, 1870, page 3576:

Senator Thurmond:

"Mr. President, times have changed when the Senator from Vermont
goes to the fugitive slave law of 1850 to find a model for legislation..."

Sen. Thurmond was referring to the fact that for the so-called civil
rights legislation, the 1850 slave law was revived to serve as a model.
The Republicans in the House and Senate were under the control of a
large group of dedicated Communists, whose hatred for the superior
whites of the South knew no bounds. The policy of the Radical
Republicans in the legislature and on every front, differed very markedly from that of Pres. Lincoln. The Radical Republicans hated the switching over of the American economy from a mercantile to an industrial one
in an atmosphere where liberty was guaranteed by the Constitution.

They were confident that the war could be won, but it had to be won, their way and that meant waging total war on the South. So they held out to the press and the pulpit that the South was antagonistic to freedom for all and a free way of life, because, they said, the politics and economics of the South was dominated by slave owners, and the war was necessary to destroy this class. Preferably, all-out war.

The Radical Republicans even held that all-out war was "the more humane way of rooting up plantation owners and their slave-labor based economy." Military leaders who were made aware of the plans of the radicals were sworn to secrecy, more because the plan called for the confiscation of plantation owner's property, followed by a program that would break up the great plantations. The Radical Republicans based their prosecution of the war on three key strategies:

(1) They would free the slaves immediately.

(2) They would then arm the freed slaves and put them in the Union Army in uniform and assign them to combat roles.

(3) They would divide the broken-up plantations into smaller land holdings which would be given to an even number of Negroes and whites, so that a new class of freeholders beholden to the Radical Republicans would defend and preserve what was won. The latter part of the Radical Republican's plan was the basis of all Reconstruction legislation.

Lincoln, who had never had any experience with Communists had as his only goal in prosecuting the war, the preservation of the Union, for which he felt he had been elected. In 1862, Lincoln told Horace Greeley that although he was anti-slavery: "My paramount objective in this struggle is to save the Union, and it is not either to save or destroy slavery." Lincoln preserved the integrity of his objective for as long as he could hold out, chastising General Hunter for freeing slaves in South Carolina and reprimanding General Fremont for doing the same in Missouri.

While the Radical Republicans obstructed him at every turn of the way, Lincoln pursued his program for ending slavery the mainstays of which were a 37-year period of gradually freeing the slaves; compensation to slaveholders in the State who said the Constitution held slaves as private property; and the colonizing of freed slaves in West Africa at government expense. It is fair to say that Lincoln was fascinated with the idea of separating the white and Negro races and in 1862 he told a delegation of freed slaves that his view was that both races would be better off, separated by water (the ocean) between them.

With unending pressure from the Radicals and the war not going well, Lincoln began to weaken and gradually began to adopt some of their still-secret agenda. The Congressional Globes and Congressional Records of the period show that the Emancipation Proclamation was the first visible sign of weakness. Lincoln knew full-well that he had no right to sign a proclamation let alone suspend habeas corpus, but while agreeing to it, he remained distinctly lukewarm to the idea of inducting freed slaves into the Union Army. There are several accounts of how many blacks actually served as combatants, but one of the more accurate ones put the number at 186,000 toward the close of the war.

Confiscation of property was the main plank of the Radical Republican plan to utterly destroy the South and to this end they rushed two bills through the Congress, but because Lincoln would not change his mind, they came to nothing and so the bitter hatred held by the Radical Republicans toward the South, never closed the gap between Lincoln and the Communists and this is clearly reflected in the Reconstruction laws.

The Slaughterhouse cases gave the death-knell to the so-called Civil Rights Act of 1866, and the justices of the Supreme Court poked fun and laughed at it. Yet, although struck down by the court, the Communists in the House and Senate revived the discredited measure and used it as a model for their 1964 Civil Rights Act.

So here we have the fraud of the 13th, 14th and 15th Amendments — passed under duress of military force, and never ratified, as the basis of the 1870 Civil Rights Act; struck down by the Supreme Court in 1888, in the Slaughterhouse case, resuscitated and used as the model of the so-called 1964 Civil Rights Act. Even if the 14th Amendment had been properly drafted and ratified by the States, it would still have been outside of the pale and the ken of the Constitution, because what it did was ISOLATE the "equal protection of the laws" of the first section of the 14th Amendment, so that it could be "interpreted" to mean anything and everything under the noonday sun, or as the Communist spirit moved. In other words, civil rights became a political football.

I cannot print the full texts of the debates about so-called civil rights legislation, which took place between 1870-1885, but there are hundreds of examples of how the Communists tried to obliterate the Constitution and Bill of Rights by consistently attempting to isolate the "equal protection of the laws" clause of the 14th Amendment. A list of some

Congressional Record sources is found in the bibliography section of this book.

The Constitution is a document of perfect equipoise; one section or clause cannot be isolated from the whole; the Constitution has to be read as a whole document and cannot be fragmented. It is worth noting that there is a very large gap in the history of the United States concerning Communist infiltration of both parties in the House and Senate, and their attempts to destroy the Constitution and the Bill of Rights, a cause taken up by the Democrat Party under Roosevelt in 1932 and which is ongoing today under Pres. Clinton.

Congressional Record, Appendix, March 15, 1948 pages A 1644-A1646.

The Hon. Rank Boykin:

"In 1888 the Supreme Court of the United States declared that a civil rights program similar to the one now sponsored by Mr. Truman, was unconstitutional. The decision was rendered by a Republican court in an era where feeling was running strongly against the South. When the United States Supreme Court declared that this so called civil rights legislation violated the Tenth Amendment of the Constitution, it rendered a judicial — not a political decision..." The court said that the three amendments violated the Tenth Amendment.

It is uncanny just how far the pretense went that the 13th, 14th and 15th Amendments were actually a part of the U.S. Constitution, when in fact, they had never been properly ratified. Why does the court not make an honest statement that the civil rights legislation is moot in view of the unratified amendments upon which it is based? Why the posturing, why the pretense?

What Mr. Boykin was saying was that in spite of a Republican Party dominated Supreme Court, and in spite of the hatred felt for the South by the Union, the court in 1888 went beyond it to render a judicial verdict, not a political one. Before this verdict was handed down, the 13th, 14th and 15th Amendments had been held out as adding something new to the Constitution, when in fact they added nothing new to it, at all. Then along came the Communists in both parties and *added something new,* the so-called "affirmative action" program, which is nowhere to be found in the 13th, 14th and 15th Amendments.

In spite of this historical fact, we have the courts of this land issuing one civil rights, affirmative action edict after another, as though it were perfectly proper. It is insane for a judicial system to be run in this altogether preposterous manner. We need a statesman who will step forward and halt this treacherous pantomime of civil rights abuse based on amendments which have never been part of the Constitution because they were not properly ratified, and nor are they properly ratified, even today.

Congressional Record, Senate, pages E 7552-E 7554:

Sen. Ervin of North Carolina:

"The Supreme Court found something new in the 14th Amendment which said the people of California could not repeal their own occupancy law..."

As previously mentioned, this kind of thing arises when attempts are made to isolate parts of the Constitution from the whole and chaos is the result. What is often lost sight of is that the 14th Amendment was addressed to the States and *not* to individual people. For instance, voter requirements have nothing to do with the 14th Amendment, yet we frequently have the federal government violating States rights by interfering with voting by invoking the 14th Amendment.

Congress cannot legislate for States legislatures. For instance, if a State legislated that a proficiency test in English is required before a voter is eligible to vote, that Congress cannot legislate against the State. In any case, even if invoking the 14th Amendment, it would be wrong, as the issue belongs in the 15th, but in the 15th, there is nothing which prohibits States from having an English language proficiency requirement for voters. The final word is, I believe, that Congress found it impossible to resubmit the 13th, 14th and 15th Amendments for ratification even knowing this has to be done to validate them. Congress knew these three amendments would not be validated because of the punishing 3rd section in the 14th Amendment, put in by the vengeful Southern Republicans would forever damn the possibility of ratification by the Southern States.

There is no court in the land that can make the 13th, 14th and 15th Amendments "the law of the land" when they have never been so and are not now. The amendments cannot be interpreted any other way. Even if it were a part of the U.S. Constitution, the 14th Amendment in the 1st section is indirect; it does not say that it gives equal protection of the law based on race. Where can the liberals point to the word "race" in the 1st section? What the last section of the 14th Amendment says is "equal protection of the laws... as to life, liberty and property...as to due process of law" meaning a trial by jury. This constitutional fact was ignored in the fraudulent Brown vs. Topeka, Kansas "desegregation" case of 1954. Due to the fact that segregation is NOT a crime, why are children bused past their local schools? For this to happen there ought to have been a jury trial or due process of the law, since parents and children were discriminated against by forced busing simply because of their race.

The so-called Civil Rights act of 1866 was nothing but hate legislation against Southern Democrats for seceding from the Union and it provided a vehicle for Radical Republicans to vent their spleen against their Civil War enemies. This so-called civil rights act had little in common with voting, rather it was a mish-mash rehash of political events. The Congressional Globe May 18, 1870, "Enforcement of the 15th Amendment," pages 3558-3571, makes this very clear. The Supreme Court found the civil rights act of 1866 unconstitutional, but the Democrats resurrected it in 1964. A careful reading of the so-called civil rights debates in the period 1866 — 1885 shows the clearest evidence of attempts made to isolate the last section of the 14th, "equal protection of the laws" from the 1section. The Constitution cannot be compromised in this was, otherwise its perfect equipoise is destroyed. The bottom line is that the 14th Amendment is badly flawed and cannot be ratified even today, as it is unconstitutional.

CHAPTER 6

REVERSED ROLES OF THE REPUBLICAN AND DEMOCRAT PARTIES

HATE CRIMES AND MINORITY RIGHTS
NATIONAL SUICIDE: THE 1965 IMMIGRATION REFORM ACT

I n the 1850s-1890s, the Republicans were more penetrated by Radical Communists than were the Democrats of the South who were free of Communist representatives and their propaganda. Excellent detail on the background of the founding of the Republican Party is found in the Congressional Globe, Dec. 21, 1869, pages 22-26. It is to lengthy to include here and an abbreviated version would not give the full impact of how rotten and crooked the radical Republicans were in 1869.

The Republican Party, founded in 1856 as the Union Party, was so filled with jealousy over the life style of the South, so filled with envy that for sixty-years the Democrats by virtue of their superior education had controlled the Congress, that when the Republicans saw a chance to take revenge on the South, they took it and plunged the two sides into a civil war which almost tore the U.S. apart. Congressional Globe, June 1866, Pages 3241-3250:

Rep. Raymond: "That time of real danger was when the Missouri compromise was repealed, and Kansas was likely to come into the Union as a slave State. If she had thus come in the number of free States would have been equal. But then the South had elements of political power which made her formidable. She had wealth. She monopolized the best cotton in the world. Her cotton, sugar, rice and tobacco swelled the vast volume of our commerce and regulated our exchanges in Europe. She had for political leaders men of great intellects, iron will, towering ambition, men fit to struggle for an empire, and able to infuse their own bold, audacious tempers into the great mass of the Southern people over whom their influence was absolute and unbounded."

"She had numerous population, active, aspiring, and bold — a generation of young men trained in the school of Calhoun and McDuffie, nursed in the doctrine of States rights and State sovereignty, taught to believe in the right of secession, and educated in the faith that the South was the victim of Northern tyranny... But sir, the southern States previous to the war had four million slaves, three million of which were represented on this floor, that is to say, they were entitled to the full representation of their white population...The slaves of the South gave the South twenty-eight additional members, taking one hundred and twenty thousand as the ratio of representation."

"How is it now? I take it to be universally admitted that the war has proved more fatal to the colored population of the Southern States than to the whites. The testimony of all who are familiar with the statistics of mortality during the war is to the effect that at least one-fifth of the Negroes of the Southern States have perished during the rebellion (Civil War)...Jefferson Davis, I see, from public prints concedes that one million of the slaves, one-fourth of the whole have probably disappeared..."

The Republican Party's conduct in forcing through the 13th,14th, and 15th Amendments, plus the Reconstruction laws that went with them, left much bitterness in the South, and, as we see from the foregoing, did little to assuage the pain and suffering and destruction of the Negro population in a war largely of the Radical Republican's making. Reading the Congressional Globes is a sobering experience as in the debates found in its thousands of pages, is the unmistakable desire of the Republican Party to settle old scores with the Democrats, clearly established.

The Republican Party of Lincoln charged that the eleven Southern States had "rebelled" against the Federal government, and had no constitutional authority to secede. In so far as my research goes, I was unable to find anything in the Constitution that would forbid secession from the Union by any of the Southern States. If such a prohibition exists, I would like to have it pointed out to me, but until I am correct-ed, I tend to believe that there is no bar to Southern States seceding from the Union, although the Northern States were apparently barred by law from so doing.

Far worse, was the violation of the Constitution committed by the Radical Republicans in forcing through the 13th, 14th, and 15th Amendments and the Reconstruction legislation. Section 3 of the 14th Amendment was vindictiveness in the extreme. The South had not taken up an insurrection nor rebellion; it went to war, a civil war, because it felt it was being unjustly treated by the system of tariffs then in opera-tion, tariffs from which the South did not reap its fair share.

Much valuable information on the subject of the Reconstruction debates is to be found in the Congressional Globe, May 30, 1864, pages 2904-2906. The various headings are misleading if not related to other matters such as contained in the Congressional Record of the period 1885-1900 and also in the period 1900-1920. Otherwise it is likely to lead to the wrong impression.

The Republicans went outside of the Constitution and violated their oath of office to accomplish their goals, a violation considered so heinous by the Founding Fathers that they decreed the death penalty as fitting punishment. It cannot be proved that the secessionist States vio-lated the Constitution, but it can most definitely be proved that the Republicans violated the Constitution and the Bill of Rights on scores of occasions to ram through their unconstitutional 13th, 14th, and 15th Amendments and the Reconstruction laws.

Then, in compounding their scores of violations of the Constitution, the Republicans went a step further and by the threat of a permanent mil-itary occupation of the South, coerced some of the eleven States into rat-ifying the three fraudulent amendments. Worse than that, the Republican-controlled Congress then violated Article IV, Sec. 4, of the Constitution by making out that the thirteen states could only be admit-ted as "new states," as if they were newly entering the Union, when as it is obvious, they were always part of the United States of America and could never, under any circumstances, have been barred by the Congress of their right to suffrage. Such blatant fraud is hard to match with the so-called violation of seceding from the Union. Section 3 of the 14th Amendment was a blatant attempt to deny right of suffrage to members of the Confederate States legislatures.

It was open trickery and knavery, no more, no less. And perhaps the worst trickery was the three amendments — 13th, 14th, and 15th — conceived in hatred and passion and totally lacking in objectivity, and then, in the crudest of a long string of crudities, attempting to force them upon the South through threats and outright intimidation.

Since the 1900s, the roles of the two political parties have been reversed. In 1913, Woodrow Wilson's administration was under strong Communist influence, but as Rep. Louis T. McFadden, a former chairman of the House Banking Committee once reminded us, the most vehemently opposed to the 1913 Federal Reserve Act were a group of Democrats who spoke out strongly against it, but it was not a Republican Party bill, although a number of Republican Party senators voted for it. Wilson was a violator of the Constitution in so far as he did not uphold the U.S. Constitution, especially in seeking and obtaining not only the illicit powers taken by Lincoln, but demanding, and getting, ten more to which he had no constitutional right. Wilson also violated the Dick Act and the Militia Act by sending State militia soldiers to die on the battlefields of Europe, a most heinous crime for which he ought to have been impeached and tried for treason. (See the chapter "What You Don't Know About The Militia.")

Lincoln didn't know that he was being set up by the Communists in his party to promote the Civil War in the hopes that Communism would be the main beneficiary; he really didn't understand what was going on, nor that their aim was the destruction of the United States. (The same tactics are being used against the American people by the Communist Democrat Party and its leader in the White House — they have confused the American people, this time using the U.N. as their vehicle.)

Once the Civil War got started, Communists by the hundreds of thousands poured into the U.S. and infiltrated Lincoln's administration and his party. These "advisors" prompted Lincoln to start the Civil War, which they expected to use as a vehicle to turn the U.S. into a Socialist state.

The Radical Republicans were responsible for much of the Reconstruction laws and they really wanted to exterminate the South. They operated mainly out of Massachusetts and New Jersey, and left behind a legacy that even today, is readily apparent. They were the ones who got two Communist generals appointed to serve under General Sherman, and these two men planned a swathe of destruction for

Sherman's march to the sea; a march where wholesale slaughter and destruction prevailed. These were communist actions against the white population of Confederated States. There was no need for the march of destruction, but Sherman, like Lincoln, fell victim to the blandishments of the Radical Republican Communist advisors.

In the 1920s, the Democrat Party was openly invaded by a large body of Communists, and in 1932, the party became the Communist Party of the U.S.A. Roosevelt set the course that would henceforth severely compromise the Constitution of the United States so as to adhere more closely to the Communist Manifesto of 1848. The Roosevelt Supreme Court moved strongly to enforce the Communist Manifesto of 1848 as we saw in its decisions on so-called civil rights cases.

The extremists in the Republican Party must be held responsible for attempting to wreck the perfect Republic left for posterity by the Founding Fathers. There is good reference to this in the Congressional Globe of January 27, 1866, pages 461-470 Rep. Boutwell made a speech which tells this. Furthermore, a reading of the thousands of pages of the Congressional Records from the 1850s to the 1880s, shows the radical extremists of the Republican Party were influenced by Communist agents among their number who held that the South was a monster which would recreate itself, if not dealt a near-fatal blow. Of course the South was never a threat to the North.

What the Radical Republicans did was search European history to see how they might introduce repressive legislation to fulfill their goal and enable them to impose bills of pain and penalties. They went to Europe and studied the history of internecine strife, civil wars, and national wars. They must have found that for centuries Europe was ruled by those born to power, who exercised it in a ruthless manner, with the help of the Communist Manifesto. The people of Europe, in lockstep with their rulers for centuries were not able to resist, nor did they have any desire to combat the ruthless rule of their masters.

But the American people were a different breed of men, a nation born in freedom and determined to keep it. The big mistake made by the Republican extremist under the influence of their Communist advisors was to believe that legislation of the repressive nature of the 13th, 14th, and 15th Amendments, and the repressive Reconstruction legislation, would be meekly accepted by the people of the secessionist States, not knowing that its leaders were well-versed in the Constitution and the Bill of Rights.

To most conservatives, the perception is that the Republican Party has always been the more virtuous, more jealous of liberty, more dedicated to the preservation of our Republic, than the Democrats. This is because the American people have never been told the whole truth about these three fraudulent so-called amendments, nor the role played by Radical Republicans in their making, nor that they were never properly ratified by the required number of the States. This view of a "good" Republican Party was lately espoused by former Sen. Malcolm Wallop, of Wyoming and it is worth excerpting here what Wallop said in a speech he made at the Conservative Political Action Conference on March 8, 1997:

"From the time of Lincoln, the Republican Party has been a party of principle. The Democrat Party lives as it has lived for most of its history as a brokerage house for government favors...Lots of people make a living out of being Democrats. The teachers' unions, the government workers' unions, the abortion industry and a host of well-connected businesses, the kind that gets the U.S. government to set up deals for them abroad or to tailor regulations for them — they make a living out of being Democrats..."

As I believe I have demonstrated, Sen. Wallop is not factually correct; Lincoln blundered badly in demanding and getting the power of habeas corpus and by allowing the Civil War to be prosecuted. It is ironic that in Lincoln's time and the period 1850-1865 the Radicals in the Republican Party, penetrated by Communists, was more under the influence of the Communist Manifesto of 1848 than was the Democrat Party, which was the party of constitutionalism and patriotism and of course it was the mass arrival of Communists in the 1920s that turned the Democrat Party into a Communist Party, starting with Pres. Wilson.

And then under the direction of Roosevelt, it became the Communist Party of the U.S. Communism is much advanced down the road toward *total communism* under Pres. Clinton, as I predicted in my work, "Clinton, The Next Four Years: An American Tragedy." In pursuit of this goal, the "liberals" who are in the majority in the Democrat Party, and in not inconsiderable numbers in the Republican Party also, had a staunch ally in the U.S. Supreme Court and politicized so-called "Federal" judges. But lest we forget, it was the Republican Party's *reconstruction* legislation that set the stage for Pres. Roosevelt's New Deal and Pres. Johnson's Great Society.

The "hand-out" legislation of the Reconstruction period was later co-opted by the Democrats in earnest, starting with Roosevelt. There were many patriotic Southern Democrats in the Senate up until 1950, men like Sen. Stennis and Sen. James Allen, who were the diametric opposites of Pres. Carter. We shall come to Carter's treason and sedition under the chapter about treaties, and especially about the Panama Canal treason.

As Rep. Raymond said: "Model republics, noble and perfect commonwealths, where no wrong shall find toleration and no man lack justice are the object of all good men's desires...They can never be the birth of passion, they can only be the steady growth of time and patient efforts of the good and the wise." The "birth of passion" by the Republican Party in the period leading up to, during, and after the Civil War, all but ruined this nation and paved the way for a Communist takeover which grew by leaps and bounds under the Carter administration and accelerated rapidly with the advent of the Clinton administration. History is mostly blank pages of this period of Communist influence in our national life, but it is written in the thousands of pages of the Congressional Record, which is impossible to reprint here in its entirety.

As previously mentioned, the roles of the two parties were reversed starting early in the 1920s and since Roosevelt, the Democrat Party has allied itself with the Communist Manifesto of 1848 and is today virtually the Communist Party of the United States of America. In their attempts to make a "level society," first by attempting to "level" education through Thomas Dewey — and later through Carter and Mr. and Mrs. Clinton — "level minds" of utter mediocrity was the outcome. Unconstitutional court rulings such as forced busing, Communist egalitarianism, magnet schools, pairing schools, and "level minds" with "equal justice" through "equal protection of the laws," were applied out of context and isolated from the rest of the Constitution. Imparted to the ignorant was the notion that this is "what the Constitution decrees." In truth badly-flawed programs are not found in the Constitution but instead, are lifted straight out of the pages of the Communist Manifesto of 1848.

Nor should we forget that it was the Democrats who gave us Pres. Wilson, who went outside of the U.S. Constitution to establish an illegal private entity, the Federal Reserve Banks system; who established Federal income tax; who destroyed our protective trade barriers thus opening our markets to every type of international "free trade" banditry in the world; who forced this nation into a European family quarrel, the First World War; who gave us Roosevelt who took this country off the Gold Standard and demonetized silver so that the Rothschilds' war debts could be paid in gold; who pushed for Communist control of his party; who gave us the bogus United Nations treaty/agreement; who gave us Pres. James Earl Carter and the equally bogus Panama Canal Treaty. The list of treacherous, treasonous disasters forced upon this nation by the Democrat (Communist) Party of America is endless. The foregoing is detailed in my book, "One World Order: Socialist Dictatorship."

The Democrats gave America a crooked Supreme Court filled with near-Communists or actual Communists, or their sympathizers, Frankfurter, Fortiss, Brennan, Douglas, Warren, Burger, to which has been added, Breyer and Ginsburg. It was the duty of the judiciary to examine the 13th, 14th, and 15th Amendment cases before ruling on them, and they failed lamentably to do their judicial duty. This resulted in further frauds perpetrated on the American people, the Civil Rights Act of 1964, the Voting Rights Act of 1965. These "laws" would almost certainly have been thrown out had they been put to a test of their constitutionality. Instead, they were palmed off on the American people as "law." It was the Democrats who gave us a bullying, hectoring Supreme Court which tried to legalize infant murder; which forced "desegregation" upon the American people through race busing. Not one of these so-called "laws" held constitutional by the Supreme Court were anything but mere hypotheses heaped upon hypotheses, a string of shams and frauds.

The Democrats gave us U.S. participation in WWI, WWII, Korea and Vietnam, at the cost of so many young American lives, something we must never allow ourselves to forget. Had the Constitution and the Bill of Rights been adhered to, none of this would have happened. I say this to highlight for posterity what damage was done by the violators of the Constitution.

The Democrats pushed "equality" to ridiculous lengths. Our society is based upon the natural law of selection, totally at variance with the "equality" of the Communist Manifesto of 1848. Let us not forget the driving force of Communism was a "level" society, an uneducated, uninspired "mass" of people, easily regimented, easily controlled and at the mercy of a totally centralized government. This was the blueprint for tyranny laid out by the Communists in 1917; the same blueprint being closely followed by the Democrat Party in the 1990s and Mr. and Mrs. Clinton are the logical successors to Franklin and Eleanor Roosevelt.

In the 1960s the Democrats created a special class of people who they said were to have unequal rights and unequal "protection of the law" and they instituted special government departments to create "cases" for the Supreme Court to try. The Democrats brought into being government departments not mentioned in the Constitution and therefore, a prohibition of such entities; the F.B.I, the Office of Equal Opportunities, the Legal Services Corp., the Civil Rights Commission, and the Department of Education, to name a few, whose task it was to prosecute "affirmative action" "equal opportunity" in housing, employment, violation of "civil rights" and all manner of concessions for the special class that came into being through the fraudulent, false and unconstitutional 13th, 14th, and 15th Amendments.

What the crooked Supreme Court did was try cases brought by the aforementioned agencies and then hand down crooked rulings which were not "equal opportunities" under "equal protection of the law" but rather opportunities to create special privileges and superior rights for minorities and more especially, for the Negroes. This is precisely what the Reconstruction legislation coupled with the 13th, 14th, and 15th Amendments was designed to do. Thus, the country is reaping a "democrat" whirlwind today, because of the actions of the Republican Party in the 1850s-1880s, a destructive force worse than the Civil War.

The Democrat Party became the Welfare State Party, a party which stays in power because of its Socialist programs, school lunches, rent subsidies, medical benefits, Social Security, food stamps child support for unwed mothers, free abortions, all of which has become a fully-fledged government industry in its own right and absolutely beyond the pale and the ken of the Constitution and the Bill of Rights.

"Oh you say so," respond the welfare generation, "but the general welfare clause says we are entitled to these benefits." The general welfare clause is totally unapplicable to personal welfare and addresses only the welfare of the entire nation and has no bearing on feeding and clothing a welfare population at public expense. This type of personal welfare is fraud, not mentioned anywhere in the Constitution and the Bill of Rights, and is, therefore, a prohibition of it. It is the Communist "leveling" process in action; taking from the productive sector and giving it to the nonproductive sector.

Only Senator East tried to do something about it as we find the Congressional Record, Senate, March 17, 1982 pages 2253-2268 which deals with the exception clause of Article III, Section 2 of the Constitution: "In all other cases before mentioned, the Supreme Court shall have appellate jurisdiction, both as to the law and the fact, with such exceptions, and under such regulations as the Congress shall make."

Extensive studies show that in the McCardle case the Congress overruled the Supreme Court. This nation should know that the 13th, 14th, and 15th Amendments are not part of the U.S. Constitution and Bill of Rights. The Communists in the Congress played a huge roll in foisting these three fraudulent amendments onto the American people. The McCardle case would have negated much of this situation, but under threat by the Congress, the Supreme Court ducked the case.

Given the sad truth that We, the People, have failed to denounce the fraud of the 13th, 14th, and 15th Amendments, we might do well to take a look at these amendments, especially the 14th which has caused more pain, strife, anguish, dissension and loss of States rights than any other amendment, at least in my opinion. In (140 — United States, 594), the court ruled that "...the power to make ordinary regulations of police powers remains with the individual States and cannot be assigned to the Federal Government, and that in this respect, it is not interfered with by the 14th Amendment." The court ruling was a victory for the 10th Amendment.

Instead, what we have today is endless legislation by the Congress that ignores the forgoing; the makers of bills promoting Socialist causes; a federal government ignoring that its powers are limited and delegated, continues to violate the laws of life, liberty and property and due process of the laws. Two of the most heinous examples of this are the terrorist assaults by the BATF, the U.S. Marshals Service and the FBI, on Randy Weaver and his family; and David Koresh and his Branch Davidian Church members. In both cases the terrorist attacks on Randy Weaver and his family and Koresh and his followers, were carried out under so-called "gun control laws" which are 100 percent unconstitutional and not laws at all, including the first such "law" passed in 1930.

Congressional Record, Feb. 26, 1792 pages 1795-1797, on civil rights, gives the meaning of the 14th Amendment in a clearer way than what is found in any law books, and it has to do with the Reconstruction debates. The Congressional Record account of the debates runs into hundreds of pages, each requiring careful scrutiny to find who the Socialists were, and how they greatly influenced the House. Note that all law books today are heavily influenced by Communist philosophy, and do not mention the foregoing facts.

The Republican Party and the whole Civil War effort was penetrated by radical Socialists and Communists, mainly from Eastern Europe, who saw in the war a great chance to advance Socialism in the U.S., the aim of the Fabian Socialists who had come over from England in 1895. They settled mainly in Massachusetts, which is why it is such a problem State as it has been ever since the 1800s. Just look at how many Communists it has returned to the House and Senate and you will get the point. President Lincoln did not comprehend or understand that the goal of these Radical Republican infiltrators was to make the Civil War a Socialist War, and he played right into their hands when he violated the Constitution through his habeas corpus executive order.

The Communists in Congress bedeviled both parties and their motives were poorly understood, if at all, by only a small number of legislators. One can say that 75 percent of Communist efforts were directed toward labor and 25 percent toward civil rights issues. The Communists were there to create friction between the Democrats and Republicans just as Albert Gore and William Clinton are doing today. In case there are those who don't know about this Communist penetration of the Congress long before the Civil War and in the post-Civil War period, be advised that there is a long list of Communists in the Congressional Records of 1926. Communists in the Congress and the judiciary, greatly influenced the case Brown vs. Board of Education, Topeka, Kansas, the so-called 1954 "desegregation" case: Congressional Record, House, March 2, 1970, pages 5570-5583.

One of the greatest constitutionalists of the time, Senator Thurmond of Ohio, stated as follows:

"And are we to interpret the Constitution by pictures of suffering, of destitution or every wrong and change its plain letters, and extend it to meet every want or necessity that may exist in the country; then, sir, you had better abolish it at once; then, sir, the limitations of the written constitution are not worth the paper they are written on..."

The 14th Amendment was written by the best legal brains of the period and every effort was made to keep the word, "race" out of it. The writers of the 14th Amendment drew on the Magna Carta for inspiration, which is equal protection of laws in a jury trial and a complete trial or due process as to life, liberty and property. There was no need for the 14th Amendment because "equal protection of laws" was already in the Constitution in Article VI, Sec. 2., and "equal protection of the laws" is also expressly implied in the 5th Amendment. "Equal protection of the laws" had a mundane meaning in the 18th century, basically, it meant that a policeman on the beat in England had to look out for all, and not only for the rich of the town. Those who wrote the 13th, 14th, and 15th Amendments tried to be color-blind, but the Communists in the Supreme Court and the Congress moved heaven and earth to make race a pillar of these amendments.

The REAL reasons why the 13th, 14th, and 15th Amendments were written are to be found in the Reconstruction debates in the 37th, 38th, 39th and 40th Congress. This information is not in the law books and I venture to suggest that 97 percent of the members of Congress in 1997 do not know anything about these matters. Unless they study the Congressional documents I have mentioned so many times, they won't know the Constitution.

The Civil Rights Act of 1866 was found unconstitutional, but some of it was revived in the civil rights acts of 1870, which was passed under the "war powers" of Congress. The 1964 Congress would have had to have the *undefined* war powers of the Reconstruction debates to have passed the Civil Rights Act of 1964, which was fraud and deception. As a run-up to the election of Socialist President Woodrow Wilson, we have the words of a prominent Socialist, a man under the sway of Fabian Socialism, Senator Boutwell. Congressional Record, Aug, 7, 1911, pages 3671-3693:

"...A slight investigation of the history and passage of the 14th Amendment will show that not only does the language of the amend-ment cover other persons, but that design and purpose as shown by the debates was that it should..."

A "slight investigation" might show this, but a proper, full, investi-gations shows it does not. The big thing to remember about the 14th Amendment is that it was drawn up in secret behind closed doors by a select, largely Socialist group of Radical Republican constitutional anar-chists from the House and Senate. Thaddeus Stevens, whose immense input into the deliberations of the secret committee is well demonstrated in this amendment. His speech found in the Congressional Record, House, Jan, 25, 1922, pages 1723-1729, demonstrates the unrestrained vindictive nature of the man.

Herein we find a blatant attempt to amend the Constitution by taking away States rights guaranteed by the Constitution, under the pretext of protecting the rights of blacks. We should note that prior to the Civil War blacks were not slaves in the truest sense of the word, as their condition of servitude differed greatly from those of Roman slaves who could not live together as a family, and were brutally treated. Slaves held by plantation owners were considered as "valuable property" purchased at a high cost. In the 1770s the cost of a Negro slave had risen to 70 English pounds — a lot of money in those days. As such, it is unlikely that they would be mistreated. This is not to say that were never any cases of ill treatment.

The Congressional Records of the era show that the 13th, 14th, and 15th Amendments sprang from the Civil Rights Act of 1866, which was found unconstitutional. Since the base on which these amendments rested was found unconstitutional by the Supreme Court, how then could the amendments still be left standing?

The cunning deception of the 14th Amendment did not always fool judges as it does today. In the Slaughterhouse decisions, the judges poked fun at the 13th, 14th, and 15th Amendments. The Republican Party saw in the 14th Amendment an opportunity to stay in power through the Negro vote. Desperately anxious to stay in power, it cobbled these three amendments together in extreme haste. One of the intentions of the 14th Amendment was to ensure that Confederate officers who served at State level and those with a rank of colonel or higher, could not hold public office. In the rush to force the 14th Amendment through, its secret committee backers forgot to give the Negro the vote, so they had to rush the 15th Amendment through to correct their error.

That the 13th, 14th, and 15th Amendments were never constitutionally ratified by the States, will be observed by reading the Reconstruction debates. The Dred Scott case, perhaps the most important Supreme Court case in two centuries, proved that neither Lincoln nor the House and Senate had the right to free the slaves as they were, legally speaking, chattels; the private property of their owners who were protected by States rights. To overcome this, the so-called Civil Rights Act of 1866 was passed. It was later struck down as unconstitutional because the 14th Amendment had not yet been passed and was unratified by the States, in which condition it remains to this day. i.e., unconstitutional to the last degree.

To make matters more difficult for those seeking to free the slaves, the Supreme Court ruled against the 14th Amendment in the McCardle case, thus voiding it. The court ruled that the Confederate States were laboring under an occupation by the Union Army, thus "free and fair" voting by the State legislatures was not free and fair, simply because the members voted under extreme duress. The Reconstruction Acts of Congress were also found unconstitutional because they violated a bill of attainder. This is found in the Congressional Globe, Senate, Feb. 15, 1871.

THE 14TH AND 15TH AMENDMENTS VIOLATE THE 10TH AMENDMENT TO THE UNITED STATES CONSTITUTION

"The powers not delegated to the United States (singular) by the Constitution, nor prohibited by it to the States, are reserved to the States, or to the people." We need to understand that in the words "or to the people" is found a large number of rights called personal rights, constantly being encroached upon by Federal, State and local government under the guise of "equal rights," "civil rights;" not to mention so-called "affirmative action laws" and "homosexual rights" and so on.

As we have seen herein, the Radical Republicans were the ones who betrayed the Constitution and the Bill of Rights in clamoring for the Civil War. In the post-Civil War era, the Radical Republicans who had so bedeviled Lincoln also forced the passage of the 13th, 14th, and 15th Amendments to the Constitution plus they were responsible for the Reconstruction laws all of which were unconstitutional. On the other hand it was the Democrats who fought most valiantly to preserve the Constitution and the Bill of Rights.

But in the early 1900s at a time when the Democrats began to turn toward Communism, first under Woodrow Wilson where it was mainly a party for "causes" and later under Roosevelt where Communism was openly embraced, the roles of the two parties showed a change of direction which eventually led to a reversal of their earlier roles. The South underestimated the determination of Lincoln to keep them in the Union never seeming to realize that it was based upon the position that as the North could not secede from the Union therefore, the South was to be kept from so doing, even if it took extreme force to keep the nation intact. We repeat the following because of its tremendous importance:

Congressional Globe January 31, 1866, pages 546-549:

"But this civil war never could have taken place if the rights of each State had been respected by the Congress and the people of every other State. We have heard so much of the first gun being fired at Fort Sumter, or by old John Brown in Virginia, but it was fired by the American Congress when that body passed the Missouri Compromise and usurped the right to legislate upon the subject of slavery, *a mere domestic issue, resting with the people of each State..."*

As the learned and renowned Judge Cooley said in his book, "Constitutional Limitations" at page 796: "In the American constitutional system the power to establish ordinary regulations of police powers has been left with the individual States, and cannot be taken away from them, either wholly, or in part and exercised under legislation of the Congress. Neither can the National Government through any of its departments or officers assume supervision of the police regulations (municipal regulations) of the States."

There are also many court cases which have supported the position that the Central Government cannot intrude into the affairs of the States and especially holding that Lincoln had no right to interfere in the issue of slavery, and holding that the Congress did not have the right, either.

Howard 14 and Howard 17: "The power to make municipal regulations for the restraint and punishment of crime; for the preservation of the health and morals of its citizens has never been surrendered by the States, but retained by them."

Wallace 41: "No power is conferred by the Constitution upon Congress to establish mere police regulations within the States."

Wheaton 303, 326: "The government of the United States can claim no powers which are not granted to it by United States and the powers actually granted must be such as are expressly given, or by implication." (Expressly implied.)

92.U.S. 542, seventh headnote: "Sovereignty for the protection of life, personal liberty; rests in the States."

113 U.S.31: "but neither the amendment (14th) broad and comprehensive as it is, nor any other amendment is designed to interfere with the powers of the States sometimes referred to as the 'police powers' to prescribe regulations, to promote health, peace and good order of the people."

So where did Pres. Eisenhower, for example, get the right to send federal troops to the State of Arkansas to enforce desegregation? The bald-faced truth is that Mr. Eisenhower had absolutely no right under the Constitution to undertake such a mission.

16 Wallace 82: "Under pressure of all excited feelings growing out of the war, our statesmen still believe that the existence of the States, with powers of domestic and local government including the regulation of civil rights of persons and of property essential to the complete working of our complete government."

The unbridled ambition of the late 20th century constitutional anarchists in the Democrat Party — a complete reversal of their role in 1865 — is to turn the Constitution on its head and do away with the Bill of Rights. Leading constitutional anarchists in the ranks of the Democrat Party, among whose number we find Clinton, Conyers, Feinstein, Lautenburg, Kennedy and Boxer are running this constitutionally-criminal enterprise. Not far behind the Democrats bent on destroying the Constitution are found a large number of Republicans holding similar aspirations. They include in their leadership, Bush, Jeffords, Gingrich, Lugar, Abraham, Specter, Lott, Longford and so on; until today we have in the United States a close proximity to a one-party political entity.

SO-CALLED "HATE CRIMES" AND MINORITY RIGHTS

This subject quite properly comes under the heading of the 14th Amendment because, as I have said, civil rights cases as interpreted by the Supreme Court since the 1950s are based on this amendment. Since the 13th, 14th, and 15th Amendments were not ratified, it follows that the 1964 Civil Rights Act is mere hypotheses heaped upon hypotheses. The federal government added "civil rights" covering women, implying that women are a minority — a bald-faced Communist lie and now, homosexuals are included as a "minority". The "additions" are ultra vires, of no effect, outside the pale and ken of the Constitution, a fraud and a hoax perpetrated upon the American people, almost as much of a hoax as the "wall of separation between church and state," hoax.

Even if the three amendments had been ratified, there is absolutely nothing in them that includes social legislation, that is to say, giving one class of persons social rights. Congressional Globe, March 15, 1870, pages 1950-1961:

"...it is impossible for a State rightfully and constitutionally to make a law which shall bear upon the social conditions or the rights of one man in a different sense or in any different way from what it bears upon another. That is obvious..."

Let us look at so-called "hate crimes." Nowhere in the Constitution and the Bill of Rights is "hate crimes" mentioned; therefore it is an inhibition (prohibition) of this term. The same holds good for such terms as "race," "national origin" "gender" "religion," "discrimination," "desegregation," "intimidation" "sexual orientation," "harassment." In law one cannot use cognates or synonyms, but the Communists in Congress are good at a play on words, which they learned from the Communist Manifesto of 1848, and they use the technique all the time, making many flexible, ordinary words, inflexible, which places an entirely different construction on them. And yet, the courts use these words and terms all the time.

Take the fatuous House Bill 2703, which purports to prohibit certain kinds of "harassment" against persons because of their sex, race, (national origin) religion, marital status. What kind of utter madness has got a hold of us? We find none of these words mentioned in the Constitution, so they are a prohibition and a prohibition against any "laws" built upon them. Such "laws" are mere hypotheses heaped upon hypotheses. Where, for instance, do we find the word, "harassment" in the Constitution? It just isn't there, yet a whole series of "laws" have been built around it to satisfy the desires of the star-gazing incendiary liberals without regard to the constitutionality of such laws.

In law we have to have strict interpretations which can only be based upon Judge Story's 15 Rules of Interpretation of the Constitution. We cannot use synonyms or cognates. A law has to be clearly written with no ambiguity attached to it. The meaning of the word "harassment" has no connection with the way it is used in House Bill 2703. Webster's Dictionary says the word means the following:

"Harass (French he'ras, herasser), worry, impeded by repeated raids by the enemy, exhaust, fatigue, to annoy persistently." The word is used clearly in a military context. "Harass" can never be used in the context of any "civil rights" lawsuits.

The Communist manifesto of 1848 specializes in a play of words, taking the ordinary usage of words and making them inflexible. In this manner, "harass" can be made to mean anything. Anti-Constitutionalist Charles Schumer and Mr. Clinton use the word "terror" in much the same way as "harass." The word "terror" or "terrorism" do not appear in the Constitution. It was the Communists who started to use words like "discrimination," "intimidation," "desegregation." Many of the race-hate laws and "civil rights laws are based on the 14th Amendment which says nothing about race as a condition of equal protection under the laws. Even had the 14th added the word "race," or any of the foregoing words, no laws could be built around them because the 14th Amendment has never been ratified.

Hate crimes are a bill of attainder violation where a person is punished by a legislative act and a legislative board takes the place of a judge and jury. So called "hate crimes" are also a violation of the 1st Amendment to the Constitution. Even though such laws are patently ultra-vires, the Federal Government by virtue of its force acts as if they were constitutional laws. So we have to be careful that we do not fall foul of these so-called "hate crime" laws and "racist" laws.

The Justice Department has no constitutional authority to compile a list of "hate crimes." The Communists intimidated the U.S. Senate to permit the Justice Department to make up a list of "hate crimes" which is based entirely upon hearsay. Also, where in the U.S. Constitution does the Justice Department have the slightest right to compile such a list? It is not there! But it is in the Communist Manifesto of 1848! If such a list were to be assembled, it would be the job of the Congress to compile it, not the Justice Department, and even then it would be of doubtful validity as it would be a violation of a bill of attainder.

The Justice Department should have had its wings clipped and its "hate crimes" catalog destroyed a long time ago as the Justice Department is not the judiciary, nor the legislative branch. Moreover, the list of "hate crimes" violates the 5th Amendment of the Constitution, as well as Article 1, Section 9, Part 3: "No bill of attainder or ex post facto law shall be passed." The so-called "hate list" is merely a device enabling the Justice Department to accuse individuals of crimes without granting them due process, a jury trial.

Due process of the law means going through the entire process leading up to a trial by jury, without any "short cuts." This was decided in the celebrated case, Cummings vs. State of Missouri, Congressional Record, Senate, Feb. 16, 1882, pages 1195-1209.

The 15th Amendment says that race shall not be a factor in the privilege to vote. Remember, voting is not a civil right, but a privilege. The

Justice Department loves to use the word "criminal" as do the Communists in the Congress, but it is worth noting that the only direct mention of criminal law is found in Article 7 of the Bill of Rights. The Bolshevik rulers called anyone who disagreed with their policies, a criminal, and likewise, Mr. Clinton attacks anyone who disagrees with him and tries to make criminals of them by having them investigated by federal agencies. If there is a difference between this kind of misuse of the law and what the Bolsheviks did, then I would like to know what the difference is.

The first section of the 14th Amendment makes no reference to political rights, and is, in fact, involved with citizenship and equal protection under the law and due process. Whereas civil rights as to life, liberty and property are guaranteed in the 14th Amendment, political rights are not guaranteed for any race or group. To suppose otherwise is nonsense. As to equal protection of the laws, found in the 14th Amendment, this does not apply to privileges and immunities of those not expressed or implied by the Constitution. To talk of "homosexual rights" and "women's rights" is to be absurd, constitutionally speaking.

To speak of women as a "minority" is preposterous as women are in fact a majority; as much as it preposterous to call homosexuals a "minority." Nowhere in the U.S. Constitution do we find the word "homosexual" nor is it expressly implied; thus it is an inhibition or prohibition and no so-called laws can be predicated upon imaginary minority homosexual rights. We need to be on our guard and take careful note how the Communists use the U.S. Constitution and associate it with the Communist Manifesto of 1848. The Communists in Congress use tautology and redundancy to make their bills plausible or to add credibility where none exists. A good example of this is found in the Socialist Sen. Feinstein's "assault weapons" ban. There is no such thing in the Constitution as " assault weapons" therefore it is a prohibition of the term. This is a good example of inflexibility being applied to flexible words in normal usage.

PERSONAL RIGHTS ALL BUT FORGOTTEN

I have not seen anything much written about or spoken of by Congress and the courts concerning unenumerated rights since the 19th century. These inalienable rights have been swept under the rug and forgotten. It is vital to our freedom that they be brought out and revived.

The 9th Amendment starts with enumerating the powers of the Federal Government and refers to other powers. We need to have a clear understanding of exactly what these other powers are. They are the States rights (sovereignty). The remaining powers are personal and private rights which may not be abridged or circumscribed or tampered with by the central or State governments in any way.

In the 1960s we saw one bill after another supposedly conferring "civil rights" on a varied collection of groups and the personal and private rights of citizens got all scrambled up with these so-called civil rights bills. These private and personal rights should never have been mixed up with the other rights expressly implied in the Constitution and Bill of Rights. The second big mistake is that the Supreme Court misunderstood the intentions of the legislators when the 14th Amendment was written up and made the first ten amendments to the Constitution a responsibility of the States, as well as the Federal Government. This is 100 percent wrong and one has to refer to the Slaughterhouse cases to see this clearly.

The 14th Amendment does not say what the Supreme Court tries to twist into it. In fact the 14th Amendment did not change Article IV, Section 2, privileges and immunities of citizens of the United States. There has always been States citizenship and U.S. citizenship. The latter refers to members of the armed services, diplomatic corps, citizens traveling abroad. There are scores of court cases where this was decided. Here is one of them:

123 United States 166: "That the first ten articles of amendment were not intended to limit the power of State Government in respect to their own people; but to operate on the National Government, was decided a half-century ago, and that decision has been steadily adhered to ever since."

Most of the so-called "civil rights" and changes in the population mix have come about since the Civil War — and it was a civil war and not a rebellion. Those civil rights are predicated on the 13th, 14th, and 15th Amendments (but mainly on the 14th Amendment) which was never ratified and could never stand constitutional scrutiny. Thus all of the so-called "statutory laws" pyramided upon these three amendments, are null and void and are no obligation upon anyone, as if such "laws" had never been put on the books. That is right: All laws predicated on the 13th, 14th, and 15th Amendments are mere hypotheses heaped upon hypotheses. Yet the government, the courts, go on, year after year, pretending that these three amendments have the force of law, when they know very well that they do not.

All that the Supreme Court does is heap hypotheses upon hypotheses, when it makes decisions based upon the fraudulent 13th, 14th, and 15th. amendments. Many of these concern "civil rights" which are also closely related to immigration and are thus, relevant and important to this study. The vapid excuse that all of the Reconstruction measures of the three amendments could have been carried out anyway through the war powers of Congress, is just so much disinformation. The United States was not at war with a foreign country: It was a civil war. This is the MOST VITAL distinction.

Congressional Record, House, May 18, 1870, pages 3558-3571:

Under "Enforcement of the 15th Amendment" we have the start of the debates on "racism" or the so — called Civil Rights Act of 1870. This legislation was HATE legislation against the Democrat Party. At that period of our history, the Democrats had not yet been taken over and subverted by the Communists and Socialists as was the case with the Radical Republicans. Hate "civil rights" legislation was designed to degrade Southern whites, which was what this legislation was about, and the Civil War was really to settle old scores between the two parties which dated back to 1818. The cause of the Civil War was not slavery. The slavery issue was raised later, after the war was in its second year.

The Southern whites were hated, not by blacks, but by Northern whites who did not think slavery wrong, but opposed it because slavery financially enabled young white Southerners to attend universities in Europe and come back with a superior education, which gave them the edge in the House and Senate. The North did not hate slavery per se — it hated the fact that because of it, whites in the Southern States were superior in education and could dominate the Federal Government. A reading of the Annals of Congress, the Congressional Globes and Congressional Records of the period confirms the foregoing.

The Radical Republicans and Communists and Socialists in the Republican Party saw in this a golden opportunity to take vengeance on the superior Southern whites and they did it in two ways: By so-called "civil rights" legislation based upon the bogus 13th, 14th, and 15th Amendments, and by changing the immigration laws that allowed non-Western European nationals to come to the United States as immigrants. The white man was fighting for his very existence in the South, but the

Democrats won the fight by virtue of their superior education versus the virulence of the vengeful Radical Republicans and their Communist allies. One has to study the Annals of Congress and Congressional Globes to be able to understand just how deep-seated the hatred for the South was, and how rotten the Republican Party was in this era. It is beyond the scope of this study to do more than make passing mention of these factors that went into so-called civil rights and Reconstruction laws.

In 1888, the Supreme Court put a crimp in the Republican Party's vendetta through the Slaughterhouse case by declaring the so-called civil rights act of 1866, unconstitutional. It was clear that the 13th, 14th, and 15th Amendments were written for the sole purpose of disadvantaging white Southerners. There is a huge void in our history books which shows absolutely nothing of the determined push by the Communists and Socialists to take over the United States between 1850 and 1870 and this phase of stripping the Confederate States of States rights was a part of it. There is a bibliography in the Library of Congress ten pages long containing the names of 150 Communist organizations and fronts active in the period for those who would query early Communist penetration of the United States.

Congressional Globe, June 16 1866, pages 3212-3218:

"I have referred to and I maintain fully the power of the State to determine and exclude all persons who it may regard as dangerous and injurious to its interests from whatever cause, real or imaginary."

A profound statement, which, were it to be published today, would be labeled as violently "racist" and "bigoted," but which nevertheless, must be read. It also shows the clear intentions of the Founding Fathers, and sheds light on those bent upon preserving Christian Western civilization in the United States. As part of our history it cannot simply be swept under the carpet because it is likely to cause pain and suffering to some of our people. In the case of Aury vs. Smith, 1 Litt. Rep 327, the court said that: "Prior to the adoption of the Federal Constitution, States had a right to make citizens of any person they pleased, but as the Constitution does not authorize any but white persons to become citizens of the United States it furnishes a presumption that none others were citizens at the time of its adoption....Again, sir, the act of Congress passed in 1790, during the second session of the first Congress which assembled after the adoption of the United States Constitution, providing for a uniform rule of naturalization confines the right to become a citizen to aliens being free white persons."

This is given an historical observation, without prejudice to any and offense to none, but the truth must be reported; history cannot be ignored because it offends, and it is fair to say that the Founding Fathers and the early legislators were clear in their intent; they wanted America to be a Christian, Western European nation. As Judge Taney put it:

"...It is true that the Declaration of Independence seemed to embrace the whole human family, and if they were used in a similar instrument at this day they would be so understood. But it was too clear for dispute that the enslaved African race were not intended to be included and formed no part of those who framed and adopted this Declaration..."

The Congressional Globes and Congressional Records make it more clear: Less still do Asian races and other non-Western non-Christian races who have been allowed to enter the United States, qualify as citizens — if the original intent of the Founding Fathers is understood and followed. This is not "racism" — only a recital of what is stated in the Annals of Congress, the Congressional Globes and the Congressional Records and this history cannot be stricken from the record, just because today, some government department, or the ACLU, says the remarks are "racist." If any reader is offended by this, then let him lay the blame for it at the door of the Founding Fathers and not those who report history.

Other non-Western European races who have come here since the 1930s have no common ground with America of the Founding Fathers, the Declaration of Independence and the Constitution; the Bill of Rights. They are not of the stock of George Washington, Lincoln, Davy Crockett, and Daniel Webster. These other races are trying their best to establish what is commonly called "multiculturalism" which is a prescription for national suicide. America is not a melting pot, at least that much has long ago been established.

The inescapable truth is: America has become *many* different nations when we look at the Asian and other non-European non-Christian races that have taken on a major role in shaping the destiny of this country. What we have today in America, clearly visible, is *cultural radicalism* which will lead the United States down the Gaderene Slope to perdition. Multiculturalism is threatening the very existence of our nation. Multiculturalism, moreover, is being legislated, and this will never work. What Frederic Bastiat wrote in his memorable essay, "The Law," is worth quoting: "Enforced Fraternity Destroys Liberty".

"Mr. de Lamartine once wrote to me thusly: 'Your doctrine is only half of my program. You have stopped at liberty; I go to fraternity.' I answered him: 'The second half of your program will destroy the first.' In fact, it is impossible for me to separate the word 'fraternity' from the word 'voluntary'. I cannot possibly understand how fraternity can be legally enforced without liberty being legally destroyed, and thus justice being legally trampled underfoot. Legal plunder has two roots: One of them, as I have said before, is in human greed; the other is in false philanthropy."

All laws about "equality" stem from a big misunderstanding. The 14th Amendment is the root of the trouble. It does not say in the first section of the 14th amendment that there is "equal protection of the law" based on race — which is what the Federal Government implies with its "race" laws — which are no laws at all. We all get our constitutional civil rights not by race, but indirectly through life, liberty and property. The Constitution is subtle and does not deal directly with race. For this reason alone, the civil rights laws of the 1980s, 1954, 1964 — 1967 and onwards are all unconstitutional. In any case the 14th Amendment was addressed to the STATES and not to INDIVIDUALS, a very important distinction, apart from an even greater distinction that the amendment was never ratified.

The Civil Rights Act, the Voting Rights Act, these are hypotheses heaped upon hypotheses because they are founded on the 14th Amendment which did not add anything to the Constitution and which, in any case, as I have said repeatedly, (it cannot be stated enough) was never ratified. These acts have no force in law, even though they are enforced by the federal government wielding its powers, especially in violation of the 10th Amendment.

The Slaughterhouse cases said very clearly that the 14th Amendment added nothing new to the Constitution, but the Socialists tried to make it seem that new "rights" had been uncovered. If we were one mass, one homogeneous nation, there would not be any need for special rights for some. National unity cannot survive when it is based on "special rights" for some and not others. In the celebrated case U.S. vs. Harris (106 West), Justice Wood rendered the following verdict:

"It, the fourteenth amendment is a guarantee against the acts of the

State Government itself: It is a guarantee against the exercise of arbitrary and unconstitutional power on the part of government and legislation of a State, not a guarantee against the commission of individual offenses: And the power of Congress, whether expressed or implied, to legislate for the enforcement of such guarantee does not extend to passage of laws for the suppression of crime within the States. The enforcement of the guarantee itself supposes it to be the duty of the State to perform." (Under the power of the 10th Amendment.)

Judge Bradley, in another civil rights case stated: "It is the State action of a peculiar character that is prohibited by the 14th Amendment: individual invasion of individual rights is not the subject matter of the Amendment..."

In 1873-1875 civil rights legislation did not succeed in the courts. Congress found the so-called Civil Rights Bill of 1866 unconstitutional, because the 14th Amendment was not passed at that time. Even if the 14th Amendment had been ratified — which it was not — so-called civil rights could not have been predicated upon it — as Attorney General Nicholas Katzenbach fraudulently attempted to pass off in 1964 in an unconstitutional manner. The privileges and immunities of the 14th Amendment were already in the Constitution before the 14th Amendment, and the 14th added nothing new.

It is generally agreed that there is just too much big government, but who will do something meaningful about addressing the problem? To find wisdom and understanding of the United States Constitution, turn to the Annals of Congress, the Congressional Globes and the Congressional Record. In the pages of these records we find debates of the highest caliber, eclipsing by far the legislators of today, who don't have the vocabulary necessary to explain the Constitution as the legislators in the period 1870-1900 were so ably equipped to do.

The Hon. Eppa Hunton said it so well, on February 3, 1875: "The World is Governed Too Much." Today, the United States is governed too much. Fully 75 percent of the Federal Government could be shut down without harm to the nation. The heinous Reconstruction period brought forth thousands of useless laws, and the present era, thousands more such unconstitutional laws. Today we border on anarchy in Washington.

The United States is not in need of the thousands and thousands of laws Congress has passed. The country is developed, the States are developed and have their own constitutions. The Federal Government is needlessly and unconstitutionally duplicating the powers of the States, especially in health, education and police powers, where the 10th Amendment to the Constitution reserves such rights to the States.

There is no constitutional provision for a Department of Education. Where in the Constitution is a Federal Government Department of Education authorized? It is not there, as education is a matter reserved by the Constitution for the States.

If a department of government is not mentioned in the United States Constitution, it is a prohibition of that department. Where in the Constitution is there empowerment for Departments of Agriculture, Education, police protection, Federal banks, Federal judges, Health? It is simply not there, so it is an inhibition or prohibition of these departments and organizations of the Federal Government. Let the Republican Party in Congress close them down. They have the constitutional authority to do it.

All that the Congress has done in the last 40 years or more is pile up on each other, thousands of laws which impinge on States rights. Congress has nothing better to do than spend its time dreaming up ways of imposing more and more federal "laws" on the States.

Then, to make matters worse, the Congress passes these so-called laws and expects the States to pay for them. There is not one single word in the Constitution that authorizes Congress to make the States pay for enforcing Federal Government legislation. There is no such provision in the Constitution that would oblige the States to pay for legislation passed by star-gazing liberals and I could cite hundreds of examples of such pieces of legislation.

The States are not obliged to fund any Federal laws. Yet here we have the State of California stuck with an annual bill of $3.6 billion dollars, because the Federal Government has failed to guarantee a republican form of government and daily allows and permits thousands upon thousands of illegal aliens to invade not only California, but dozens of other States also.

The powers of Congress are not absolute; they are delegated powers found in Article 1, Section 8, clauses 1-18. This is the total sum and substance of the powers of Congress, which is why the Brady bill and Feinstein's assault weapons bill are so ludicrous. The 2nd Amendment to the United States is a *right* that *cannot* be legislated against. And nowhere in the Constitution is the type of gun we are allowed to own and bear delineated.

The Congress should consider appointing a commission of qualified persons to look into the question of civil rights. Such a commission would have to be made up of persons who have made a diligent study the Annals of Congress, the Congressional Globes and the Congressional Record for at least ten years. It is only persons who are thus qualified who understand the question of civil rights. Judges should be excluded.

Senator Turnbull was a members of the Senate Judicial committee that helped draft the 14th Amendment to the U.S. Constitution. On January 5, 1874, Sen. Turnbull said: "The 14th Amendment was to secure all of the people of the U.S. with freedom." The 14th Amendment does not contain any of the fantasies attributed to it by star gazing liberals. There are no fancied, exotic rights in it.

In any case, the Slaughterhouse cases judges stated that the 14th Amendment is redundant to the Constitution. So called affirmative action legislation violates the civil rights of whites. The so called Voting Rights Act also violates the 5th Amendment.

The great constitutional scholar, the late Senator Sam Ervin put the position very well in the Congressional Record, Senate, pages S 3287-S3294, March 9 1970:

"Now what is a bill of Attainder which is reported in Wallace 333? It is defined in Cummings vs. the State of Missouri which I have just quoted. It is also defined in the case of U.S. vs. Lovett 328 U.S. 303...Legislative acts no matter what they arc from that apply to individuals or easily ascertainable members of a group in such a way as to inflict punishment on them without a judicial trial are bills of attainder prohibited by the Constitution. This is clear. It is clear the Voting Rights Act of 1966 constitutes both a bill of Attainder and expost facto law which punishes someone (or a class) for an act which was not a crime at the time the crime was committed."

The Voting Rights Act precisely states, "the people of 39 counties of my State (North Carolina) by denying them the power to exercise a constitutional right which is secured to them by four distinct provisions of the Constitution. These cases say that you do not have to punish people criminally. You punish people within the prohibition of a bill of Attainder whenever you deny them the power to exercise a right, whatever that right may be."

The original civil rights debates lasted 13 years and started in the middle of the Civil War, which in spite of the hundreds of books written about the war, the issues that started the war have never been clearly defined. Mixed in with these civil rights debates of the period was voluminous Communists and Socialist propaganda. American history books by and large have glossed over or did not even mentioned the incursion of Communist agitators into the scene.

The 13th, 14th, and 15th Amendments are complex and surrounded by much Communist propaganda and the sad truth is that very few judges — even the best of them — really do not know what is involved. Space does not permit me to publish them here, but the speeches made by the Hon. A.S. Merrimon of North Carolina, a senator who really understood these amendments should be compulsory reading for every judge and also the justices of the Supreme Court. Sen. Merrimon was most emphatic on the limited powers of Congress:

"Mr. President, in the first place, in my judgment Congress has no power in the Constitution to pass the pending bill commonly called the civil rights bill" and he was referring to the bill of 1866.

Incidentally, "Brightly's Digest of the Laws of the United States" also says that Congress has no authority to pass civil rights bills. We also know that the Socialist/Marxist Earl Warren Supreme Court nullified the Constitution in forcing and subverting of the equal protection of the laws clause in violation of the balance of the Constitution. In other words, the Socialist/Marxist Earl Warren Court did its best to destroy the equipoise of the Constitution which means that any part of the Constitution has to be interpreted in the light of the complete document, and not just isolated to suit the particular purpose of the occasion.

The Earl Warren court took treason cases away from States courts where they properly belonged, thereby robbing the States of their police powers which is 100 percent unconstitutional. Warren isolated the 1st Amendment and made it mean anything and everything the Socialists and Marxists wanted it to mean. Justices Frankfurter, Earl Warren and Warren Burger did inestimable damage to the States rights of police powers and police protection, and it ought to be a the highest priority of the Republican Party-dominated Congress to at least make a start toward rectifying the many palpably unconstitutional rulings handed down by these three justices, whose main job in life was to subvert the Constitution by amending it through judicial fiat, under the guise of interpreting it.

NATIONAL SUICIDE: THE 1965 IMMIGRATION REFORM ACT

This is a subject considered too hot to handle by many politicians and writers, because they fear the invective of "racist" and of falling foul of unconstitutional so-called "race" and "hate" laws. Let me say that so-called "hate laws" are the work of the radical Socialists and Communists embedded in both political parties. There is no need for a special category of crimes such as are dealt with under "hate crimes." This only further divides and inflames passion. In any case, such laws are unconstitutional. There are scores of laws already on the statute books that deal with all manner of criminal activity. Why the need to "specialize?" Could it be purely a political ploy?

This work is about the fundamentals of the United States Constitution, who wrote it, and for whom it was written. Unavoidably, race will come into the discussion, but this is not a work about party politics "race" which has bedeviled the United States since the Reconstruction period following the Civil War, and which is still with us. The careless treatment of the Constitution by the legislators and the Supreme Court, is part of a pattern to denigrate and make of no effect the provisions of the Constitution. This pattern began to emerge in the runup to the Civil War, during its disastrous years, and all through the post-Civil War era, particularly in the "Reconstruction" laws forced upon the secessionist States.

Only those few scholars who have made a diligent study of the Annals of Congress, the Congressional Globe, and the Congressional Record, (and they ARE few in number) know there was a tremendous effort made by the Communists and Socialists to infiltrate the United States in the period leading up to the Civil War, and in its aftermath. Their success with the Republican Party whose radical members of Congress so bedeviled Lincoln, has already been mentioned.

In the 1920s — 1930s, there was a resurgence of an attempt by the Socialists to take over the U.S. government, and nowhere more so than in the court system, the legislature and, in the 1960s, in the field of immigration. What the Socialists were unable to accomplish by a frontal assault on the U.S. through the Civil War, they tried to accomplish in the 1930s by massive infiltration of constitutional anarchists planted among the judiciary. Their efforts were largely a continuance of the Reconstruction period's civil rights efforts, but, in the 1930s and 1960s, the thrust was to a more subtle means of overthrowing the Union, in which immigration from non-Founding Father countries played a major role.

The United States Constitution is the oldest written Constitution surviving in the world, a hindrance to world Socialism and as such, it remains under daily assault from constitutional anarchists — Communists and Socialists. But thus far, that marvelous document signed in Philadelphia in 1787, is meeting all tests and still stands as the supreme law of the land, although under ongoing savage and relentless attack by its enemies.

The United States Constitution was written to avoid the pitfalls of democracy (majority mob rule under a Napoleonic Code) autocracy; it was written for a confederated Republic. The fifty-five men who met at Philadelphia were all of Anglo-Saxon nationality. Hence it follows that the Constitution was written in the collective light of their national identity, experience, heritage and culture, and as an expression of their wishes that the United States be thus constituted.

The peoples of Europe, particularly England, Ireland, Scotland, Germany, France, Norway, Sweden and Denmark, desired to move to the "new country" and when this desire spilled over to other non-European nations, there was planted the seed which has grown to threatening demographic proportions in a manner never envisaged nor intended by the framers of the Constitution. The cement that bound the framers of the Constitution together was the fact that all came from white, Western European Christian countries. This is no reflection upon any other group; nor is it casting aspersions on any other group. It is simply a matter of cold, hard fact, which cannot be presented in any other way. Many students of the Constitution, myself included, believe that the "common heritage" factor, more than anything else, is what made the Convention the great success it turned out to be, and what made the United States such a great country.

In their deliberations the delegates to the constitutional convention frequently referred to "law of nations". They were referring to Vattel's "Law of Nations" the "Bible" on which they based much of the policies later written into the Declaration of Independence, the United States Constitution and the Bill of Rights. As a final safeguard, Clause 18 of the delegated powers was accepted: "To make all laws which shall be necessary and proper for carrying into execution the foregoing powers and all other powers vested by this Constitution in the government of the United States, or any department thereof."

The violation by the Federal Government of Section 9 (1) of the Constitution is what concerns us here:

"The migration of such persons as any state now existing shall think proper to admit shall not be prohibited by Congress prior to the year 1908 but a tax or duty may be imposed on such importation, not exceeding ten dollars per person." Conversely, it was presumed that the States had the right to EXCLUDE such persons they did not think proper to admit. This premise was borne out by the Chinese Exclusion Act. (This was later repealed by Congress.)

States rights to exclude those they did not want to admit has been ignored by federal immigration laws which allow nations whose nationals are not Western European and whose antecedents did not take part in the framing of the Constitution, preference over immigrants from Founding Father nations. These observations, naturally, exclude the Negroes, territories and people who were later made part of the United States, and very specifically, do not apply to Hawaii and the Pacific Island territories. The Founding Fathers obviously thought that it would make no sense to let people of every nation on earth emigrate to the United States. It is clear from a reading of the Annals of Congress, the Congressional Globes and Congressional Records that mass immigration of nationals other than from Christian European nations was never contemplated, considered nor planned, and would not have been permitted by the framers.

But then, who among the Founding Fathers could have envisaged that large numbers of Socialists, Communists and constitutional anarchists were to invade the United States in the 1920-1930s, and that traitor Roosevelt would set an agenda for national suicide by opening the immigration gates to all and sundry? Not one of the distinguished delegates to Philadelphia would have agreed to such a policy, had it been brought up at the time, which is why the right of immigration was reserved to the States as to who they would admit, or not admit. An open immigration policy is in violation of the Constitution and of States rights. This error was compounded by the astounding, unconstitutional, Immigration Reform Act of 1965.

Americans are entitled to know their constitutional history and how their country was established as a Western European Christian nation, by Western European Christian white people and that the U.S. was envisaged and expected to be a culturally particularist nation. Without attaching ourselves to this cultural particularist heritage — in accordance with the ideals of the Founding Fathers — we would never have become a nation in the vision of the Founding Fathers, and if we depart from their blueprint and go on in the way of a multi-ethnic divided nation, we will soon cease to be a people and a nation. We have the examples of ancient Greece and Rome to contemplate.

Frederic Bastiat, whom I have already quoted, put paid to the idea that brotherly love for other than our own, can be legislated. Why should expression of our particularist heritage be denied or classed as "racism" and "bigoted" except to silence our legitimate right to be heard? When we dare to defend our traditional heritage it is called "reactionary and racist." What is our traditional heritage? It is what the Founding Fathers clearly spelled out and what the framers of the Constitution carved in granite: It is that we are a Western European and Christian nation.

Now comes the Communists, Socialists — constitutional anarchists in Congress and the Supreme Court, and they say, "you are a diverse nation," and they try to stress diversity, and then they talk about "equal protection under law based on race." This sentiment is based upon the 14th Amendment which has never been ratified and is merely hypotheses heaped upon previous heaps of hypotheses of the Supreme Court.

Writing in his work, "Immigration and Migration — A Historical Perspective" published by the American Immigration Control Foundation, John Lukacs states there are those who are deeply concerned that if matters continue as they are at present, "it would lead not only to a gradual but a radical mutation in the composition of the American people (i.e. as a basically Christian West European nation), and the transformation of the very essence of the present civilization of the United States." As we shall see in the next chapter, the "transformation of the very essence of the present civilization of the United States" has already progressed so rapidly and so far, as to be impossible to turn back. America, as envisaged by the Founding Fathers has got less than 80 years left before its Constitution is destroyed and the nation is swallowed up by those for whom citizenship was never the intention of the framers of the Constitution.

CHAPTER 7

THE FOUNDING FATHERS NATIONAL LEGACY FOR THE UNITED STATES

1965 IMMIGRATION REFORM ACT IS DESTROYING IT. PROCLAMATIONS, EXECUTIVE ORDERS UNCONSTITUTIONAL

Nowhere was this ideal of the national heritage left to us by the Founding Fathers expressly implied so well and in such a forceful manner as it was by Edmund Burke, in 1790:

"But one of the first and most leading principles on which commonwealth and the laws are consecrated, is lest the temporary possessors and life-renters in it, unmindful of what they have received from their ancestors, or of what is due to their posterity, should act as if they were the entire masters; that they should not think it amongst their rights to cut off the entail, or commit waste on the inheritance, by destroying at their pleasure, the whole original fabric of their society; hazarding to leave to those who come after them, a ruin instead of a habitation — and teaching these successors as little to respect their contrivances as they themselves respected the institutions of their forefathers. By this unprincipled facility of changing the state, as often, and as much, and in as many ways as there are floating fancies or fashions, the whole chain and continuity of the commonwealth would be broken. No one generation could link with another. Men would become little better than the flies of a summer." (From "Reflections on the Revolution in France.")

The 1965 Immigration Reform Act written by Constitutional Anarchist Socialists is indeed based upon "floating fancies or fashions."

Before this bill was passed, 89 percent of the population of the United States was of Western European, Christian origin. Since passage of the bill, 90 percent of immigration is from non-Western, non-Christian countries. Given the cultural heritage left to us by the Founding Fathers, we need to ask the question: WHY? Why the drastic change? Why did Lyndon Johnson sign into law on October 3, 1965, a bill that seeks to undermine our Founding Fathers cultural inheritance? Why did the United States from that day onwards have to open its doors to every nation on earth — and their extended families — nations who have absolutely no cultural heritage in common with the Founding Fathers America?

In his book, "A Turn to the South," V.S. Naipaul shows conclusively that it is not only whites who are concerned about the catastrophe in the making. Blacks also are very uneasy about this new mass migration of other cultures and other people not of Founding Fathers stock and origin. One of the first to voice concerns about the Federal Government intervention with the rights of the States to resist such policies, was the late Senator Sam Ervin, one of the greatest constitutional scholars of the 20th century. On pages E7552-E7554, Congressional Record, Senate, August 22 1968, Ervin states:

"The Supreme Court found something new in the 14th Amendment that said the people of California cannot repeal their own open occupancy law enacted. In another, most amazing case, the court held in Katzenbach vs. Morgan that the 14th Amendment empowers Congress to abolish New York's English language voter requirement and substitute it for a newly created Federal voting qualification, even though the Court conceded that the English language requirement was reasonable and non-discriminatory."

Here we see the Federal Government busily undermining States rights, especially the 10th Amendment, and even more ominous, we see newly arrived non-European, non-Founding Fathers groups seeking "rights" for their languages and customs. In another equally astonishing case, Kevishon vs. the Board of Regents in New York City and in the Robel case, the Court held it "constitutional" for Communists to teach in our schools. This was done at the behest of constitutional anarchists who were not judges but "Social Fixers" appointed by Socialist Franklin D. Roosevelt, to circumvent the Constitution. I refer to Justices Frankfurter, Fortas, Douglas, Black, Warren, Burger, and later,

Eisenhower appointee Brennan, among others, who perfectly fit the definition, "Social Fixers."

No wonder that the New York State Commissioner of Education said, "we are becoming a different people." If we examine immigration population statistics, there emerges the inescapable fact that unless the trend is halted immediately, by the year 2085 — a scant 88 years from now, America will have been transformed into an Asian/Hispanic/Other/nation in which Founding Fathers Americans will be a minority — absolutely not what the Founding Fathers intended, nor is it what the African American population wants. It was Clinton himself who gleefully expressed his satisfaction with this prospect in a recent television news broadcast.

What is the aim of the constitutional anarchist-communists-Socialists and Nihilists? In short, it is to drown the nation founded by the framers of the Constitution in a flood-tide of peoples of a different racial and ideological background who were not included in the Declaration of Independence, the Bill of Rights and the U.S. Constitution. A fearlessly outspoken Judge Roger Taney, the most learned and incorruptible judge ever to grace a judicial bench, made the intention of the Founding Fathers crystal-clear. Page 3216, Congressional Globe:

"The words 'people of the United States' and 'citizens' are synonymous terms and mean the same thing. They both describe the political body who, according to our republican institutions, form the sovereignty and hold the power and conduct of Government through their representatives...They are what we familiarly call 'the sovereign people' and every citizen is one of these people and a constituent membership of this sovereignty. The question before us is whether the class of persons described in this plea abatement compose a portion of this people and are constituent members of this sovereignty? We think not. They were not included and were not intended to be included under the word 'citizens' in the Constitution and cannot claim the rights and privileges which the instrument provides for a secure United States..."

The granting of citizenship to such persons would fall in with the plans of the constitutional anarchists, changing forever the way the United States was envisaged and construed by the Founding Fathers through the Constitution, in a manner most detrimental to their expressed wishes and desires. We are duty-bound to face up to reality: Such changes are already having the most profound consequences for

our national heritage. America has nothing to do with Asian-Indian cul-
ture, or Zulu culture, or Kurdistan culture, or Taiwanese culture, or
Congolese culture or Vietnamese culture. America of the Founding
Fathers had one culture in mind, that being Western Christian culture.

Not that we have anything against these other nations and their culture; it is simply not America's culture and America has nothing in common with Mahatma Ghandi's philosophies which are an anathema to our
Declaration of Independence, our Constitution and the manner in which
the Founding Fathers structured the United States. What communion do
we have with these people? The answer is none, yet it is they who will
have the majority, not us, by the year 2085. It is they who will have the
majority, and the Socialist/Marxist/Communists are looking forward to
the day when they will be able to destroy the Constitution by way of
constitutional amendments, voted on by democratic mob rule, people
totally in ignorance of the Constitution. That was, of course, the intent
and purpose of the sponsors of the 1965 Immigration Reform Act.

The deceitful Immigration Reform Act of 1965 was deliberately
written to change the racial oneness and identity of the United States.
Whenever we see the word "reform" we can be sure that the
Communists are hard at work underground, helped by the miners and
sappers of the judicial branch. Unlimited diversity is not wonderful for
this country. It is a wreckers ball. Yet, we who have the most to lose have
been silenced by threats of "race hatred" prosecutions, a bill of attainder
forbidden by the Constitution. Our right to free speech has been trodden
underfoot by smears of "bigots" and "racists." Nationally, we are afraid
to exercise the right of free speech handed down to us by our Founding
Fathers lest we fall foul of the ACLU.

As Sen. Ervin pointed out during the debate on the 1965 bill, it did-
n't eliminate discrimination against other nationals but it ushered in a
new era of discrimination against immigrants from Western Europe.
Ervin said most emphatically that it was right and proper to defend the
immigration quotas of Western European Christian nations against the
inroads of non-Founding Fathers nations. He emphasized again and
again; it was the former who had built America. No one chose to smear
Sen. Ervin with "racist" epithets at the time he made his profound observations, and none dare do it today. *The Act also discriminates against
African-Americans.*

Before 1965, in spite of the efforts of the Roosevelt constitutional anarchist "fixers," the bulk of immigrants — 89 percent — were still coming from Western Europe. But in 1965, the trend was reversed: we now have 90 percent of legal immigrants coming from non-Christian non-Western non-European countries. This amazing number of what I call non-Founding Fathers immigrants is twice the number of immigrants allowed *by all other countries of the world, combined.* America's *national* suicide immigration policy has got to be halted immediately. It is that, or death of the nation as structured by the Founding Fathers.

Constitutional anarchists would have us believe that America is merely a political entity, and in the words of one of the purveyors of this notion, Justice Cruz Reynoso of the California Supreme Court: "America is not a cultural, linguistic, religious or racial union." That being the case, why not admit Iranians, Ghanaians, Algerians, Brahmins, Congolese, Sudanese, Moroccans, Indonesians, Tibetans, Zulus, Libyans, Mongolians, Berbers, Taurags, Sinhalese, and every nation on earth, and why not let us have a Federal Tower of Babel Civil Rights Division for all languages each with equal rights to see that none is "discriminated" against?

In 1921 Congress passed a national origin quota with the intention of slowing down the rush of non-Founding Fathers immigrants from Eastern Europe. The act was not disguised in any way: It was intended to secure for posterity that immigrants coming from Western European Christian nations remain in the majority. It was intended to preserve America's composition, reconfirmed by the McCarren-Walter Act of 1952, which substantially limited immigration from countries outside of Western European Christian countries. Asian countries were limited to 100 persons a year, but "refugees" swelled their numbers by thousands more.

What could be clearer than the 1921 national origin quota laws? Was Judge Taney a "bigoted racist?" Or was he merely spelling out what the Founding Fathers and the framers of the Constitution held desirable for the United States? Under the Taney ruling, none of the masses of non-Western European "immigrants" who have flooded these shores since Franklin Roosevelt-packed the Supreme Court, could be included in "We the People."

Washington Times writers Sam Francis and Paul Craig Roberts, see the problem in this light. Roberts wrote a piece in which he said:

"Not since the Roman Empire was overrun by illegal aliens in the

fifth century has the world experienced the massive population movements of recent years." Both writers talk about the growing danger of
"Third Worldization of America's cities;" Roberts says that in excess of
3 million illegal aliens come to the United States each year. And they
probably have five million children or more, swelling the total to at least
eight million a year.

Immigration, more so legal immigration, is the most pressing problem of the late 1990s, and if the United States does not scrap the
Immigration Reform Act of 1965, we will end up with untold millions
of non-Founding Fathers immigrants denied entry into France, Britain,
Germany, Spain and the Scandinavian countries. With populations of the
non-European nations doubling every 25 years, what we are looking at
is a veritable nightmare scenario. The 1965 Immigration Reform Act is
an invitation to the world at large to send their unwanted human cargoes
to our shores at the cost of Founding Fathers Americans.

When pushing his bill S500, Senator Edward Kennedy blatantly and
purposefully lied about the intentions of the measure:

"...Contrary to the charges in some quarters, S500 will not inundate
America with immigrants from any one country or area, or the most populated and economically deprived nations of Africa and Asia...In the
final analyses, the ethnic pattern of immigration under the proposed
measure, is not expected to change sharply as the critics seem to think."

Yet, that is exactly what has happened. Kennedy knew it; he was
lying to the Senate and the American people and he did it deliberately
and with full knowledge that he was lying. Kennedy is a consummate,
professional liar and a man who can never be trusted. Another Socialist
liar was Nicholas Katzenbach, an unelected official who announced to
the Senate subcommittee on immigration that the object of the bill was
to eliminate the national origins quota system, but not to increase immigration. What right did Katzenbach have to change our national origin
quota system? The answer was that he had absolutely no right to do any
such thing, but he did it just the same:

"We don't care about the place or circumstances of your birth.
(Ignoring the Founding Fathers). What we care about is what you can
contribute." This was conniving deception at its worst. Naturally, the
Founding Fathers would have cared about the national origin of the
flood of immigrants. This was of paramount importance to the survival
of their descendants. Added to the problems raised by the 1965 Act was

the provision that allowed admittance of hundreds of thousands of relatives in unprecedented numbers. They came from China and other Asian countries (particularly India and Pakistan) and the percentage of Christian Western Europeans (and families) fell to less that four percent of the total.

Bill S 500 is a national disaster for Founding Fathers Americans. To this day there is no ceiling on these extended families, which in the case of Asians (especially Indians and Pakistanis) runs into hundreds of members per family. This has created an immigration situation which will lead to the demise of Founding Fathers America in a short space of time. Family preference continues to hog immigration quotas and 99.9 percent of the quotas are allocated to non-Western European, non-Christian countries.

Western European Christian countries have been blanked out by immigrants from China, India, Nigeria, Vietnam, Mexico and Korea. Surely this is discrimination against Western European Christian nations? Senator Ervin, a voice crying in the wilderness, took on Socialist traitor, Secretary of State Dean Rusk, and this is what transpired:

Senator Ervin: "That racial and national origin discrimination, I think it is a very important thing for us to pursue...The fact that the McCarren-Walter Act gives preference to these ethnic groups I have mentioned (Western Europeans) is the objection to it, isn't it?"

Secretary Rusk: "Yes, as opposed to others all over the world."

What an audacious admission by yet another *unelected* official! What obligation was there upon American citizens of Western European descent who populated and made great the United States, the people whose national origin was the underlying reason for the success of the United States; what reason was there for them to be looked upon as second-class citizens to make way for immigrants from non-European, non-Christian countries; those who had contributed exactly nothing to the success of the United States?

They were a thousand miles apart and alien to it. Their cultures had no conception of such things as liberty and justice for all. They had absolutely no idea what the Constitution was about. The ideals of the Constitution were and are, foreign to them, and will forever so remain. There was no reason for traitor Rusk to be concerned about such alien nations.

Senator Ervin: "Mr. Secretary, do you know of any people in the world that have contributed more to making America than those groups?" (Western Europeans.) In other words, you take the English-speaking people; they gave us our language, they gave us our common law, they gave us a large part of our political philosophy...The reason I say this bill is discriminatory against these people is because it puts them on exactly the same plane as the people of Ethiopia are put, where the people of Ethiopia have the same right to come to the United States under this bill as the people from England, the people of France, the people of Germany, the people of Holland, and I don't think...I don't know any contributions that Ethiopia has made to the making of America."

Now Senator Ervin could have said exactly the same thing about China, Zululand, Nigeria, Iran, India, Pakistan, and Egypt, and no one in their wildest dreams would have called this distinguished constitutional scholar a "racist." Continuing in the same vein, Sen. Ervin stated:

"The point I am making is, we discriminate in every day in every phase of life, we discriminate in law, we make them in our personal actions, we discriminate in our opinions...we discriminate by the girls we marry, choose one and object to the other, or they object to us. The only possible charge of discrimination in the McCarran-Walter Act is that it discriminates in favor of the people who made the greatest contribution to America, (the Christian white Western European races) and this bill puts them on the same plane as everybody else on earth."

"I do not think you could draft an immigration bill in which you do not discriminate. I think discrimination is ordinarily the exercise of intelligence to make conscious choices...we always discriminate, only the basis of it is different, each of us thinks our way is wise and right...I think there is a rational basis and a reasonable basis to give preference to Holland over Afghanistan, and I hope I am not entertaining a very iniquitous thought when I entertain that honest opinion."

In his statement of fact, Sen Ervin lifted the debate above and beyond where it could be called "racist" or "bigoted." But an honest opinion in favor of Founding Father Western European immigrants was the last thing the constitutional anarchists, the Communists in control of the Democrat Party wanted to hear, and so the wisdom of the great constitutional scholar Ervin, was lost in the irrational, irresponsible babble from the Tower of Babel — as was the intention of the Socialist-Communist constitutional anarchists.

Sen. Ervin did not need to make an apology then and none is needed today. In fact his statement should have reverberated across the land.
Millions should have heard it, but it got buried in the Congressional
Record. We must recognize for once and for all, above the Socialist slan-
der and name-calling: America has the moral and legal right and obligation to control immigration on one basis and one basis only, that basis
being its distinctive Western European Christian make-up, its English
language, its cultural heritage which produced the Founding Fathers and
the Constitution, the Declaration of Independence, the Bill of Rights.

I will say it more than once in this book; when we read or hear the
word "reform," then we know we are dealing with Constitutional anar-
chist-socialist nihilist change-agents, whose motives are always inimical
to the best interests of the United States. Among such malevolent
Constitutional Anarchists were Dean Rusk and Nicholas Katzenbach,
the "reformers" of the 1965 Immigration Act. They used Kennedy as
their tool. That was Kennedy's sole function in the Senate and he would
not have lasted five minutes had he not obeyed his masters.

Although Sen. Ervin chose an African country to make his point, he
could have chosen any non-Western European, non-Christian nation.
Starting in the 1880s, a conscious attempt was made to exclude Asians
from coming to the United States. In 1943 a quota of 100 per Asian
country was set, and the McCarran Act of 1952 further reinforced the
intention of the Founding Fathers by limiting to 2000 the total number
of Asians admitted in any one year from all Asian countries. It was principally this stumbling block to the Socializing of America that socialist
constitutional anarchists Dean Rusk, Kennedy and Katzenbach sought to
remove.

To disguise what they were doing, the Socialists had every left wing
professor, every newspaper and magazine in the country, and the three
main television stations begin to extol the virtues of "multiculturalism."
Now, bear in mind, this is an old Communist trick taken straight out of
the pages of the Communist Manifesto of 1848: destroy and break down
the national character, thereby weakening the country's national sovereignty and make it ripe for a takeover. The left wing mouthpiece for
Communism, "The Nation" put it this way:

"America is being overrun by immigrants. In one sense, of course,
this is true, but in that sense it has been true since Christopher Columbus
arrived. Except for the real Native Americans, we are a nation of immi-

grants...Much of the anti-immigration fervor is directed against the undocumented, but they make up only 13 percent of all immigrants residing in the United States..."

The point is not that the illegal immigrants make up "only 13 percent" but that they are here at all. How can we defend people who break our laws and continue to break them by excusing them because they are a small percentage of the total? To do this is to miss the point. In California these lawbreakers are costing the State in excess of $3.6 billion annually. That is a huge sum of money by any standards. The question is: Why should the situation be tolerated at all? The simple answer is, it shouldn't. To quote Alexander Hamilton:

"Where, then, is the virtuous pride that once distinguished Americans? Where the indignant spirit, which in defense of principal, hazarded a revolution to attain that independence, now insidiously attacked?"

Where indeed, when no national outcry followed the outrageous "reforms" to immigration slammed through the legislature in 1965 without public debate and without We, the People, ever having had a chance to gainsay the Socialist-Communist Democrat constitutional anarchists? A most profound event occurred in 1965, one that forever changed the face of Western Christian America. Had a foreign army invaded the United States in 1965, it could not have accomplished as much nor done as much damage as Katzenbach, Rusk and Kennedy accomplished, and it was done without firing a shot. So subtle, so evil was the this attack that few appeared to notice it. Imagine how Americans would have rallied to repel invading armies from India, Pakistan, China, etc?

Moreover, instead of the so-called melting pot, what is developing in the U.S. is multiculturalism in which each group seeks to keep to its own habits and customs, all the time demanding "equal rights" for its culture. In effect, the United States has become an extension of China, India, Haiti, Nigeria, Mexico, Pakistan. Is this what the Founding Fathers intended? That America should be Balkanized? I seriously doubt it.

Supreme Court Justice Stephen Field noted this in 1884 when he wrote that the Chinese "have remained among us a separate people, retaining their original peculiarities of dress, manners, habits, and modes of living which are as marked as their complexion and language." Five years later, he upheld the exclusion of Chinese immigrants. Can it be said of Justice Field that he was a "racist?" I believe not. He was, after all, looking to preserve America's Anglo-Saxon, Nordic Alpine, Franco, Germanic heritage, in the best traditions of the Founding Fathers.

This does not mean depriving the American Indian and Negro of their rights. They must continue to enjoy full protection and all rights accorded the majority. Those of other races who are admitted, however, must be absolutely willing to adopt the civilization and the heritage and the English language of the Founding Fathers as African-Americans have done and not try to start their own colonies inside the United States. And there must be no more immigration allowed from countries other than Western European countries.

It is now politically correct to talk of multiculturalism as a benefit. But what nation has been able to survive an infusion of many different cultures and survive as the ORIGINAL nation? Neither ancient Rome or Greece were able to survive "multiculturalism" and neither will the United States, which is, of course, the goal of the constitutional anarchists based upon the Communist Manifesto of 1848. And in pushing multiculturalism, our Founding Fathers heritage is constantly under attack, and this is going on in our schools.

Look at the report from the New York State Commissioner of Education, which is titled: "A Curriculum of Inclusion." It states: "African Americans, Asian Americans, Puerto Ricans and Native Americans — the Socialist name for American Indians — have all been oppressed. This oppression consists of the fact that a systematic bias toward European culture and its derivatives (has) a terribly damaging effect on the psyche of young people of African, Asian, Latino and Native American descent."

To correct this alleged "oppression" — and it is worth mentioning that this kind of thing is not encountered in the schools of Britain, Denmark, Germany and France, but only in the United States — Asian, Hispanic and African history and culture must be "equally valued." Why not then equally value the culture of the Zulus, the Malays, the Papuans, Pathans, Hottentots, Bushmen, Iranians, Ugandans, Kurds, the Sudanese, Kenyans, Mongols, Tibetans, Laotians; the Libyans, the Algerians, the Sudanese? Why limit "equally valued" culture?

Of course what the report really means is that "equality" is to be achieved through a never-ending attack on Western European Founding Fathers Americans and a constant vilification of all that our Western

European descendants left for posterity, with constant concessions —
giving up their constitutional rights — by the original Founding Fathers
group. The Pilgrims are explained away as the product "individuals and
nations that were ready to 'discover' and invade and conquer foreign
land because of greed, racism and national egoism."

The "inclusion equality" idea burst upon the education scene like an
out-of-control forest fire, and of course, it is very much related to immigration, because if carried to its logical conclusion it calls for more and
more non-Western European non-Christian nationals to be allowed into
the United States, to redress the "inequality oppression." The intention
is clearly to blot out the Western European heritage entrusted to the
United States by our Founding Fathers. This we cannot permit.

Writer Molefi Kete Kamiya says: "There is no common American
culture as claimed by the defenders of the status quo," read U.S.
Constitution. "There is a hegemonic culture to be sure, pushed as it were
as a common culture." This is a more forthright view of "multiculturalism" which past civilizations show, fragmented into different cultures. It
does not unite, but rather divides a nation. Veering away from his praise
of multiculturalism, Kamiya finally concludes as follows:

"It is an inescapable fact that throughout most of the history of the
West, a constellation of forces, including but not limited to sexism" (a
modern inflexible-word invention of the Socialists and taken directly out
of the hard core Communist Kollontay's writings) "and racism, largely
restricted cultural access to European males of the upper classes. But
one can deplore that, and still return with ever-renewed wonders to the
great achievements of the Western tradition — a tradition, as many
observers have pointed out, that itself created the freedom that allows its
opponents to attack it." This is precisely what the great constitutional
scholar Ervin told the disreputable constitutional anarchists, Edward
Kennedy and Dean Rusk.

Social scientist Andrew Hacker is quoted by Kamiya as believing,
"America is two nations" and law professor Derrick Bell says that
"racism is permanent and that American society is racist in its essence."
Kamiya goes on to say: "If this is true, it logically follows that if whites
refuse to acknowledge that they are racist, they are in denial...(which is)
taken as prima facia evidence of racism." These quotations from the left
show just how difficult it is to lift the issues posed by unlimited, uncontrolled immigration spawned by the 1965 Immigration Reform Act,

above a name-calling level, and to deal with it, without falling foul of so-called "race laws" and "hate crimes." (Not mentioned in the Constitution and Bill of Rights, expost facto and violation of a bill of attainder and therefore a prohibition of "hate crimes.)

Senator Ervin's position was that the United States could not afford to depart from its existing Western European culture and racial make up, but the enemies of the United States had other goals in mind. Edward Kennedy, one of the constitutional anarchist's most radical, most rabid members whose "Bible" is the Communist Manifesto of 1848, lied to the committee on which Ervin sat:

"...S500 would make no such radical changes...But the extreme case should set to rest any fears that this bill will change the ethnic, political or economic make up of the United States."

Yet, a scant 31 years after Kennedy uttered his lie, there IS an extreme change in the ethnic, political, and economic make-up of the United States, the end of which is not yet in sight. The immigration issue is not behind us, it lies ahead of us, to paraphrase France's minister of immigration affairs. In reply to further question by Sen Ervin, Labor Secretary Willard Wirtz — another unelected official, said:

"I just want to make this point because the argument that the cultural pattern of the U.S. will change needs to be answered. Our cultural pattern will never be changed as far as America is concerned."

Again, this was a monumental falsehood and Wirtz must have known it. As for Dean Rusk, his reason for opening the immigration doors wide to other nations was that we had offended some of them. He said our relations with Asian countries was being damaged by our immigration laws, and he went on to assure the committee: "We're not complaining about numbers but about the principal of total exclusion which they considered discriminatory." Here Rusk uttered an outrageous lie.

Rusk further assured the committee that the bill would not result in massive Asian immigration to the United States, another flat-out lie which Rusk uttered knowing it to be utterly false and misleading. Rusk assured the committee — and it was likely that he was committing perjury at the time — that the United States would not be asked to take in more than 16,000 Asian immigrants a year.

Yet, by 1985, Asian immigration reached 250,000 a year. Unless this is checked, by the year 2035 we will have an Asian population of 9.86 million, or put another way, an increase of 600 percent in the number of

Asian immigrants over 35 years. No nation can stand that kind of a dilu-
tion and still survive as an original nation. What would happen to France
if almost 10 million Asians were admitted to that country? France would
no longer be France! Why not just admit 10 million Iranians, Turks,
Kurds and Zulus, Patagonians, Tibetans, Algerians, Berbers, Bushmen,
Hottentots, and Papuans while we are at it? Why stop at Asians being
allowed unlimited entry into the United States? Isn't that discriminating
against other nations?

We need to pause and take note of the type of ammunition used
against those who would seek to bring the truth about immigration to the
American people. They are falsely accused of harassment, intimidation,
and the favorite, discrimination, all flexible words turned inflexible by
the Communist and anarchists. Let me say that not one of these words is
in the Constitution, yet they are used by courts on a regular basis as if
they were. Take the fatuous House Bill 2703. This bill purports to prohibit certain kinds of harassment against a person because of his or her
race, color, religion, ancestry, sex, marital status, national origin, etc.
What utter madness has a hold of us?

We find none of these words mentioned in the Constitution, so they
are a *prohibition,* and, therefore, there can be no laws built upon them.
Such laws are merely hypotheses heaped upon hypotheses. Where do we
find the word "harassment" in the Constitution.? It just isn't there, yet a
law is built around it because of the wishes of star-gazing incendiary liberals who know nothing about constitutional law.

The Communist Manifesto of 1848 specializes in a play on words,
so that the word "harass" can mean anything. Today, constitutional anarchist Charles Schumer and Clinton use the word "terror" in the same
indiscriminate way, even though it is NOT in the Constitution. It was the
Communists who started the use words like "discrimination, intimidation and harassment." Another Communist word is "desegregation."
None of these words are found in the Constitution; thus they are inhib-
ited by the Constitution. So many of the so-called "civil rights" laws are
based on the 14th Amendment, but the 14th Amendment for instance
never mentions "race" as a condition for equal protection of the law, nor
can anything be based upon it, because the 14th Amendment was never
ratified. This is a mere excuse to make a case for "special rights" for
immigrants not of the Founding Fathers Western European races.

The 1965 Immigration Reform Act goes a long way toward fulfilling Socialist dreams and aspirations, as explained by Kotkin and Kishimoto, who demanded that the U.S. forget its Western European-British history and "pay more attention to Asian history and culture." Without giving one single valid reason why the United States, in violation of its Western European Christian culture and heritage, should aspire to be a "world nation?"

The 1965 Immigration Reform Act was revolutionary and only Senator Ervin stood like Horatio at the Bridge trying to hold back the flood tide from India, Asia, Africa, South America. This far-reaching piece of constitutional anarchy legislation escaped public scrutiny and public debate. In contravention of the Constitution, We, the People, were not given any say or allowed to participate in what should have been a national debate. States rights were also utterly, violated. This Act must be repealed post-haste. Above all, the 1965 immigration act is illegal. It would have required a constitutional amendment properly ratified by the States, to become law.

The tragedy of the 1965 Immigration Reform Act is that We, the People, were allowed absolutely no input, no say in the matter, of how we want our country to look by the year 2085. The measure should have been put forward as a constitutional amendment. Using arbitrary power, forbidden by the Constitution, the Democrat (Communist) Party majority in the House and Senate, without public participation in the debate or consultation, brought about a revolution in the United States. It was one of the dirtiest, most sneaky below the belt blows ever dealt to this nation by Dean Rusk and his fellow Constitutional Anarchists and shows just why democracy has such a history of failure. History shows that diversity weakens nations, and eventually, it is their undoing. This will happen in the U.S. unless we take decisive action against the enemies who constantly threaten U.S. sovereignty.

To the rest of the world, America is typified by what theologian Will Herberg said:

"The American's image of himself is still the Anglo-American ideal it was at the beginning of our independent existence. The "national type" as ideal has always been and remains pretty well fixed. It is the Mayflower, John Smith, Davy Crockett, George Washington and Abraham Lincoln that define America's self image, and this is true whether the American in question is a descendant of the Pilgrims or the grandson of an immigrant from Eastern Europe."

This was the vision of the Founding Fathers also, who had nothing to do with Mahatma Ghandi or some other Indian leaders or foreigners. To pretend that the United States can have "multiculturalism" and still be a Founding Fathers nation, is without merit and is the product of the Socialist incendiary star-gazers. "Multiculturalism" has a history of violent failure as one of the worst aspects of democracy by mob rule. Cultural diversity is a myth; it can never be sustained. It is a vacuous idea to repeat parrot-fashion, "this country was built on diversity." It was *not!* If there was any diversity, it was contained in the mold and form of differences among the family of Western European Christian nations. Non-Western, non-Christian nations were never considered by the Founding Fathers. They never featured in the discussions of the framers of the Constitution; in any case such an idea would have been rejected, outright, even if non-Western people had been a part of the population in 1776.

Just in case we think that those other races now flooding the country are on par with our Western European ancestry, see what John Lukacs, an Hungarian-born immigrant had to say on the issue:

"...the English-speaking character of the United States must not be taken for granted...The still extant freedoms of Americans — all Americans — are inseparable from their English-speaking roots...The freedoms granted by the Constitution and the consequent prosperity and relative stability of the country flowing therefrom — were not abstract liberties, but English liberties, dependent on practical as well as sentimental attachments and habits of English law."

Thus it follows that these English-speaking roots and branches are what developed the country and made it a great, strong national tree. There is nothing in common here with the customs of India or China, Kurdistan, Zululand, Thailand, Pakistan or Nigeria, Mongolia, Punjabi, or Tibet, for example. Now come the diversitists and they tell us: "You have to forget about your West European, Anglo Saxon heritage," but they make no effort to explain why we must eschew our heritage, nor do they tell us that the attachments and habits of Western European traditions have nought to do with Indians (Asian Indians), Malays, Chinese, Kurds, Zulus, nor that these distinctly Anglo-Saxon traditions are barely understood by the other non-European nationalities.

There is already a denial that there is such a thing as our Anglo-Saxon heritage. Americans are not being given the facts. Uncontrolled immigration made possible by the 1965 Immigration Reform Act has led to a moral decline. A divided society is making for the degeneration of morality from which we will not recover. Liberals point to the recovery of France after the French Revolution, but that was only possible because France continued to be a single nation; its people were French, not a mixture of almost every other nation on earth as is the case with America of the 1990s. As Christopher Lasch put it in his work, "The Obsolescence of Left and Right" published in 1989, America is continuing "the slide into apathy, hedonism and moral chaos." There will be no return from this condition unless drastic measures are adopted to end mass immigration from non-Western European countries — legal and otherwise, without a moment's delay.

We have already seen in California what will be the fate of the United States, where the totally out-of-proportion numbers of non-Western European immigrants are causing a collapse of the State and where Western European Founding Fathers Americans are soon to be in the minority. The American Control Foundation and the Federation of American Immigration Reform (FAIR) have joined forces to try and awaken Americans to the danger of the Communist-inspired Immigration Reform Act of 1965:

"A traditional moralist may object asserting, 'I am my brother's keeper.' We must ask him: And what about your children? And your children's children? What about the children of your neighbor next door? Must we subsidize and distribute our patrimony among all children of all the world? Americans are already outnumbered twenty-to-one by the rest of the world. Our grandchildren will be outnumbered even more. Must we condemn them to the poverty of an absolutely equal distribution? How would that benefit them or the descendants of other people? Total poverty can be avoided if only people agree that the ancient admonition, 'Charity begins at home' is still the best guide to philanthropic action."

Only by informed opinion can this issue be made into the hottest political issue, one the Republican majority in the House will be forced to confront. As "Washington Times" staff writers Samuel Francis and Paul Craig Roberts put it: "Let's regain control of our borders...Not since Genghis Khan rode out of the Asian steppes has Western-Europe and the United States encountered such an alien invasion... Not since the Roman Empire was overrun by illegal aliens in the fifth century has the world experienced such massive population movements of recent years."

A recommended reading is Martin Van Creveld's "The Transformation of War." Author Van Creveld shows in stark, grim reality, the consequences of allowing the 1965 Immigration Reform Act to remain in force. To continue to allow millions of non-traditional non-Founding Fathers nations to send their excess populations to the United States is a guaranteed suicidal policy. The cultural and economic fault lines of the United States are already rupturing!

In their book "Citizenship Without Consent," Peter H. Schuk and Roger M.Smith state that we need to change the current utterly false notion that the Fourteenth Amendment gives automatic citizenship to children born in the United States of illegal aliens. This gross distortion has no constitutional basis. Congressional Record, Senate, March 1926, pages 327-329:

"The Constitution has established citizenship in this Republic in which race questions are not present and cannot be introduced. (Therefore no so-called civil rights act can introduce race as a group or any other group, either.) The proclamation of the Constitution is: "All persons born or naturalized in the United States, and subject to the jurisdiction thereof, are citizens of the United States and to the States wherein they reside." The term, "and subject to the jurisdiction thereof," rules out children born on U.S. soil of parents who are illegal aliens, as such illegal aliens are not "subject to the jurisdiction thereof (the United States) or "the State wherein they reside."

Under unbearable pressures from constitutional anarchists Dean Rusk, Franklin Roosevelt, the Kennedys, Metzenbaum, Boxer and Feinstein, Americans of the traditional Founding Fathers, Davy Crockett, George Washington, Daniel Webster, Patrick Henry, have been denied their cultural heritage ever since the advent of the 1965 Immigration Reform Act; in short, they are discriminated against and today, we stand at the point so clearly defined by Alexander Hamilton in 1802:

"The safety of our republic depends essentially on the energy of a common national sentiment; on a uniformity of principles and habits; on the exemption of the citizens from foreign bias and prejudice; and on that love of country which will most invariably be found to be closely connected with birth, education, family. The opinion...is correct that foreigners will generally be apt to bring with them attachments to the persons left behind; to the country of their nativity, and to its particular customs and manners...The influx of foreigners must, therefore, tend to produce a heterogeneous compound; to change and corrupt the national spirit; to complicate and confound public opinion; to intrude foreign propensities. In proportion to their numbers, they will share with us the legislation. They will infuse into it their spirit, warp and bias, its direction, and render it a heterogeneous, incoherent, distracted mass... Suppose 20 million republican Americans were thrown all of a sudden into France, what would be the condition of the kingdom? If it would be more turbulent, less happy, less strong, we believe that the addition of half a million foreigners to our present numbers would have the same effect here."

Again, the 1965 Immigration Reform Act will bring about the very conditions which Hamilton warned so strongly against, in less than a hundred years from now. Had Hamilton made his very valid arguments against non-Founding Fathers immigration today, he would have been hailed before the Courts on charges of "hate crimes" and called a "racist" and a "bigot," the two most inflexible words the Communists love to use against traditional Americans — and by now you know what I mean by this term.

Are Hamilton's observations "racism?" Or "bigotry?" No, they are mere intellectual common sense and let us not forget that the basis of the Constitution of the United States is common sense. We have seen the problems unleashed by the Federal Government rashly giving privileges to other cultures, simply because they are in the minority. The Voting Rights Act, the establishment of the Department of Education, the Civil Rights Act and Affirmative Action; these things have torn and rent the fabric of American society. They have not made of us "One Nation Under God" nor engendered feelings of brotherly love. Nor will that ever happen. Instead, to paraphrase Burke, "We have become a nation of summer flies."

Biblical theism is expressed in the Declaration of Independence in the words that God has endowed men with inalienable rights. But this is not the true meaning of the words "inalienable rights." The true meaning is that when the colonists left England, they left behind bad and corrupt laws and took with them the best, most honest, reliable, upright, proper laws with integrity, which they brought to America. This is all the words "inalienable rights" mean.

If America continues as it is at present, we shall have sets of rights for about fifty different cultures and languages, all of which will demand that laws and regulations be printed in their particular language and that their languages must have "equal rights" in schools. We will have radical pluralism in full cry and this will give rise to a new threat to our liberty, by reason of the demands that the inequality of cultures must be overcome by legislation. One cannot begin to imagine what kinds of legal battles are going to arise before the year 2085 over "rights" issues.

What I foresee is an America, sinking into the morass of "rights" in the name of "democratic" multiculturalism and diversity as "cultural equality" swallows up America of Western European Christian white descent, the America of the Founding Fathers. The preposition here is that the Western European Founding Fathers Americans will have to lose their identity in order to grant Hispanics, Chinese, Indians, Laotians, Nigerians, Vietnamese, Zulus, Kurds, Iranians, Tibetans, Mongolians and Filipinos their alleged "rights;" rights which they did nothing to help establish in the early history of the U.S., and a Constitution and Bill of Rights of which they have little or no understanding and care even less about.

If 20 million Americans were forced upon Laotia, Cambodia, Mexico, it would be called "American imperialism." William McDougall's book, "Is America Safe for Democracy" says it better than anything I have encountered:

"As I watch the American nation speeding gaily with invincible optimism down the road to destruction, I seem to be contemplating the greatest tragedy in the history of mankind."

One wonders when Western European Founding Fathers Americans are going to wake up and realize just what is happening to the nation they built on this continent? Immigration is indeed the road to national suicide; its purpose perfectly clear: The United States is being turned into a "global" Third World nation. It is up to We, the People, to decide whether we want to stay on that road or get off it as a matter of extreme urgency.

PROCLAMATIONS, ALSO KNOWN AS "EXECUTIVE ORDERS" ARE UNCONSTITUTIONAL

The Communists festering inside the Congress, the Legislature, the Judiciary and the Executive, have in thousands of instances tried to nullify the U.S. Constitution through the expedient of so-called "executive orders." All U.S. Presidents since Lincoln are guilty of violating their oath of office by issuing "executive orders." It amazes me why this is allowed to stand, year after year, for if the President can act like a

"King," and pass any "law" his heart desires, then what need do we have of a Senate and House of Representatives? If the American people are satisfied with a king in the White House, let us send the Senators and Representatives home and save vast amounts of money!

This is no idle statement. "Executive orders" are *proclamations!* If the President is allowed to get away with issuing proclamations on every whim and fancy that enters his head, then indeed, he assumes the function of a king. The President of the United States has no authority to issue proclamations for he does not stand "where kings stood" to quote Lincoln, who, unfortunately is the father and originator of "executive order" proclamations. "Executive order" proclamations violate the oath of office taken by the President to support and uphold our Constitution and tramples the Constitution and the Bill of Rights underfoot. This makes the President a law-breaker, like any other common criminal, and never was there such a dire need to watch the criminal activities issuing forth from the White House in the form of proclamations, than there is in the term of office of Pres. William Jefferson Clinton.

If we are to uncover the truth about proclamations we have to go to the Founding Fathers, one of whom was Judge St. George Tucker, a soldier-hero of the American Revolution and a professor of law at the William and Mary University. His book, "Blackstone's Commentaries" (title shortened) is the ultimate authority for much of what the Founding Fathers wrote into the U.S. Constitution. Published in 1803, and since that year, mentioned on enumerable occasions in the Congressional Record. Here is what Judge St. George Tucker had to say on the subject of proclamations, on pages 346-347:

"The right of issuing proclamations is one of the prerogatives of the crown of England. No such power being expressly given in the Federal Constitution, it was doubted, upon a particular occasion whether the president possessed any such authority."

About the only thing a U.S. President can proclaim, is in the realm of a day of mourning, a day of Thanksgiving, and this is how George Washington used it. He never, ever, attempted to usurp it for other purposes to which he was not entitled. On page 547:

"But if a proclamation should enjoin any thing to be done, which neither the law of nations, nor any previous act of the legislature, nor any treaty or compact should have made a duty, such an injunction would not only be merely void, but (also) an infringement of the Constitution."

There need be no further discussion as to whether a U.S. President may issue a proclamation, also known as an "executive order" which is not mentioned nor expressly implied in the Constitution in the same way that the word "proclamation" is not mentioned; therefore both "executive order" and "proclamation" are prohibitions of the power, null and void and no law at all and of no effect. The ONLY "executive orders" President Clinton can issue would be to order his White House staff to put their desks in order, come to work on time, and have fresh flowers in his office every day; things of that nature.

We need to strengthen the foregoing contention by noting that the word, "proclamation" was expressly kept out of the Constitution for the reason that the word was always associated with monarchs and the aristocracy of Europe at the time the Founding Fathers were discussing the Constitution, and they deemed it advisable to expressly exclude "proclamations" because of this association, plus the reason that aristocracy and titles of aristocracy are forbidden by the U.S. Constitution. The term, "proclamation," was not abused up until the Civil War, and would most probably never have been abused but for the false step taken by Lincoln. This contention is spelled out in the Congressional Record, Appendix, House, Feb. 12, 1917, under the title, "War Legislation in Lincoln's Time" by William J. Graham, pages 134-137:

"Habeas Corpus — Suspension of the writ, Pres. Lincoln was authorized by an act of March 3, 1863 (12 State. L., 755-758), to suspend the writ of habeas corpus: That during the present rebellion (note the use of the word, rebellion, instead of war) the President of the United States is authorized to suspend the privilege of habeas corpus in any case throughout the United States or any part thereof."

This action was based upon Article 1, Section 9, Clause 2 of the U.S. Constitution. But is was, nevertheless, a clear violation of the Constitution for Lincoln to take this power, and of course he had other powers and did not need to resort to the treachery of proclamations. The misuse of the word "rebellion," whereas it should have been "war," is the key to Lincoln's unconstitutional action. By so doing, Lincoln set himself up as a king, and he knew full-well that what he was doing was a violation of the U.S. Constitution and the Bill of Rights. What is not so well known is that he tried and failed to use the emancipation proclamation to get the slaves of the South to rebel against their masters. It failed because the slaves stayed loyal to their slave owners.

The next power-grabber to come along and take powers not delegated to the government in the Federal Constitution, Sec. 8, Art. 1, Clauses 1-18, was the tool of the Fabian Socialists and the Wall Street bankers and European bankers, Pres. Woodrow Wilson, who issued one proclamation after another, all of them unconstitutional, and on top of his bibulous excesses, he demanded — and got — ten additional powers, to which he was not entitled under the Constitution. The upshot was that the U.S. was dragged into WWI, and Wilson grossly violated his oath of office by sending conscripted National Guard units to battle in France. The sordid story of this weak, blackmailed man, who scores of times broke his oath to uphold and defend the Constitution, for which he should have been impeached, removed from office and hanged for treason, is told in the chapter, "What You Don't Know About the Militia." Wilson was directly responsible for the casualties we suffered in WWI: 115,000 killed, and 206,000 wounded.

After Wilson, came the next major violator-proclamation issuer, the butcher of Hyde Park, Franklin D. Roosevelt, who went further than his predecessors, usurping all of the powers of Pres. Lincoln under habeas corpus, plus the ten powers usurped by Wilson and then several more. One of Roosevelt's anti-constitutional proclamations was taken under a contrived "financial emergency," and there are those who today, still believe in the fable that Roosevelt's War Powers Act, actually suspended the Constitution! Of course not the President, nor the Congress, nor the courts can "suspend the Constitution." There is in fact and in law, no judicial or congressional power that would allow it. Perhaps a dictator could say, "I am suspending the Constitution" but such a statement would be ultra-vires, without any validity and totally, unconstitutional under the American system.

Republican presidents were also guilty of violating their oath of office: Reagan and Bush were not shy about issuing proclamations, and Bush once thought about declaring "martial law" during his private war with Iraq. Perhaps the chief offender when it comes to issuing proclamations is Pres. Clinton. This man thinks nothing of daily trampling over the Constitution and the Bill of Rights, and a weak, divided, leaderless Republican Party majority in the Congress, not only stands aside, but in several instances, actually helps him to break the law. We quite properly punish shoplifters when they are caught, and we think of them as criminals, yet, here is a man who commits the heinous crime of violating the Constitution and the Bill of Rights on an almost daily basis, and he is not called a criminal, a scofflaw, although none is more qualified than violators of the Constitution to be thus branded. Instead, Pres. Clinton goes about his business of wrecking the Constitution without a peep from of the moribund, defunct Republican Party.

Where in the U.S. Constitution does it say that the President can issue a proclamation authorizing a huge land grab? I say, it is nowhere to be found. That is what happened in 1997, when Clinton "set aside" vast tracts of land belonging to the American people under the so-called "The American Heritage Rivers" proclamation. Clinton sealed off lands containing vast deposits of coal and other minerals. The president has no authority to take over lands in Utah belonging to the people of the State of Utah or any other American state. On the basis of a fraudulent proclamation, (they are all fraudulent, only this one is more so than most) an article of impeachment should be issued.

Clinton claims that Teddy Roosevelt gave him the right to act in the manner of a Bolshevik dictator. During his tenure in the White House, Teddy Roosevelt gave us the unconstitutional FBI by proclamation; then he and a man named Gifford Pinchott, conspired together to rob the American people of millions of acres of land by establishing "national parks." Pinchott was the first of many bogus "environmentalists" that followed. Actually, what Roosevelt and Pinchott conspired to do, was to preserve these lands for the exploration of oil which was to follow, so that the lands could never fall under general public use. Roosevelt should have been impeached for his grave crime against the people, but once again there appeared to be no one who knew the U.S. Constitution well enough to charge Roosevelt and Pinchott with high crimes and misdemeanors of which both were guilty a thousand times over.

Thus, the basis of Clinton's claim that he took the power to grab land in Utah from Teddy Roosevelt, is puerile, banal, venal and utterly false. Roosevelt never had any such powers, as he did not have the power to issue proclamations and, in any case, Mr. Clinton as a lawyer must surely know that the acts performed by one president cannot be held over into the term of another. That is why the presumption that the U.S. is still under martial law is untrue; the power of habeas corpus granted to Lincoln *died with him* and was not and could not be carried over into the term of a succeeding president. That is the law! Now let Mr. Clinton obey it, or suffer for his crimes through the process of impeachment.

CHAPTER 8

INTERSTATE COMMERCE CLAUSE

FOOD AND DRUG ADMINISTRATION, CENTRALIZING COMMUNIST
CONTROL OF CHILDREN, GENERAL WELFARE CLAUSE, FOREIGN AID,
TREATY POWERS VIOLATED, LETTER TO SENATOR TRENT LOTT

S tarting in the 1920s the Communists and their fellow-travelers in
the Federal Government have consistently tried to use Article 1,
Sec. 3, Clause 3, "To regulate with foreign nations and among the
several States and the Indian tribes," to mean anything and everything
under the sun. The Congress has surrendered its right to negotiate on foreign commerce to the executive, one of the most damning things it could
have done to the Constitution and which surrender of legislative powers
to the executive is happening more frequently with each passing year, as
part of the Communist drive to centralize power in the hands of a single
central government. In the 1920s the Communists even tried to make
children part of interstate commerce.

The true and only interpretation of the interstate commerce clause is
that its purpose was to appropriate sufficient funding by the House and
Senate, for the building of roads, canals, bridges, and in certain
instances, railroads for the purposes of improving transportation
between the States and thereby facilitating interstate commerce. There is
nothing whatever that would suggest it covers *individual* products, save
and except in the case of guns which are particularly exempted from
being regulated by the interstate commerce clause, both in states
Constitution and the federal Constitution. But the Communists came
along in the 1920s, and with their talent for twisting words, imputing

inflexibility to ordinary meanings of words and grafting on shades of meaning, and by employing every piece of chicanery known to mankind, they tried to make the clause fit personal products and firearms of all types.

Every one of the several States has its own distinctive commerce clause, and generally, each follows the federal constitution but apply laws to commerce only inside State boundaries. And State commerce clauses control rivers, canals, lakes, railroads, highways, and bridges inside the State. Nowhere is it applicable to individual products in States constitutions, any more than it is in the federal Constitution, and as I have already stated, it does not and cannot ever be used regulate firearms. President Monroe was the first to use the act to build roads, notably the Cumberland road project; then came the Erie canal, steam boat regulations applicable to the Mississippi River commerce, railroads, and today, aircraft traffic, radio, television channels.

I could find nothing in the federal interstate clause that concerns itself with individual products. For instance; interstate commerce cannot control canned food products shipped from one State to another and there are literally millions of such items and certainly not firearms which are governed exclusively by the 2nd Amendment. The Communists tried to make out that guns can be regulated by the interstate commerce clause, but show me where it says that in the clause or in any other clause in the Constitution! Would any lawyer, legislator, federal judge, member of the Supreme Court, care to take up this challenge?

In fact, nowhere in the interstate commerce clause is it expressly implied that the Federal Government has the power to regulate guns, or regulate guns under any other clause of the Constitution and there is no expressly implied power written into the commerce clause that would permit it. In fact the Federal Government cannot regulate *anything* under the interstate commerce clause, because products and services originate in the several states and are, therefore, subject to STATE regulations (with the exception of guns) of the States where such goods were produced and or services rendered.

As we see, the Communists constantly try to invoke the Interstate Commerce clause, but the Constitution was never meant to be everything to everybody under the sun, the moon and the stars! They also try to hoodwink the judiciary by isolating the Commerce clause from the rest of the Constitution, thereby destroying its perfect equipoise.

The Communists have fallen back on the cynical position that they can pretty much apply all things they don't like about the system to control by the interstate commerce clause and connived the lawmakers to believe that they can impede, hinder, obstruct and interfere with commerce between the States, which Congress cannot do, as the power is not contained in the delegated powers of the Federal Constitution found in Sec 8., Art. 1, Clauses 1-18, nor is it anywhere expressly implied, and Congress cannot add one period, one comma, nor subtract the same from the Constitution and the Bill of Rights. The Food and Drug Administration (FDA) has even taken to harassing citizens and making them believe that they can restrict their activities in commercial enterprises, to their home State, which is a blatant falsehood. The right to keep and bear arms under the 2nd Amendment is an ancient right which can be traced back to Athenian and Roman law, and can never be abridged, circumvented, or set aside, especially not but trying to bring guns under interstate commerce laws.

THE UNCONSTITUTIONAL FOOD AND DRUG ADMINISTRATION (FDA)

The Persecution of Dr. Burzynski; The Interstate Commerce Clause and Centralizing Child Welfare, Education and Health.

In the first instance there is no mention of the FDA in the Constitution and the Bill of Rights, so it is a prohibition of this term. Therefore, anything the FDA enacts is no law at all because it lacks a constitutional mandate in the same way as the FBI, the BATF and other central government agencies, have no constitutional mandate. How can an unconstitutional body make and enforce laws which are based on authority it does not possess?

The persecution of individuals who do things the FDA does not like needs to be the subject of a Congressional committee hearing. A perfect example of what is under discussion here is the case of Dr. Stanislaw Burzynski, a Houston doctor who has cured hundreds of people of the scourge of cancer. For years, the FDA persecuted this good servant of humanity, for the simple reason that the establishment cancer "treatment" centers did not like the fact that he could do more than slash, cut and burn cancer sufferers, so their FDA watchdog, said Dr. Burzynski's treatment was not acceptable, unethical and unlawful.

Consequently the FDA staged a trumped up charge against Dr. Burzynski, that he had violated federal interstate commerce rules,

Article 1, Section 8, Clause 3: "To regulate with foreign nations and among the States and the Indian tribes," but much to its chagrin, the judge ruled against the FDA — a rare victory for the people over the FDA. The FDA told the court it was acting on a case law precedent they had found in 1880, but a search turned up no such case in the Congressional Record of that year, at least not that I was able to find.

What the State of Texas did was acquiesce to the F.D.A.'s efforts to put up barriers around Texas and say that people could not come from other States to be treated by Dr. Burzynski. In so doing, the F.D.A. and the State of Texas violated another part of the U.S. Constitution, that is to say, they tried to separate the interstate commerce clause from Art. IV, Sec.2, Part 1: "The citizens of each State shall be entitled to all the privileges and immunities of the several States." This relates to the question of State citizenship, over which the Federal Government has no say and absolutely no control.

Even though the 14th Amendment is null and void, it is still cited by the Federal authorities, but the Federal Government cannot have its cake and eat it. In the 14th Amendment it says, inter alia. "... No State shall make and enforce any law which shall abridge the privileges and immunities of the citizens of the United States..." The intent was to make citizens, first, citizens of the United States and then, citizens of the several States. The intent and purpose was of course to protect the civil rights of the Negroes. Now comes the State of Texas egged on by the F.D.A. and Texas says it has the right to "enforce any law which shall abridge the privileges and immunities of any of the citizens of the several States" and then proceeds to interfere with Dr. Burzynski's civil rights and restrict him to Texas and limit him to patients who reside in the State of Texas. This is a bill of attainder and expost facto law of which the State of Texas is guilty, a vile attack on the whole Constitution.

Dr. Burzynski's patients had the right to go to any State they pleased and the interstate commerce clause cannot be used to impede and circumscribe their rights. Those responsible for the prosecution of Dr. Burzynski *must be impeached* and charged with failing to uphold their oath to protect the U.S. Constitution, by bringing a bill of attainder and expost facto law against Dr. Burzynski, and if found guilty, be severely punished and forbidden to serve in any governmental capacity for the rest of their lives. The bottom line is that no so-called Federal judge has any jurisdiction to place limits on the State citizenship of Dr. Burzynski less still to make a bill of attainder and expost facto law against him. Any judge who is guilty of such action, should be impeached and removed from the bench and disqualified for life.

CENTRALIZING CONTROL OF CHILDREN :
A COMMUNIST GOAL SINCE THE 1920S

In the 1920s the Communists in the federal government — and there were hundreds of them — tried to include children under the interstate commerce clause, but they were not successful. Congressional Record, House, July 3, 1926, pages 12918 - 12951 :

"It was not until the Supreme Court held the first child labor law unconstitutional on June 3, 1918 that the "Maternity act drive" started. (It is this line which Mr. and Mrs. Clinton are following today.) And then the campaign for control of subsidies began at once, with the introduction on July 1, 1918 of the original maternity bill (HR 12634-65 Congress) by Miss Jeanette Rankin. Miss Rankin is the field secretary of Mrs Florence Kelly's national Consumer League, since Montana refused to reelect Miss Rankin (for taking blatant Communist positions.) The second national labor law was passed instead, on Feb. 24, 1919..."

"It is noted that all this political campaigning by the Children's Bureau (where the Clintons are coming from) to enlist the National League of Women Voters, the National Women's Party and various women's clubs through the Women's Joint Congressional Committee, in aid of the (Childrens') Bureau drive for complete power over children, took place while the second child labor law was pending before the Supreme Court, with the outcome in doubt, as the Court had already found the first law unconstitutional, May 15, 1923 (Bailey vs. Drexel Furniture Company) the drive for the amendment began, Mrs. Kelley and Miss Abott leading the agitation."

What is worth noting is that Rankin, Kelly and Abbott were about as hard core a Communist threesome as one was likely to find. The similarity between what the were trying to achieve, i.e., centralization of child welfare and standardizing of education and what Mr. and Mrs. Clinton are doing, is so strikingly similar as to require no further explanation.

In any event, the Communists fought hard to make it seem as the interstate commerce clause could be invoked at any time and for any cause they deemed worthy for the furtherance of Communism in the

United States, which would tend to explain much of what has transpired during the Clinton presidency.

On pages 12928 and 12933 of the Congressional Record, House, July 3, 1926 are listed the Communist-front women's organization who enlisted in the battle to centralize child welfare (control) and education:

"The National League of Women Voters; National Consumer's League; Congress of Mothers; Women's Christian Temperance Union; American Association of University Women; National Federation of Professional and Business Women; Parent Teachers Association; Union Girls Friendly Society of America National Women's Trade Union League..."

"The Communists put in a mighty effort to get around the Constitution, but the Supreme Court, totally different in outlook from the Warren Court, stood in the way..." In spite of the fact that the Supreme Court held the view that "the fundamental theory of general liberty upon which all governments (the several Sates) in this Union repose excludes any general power of the State to standardize its children; the Children's Bureau is obsessed with the idea of standardizing connected with children." I hope this makes it clear just what the goal of "standardizing children," which is being pushed by Mr. and Mrs. Clinton remains almost unchanged.

On page 12930:

"But the Constitution of the United States and the Supreme Court (loyal to its oath to uphold the Constitution) stood in the way of direct control by the central government, of education, local health administration, maternity, and other doles, rural and other child labor as in England, in Germany, and before Germany, the Communist Manifesto of 1848. Of the three great Socialist features, 1) equalizing education throughout the Nation, 2) for centralizing of local affairs by a dictatorship (destruction of States rights) and 3) for doles system (today called "Federal aid").

And on page 12936:

"International control of children. Not only did the Childrens' Bureau call for an international conference of foreigners to frame minimum standards for health, education in the United States (Childrens' Bureau Annual Report for 1919) but it has constantly sought to subject American legislation for children to foreign standardization. Hence the Children of the world will be under the protection of the League of Nations..."

I hope we can see the unmistakable origin of the efforts of the Clinton administration, and especially that of Mrs. Clinton — the "Florence Kelly" of our times — and especially how the Clintons are striving to "standardize" children in the true Communist way. Now I hope we can see where Mr. and Mrs. Clinton got the idea to call in the United Nations to interfere with the health, education and welfare of the children of America, and subject them to foreign standards, in gross violation of their States rights in these areas, guaranteed by the 10th Amendment to the U.S. Constitution. If ever there was a case to be made for the impeachment of Pres. Clinton, there is enough evidence in the pages of this portion of the Congressional Record to force him from office.

On Page 12940:

"Now will it be shown that the exact things contained in the child labor amendments are the aims of the economic program of the Communist International at Moscow as well as part of the Socialist program in the Communist Manifesto of 1848 by Marx and Engels."

Let us take note and make sure that we know and understand where the Clinton administration is coming from and where it is trying to go with its centralizing (communizing) of the children of America. This treasonous, traitorous move to communize the children of America must be halted before it goes any further. Now we have Mr. and Mrs. Clinton pushing for the same goals as Miss Rankin, Florence Kelly and Miss Grace Abbot, which stripped of polite words, is simply to make COMMUNISTS of the children of America, supposedly out of concern for their welfare. This mendacious conduct should not impress any one who knows the history of the drive the Communists made in the 1920s to wrest control over children from the States. The Clinton's efforts are manifestly spurious; without any real feeling for children, but rather should be seen for what they are; an attempt to mask what they are really up to; that being to carry on where The Childrens' Bureau left off.

Besides everything else, the Federal Constitution says quite clearly that the welfare of children is the responsibility of the several States as set out in Article 10. Child welfare is part of State's rights and the federal government has no constitutional authority to meddle in the police powers of health, education, welfare and police protection covering States rights in these areas. Mr. and Mrs. Clinton know they have zero authority to go into the several States and claim jurisdiction over the children residing in those States. Let us call their bluff and expose them as agents for International Socialism.

GENERAL WELFARE CLAUSE

The General Welfare Clause is another of those misunderstood clauses in the Constitution and the Bill of Rights. Congress has wasted valuable time trying to "balance the budget" when there is no need for it. The general welfare clause of Article 1, Sec. 8, Clause 1 can be used to correct the problem of overspending. Instead, Congress has tried to make an independent power of Article 1, Section 8, Clause 1, but it is a general clause which relates the powers of clauses 2-17. The Socialists have interpreted this clause to mean that those who need food stamps, rent subsidies, child support, welfare money and "benefits" are entitled to it; and something called the Legal Services Corporation, when in fact the Constitution is silent on these words and therefore the power sought to implement the Socialist notion — for that is all it is — is simply not there! There is not anything the Constitution and the Bill of Rights that says anyone is entitled to these "benefits." Where do the liberals get this word "benefits" in this context? It is not thus stated in the Constitution and the Bill of Rights.

Congressional Record, Senate, Jan. 3, 1924, pages 549-558 is too long to quote here except to say that in it we find a learned discourse about the meaning of the clause, by Judge Story and Judge Ticknor, in which it is concluded that for the Federal Government to engage in individual welfare would require a constitutional amendment to be passed before it could hand out rent subsidies, food stamps, child support, etc., to individuals.

There is no mention of a Legal Services Corporation in the Constitution and the Bill of Rights and 245 members of Congress committed the heinous crime of violating their oath of office, one which our Founding Fathers said should be severely punished. Under this category of a betrayer of the Constitution come those who voted for establishing a Legal Services (Plundering) Corporation, notable among whom were Aucoin, Weaver and Wyden.

The 1st Amendment was subverted by Justice William O. Douglas and government has gone on subverting it ever since. The enumerated powers begin with a general clause and end with a general clause, but a general clause in which the powers delegated to Congress are enumerated in 2-17. There is a statement which makes it clear that the government cannot continue to operate if expenditure exceeds income, and if this real prohibition was applied, there would be no need for Congress to spend hours and hours in asinine debate about "balancing the budget" they would very quickly resolve the issue or have to shut down and go home.

The radical Republican extremists ventured well beyond the pale and the ken of the U.S. Constitution in the Reconstruction debates and they used European history as their model for dealing with the "rebels." Of course the South was not some conquered European nation but part and parcel of the United States. Revengeful Republicans were motivated by hate in comparing a conquered European nation with the South and they searched everywhere for a model on which to base the 13th, 14th and 15th Amendments — that is to say, everywhere except the U.S. Constitution itself.

Radical Republicans held out the premise that they got their authority for the three amendments from the general welfare clause of Article 1, Sec. 8, Clause 1. This was utterly fatuous and ridiculous, and shows how men will attempt to twist and subvert the U.S. Constitution and the Bill of Rights when they want something badly enough and when that something is outside of the Constitution. It is ridiculous because Clause 1 is followed by *specific* clauses 2-17 and there is not a single power that tells the Congress what to do in a civil war. As previously stated, Reconstruction laws were an infinitely worse violation of the U.S. Constitution than was seceding from the Union — if ever, this was a breach of the Constitution.

FOREIGN AID

One of the devices which enabled the Socialists/Marxists/Communists to rob billions of dollars out of the pockets of the hardworking middle class of America, was the Rockefeller-designed Foreign Aid Act of 1946, which is 100 percent unconstitutional. Congressional Record, April 21, pages 6548 - 6561: we read that President Monroe struggled to justify foreign aid but he could find no constitutional empowerment for it. Pres. Monroe really knew the Constitution, and he was not prepared to violate his oath of office to uphold and support the Constitution, even though he desperately wanted to help the South American countries to secure independence from Spain. Yet, search as he might, this man who knew the Constitution better than any other president, could not find any provision in the Constitution that would allow it. Where the Constitution is silent on a power and it is not expressly implied or incidental to another power already in the Constitution, it is a prohibition of that power.

Foreign Aid is thus prohibited by the Constitution and that makes the Foreign Aid Act of 1946 null and void and of no effect and no law at all. If anyone in the Supreme Court, the ABA, the Justice Department, the Congress or the White House can show just where its states in the Constitution that foreign aid is constitutional, then let them prove it, but no one can do that, because it just isn't there! Yet in spite of this, the secret upper-level parallel government of the United States goes on year after year, doling out billions of dollars to foreign countries in defiance of the law of the land. Foreign aid is merely a device used by the international banks to fill their bottomless pockets at the expense of the American people so that they will not lose their mineral rights and other benefits in foreign countries accruing to the Committee of 300. Foreign aid is a backup for the loans banks give these mineral-rich but otherwise impoverished countries, whose people have their national resources stolen from them through this device. Then, if the bank loans sour, there is always "foreign aid" to see that the banks don't lose their shirts on their bad loans.

TREATY-MAKING POWERS VIOLATED BY THE CENTRAL GOVERNMENT

The corrupt judicial system had nearly always sided with the so called "treaty is the law of the land" falsehood, and ruled more often than not that treaty powers are superior to the U.S. Constitution. In the case of Fugii vs. California (1950) the high court struck down a California law on the grounds that it conflicted with the U.N. Treaty! As I have said hundreds of times before all across this country, one of the main purposes of establishing the U.N. inside the United States was to be able to use the U.N. to break down State law. Ramsey McDonald, the Fabian Socialist, after returning from a spy mission to the U.S. in 1895, said that Socialism would not become the leading political creed in the U.S. unless and until the states constitutions were destroyed, and then, likewise, the Federal Constitution.

"Treaty-like" agreements which are neither treaties nor agreements have in most cases found a friend in the courts of this country. These so-called "treaty-like agreements allegedly give the President the authority to bind the U.S. to another country without the "advice and consent of the Senate." As far as I was able to ascertain in 1994 when I searched the records, nearly 12,000 of such so-called "treaty-like" agreements were being called the "law of the land." No wonder Thomas Jefferson castigated the judiciary as "miners and sappers" working silently to overthrow this nation. And no wonder Davy Crockett said that "the executive, like a lion, must be caged." A rampant President Clinton is raping the Constitution on an almost daily basis with his "executive orders" and "treaty-like agreements," all unconstitutional and null and void.

Letter To Senator Trent Lott. May 3, 1997.

Senator Trent Lott
Russell Building, Room 404
Washington, D.C. 20510.

Dear Senator Lott,

I almost never write to our representatives in Washington anymore, because recently I came to the realization that such action is an exercise in futility. However, I am so deeply disturbed, dismayed, disillusioned, depressed and despairing of what I perceive as your departure from the Constitution and Bill of Rights, that I decided to write to you, anyway. I don't know if you will ever receive my letter, because today, our Representatives surround themselves with aides and helpers who censor what they think their bosses should see. This is not right, nor proper. It is part of what is wrong with Washington. Senators and Representatives have a duty and an obligation to read all letters written to them by their constituents.

Confounded, concerned, filled with consternation, begins to describe my feelings about your acceptance "with reluctance" of the Chemical Weapons Convention treaty, a sham of a treaty if ever there was one, a mockery of our Constitution and of States rights. But whether qualified by "reluctance" or not, your vote was still a vitally important vote in favor of this anti-Constitution "treaty," which "treaty" is a fraud and a sham because, apart from scores of other reasons, it is purportedly made with a foreign entity having no sovereignty, and worse yet, an entity which is no more and no less than a front for the expansion of Communism, which, far from being dead, is alive and well, flourishing under the guidance of the Clinton administration, which administration continues to expand the Communist Manifesto of 1848 in the United States, begun by Pres. Franklin D. Roosevelt.

If you do not believe that Roosevelt was a Communist, view the footage by C.N.N. covering the dedication of the F.D.R. memorial in Washington, D.C., and you will see the designer of the memorial, giving the Communist salute, a raised clenched fist of the left hand, not once, but at least three times, as a signal that Communism has triumphed in the United States. This so-called Chemical Weapons Convention (CWC) "treaty" is about the most blatant violation of the U.S. Constitution among a whole slew of a such violations to come along in recent months to which members of your Republican Party have greatly contributed. Others which come to mind are NAFTA, GATT, the Panama Canal treaty, which were without exception put over the top by "moderate" (Socialist) Republicans upon whom the Democrats have always been able to count at times of need.

The columnists, Evans and Novak, say that you voted with Clinton because of advice you received from the "Republican Party's arms control wing." It seems to me that this Republican Party is joining with the Clinton administration to grind the U.S. Constitution and the Bill of Rights into dust, of which the CWC gross violation of the U.S. Constitution is the latest example, one which is as serious as the so-called "line item veto powers," another instance where "moderate" (Socialist) Republicans put the Democrat (Communist) Party over the top.

How could anyone who knows the Constitution, as I believe you do Senator, vote for a United Nations treaty which allows the U.N. to come into our country and violate our sovereignty and meddle in States rights? And incidentally, constitutionally, we do not belong to the U.N. As I have said, the U.N. is in any case totally lacking in sovereignty and has no power whatever to negotiate treaties with the U.S. Sen. Lott, you probably know the Constitution better than I do, so I respectfully request that you please show me just where in our Constitution do you find the authority that allows a treaty to take precedence over our Constitution and States rights?

Many years of the study of hundreds of treaties, has led me to the conclusion that treaties are baneful in the majority of cases. I don't want to give you a history lesson, but one treaty, the Treaty of Paris of 1259 led directly to the Hundred Year's War; the Treaty of Utrecht of 1713, gave Spain the right to supply slaves to Spanish America, the "grant of Asiento;" the Treaty of Navigation and Friendship of 1814 between Britain and the Argentine resulted in the Falklands War a few years ago. Then there was the Treaty of London of 1825, which "granted" the governments of Britain, France and Russia "permission" to interfere in the internal affairs of Turkey, and a more baneful treaty would be hard to find.

There are many examples like the few I have cited, which led to conflict as one or other of the parties began to realize it had been sold a false bill of goods. The other notable treaty which led to WWII, was of course, the Treaty of Versailles of 1919. The only saving grace about these treaties, is that by and large, they were between countries with total sovereignty, a most glaring omission in the so-called CWC "treaty."

The great Judge Cooley is quoted in the Congressional Record, House "Trade with Puerto Rico" pages 2273-2279 and pages 2287-2289: "Judge Cooley in his work on Constitutional Law, page 35, says: The Constitution itself never yields to a treaty or enactment. It neither changes with time nor does it in theory bend to the force of circumstance."

I am not a lawyer, and I don't know if you are, Senator Lott, but I do believe that your vote was one based on expediency. Apparently, if press reports are correct, you voted for the CWC "treaty" in order to get some concessions from the President in unrelated matters to do with the farcical balancing the budget efforts going on in the Congress. It is farcical because it is not needed; the general welfare clause already takes care of the problem of excess of government spending over income, but the real problem is that the Constitution is being ignored.

Having researched the question of expediency taking precedent over the Constitution — which in my opinion is what happened here with the Republicans who voted for the CWC "treaty" — I know of two excellent decisions by the Supreme Court where it says that temporary expediency has no validity and cannot circumvent the U.S. Constitution, or words to that effect.

There is also given, fifteen reasons why the Panama Canal Treaty is bogus, and this is relative today, because like former Senators De Concini and Baker, you are apparently seeking to reassure your critics by placing reliance on certain guarantees given by the President, which will, in my opinion, turn out to be as worthless as the De Concini reservations attached to the Panama Canal "treaty," i.e., not worth the paper they are written on, and in my opinion, when it comes to push and shove, the CWC "treaty" wording will prevail, not President Clinton's written assurances.

No part of the wording of a foreign treaty can be intermingled with the U.S. Constitution. In Vattels' "Law of Nations," we find examples of how a treaty can ruin a nation. The treaty between Rome and Carthage reminds me of the unclear, flawed CWC "treaty." The point I am making here is that laws are supposed to be written up in a precise manner, but the CWC "treaty" is all scrambled up. The problem today is that history is badly neglected — and it is no longer taught in our schools having been replaced by Communist Manifesto of 1848 "social studies" — so that the majority of new, young, members of the 105 Congress simply ignore history, when they should be guided by it.

The similarities between the Rome — Carthage treaty of 508 B.C. and the CWC "treaty" should have rung alarm bells in the Senate when the CWC "treaty" came up, but it did not, possibly because with a few notable exceptions, in my opinion, the Senators do not know the Constitution and the Bill of Rights, and less still do they know the history that led up to the making of our Constitution, because of their neglect of history, generally, and also neglecting to read up of the Annals of Congress, the Congressional Globe and the Congressional Record.

Of course there are several Senators who are a notable exceptions to these observations. Because of the lack of such fundamental knowledge, the minds of many in Congress appear to have become moribund, at least in my opinion, and it is one of the main reasons enabling the Communists to advance the cause of the Communist Manifesto of 1848, and put their plans over on this Republic, an example of which is the CWC so-called "treaty."

I quote what one of the great Representatives of the period 1880-1887 had to say, and we can all learn from it: The Hon. George Seney, House of Representatives. March 1, 1857:

"The measure ought not to become law. The very title of the bill is suggestive of improper and unauthorized legislation. As to the bill itself, it would be difficult, in my opinion, to put upon ten pages of paper more repugnance to the Constitution of the United States..."

Although Rep. Seney was talking about a bill which was being forced through the House to bring the Federal Government into the common schools of the States in violation of the 10th Amendment, the same words, in my opinion, may be applied with equal repugnance and force to the CWC "treaty" to which you and 29 Republicans gave your consent.

Congressional Record, House, May 16, 1922, Pages 7060 - 7084, a superb constitutionalist, Rep. Tucker, speaking:

"... Judge Storey said with great power that no one power in the Constitution can annihilate another (Storey, on the Constitution). In other words a treaty cannot be used to annihilate the Constitution. A treaty is no greater than an Act of Congress and Congress is bound to the U.S. Constitution and therefore a treaty cannot be greater than its creator or those who wrote the U.S. Constitution. The case of Heim vs. McCall (239 U.S. 175) is the last case on the subject..."

How then, Senator Lott, I respectfully enquire, could you assent to a treaty which on the face of it, sets itself up as greater than the Constitution? Then there is the question of States rights which take precedence over any and all treaties and it is the CWC "treaty" which the Communists are using to try and overcome the stumbling block of States rights on their road to transforming this nation into a Communist State.

Justice McKenna, in the case Patsome vs. Penn (232 U.S. 145):

"...then clearly rights claimed under a treaty against such power of the Senate are void, and if void, they are void because *state power collides with treaty power and is superior to it.*" (Emphasis added.)

Page 7072, Congressional Record, House, May 16, 1922. In his work, "Principles of Constitutional Law" Judge Cooley held as follows:

"The Constitution imposes no restriction upon this power (meaning the enumerated powers), but it is subject to the implied restrictions that nothing can be done under it, which changes the Constitution of the country, or robs a department of the Government or any of the States of its constitutional authority."

This is what the bogus Panama Canal treaty and the bogus Genocide treaty and the bogus SALT treaties tried to do as does the pernicious CWC "treaty." On this ground alone, the CWC "treaty" is bogus and one hundred percent unconstitutional, and rolls right over Judge Storey's 15 Rules of Interpretation. In my opinion, all who voted for it may, and I say may, have violated their oath to uphold the U.S. Constitution.

The United Nations has no authority to pry into the affairs of other nations, and in the U.S. our Constitution (State and Federal) forbids it. All nations keep their sovereignty and this dates back to ancient international law, the only exception being that after the Napoleonic wars and WWI, the Communists tried to empower a league of nations, which in both cases was short-lived. The CWC "treaty" also purports to allow the U.N. to interfere in States rights and the internal affairs of the United States.

In the plainest of plain language, Senator, the CWC "treaty" is going to do in the States and the United States, what the U.N. "inspectors" are doing in Iraq, if We the People, are foolish enough to let it stand.

How can any legislator take seriously a treaty in which one of the parties, the United Nations (U.N.) is totally lacking in sovereignty? Such a treaty can only be regarded as a bad joke, a mockery, an engagement in mendacity, frivolity, an exercise in absurdity, a laughing stock, having no force under the supreme law of the United States, the Constitution and the Bill of Rights. May I respectfully suggest that the 29 Republicans who voted for the CWC "treaty" read what Thomas Jefferson said: the U.S. is not bound by any treaty which requires funding by the Congress or any Federal Government department. Who is right, the "Demorepublicans" or Thomas Jefferson?

I quote now from Glenn's International Law: Essentials of a Valid Treaty or Contract Between two or more Independent States:

a) Capacity of the party to contract.
b) Duly empowered agents to act on behalf of other states.
c) Freedom of consent.
d) The object of the contract to be in conformity to law. (In the CWC "treaty" the law is the U.S. Constitution.)

Neither the U.N. treaty/agreement nor the CWC "treaty" conform to the above. Let us deal with (d) above, just one of the necessary attributes to a treaty which both the U.N. treaty/agreement and the CWC "treaty" fail to meet. Neither "treaty" is in conformity with U.S. law, the only law which we are bound to obey. According to our fist chief justice of the Supreme Court, John Marshall, where the U.S. Constitution is silent on a power, it is a prohibition of that power. Inasmuch as the U.S. Constitution does not mention the U.N. it is a prohibition of the U.N., hence the 1945 U.N. treaty is ultra vires, a mere hypotheses of no effect, and nor can anything built upon it be a law, and this includes the CWC "treaty."

Would you please sir, elucidate on this point and explain to me how you were able to reconcile the many, many, constitutional prohibitions against this treaty when you voted for the CWC "treaty" and also how you reconciled your vote with the prohibitions in the Constitution which are that no State need answer ANY enquiry about its internal affairs made by any foreign government or a foreign entity, and that no State need comply with questions from any foreign entity, and much less one lacking in sovereignty. As far as I am able to ascertain, States, under this condition of imposed "treaty" conditions have the right to thrust out such intruders. May I remind you of what I said earlier: Judge McKenna ruled, "State power collides with Treaty Power and is superior to it."

Senator, I respectfully request that you show me just where in the U.S. Constitution is there an obligation to allow U.N. agents to contact any official or person residing in the States and to question them about anything regarding the internal affairs of their State? It is a monstrous intrusion, and I believe there is no such provision in the U.S. Constitution which would permit it. On the contrary, it is stated time after time that no treaty can override the superiority of States rights!

Inasmuch as the CWC "treaty" does not conform to the U.S. Constitution, and is therefore void, please explain how you and the other Republicans address this most telling objection to the CWC? Senator Thurmond, another of the great constitutionalists of the period (1880-1900) put his objection most succinctly:

"...If a treaty is not in consonance with our U.S. Constitution, it is void." He also said that far from being the law of the land — as some would have us believe — "a treaty" (with a foreign nation with clear sovereignty) "is only a law at best, and like any other statute passed by Congress, must be constitutional." A treaty with a body lacking sovereignty is no treaty at all and is null and void, with obligation upon none.

This so-called CWC "treaty," is in fact diametrically opposed to the U.S. Constitution, so how in God's name can it be in consonance with it? This treaty is just another example of one hypotheses stacked upon another; the U.N. treaty of 1945 is exactly that, hypotheses heaped upon hypotheses, and to my way of thinking, all the codicils, promises, notes attached to it by Clinton are mere conjecture, as the original instrument, the U.N. treaty — or is it an agreement — of 1945, is invalid, ultra vires, and incumbent upon no legislator to respect.

It would take at least two, and possibly three, amendments to the U.S. Constitution to make our supposed membership of the U.N. legal, and so in plain language, the CWC "treaty" is fraud, stacked upon the fraud of the United Nations "treaty"/agreement. The U.N. "treaty"/agreement of 1945 and the CWC "treaty" of 1997, are both deep insults to the Founding Fathers and to the U.S. Constitution and the Bill of Rights they gave us, which these iniquitous "treaties" are intent upon destroying! Quad Erat Demonstrandum (QED.)

Are we not all duty-bound to obey the Constitution? I recall what the great constitutional scholar Rep. Raymond had to say about this point, and if you have read the Congressional documents I mentioned, you will agree that here was a man who was at least one hundred years ahead of his time on knowing the U.S. Constitution and the Bill of Rights. The Congressional Globe, June 1866, pages 3241-3250:

"...The Constitution is today for us, for Congress, for the President, for every State, and for every Legislature and for every court in every State, the supreme law of the land..."

Senator, would you please be kind enough to explain how in the face of the foregoing, 29 Republicans sided with the Democrat President on the CWC "treaty" in what seems to me to be a gross violation of the supreme law of the land? I don't see one single provision in the U.S. Constitution that would allow the Republicans who voted for this pernicious "treaty" to do so with out violating the U.S. Constitution? The CWC "treaty" does not defend the U.S. Constitution; rather it seeks to destroy it.

To me it is just inexplicable that you and 29 other members of this Republican Party could be in favor of the CWC "treaty" which violates the sovereignty of this nation. In this I am reminded of the way in which former Senator Baker sided with the Democrats against President Nixon at the Watergate hearings and how he and Sen. Di Concini stood with Carter in giving up U.S. sovereignty at the Panama Canal, and these are not pleasant memories.

I think the CWC "treaty" is about the last straw, and shows me, at any rate, that this Republican Party is fast approaching the point where it is as untrustworthy as was the Republican Party which began the Civil War; the authors of the unconstitutional, bogus, 13th, 14th, and 15th Amendments to the United States Constitution, and the unconstitutional Reconstruction legislation, not to mention the unconstitutional Gulf War, unconstitutional in that it lacked a properly drawn up declaration of war as mandated by the Constitution. For clarification — and it is too long to include here — I suggest that you read the model declaration of war by the Congress which preceded the Spanish-American War.

Pres. Bush failed utterly to comply with what was constitutionally required to take this nation to war, and the Republicans backed him. The fact that they thought the war a just cause, had no validity, and did not excuse violating the U.S. Constitution. The Constitution cannot be bent and twisted to meet expediencies, therefore, it did not surprise me in the least to find Bush in the Clinton camp.

As the leader of this Republican Party in the Senate, you proved to me that political parties are baneful, which is why I do not belong to either party. Although favoring the Republican Party when it behaves, I will never again contribute one red cent more to it until Republican legislators stop violating the U.S. Constitution and the Bill of Rights and halt "bipartisanship" (which usually means taking part in some unconstitutional act) in cooperation with President Clinton and the Democrat (Communist) Party. In my 26 years of intensive study of the Annals of Congress, the Congressional Globe and the Congressional Record, (and I still study them as one would read at a good university), never have I ever come across anything quite as heinous to the Constitution as the so-called CWC "treaty."

What the CWC "treaty" does is take the language of the Constitution and mingle it with the language of a One World Government body, the United Nations. This is an unconstitutional travesty which must be making our Founding Fathers writhe in their graves! Never has such a preposterously unconstitutional document been presented to the Senate for its assent, than the CWC "treaty," one which should have been declared dead on arrival.

The measure should have been declared dead on arrival as it fails dismally, deplorably, to meet the test of constitutionality. I am sure you know this to be true, because you must be acquainted with Judge Joseph Storey's 15 rules of interpretation of the U.S. Constitution, which Justice Frankfurter always ignored, thus proving how important they are. The trouble with the members of the Congress is that with a few notable exceptions, they do not know how to test a measure as to its constitutionality, consequently, measures and or bills are almost never, constitutionally debated. Looking back over the debates in the Congress during the "golden years of debate" (1880-1900) I am appalled to see how the standards of debate of that period have fallen into disuse and decay.

It is my contention that every person who runs for Congress should have to prove that he or she has spent a minimum of ten years reading (studying) the Annals of Congress, the Congressional Globe and the Congressional Record. Then, and only then, would candidates for office be fit to represent the people. Going to Washington on the strength of a law degree is not the same thing as knowing the Constitution and Bill of Rights through the documents I have mentioned; law schools teach a minimum of the Constitution in the one semester allotted to the subject. No wonder our judiciary, including the Supreme Court is in such a mess with only an inkling of what the Constitution is about.

Not for the life of me can I figure out how 29 Republicans could vote for a treaty which, in my opinion, violates our sovereignty, especially our States sovereignty? The Communists said long ago that States rights are a big stumbling block to their aspirations of socializing the United States, even a bigger impediment than the Federal Constitution. They also said that the United Nations would be the instrument whereby they would circumvent States rights. It looks to me that 29 members of this Republican Party went and handed the Communists what they have always sought.

How could the 29 members of this Republican Party believe that a treaty which allows an international body to meddle in our internal affairs is constitutional? And I would truly appreciate an answer to this question, if to nothing else herein. I am sure you know that State power is superior to any treaty power, but by the actions of the 29 Republicans, Pres. Clinton was handed a great victory and our Constitution was dealt a resounding blow by this sacred principle being ignored.

Senator Lott, I could go on giving you chapter and verse as to what makes this treaty unconstitutional, but it would be merely repetitive. Rather, I am suggesting that this Republican Party's Congressional delegation go and read Vattel's "Law of Nations," St. George Tucker's "Blackstone's Commentaries;" Judge Joseph Story's 15 rules of interpretation of the Constitution; the works of Judge Cooley; the works of

Judge Roger Taney, and particularly, The Appendix to the Congressional Record, House, March 1, 1887, pages 102-105 and then it will become apparent to them what it means to uphold the U.S. Constitution and the Bill of Rights.

You might ask on what authority do I write thus, since I am not a lawyer: I will answer you by saying that for the past twenty-six years, with tenacity of purpose and dedication to my cause, I have read (studied) the Annals of Congress, the Congressional Globe and the Congressional Record. In my opinion, this is the only way to get to know the layer upon layer of complexities and profundities which go to make up the U.S. Constitution.

How did it come to pass that the Senate even considered a U.N. treaty, when, as I said before, the U.S. does not and cannot belong to the U.N., and how can the Senate go on perpetuating the myth that we do? President Roosevelt violated the U.S. Constitution by allowing the United Nations to set up shop on U.S. soil. It would have taken two or three amendments to the U.S. Constitution to do what Roosevelt did without any constitutional authority whatever. The U.S. Constitution FORBIDS the U.S. to belong to any world body, league, such as the United Nations. Vattel's "Law of Nations" is very clear about it.

Another detail worthy of your attention, Senator Lott, and I hope that you will call what follows to the attention of the Republicans who voted with you in favor of the CWC: Congressional Record, May 25, 1892, pages 4653-4665:

"..Provost v.s. Greenaux, 19 Howard: That a treaty is no more the supreme law of the land than is an act of Congress is shown in the fact that an act of Congress vacates pro tanto an existing treaty. Whenever, therefore, an act of Congress would be unconstitutional as in invading — mark you — as invading the reserved rights of the States, a treaty to the same effect would be unconstitutional."

"Senator Lott, I think you will have to agree with me that the CWC "treaty" violates those rights reserved to the States, more especially the right that no foreign body, entity or organization can meddle in the private affairs of the States, nor can any entity like the U.N. erode the sovereignty of the United States. By this definition alone, the CWC "treaty" is one hundred percent unconstitutional, not binding upon any of the several States."

CHAPTER 9

THE KOREAN WAR, THE VIETNAM WAR AND THE UNITED NATIONS

I wrote this chapter of the book out of deep concern for the failure and or neglect of the Members of the House and Senate to study and become be fully qualified and proficient in the U.S. Constitution and the Bill of Rights. Many of the legislators are lawyers; they had to pass exams to qualify to practice law. How then is it possible that such men don't know the first thing about the U.S. Constitution and the Bill of Rights? How strange that while the legal requirement for them to practice law in the courts is a degree in law, when it comes to the HIGHEST law of the land, the U.S. Constitution and the Bill of Rights, these lawyers/legislators are not required to have a degree in the U.S. Constitution and the Bill of Rights, and in most cases, have only a smattering of education in the Constitution. Any test-exam would soon reveal them to be hopelessly incompetent in this vital area.

The American people cannot and must not allow this to go on. A constitutional amendment must be passed requiring would-be legislators to have completed a minimum of 10 years of intensive study of the Annals of Congress, the Congressional Globes and the Congressional Records, after which they will be required to pass a written and oral proficiency test, and only then, would they be allowed to run for office. The United States of America is on a course of destruction, simply because the vast majority of those elected to the House and Senate are almost totally ignorant of that which they take an oath to uphold.

Abysmal ignorance of these documents and consequent failure of the House and Senate to kill proposed bills that are unconstitutional, has led to the loss of thousands of American servicemen killed, and hundreds of thousands, wounded, in the Korean War and the Vietnam War, and billions of dollars wastefully and needlessly expended; two wars that could have and should have been prevented, had our legislators been qualified to practice in the Constitution and the Bill of Rights.

It is impossible to write about the Korean and Vietnam Wars without including the role played by the United Nations (U.N.) Let us, therefore, deal with the salient features of the U.N. again. Having covered the subject elsewhere in some depth, I find there is still more to be said. At the outset, it is necessary to reiterate that the United States never constitutionally joined the U.N. in 1945.

Those who signed the 100 percent treasonous U.N. treaty/agreement document, betrayed U.S. sovereignty; those who knew what they were doing should have been forced out of office, tried on charges of treason and when found guilty, made to pay the price for treason demanded by our Founding Fathers. At the head of the list of traitors stood John Foster Dulles, Secretary of State, without whose intervention in the Senate debate, the U.N. agreement/treaty would have been rejected. As to the innocent senators, those who were all at sea, bewildered and confused, of them we can only say: "Your ignorance cost the lives of thousands of our young servicemen and left thousands more wounded and mentally scarred for life."

Without the U.N. vulture roosting on U.S. soil, there is every likelihood that there would have been no Korean War, no Vietnam War. Acting under the auspices of the U.N., the Senate approved the unconstitutional Gulf of Tonkin Resolution after only *one day* of debate on August 10, 1964. Two months later, on October 21, 1964, in Akron, Ohio, while campaigning for reelection, Democrat Pres. Lyndon Johnson said: "We are not about to send American boys nine to ten thousand miles away from home to do what Asian boys ought to be doing for themselves."

Johnson ignored the fact that even as he spoke, 20,000 "American boys" were fighting in Vietnam, "nine to ten thousand miles away from home," and before his tenure in office would pass, the number of American "boys" engaged in hostilities in Vietnam would swell to 500,000. We could say the same thing about Wilson, Roosevelt, Bush et al; all Socialists posing as Democrat or Republican American leaders. We could have included Reagan in the gallery of American Socialist

Presidents, but then again, Reagan had a change of heart and went from a New Deal-Roosevelt Democrat to a conservative Republican. Although I can offer no proof, it is my belief that Bush is a hard-core Communist by virtue of his actions which speak louder than his words.

And all those wars they generated! One thing emerges from the studies I have made, and that is, the Presidents would never have gotten away with it had the Representatives and Senators known the U.S. Constitution. But they did not, with the exception of those Senators who rejected the League of Nations "treaty," they really did not know the Constitution. Another thing worth mentioning; no Senator or Representative can be an integral member of the Republic of the United States as long as he or she remains in this state of ignorance. The Senators and Representatives in the House and Senate today, don't know anything about how a declaration of war has to be written up. Ask them, as we did, and see how the majority fail this test.

Take as an example, the Gulf Of Tonkin Resolution. In 1964 when Johnson was gearing up for full-scale war in Vietnam, among the Senators voting on this badly-flawed declaration of war, only two recognized it as a full declaration of war. Senator Morse knew it was, as did Senator Gruening. The remaining 98 senators didn't recognize it as such, because they did not have the slightest idea of what a constitutional declaration of war looked like. Congressional Record, Senate, Oct. 9, 1975, pages 32682 - 32683:

"Resolved by the Senate and the House of Representatives of the United States of America in the Congress assembled; that the Congress approves and supports the determination of the President, as Commander and Chief, to take all the necessary measures to repel any attack against the armed forces of the United States...Consonant with the Constitution of the United States (an outrageous lie) and in accordance with the Charter of the United Nations and in accordance with its obligations under the Southeast Asia collective Defense Treaty etc." If there is a standardized Communist word, it is "collective." The red flag of "collective" was ignored. The whole wording of the resolution was garbled, unclear, imprecise, useless, a shambles, an example of how such a document should never be written up. Moreover, Pres. Johnson knew that the Gulf of Tonkin resolution had no validity.

Elsewhere, I have gone to some lengths to explain why the Gulf of Tonkin treaty was a fraudulent document, not only because it was written by the State Department, which has no legislative powers, but secondly, because it co-mingled the Constitution with the United Nations agreement/treaty prohibited by the Constitution, and falsely claimed the Gulf of Tonkin Resolution as a valid declaration of war. There was just one day allocated for debate on the resolution; another unconstitutional violation: The Constitution says that all measures brought to the floor for a vote must be fully debated as to their constitutionality, and in this case, proper debate would have taken at least fourteen days.

Judge Story wrote three volumes on the U.S. Constitution in which is found one of the best examples of what a declaration of war should be; and one thing which becomes clear upon reading the work of the learned judge is that only an amendment to the U.S. Constitution, would have permitted the Senate to intermingle its Gulf of Tonkin declaration with that of the U.N. Since there is no such amendment to the U.S. Constitution, the Gulf of Tonkin resolution should have been killed on the floor of the Senate as it was ultra vires and outside the pale and the ken of the Constitution.

When the State Department wrote its Gulf of Tonkin resolution, it short-changed the process of a constitutional declaration of war, deceived the American people, and cost thousands upon thousands of dead and wounded in the Korean War and the Vietnam War. What a national disgrace that this treasonous document ever cleared the Senate, because of the sheer constitutional ignorance of its members.

The Gulf of Tonkin resolution did not state what type of war was to be fought; whether a perfect war or an imperfect war, a further reason why its was so grossly unconstitutional. Neither Truman nor Johnson had the slightest constitutional authority to send our troops to foreign lands on "peace keeping" missions at the behest of the United Nations. The United Nations charter Article 43 is an article for war, not peace, and the United Nations wants the blood of American servicemen to be shed and the dollars of the hard-working American people to be squandered in such endeavors. Look at how foolishly we carried 95 percent of the costs in casualties of these two Asian wars, and see if you can find "equity among member nations" anywhere in this ghastly toll. Again, Clinton has no authority to keep American forces in Bosnia or the Middle East. These forces must be brought home without delay, and the way to do it is for the House and Senate to cut off the necessary funding for these misadventures.

It is painful and distressing to think that if only the Representatives and Senators had a full knowledge of the Constitution in 1945, the U.N. agreement/treaty would have been rejected and thousands of lives saved in Korea and Vietnam, and hundreds of thousands of the wounded would have been spared; not to mention the huge financial cost of both wars. As a safeguard against a similar tragedy happening in the future, there must be legislation passed, making it mandatory for those who run for a seat in the House and Senate, *to be fully qualified in the Constitution, before they offer themselves as candidate.,*

NEVER AGAIN must We, the People, stand aside and allow a House and Senate full of constitutional ignoramuses to grant the desires of the Communist cadre inside the White House and the State Department. We can start today by impeaching Pres. Clinton for the unconstitutional, unauthorized deployment of the armed forces of the U.S. in Bosnia and the Middle East.

A total of 98 Senators voted for the U.N. agreement/treaty out of sheer and total ignorance of the Constitution. I can think of no other country where such ignorance of the law of the land would be tolerated! By this ignorance the Constitution and the Bill of Rights are made of no effect! Can't we see this? President Bush's Gulf War was another BIG LIE and again, the Senators failed their constitutional exam here. The law of the land should have stopped the illegal Gulf War before it got started. As a result of that huge unconstitutional error, thousands of our Gulf War veterans are suffering from serious illnesses which are being passed on to their families, also. Is it any wonder that we must DEMAND that constitutionally illiterates not be allowed to run for office? How many more Korean, Vietnam and Gulf wars are we going to suffer before this nation learns its lesson?

Had the Senators known about, and followed a constitutional declaration of war, the Korean War, the Vietnam War and the Gulf War could never have taken place. Because of the almost complete ignorance of the five steps to be taken for a constitutional declaration of war, the House and Senate has three times allowed the American people to be plunged into foreign wars which were not in America's interests and in which George Washington in his Farewell Address warned us not to become entangled.

The U.N. is an evil legacy left to the United States by Communists Alger Hiss, Harry Dexter White, John Foster Dulles, Nathan Witt, Owen

Lattimore, Gregory Silvermaster, Laughlin Curry, John Stuart Service, and of course, Franklin D. Roosevelt, all of whom should have been tried for treason.

The United States cannot, under its Constitution, furnish armed forces to fulfill U.N. goals. The Constitution forbids it! Where does the non-commander in chief draw his non existent authority to have U.S U2 spy planes constantly overflying Iraq on behalf of the U.N.? Someone in the Senate should rise up in indignation and demand that President Clinton show where in the U.S. Constitution does he have such authority? All of his spin doctors and professional liars would not be able to put a gloss over this vile desecration of the U.S. Constitution!

What Dulles succeeded in doing on behalf of the Communist New World Order was to persuade the Senate to violate Article 1, Section 8, Clause 11 of the U.S. Constitution, in which article is found the power of Congress to declare war. What the U.N. charter Article 43 says is that the U.N. has this power, not the U.S. Congress. This abhorrent violation which arose from the ignorance of the Senators in 1945 and the treachery and chicanery of Dulles and a handful of co-conspirators, has no validity under our U.S. Constitution, for nowhere in the U.S. Constitution is there any power that authorizes the Congress to give or share war-making powers with the Communist U.N. Security Council, or with any other body. For the Senate to have authorized such a declaration of war power-sharing agreement with the U.N., would have required at least two amendments to the U.S. Constitution to be passed.

Sending U.S. troops to Bosnia was a declaration of war ipso facto but not a declaration of war by the U.S., but one given to the U.N. by our government to make on our behalf, and there is not one single place in our Constitution where such a power can be delegated. Sending U.S. troops to Iraq under Article 43 of the U.N. charter, was a declaration of war without a *Constitutionally mandated* declaration of war by the Congress. This is *high treason*. Where does the U.N. draw its power to send troops anywhere? The answer must by now be obvious: From the Communist Manifesto of 1848. Vattel's "Law of Nations" says no entity like the U.N. has no authority to interfere in the sovereign affairs of sovereign states.

The Communists in the State Department sent Dulles to "explain" the U.N. agreement/treaty to the Senators, but Dulles knew absolutely nothing about the treaty-making powers of the Congress (he being as constitutionally ignorant as they were), and by lying, he confused the Senators until the debate (such as it was) turned into a veritable nightmare of confusion.

In the end, what the Senate gave to the U.N. under Article 43 was the power to make war against the United States! How could anything so bizarre ever be constitutional? The U.N. agreement/treaty was bogus! It remains bogus! What is significant is that in the U.N. agreement/treaty these words are mentioned only once in the introduction and the introduction is not a part of the charter, any more than is the preamble to the U.S. Constitution a part of the U.S. Constitution. Moreover, as the U.N. interferes in the sovereignty of other nations, it can have no validity under the U.S. Constitution.

"Other nations" includes the U.S.! Yes, the treaty/agreement allows the U.N. to make war against the U.S.! What does this do to our sovereignty? It destroys our sovereignty, the very foundation upon which our Constitution and the Bill of Rights rest. Without sovereignty we are not a nation. Congress has not got the power to destroy our sovereignty; thus, not only must we NOT obey the U.N. charter, we must oust the U.N. from our shores and demand of our Representatives and Senators that a law to this effect be passed and executed as a matter of extreme urgency.

It is worth repeating, over and over again: The U.S. did not sign a treaty with the U.N. in 1945; it signed an agreement which was, and remains, altogether unconstitutional, if for no reason other than that the U.S. Constitution does not address itself to "agreements." The U.N. "treaty" is so badly flawed in scores of places that it is of no more validity under our constitutional laws than is a blank piece of paper. Yes, the U.N.treaty/agreement is of lesser validity than is a blank piece of paper, because of the inane, vacuous, manner in which it is written, i.e., to mean all things to all men.

To mention but one example: The bottom line of the U.N. agreement/treaty centers around Article 43 of the charter and yet nowhere in Article 43 is "treaty" or "agreement" mentioned nor expressly implied. "Special agreement" is in the charter but what does that mean? It means anything under the sun and anything the Communists in Washington and the U.N. want it to mean. The U.S. Constitution does not recognize "agreements," only TREATIES. There is no 5th Amendment or "equal, protection of the laws" in this U.N. document, so how in God's name can anybody tell us that the U.N. agreement is superior to the U.S. Constitution and expect the American people to go on throwing away their freedoms expressly guaranteed by the U.S. Constitution, by being forced to adhere to this vile Communist-inspired document, this U.N. treaty/agreement which is not worth the paper on which it is written.

If it is argued that the U.N. agreement is a treaty, then let it be known that a treaty is no more than an ordinary law, and just like an ordinary law, it has to be in consonance with the Constitution: Cherokee Tobacco vs. United States (11 WWall, page 616) Justice Swayne: "A treaty cannot change the Constitution, or be held valid, if it be in violation of that instrument. This results from the nature and fundamental principles of our government."

Judge Cooley in "Constitutional Law" page 35: "The Constitution itself never yields to a treaty or enactment. It neither changes with time nor does it in theory bend to force of circumstances."

Senator Thurmond, Congressional Record, Feb. 14, 1879, pages 1300 - 1312: "A treaty is a law according to the Constitution and its modification or its abrogation belongs to that department of Government that makes and unmakes laws." Note it does not belong to the United Nations acting under Article 43.

Now, here comes U.N. Article 43 and rips the foregoing all to pieces; essentially, it VOIDS our Constitution. Article 43 of the U.N. treaty is called a "special agreement." Where in the Constitution is there any provision for a "special agreement?" It is just not there. Such "special agreement" exceeds the bounds of the Constitution. Senator Fergusson, although confused on several points and issues, hit the nail on the head when he stated as follows, during the three-day debate in 1945:

"Mr. President, the reason I am compelled to disagree with some of the opinions expressed here today that this must be a treaty is that if we are required — and we are to make this agreement with the United Nations Security Council, we must realize that it is not a sovereign state, and we will agree that it is not a Superstate. Treaties as we in law understand them, Mr. President, must be made between sovereign nations. A treaty cannot be an agreement as it is contemplated here with the Security Council etc."

Because the Senate was totally ignorant of this fact, i.e., this was not a treaty but an agreement, they allowed the U.N. agreement to be confirmed. That act of folly and disgrace cost 54,000 killed in Korea and 58,000 killed in Vietnam. That display of total ignorance of the Constitution by the Senators in 1945, cost at least 112,000 American lives and hundreds of thousands of wounded! We need to pound this information into our heads, so that the next time some Communist in the White House or the Senate, wants to embroil us in U.N. war, We, the People, will let our representatives in Washington know that it won't be tolerated! The U.S. cannot allow itself to be drawn into the role of policing the world for the Committee of 300. The U.S. must abrogate the U.N. agreement or refuse to fund it with one single dollar more. And that must be done immediately. Anything less is treason and those who are guilty of prolonging our so-called membership of the U.N. deserve to be branded as traitors.

CHAPTER 10

WHAT YOU DON'T KNOW ABOUT THE MILITIA

A s we see in the Dick Act, also known as the Efficiency of Militia Bill H.R. 11654, of June 28, 1902, this law invalidates all so-called gun-control laws. It divides the militia into three distinct and separate entities, and that the information can be found in the Congressional Record, House, pages 7706-7713 and 321-353, 7594 - 7595.

The three classes H.R.11654 provides for are the organized militia, henceforth known as the National Guard of the State, Territory and District of Columbia, the unorganized militia and the regular army. We also know that the militia encompasses every able-bodied male between the ages of 18 and 45; although some contend that this provision concerning age, was later altered. It is estimated that today, the unorganized, free-lance militia group, the militia reserve, comprises 45 million men, not including the organized militia, the National Guard and the standing, regular army, and that all members of the unorganized militia have the absolute personal right and 2nd Amendment right to keep and bear arms of any type, and as many as they can afford to buy.

The Dick Act of 1902 cannot be repealed as to do so would violate bills of attainder and expost facto laws which would be yet another gross violation of the U.S. Constitution and the Bill of Rights, but just wait and see how desperate will become the efforts of the Socialists/ Marxists/Communists in the Federal Government to circumvent it; indeed, our history is punctuated with one series of events after another, when those with devious minds and in total disregard of the Constitution, finding it inconvenient to obey the Constitution, engage in desperate, even ridiculous, efforts to allow expediency to prevail over the law of the land.

Such is the current effort of the Livermore City Council of California, which has banned "Saturday Night Specials" and "cheap handguns," as the thin edge of the wedge to circumvent the constitutional provision forbidding any such "gun control" efforts. Witness some of the most stupid so-called "gun control" laws which only succeed in further violating the Constitution — making the proponents of such laws look utterly ridiculous and quite pitiful in their ignorance of the Constitution and their zeal in pursuing the aims of the Communist Manifesto of 1848 — being the origin of all "gun control laws." The aim of the "gun controllers" is quite transparent; it is to banish private ownership of all types of guns.

That there has been an effort to conceal from the American people their personal right, their 2nd Amendment right, and their militia right to keep and bear arms, in a conspiracy of silence by government, is becoming apparent. With help of the jackals of the media, the American people have been connived, cheated, lied to, in order to make them believe that 2nd Amendment rights apply only to the organized militia. Their personal right to bear arms is carefully, never mentioned. This is a damnable a conspiracy by the Communists and their fellow-travelers in the Washington government, and several State governments, the purpose of which is to disarm We, the People, the sovereigns, so that we will be powerless to enforce our sovereignty against a tyrannical central government.

CAN THE MILITIA BE ORDERED BY THE PRESIDENT TO SERVE ACROSS THE SEAS?

To the foregoing must be added that 98 percent of the members of Congress know nothing about the Dick Act, nor the fact that the President has zero authority without violating the Constitution to call the National Guard to serve outside of their State borders: The speech by Charles Hughes of the American Bar Association (ABA) contained in the Appendix to Congressional Record, House, September 10, 1917, pages 6836-6840:

"The militia, within the meaning of these provisions of the

WHAT YOU DON'T KNOW ABOUT THE MILITIA

Constitution is distinct from the Army of the United States." At these pages is also found reference to a statement made by Daniel Webster, "that the great principle of the Constitution on that subject is that the militia is the militia of the States and of the General Government; and thus being the militia of the States, there is no part of the Constitution worded with greater care and with more scrupulous jealousy than that which grants and limits the power of Congress over it."

At pages 6836 - 6840 Mr. Hughes goes on to say:

"In order to execute the laws of the Union to suppress insurrection and to repel invasion, it would be necessary to employ regular troops or the militia, and the power given to Congress with respect to the militia was manifestly to make a large standing army unnecessary. But as the service of the militia can only be required by the National Government for the limited purposes specified in the Constitution (to uphold the laws of the Union; to suppress insurrection and repel invasion) — and these are the *only* purposes for which the General Government can call upon the National Guard — as Attorney General Wickersham advised President Taft — 'the Organized Militia (the National Guard) can not be employed for offensive warfare outside the limits of the United States."

The Hon. William Gordon, in a speech to the House on Thursday, October 4, 1917, proved that the action of President Wilson in ordering the Organized Militia (the National Guard) to fight a war in Europe was so blatantly unconstitutional that he felt Wilson ought to have been impeached. Appendix to the Congressional Record, House, October 4, 1917, pages 640 — 642:

"The term 'militia' as used in the Constitution of the United States includes all able-bodied male citizens capable of bearing arms and these have further been defined by the statutes of the United States since the adoption of the enactment as 'all male citizens capable of bearing arms, between the ages of 18 and 45 years.'"

"After the War of 1812 with England had been in progress for two and a half years, an attempt was made in Congress to pass a Bill authorizing the President to draft by lot from those between the ages of 18 and 45 years 100,000 men, with whom it was proposed to invade Canada, the enemy's territory. This bill was defeated in the House by Daniel Webster upon the precise point that Congress had no such power over the militia as to authorize it to empower the President to draft them into the regular army and send them out of the country."

Four vitally important constitutional issues were spelled out by the brilliant, patriotic, men of the time, men like Daniel Webster:

1. Although invading Canada was deemed a worthy objective, it was turned down on the constitutional grounds that no authority existed whereby the militia could be called upon to fight outside of their respective States. There was no bowing to expediency as was the case with the Republicans when the Gulf War "worthy objective" was instigated by their President Bush in violation of his oath to uphold the Constitution.

And, again, when Sen. Trent Lott broke his vow to uphold the Constitution by standing with Pres. Clinton over the unconstitutional Chemical Weapons Convention Treaty (CWC), on the grounds that the Republicans were thereby going to get concessions from the President on the utterly banal and vapid "balancing the budget" circus then meandering its way through Congress; nor the expediency that made Sen. Stevens break his vow to uphold the Constitution, when he voted to grant Pres. Clinton so-called "line item veto powers," as flagrant a violation of the Constitution as has ever come along, equal to the Radical Republican's unconstitutional 13th, 14th, and 15th Amendments and Reconstruction laws, were again a matter of putting expediency above the U.S. Constitution.

2. It established the fact that the President had no constitutional right under any circumstances to draft men from the militia to fight outside the borders of the U.S.A. — and not even beyond the borders of their respective States — a constitutional LAW which still stands; waiting for the legislators to obey the Constitution which they swore an oath to uphold.

3. The members of the House and Senate in the period 1880-1900 knew that the prohibitions of the 9th Amendment to the Constitution could not be twisted and squeezed to suit a particular purpose, no matter the merits of the case, and they obeyed their oath to uphold the Constitution. Let every member of the 105 Congress go and do likewise and stop doing what Rep. Longworth, Sen. Trent Lott and Sen. Stevens did. There can be no putting unconstitutional expediency above the Constitution and Bill of Rights. To do so is to make the legislators no better than scofflaws deserving of severe punishment.

4. After those in Congress who did not respect the Constitution, in their 2-year efforts to make expediency become the law of the land were defeated in 1917, they resorted to the dirty trick of getting CONGRESS

to "authorize" the President to call out the national militia, knowing full-well that Congress had no authority to take such an unconstitutional course of action. It was this kind of dirty trickery that so much characterized the lives of the Republican-dominated Congress during the Civil War. While mainly instigated by the Democrats, the "moderates" in the Republican Party have been more than willing to defile their oath to uphold the U.S. Constitution and the Bill of Rights, an act of treason no less, which the Founding Fathers described as a heinous crime. Certainly, in my opinion based upon constitutional facts, Sen. Lott and Rep. Stevens were both guilty of treason.

To continue with the admirable lesson in testing the constitutionality of a measure before the Congress in 1917, Rep. Gordon speaking:

"While Roosevelt (Teddy Roosevelt, the same Roosevelt who violated the Constitution with a so-called 'executive order' which established the FBI) thought he wanted more troops for the Philippines than the Regular Army could afford, he induced Congress (by diplomacy and deception) to pass a law which provided that when the Organized Militia — National Guard — had been called into Federal service for either of the three purposes specified in the Constitution (suppress insurrection, repel an invasion, uphold the laws) the President might then send them out of the country; but when this statute was submitted to Attorney General Wickersham (thank God it was not Janet Reno), it was declared by the Attorney General to be beyond the power of the Congress to enlarge its power and that of the President over the militia by legislation, this attempt to do so was adjudged to be null and void."

There is a lesson here for every Republican and Democrat legislator who loves the Constitution and the Bill of Rights: When George Bush came with his unconstitutional proposal to go to war against Iraq, it should have been rejected out of hand by the Congress. Instead, Congress "gave permission" — and there is no such thing as "giving permission" to make war in the Constitution, therefore, like Daniel Webster, they were bound by the Constitution to send Bush packing, just as Teddy Roosevelt was sent packing when he tried to get the National Militia to fight in the Spanish American War. Our troops currently stationed in the Middle East and in Bosnia, have not the slightest constitutional authority to be there, and if we had any real statesmen in the 105th Congress, they would refuse to fund this unconstitutional position and force the return of our servicemen to the U.S.

The Constitution must be obeyed at all times, no matter the merit of the cause for which it is enlisted. Inasmuch as we desire to make the Constitution fit a cause we deem necessary, it cannot be twisted and squeezed to make the Constitution fit that cause. This is what is decreed by the 9th Amendment. To continue with the speech by Rep. Gordon:

"Mr. Hughes" (a spokesman for the A.B.A.) in approving this opinion of Attorney General Wickersham, concedes that no member of the National Guard now in the Federal Service can be sent to France or any other foreign country unless he volunteers for that service; and if he will read the argument of Daniel Webster, delivered in the House of Representatives on December 9, 1814, he will be convinced that the same rules apply to drafted men; and if he will read paragraph 12 of section 8 of Article 1 of the Constitution of the United States, the first five words of which he quotes, he will observe that the balance of the paragraph reads as follows: 'But no appropriation of money for that purpose shall be for longer than two years.'"

If President Bush had read any of the above, he would have realized that his Gulf War project was unconstitutional; if President Clinton were to read the above, he would realize that his Balkans and Middle East adventures were absolutely unconstitutional. Would that the entire membership of the 105th Congress, the President, the Attorney General, the justices of the Supreme Court read and heed these words: Rep. Gordon, on page 640:

"This limitation upon the power to raise and support armies clearly establishes the intent and purpose of the framers of the Constitution to limit the power to raise and maintain a standing army to voluntary enlistment, because if the unlimited power to draft and conscript was intended to be conferred, it would have been useless and puerile thing to limit the use of money for that purpose. Conscripted armies can be paid, but they are not required to be, and if it had been intended to confer the extraordinary power to draft the bodies of citizens and send them out of the country in direct conflict with the limitation upon the use of the militia imposed by the same section and article, certainly some restriction or limitation would have been imposed to restrain the unlimited use of such power."

"The only time in our history that Congress has authorized the President to draft citizens into the military service prior to the present emergency (WWI) was during the Civil War and that draft act specifically recited in its title that it was resorted to for the purpose of 'suppressing insurrection and rebellion' which is one of the express purposes for which the Federal Government is authorized to use the militia."

It is worthy of note that Lincoln was obliged to class what was a civil war an "insurrection" and a "rebellion" otherwise he would not have been able to call the militia into the service of the Federal Government. In actual fact this was one of those dirty tricks which so characterized the Republican-dominated Congress, because the war was a civil war, not an invasion by a foreign army, nor was it in any way, shape or form, a "rebellion." It is clear from the foregoing that Lincoln, like Kennedy, Johnson, Carter, Bush and Clinton, was not above playing fast and loose with the nation and fast and loose with the Constitution.

Rep. Gordon continuing, still on page 640:

"In further support of the proposition that under the Constitution of the United States, no troops outside of the Regular Army may lawfully be sent out of the country unless and until they volunteer for foreign service, and that the Regular Army may only be recruited by voluntary enlistment, I append, hereto, a petition to the Congress of the United States by Hannis Taylor, late ambassador of the United States to Spain."

On page 640-641, appears one of the most remarkable documents of the 20 century, one which throws great light on the perversity of the Socialist/Marxist/Communists who even in 1917 infested the Congress and one which shows that President Woodrow Wilson, a professional liar, acting under the duress and the influence of the sinister Colonel House and Sir William Wiseman, MI6 representative of the British intelligence agency's North American Desk, sent thousands of young American soldiers to their deaths in France, in absolute contradiction, and willful disobedience of the U.S. Constitution, a most heinous act of treason, for which Wilson should have been tried and if found guilty, hanged. The same British groups have President Clinton in their thrall, and the consequences for such a condition are going to be a disaster for this nation, unless the British hold is broken and the Federal Government is returned to the control of We, the People, the sovereigns who reside in the several States.

"A PETITION TO THE SENATE AND THE HOUSE OF REPRESENTATIVES OF THE UNITED STATES OF AMERICA IN CONGRESS ASSEMBLED"

"(Presented by Hannis Taylor in behalf of himself and as next friend of the half a million and more of America's youths now under military duress, conscripted under Sec. 8, Art. 1 of the Constitution which provides that 'the Congress shall have power to provide for calling forth the militia to execute the laws of the Union, suppress insurrection and repel invasions' which provisions, as construed by the Supreme Court, forbids the sending of the militia, so called (meaning so delineated), beyond the territorial limits of the United States.")

"AN APPEAL TO THE CONGRESS TO PREVENT THE SENDING OF THE CON-SCRIPTED NATIONAL MILITIA TO EUROPEAN BATTLEFIELDS IN OPEN DEFI-ANCE OF THE CONSTITUTION OF THE UNITED STATES."

"Your petitioner, Hannis Taylor, a citizen of the United States and a resident of the District of Columbia, in behalf of himself and as next friend of the half million or more American youths now under military duress because conscripted under Sec. 8, Article 1 of the U.S. Constitution, represents that he hereby asserts the constitutional right of petition solemnly guaranteed to him by the first article of amendment to the National Constitution, which right as an attribute of national citizenship entitles him to petition Congress for redress in regard to any matter of 'great moment and general concern.' Your petitioner avers that no matter of greater moment or more general concern was ever presented to the Congress of the United States than that involved in the threatened transportation to European battle fields of hundreds of thousands of conscripted American youths."

"First, because no such thing was ever attempted in our entire history as a nation. In asserting that fact in his Flag Day address of June 14, President Wilson said: 'We are about to bid thousands and thousands it may be millions of our young men, the strong and capable men of the nation, to go forth and die beneath the [flag] on fields so far away...'"

What constitutional authority did Wilson have to send hundreds of thousands of young American to their deaths in Europe? Exactly no Constitutional authority! Yet, in open defiance of the Constitution, this autocrat, controlled out of Britain through the sinister Mandel House, wiped his boots on the Constitution, boots that were soon to be stained by the blood of hundreds of thousands of young Americans, and unfortunately, he was permitted to get away with such heinous treachery and escape entirely any blame or punishment. According to the Founding Fathers, Wilson should have been impeached for treason, and if found guilty, hanged. I cannot restate the penalty for treason often enough in view of the blithe manner in which our legislators and the President violate their oath of office as if it were of no moment.

Because this nation refuses to enforce the penalty for treasonous conduct of its presidents as laid down in the Constitution, and because this nation refuses to learn from history, this violent rape of the Constitution by Wilson was permitted to continue under Roosevelt, Kennedy, Johnson, Truman, Nixon, Reagan, Bush and Clinton. And unless we learn this vital lesson in time, it will end in disaster for this nation as it is hurled into the maws of a One World Government of the New World Order.

On page 641, the petition of Hannis Taylor is continued:

"...American armies were never before sent across the seas. Second, because the Congress in enacting the legislation under which said conscription has taken place, has not only not authorized, directly or indirectly, the transportation of such conscripted youths 'across the seas' but it has manifested no conscience whatever that any such unprecedented and fateful act would be attempted by any one. Thirdly, because the transportation of the militia of the National or State, beyond our territorial limits, is strictly forbidden by the Constitution of the United States."

"EXEMPTION AS DEFINED BY THE FEDERAL CONVENTION OF 1787"

"Your petitioner further represents that the Federal Convention of 1787, after long and stormy debate, so clearly and positively fixed the exemptions of the militia, National and State, from military service beyond our territorial limits that it was never questioned during the century and a quarter that preceded the year 1912. In all of our wars preceding that date the exemption was always frankly recognized not only by jurists but by all writers on our military system."

"In his recent work entitled 'Our Military History' (1916), Gen Leonard Wood says that we have been compelled to fight our wars with volunteers 'because the militia was not available for service outside of the United States.'" Hannis Taylor then cited two other authorities and pointed out that the Mexican War was conducted with the service of volunteers. Hannis Taylor then went on to say:

"Strange it is that at this late day any man calling himself a jurist should dare even in a moment of hysterical excitement to deny the existence of an exemption recognized from the beginning of our national life not only by all lawyers but by the military experts."

"EXEMPTIONS CONFIRMED BY ATTORNEY GENERAL
WICKERSHAM IN 1912"

"Your petitioner further represents that the inconvenience of the constitutional exemption in question arising out of the territorial expansion incident of the Spanish American War, prompted certain persons, more ingenious than loyal to the Constitution, to attempt by the act of January 21, 1903, as amended by the act of March 27, 1908, to circumvent and destroy such exemption, by providing that the militia, so called, shall continue to serve during the term so specified either within or without the territory of the United States."

From this it would seem evident that preparations for U.S. entry into the First World War began several years before that war started, with certain Communists in the Congress trying to circumvent the U.S. Constitution and so open a door that would purport to make it lawful for future presidents to order transportation of the Organized Militia, "over the seas" in open rebellion against the U.S. Constitution which they had sworn to uphold.

It would become apparent in the 1930s, 1960s and onwards, that the very same persons or their descendants, "more ingenuous than loyal to the Constitution" would try to destroy the personal rights and 2nd Amendment rights of We, the Sovereign People, by "all manner of stupid devices" in open rebellion against the Constitution they swore to uphold and defend.

Hannis Taylor went on to state:

"By that stupid device such evil-minded persons attempted to make Congress confer upon the President the power to rob the militia of its constitutional exemption from service abroad in defiance of the elementary principle that the legislative department of government can not confer upon the Executive a power it is expressly forbidden to exercise itself. When that stupid device was submitted by President Taft to Attorney General Wickersham, a learned lawyer whose mind was then unclouded by prejudice and passion, he trampled upon it in an elaborate official opinion delivered under the oath of his office and dated February 17, 1912, in which he said:

'The Constitution, which enumerates the exclusive purposes for which the militia may be called into the service of the United States affords no warrant for the use of the militia by the General Government, except to suppress insurrections, repel invasions, or to execute the laws of the Union...This has always been the English doctrine and in some instances acts of Parliament have expressly forbidden the use of the militia outside of the Kingdom. Our ancestors who adopted our Constitution and early wars, got their ideas of a militia, its nature and purposes from this, and must be taken to have intended substantially, the same military body..." If authority is needed for the conclusions here reached, the following may suffice: In Ordronaux Constitutional Legislation, page 501, it said:

'The Constitution distinctly enumerates the three exclusive purposes for which the militia may be called into the service of the United States. These purposes are: First, to execute the laws of the Union, second to suppress insurrections; and third, to repel invasions.'"

"These three occasions, representing necessities of a strictly domestic character, plainly indicate that the services of the militia can be rendered only on the soil of the United States or its territories... In the history of this provision of the U.S. Constitution there is nothing indicating that it was even contemplated that such troops should be employed for the purposes of offensive warfare outside of the limits of the United States. And it is but just to infer that the enumeration of the specific occasions on which alone the militia can be called into the service of the General Government was intended as a distinct limitation upon of their employment..."

"And in Von Holtz, Constitutional Law, page 170 it is said, 'the militia can not be taken out of the country'... It is true that the act of January 21, 1903, as amended by the act of March 27, 1908, says, 'whenever the President calls forth the Organized Militia of any State, Territory or of the District of Columbia, to be employed in the service of the United States he may specify in his call the period for which such service is required, and the militia so called shall continue to serve the term so specified, either within or without the territory of the United States, unless sooner relieved by order of the President.'"

The important point to note here is that both the acts of 1903 and of 1907 purporting to give the President power to call forth the militia and send it overseas are null and void, and no law at all, because the Congress itself must act constitutionally, and the Congress is forbidden by the Constitution to give itself powers other than those delegated to it in Art. 1, Sec. 8 Clauses 1-18, and that the power to enact the said amendments of 1903 and 1908 is outside of the powers delegated to

Congress, the 1903 and 1908 amendments are not law for this reason, and can never be law, save and except a constitutional amendment to this effect be passed and submitted to the States for ratification. The same strictures apply to any *future* legislation the Congress may see fit to pass.

Had the Congress stood upon the Constitution in 1917, Wilson would not have been able to send hundreds of thousands of young American men to their deaths in France, and likewise, would Roosevelt have been so interdicted in the Second World War. Millions of young Americans were needlessly killed on the battle fields of Europe and the Pacific region, simply because the Congress refused to obey the U.S. Constitution and the Bill of Rights. And Attorney General Wickersham proceeds in his opinion to tell us precisely this:

"But this must be read in view of the constitutional power of the Congress to call forth the militia *only to suppress insurrection, repel invasions and execute the laws of the union.* Congress can not by its own enactment enlarge the power conferred upon it by the Constitution; and if this provision were construed to authorize Congress to use the Organized Militia for any other than the three purposes specified, it would be unconstitutional..."

Again, this applies to any and all future legislation which Congress may try to pass to make it more convenient for subversion of the Constitution to become law.

"I think that the constitutional provision here considered not only affords no warrant for the use of the militia by the General Government, except to suppress insurrection, repel invasions, or execute the laws of the Union, but by its careful enumeration of the three occasions or purposes for which the militia may be used, it forbids such use for any other purposes; and your questions answered in the negative. Respectfully, George W. Wickersham."

On Page 641, Hannis Taylor continues:

"After citing the decisions of the Supreme Court of the United States (Houston vs. Moore, 5 Wheat., 1, and Marriott vs. Mott, 12, Wheat., 19, 27) as irrevocably settling the exemption of the militia from service abroad, the Attorney General exposed with striking emphasis, the emptiness of the stupid contention that, although the Congress is expressly forbidden to authorize the sending of the militia, National or State, abroad, it may authorize the President to do so. Speaking of the act before him, he (Wickersham) which attempted to authorize the

President to use the militia, 'either within or without the territory of the United States', he said; 'if this provision were construed to authorize Congress to use the Organized Militia for any purposes other than the three purposes specified, it would be unconstitutional.' "Thus, in advance he put the stamp of nullity upon any clause or phrase in the conscription act of May 18, 1917, which may be construed to as to express such an unconstitutional purpose."

What a scandal, what a disgrace, what a national tragedy, that the Congress did not have enough men of courage in 1917 to put the Wilson proposal in the trash can, where it rightfully belonged. Instead, Congress chose to put hundreds of thousands of young American soldiers in their graves!

I believe it to be of the utmost significance that not once during the discourse by Rep. Gordon or petitioner Hannis Taylor was it ever maintained whether the National Government had any control or influence whatsoever over the *unorganized militia,* which it is estimated to number 45-50 million men in 1997, nor is it stated anywhere that the various departments of State government have any constitutional authority to interfere with the right of the unorganized militia to keep and bear arms in whatever quantity and type, nor is any local or State police agency allowed to interfere with the 2nd Amendment rights of such members of the unorganized militia.

I repeat: There is no constitutional provision for the gross intimidation of the unorganized militia now reaching a fever-pitch in several States, and it is important to remember that ALL government — including State government, local town board, county boards, are duty-bound to obey the Constitution and that means they must refrain from passing "laws" which inhibit the 2nd Amendment rights of the members of the unorganized Militia and all citizens and that such laws, ordinances, are constitutional nullities. To return to the Hannis Taylor petition:

"EXEMPTION AFFIRMED BY PRESIDENT WILSON IN 1916"

"Your petitioner further represents that after the foregoing opinion of Attorney General Wickersham had become the law of the Department of Justice, and as such, binding in this vital matter upon Pres. Wilson, he affirmed it, with great emphasis, in four speeches delivered in January and February 1916 when he was called upon to explain why he could do no more for the development of the State militia, now euphoniously called the National Guard."

The name change to "National Guard" was only a part of the dirty tricks campaign to get the U.S. into WWI. The name "National Guard" carries with it an implication that it is a Federal Government body, when in actual fact, it is solely and uniquely, a STATE body, in which the National Government is forbidden to intervene in any shape or form whatsoever, less still have the power to call it into service for duties beyond the borders of the several States, a point which Pres. Wilson made perfectly clear twice in 1916, before he fell victim to his British controllers and their sinister agent, Colonel Mandel House. No matter that *future* efforts were made by the Congress in later years, or which it will make in the future, let us remember that the Congress *has no such powers* to change the Constitution.

"In an address delivered at New York, January 27, 1916, he said: 'I believe it is the duty of Congress to do very much more for the National Guard than it has ever done heretofore. I believe that the great arm of our national defense should be built up and encouraged to the utmost; but you know, gentlemen, that under our Constitution of the United States the National Guard is under the direction of more than two-score States; that it is not permitted to the National Government directly (and note the cunning qualifier "directly" which is not in the Constitution — what Wilson should have said instead of "directly" was "under any circumstances whatsoever") to have a voice in its development and organization; and that only upon occasions of actual invasion has the President of the United States the right to call upon these men to leave their respective States." (But *not* to call them to serve outside of the geographical boundaries of the United States of America.)

"In an address delivered at Cleveland, Ohio, January 29, 1916, he said: 'The President of the United States has not the right to call upon these men — the National Guard — except in the case of actual invasion, and therefore, no matter how skillful they are, no matter how ready they are, they are not *the instruments of immediate national use.'*" (Emphasis added.)

"In an address delivered at Milwaukee January 31, 1916, he said: 'The National Guard, fine as it is, is not subject to the orders of the President of the United States. It is subject to the orders of the governors of the several States and the Constitution itself says that the President has no right to withdraw them from their States even, except in the case of actual invasion of the soil of the United States.'"

"In an address delivered at Topeka, Kansas, February 2, 1916, he said: 'The Constitution of the United States puts them — the National Guard — under the direct command and control of the governors of the States, *not the President of the United States,* and the national authority has no right to call upon them for any service outside of their States unless the territory of the Nation is actually invaded.'"

Continuing, petitioner Hannis Taylor said:

"Here we have conclusive documentary evidence of the fact that long before the conscription act of May 18, 1917, was passed, President Wilson had complete knowledge of this entire subject, as expounded by Attorney General Wickersham in his official opinion of February 17, 1912, now binding upon the President as the law of the Department of Justice. No one knows quite so well as President Wilson that the sending of our National Militia abroad by the Executive will constitute a flagrantly unconstitutional act, and as such an impeachable high crime and misdemeanor."

Personally, I look back in amazement when I think that Wilson got away with the heinous crime of violating the Constitution and his oath to faithfully execute the laws of the United States, and even more so, I am amazed that there was no one in this great country, to stand like Horatio at the Bridge and say, "thus far and no further. You shall not cross the bridge that will cost the lives of hundreds of thousands of young Americans on the battle fields of Europe."

Where were the legislators who swore to uphold the Constitution; how did it come to pass that Wilson was able to force our young men to throw away their lives, and worse yet, how could the American nation — supposedly a highly-educated nation — stand by and allow Roosevelt to repeat Wilson's crime; what must surely have been the worst crime against the Constitution since the Civil War? Where were our legislators when this was going on? And where were our leaders when George Bush was lying to the nation about his non-existent power to lead the nation to war against Iraq? Unless We, the People, take charge of government as we are empowered to do by the Constitution, very soon, we shall have to fight a bitter battle for our sovereignty, or lose it. The rule which we must enforce against legislators is: Obey the Constitution at all times or be forced out of office. To continue with the Hannis Taylor Petition:

"NATIONAL MILITIA CREATED BY FEDERAL CONVENTION OF 1787."

"Your petitioner further represents that when the convention of 1787 those who may be called Nationalists, with Washington at its head contending that the State Militia had proven too 'inefficient under the Confederation' demanded the creation of a new militia system, entirely apart from the State systems, which would be under the exclusive control of the new Federal Government...The proposal was so bitterly opposed by States rights faction that a deadlock arose which was broken at last by a compromise arranged by a grand committee of the States (Elliott vs. 445.) The States rights faction was told that the ancient systems of State Militia might continue to exist, subject to the following limitations now embodied in Section 8, Article 1: 'The Congress shall have the power... to provide for organizing, arming and disciplining the-State Militia — and for governing such part of them as may be employed in the service of the United States reserving to the States respectively, the appointment of the officers, and the authority of training the militia according to the disciplines prescribed by Congress.'"

Note that not one word was said nor was anything implied that would have brought the unorganized free-lance militia under the discipline prescribed by the Federal Government, and further note that the unorganized free-lance militia was by far the largest of the States militia, as it is today. In return for that concession the States rights faction agreed to the creation of a new National or Federal Militia, entirely distinct from the States systems — subject, however, to the three severe limitations now embodied in Section 8, Article 1 "the Congress shall have the power... to provide for calling forth the national militia to execute the laws of the Union, suppress insurrection and repel invasions." These are the *sole conditions* under which the National Militia may be called forth to serve under the Federal Government, and there is no exception or exceptions to this rule of law, but as we shall see, in no way did the concession made by the States rights faction extend to allowing the Federal Government to send the National Militia out of the United States.

Petitioner Hannis Taylor then went on to say:

"Every student of constitutional history knows that the last limitation, 'and repel invasions' was simply a transplanting into the new American Constitution of the exemption of the English Militia from service abroad, which had been a vital part of the English constitution for a thousand years, prior to our severance from the mother country. In order to make it possible to take the English militia over the Channel to France during the present war (1914-1918) it became necessary to change the English constitution in that respect."

"Mr. Dicey, one of the most eminent modern commentators on the English constitution said in his edition of 1908; 'The militia is the constitutional force existing under the law of the land for the defense of the country...Embodiment indeed converts the militia for the time being into a regular army, though an army which cannot be required to serve abroad.' (Law of the Constitution, pp. 287-288.) And so, even if it could be claimed that our national Militia, called forth by conscription, constitutes a regular army, it is an army that cannot be required to serve abroad."

"ONLY TWO CONSCRIPTION LAWS EVER ENACTED BY CONGRESS"

"Your petitioner further represents that it is a notable fact that the national Militia as such, as a national force entirely distinct from the militia of the States (and the unorganized free-lance militia of the States) has only been called forth on two occasions and on each by conscription. The first conscription act was approved March 3 1863; the second on May 18, 1917. As the first was enacted during the Civil War (on the false premise that it was a rebellion and not a civil war) it declares with great emphasis in the preamble that it was enacted under Section 8, Art 1 of the Constitution which provides that 'Congress shall have the power to provide for calling forth the militia to execute the laws of the Union, suppress insurrections and repel invasions.'"

"After a lapse of half a century, the National Militia, as such, was called out a second time by the act of May 18, 1917, under which the National Militia is now being drafted, is not an original measure; as it appears on the face of it is simply an extension or supplement to carry into effect the national defense act of June 3, 1916. By section 57 of that act the National Militia is thus defined:

' — Composition of the militia — The militia of the United States shall consist of all able-bodied males who have or shall have declared their intention to become citizens of the United States, who shall be more than 18 years of age, and except as hereinafter provided, not more than 45 years of age, and the said militia shall be divided into three classes, the National Guard, the Naval Militia, and the Unorganized Militia.'

"The primary and avowed purpose of the conscription act of May 18, 1917, is to organize the *unorganized militia* of the United States by extending its provisions to 'all male citizens or male persons not alien enemies...between the ages of 21 and 30 years.' Thus the fact is fixed with mathematical certainty that the act of May 18, 1917, was passed in order to call out the National Militia, as such, 'to execute the laws of the Union, suppress insurrection and repel invasions; first, because it is little more than a copy of the first conscription act of March 3, 1863; second, because its avowed purpose is to organize the Unorganized Militia of the United States by extending its provisions to 'all male citizens or male persons not alien enemies...between the ages of 21 and 30 years.'"

"Of all the *shallow pretenses* devised with a view to confusing this very simple subject, *the most pitiful* is that which attempts to deny that the conscription act of May 18, 1917, was part of Section 8, Article 1, which authorizes the Congress to call out the national Militia to 'execute the laws of the Union, suppress insurrection and repel invasions.'"

"DESPERATE EFFORT TO GIVE RESPECTABILITY TO A RIDICULOUS CONTENTION"

"Your petitioner further represents that the history of our Constitution, taken as a whole, is made up of a series of efforts to evade it whenever its provisions become inconvenient to a particular class at a particular time. But never has the struggle to find a loophole been so desperate as that involved in the present attempt to invent a pretext for denying the immunity of the militia, National and State from service abroad; first, because such immunity was a thousand years old before our severance from the mother country took place; second, because the language in which it is embedded in our Federal Constitution is too plain for cavil or question; third, because the immunity was expressly affirmed by the Supreme Court of the United States in 1827; fourth, because of an exhaustive review of the whole subject by Attorney General Wickersham in 1912, in an opinion accepted by President Taft as final; fifth, because it was again solemnly reaffirmed by President Wilson in four speeches delivered in 1916."

"And yet some kind of a pretext is indispensable to those who are now proposing to send the National Militia, conscripted under the act of May 18, 1917, to European battlefields *in open defiance of the Constitution,* a ridiculous claim is being made in certain quarters that such act was really passed under that part of Section 8, Article 1, which authorizes Congress 'to raise and support [volunteer] armies, but no appropriation of money to that use shall be for a longer term than two years...'"

Petitioner Hannis Taylor then went on to give a lengthy discourse as to why the conscription act of May 18, 1917, was unconstitutional, and not all of it can be included here, but the following extracts are indeed enlightening:

"That provision ...has no more connection with the subject matter before us than an extract from the Talmud or Pentateuch...But far more important is the fact that the ranks of the Regular Army, which can only be composed of volunteers can not be filled up by conscription. When a proposal to swell the ranks of the Regular or Volunteer Army in that way was embodied in the conscription act offered in Congress in 1814, Daniel Webster so trampled it under foot in a masterful speech that it was never revived in any form."

"There is but one precedent to support conscription in our entire history, and that is the conscription act of March 3, 1863, which declares in *express terms* in its preamble that Congress enacted it to suppress 'an insurrection and rebellion.'" (Again, the Civil War was called a "rebellion" for this purpose — had the word "war" been used, the act would have been deemed as unconstitutional.) Taylor went on to denounce the reorganizing of the militia and the conscription act of May 18, 1917, in ringing terms as flagrantly unconstitutional, and gave a shattering account of how the defilers of the militia and the Constitution, brought forth a single ex Federal judge by the name of Hughes, who went before the American Bar Association — the A.B.A. — to declare that the conscription act and reorganization of the militia was constitutional. On page 643, Hannis Taylor stated as follows:

"Was there ever such a dreadful spectacle? There stood an ex justice of the Supreme Court as the prosecutor of half a million American youths, under military duress and on trial for their lives, with no one to defend them. The idea was that in that star chamber proceeding the mere ipse dixit of a great legal functionary would deprive our sons of the protection guaranteed by thousands of years of English and American constitutional law. *The undertaking was too great for any one man.* It would have been too great for Lord Bacon or Chief Justice John Marshall. The solemn guarantees of the U.S. Constitution cannot be destroyed that way." Each and every political activist judge in the U.S. should take note of this ringing denouncement of their activities.

The foregoing puts me in mind of the shameless way the adversaries of the enshrined right of citizens to keep and bear arms were assaulted by the knaves who brought forth James and Sarah Brady to intone that this right should be abrogated because James Brady was shot by a gunman intent upon assassinating President Reagan, as preposterous a proposition as the one put forward by ex-justice Hughes. The gun grabbers fit perfectly the portrait of them painted by Hannis Taylor: "...that the history of our Constitution taken as a whole is made up of a series of efforts to evade it (the Constitution) whenever its provisions become inconvenient to a particular class at a particular moment."

That the 2nd Amendment right and the personal right of citizens to keep and bear arms of whatever type and in any quantity is an "inconvenience" to Sen. Feinstein, Sen. Lautenberg and Sen. Barbara Boxer, not to mention Congressman Schumer, is unquestionable, and what is also unquestionable is the glaring reality that these persons are working toward their goal of making the Communist Manifesto of 1848 the "law of the land" and trampling underfoot the Constitution of the United States and the Bill of Rights, of which stripping citizens of the right to arm themselves is an essential element, if progress toward their goal is to be realized. To continue once more with petitioner Hannis Taylor:

"A CENSORED PRESS DISLOYAL TO THE PEOPLE"

"Your petitioner further represents that the cruel and remorseless conspiracy against the lives of half a million of defenseless American youths which opened with ex-Justice Hughes prosecuting speech is being carried on by the *censored and disloyal press that spread its broadcast throughout the land under a compact that no one be permitted to reply to it.* Your petitioner says 'compact' because when he applied to nearly one hundred and fifty newspapers for leave to expose atrocious fallacies and misrepresentations, without a single exception the door was brutally closed in his face."

"A very distinguished editor who refused him the right to be heard in the Capital of the Nation, said with perfect frankness, 'No matter if he is correct, a resolve has been reached to send the National Militia abroad in any event, in defiance of the Constitution!' That is the clean-cut fateful issue that now confronts the American Congress and the American people in this land, once known as the land of liberty and fair play. Upon its solution the life of this Republic depends."

In the foregoing we see the justification for, and the reason why for two decades, I have called the news media "jackals of the press" and in the light of what the press did to the Constitution in 1918 and thousands of times since then, to call its members "jackals" may actually be insulting to the jackal which acts out of its natural instincts, and not out of motives of base treachery, appalling deception, and treason.

A replay of the disgraceful conduct of the jackals of the American news media took place in the runup to the Gulf War in which the press lied and misrepresented the goals of that proposed war against Iraq, and as they did in 1918, the jackals of the media made a compact to block any attempt to inform the American people as to the REAL objectives behind the shocking violation of the Constitution then being carried on by former President George Bush, and which shocking violation was condoned by most members of the Congress, and who, like Woodrow Wilson, should have been impeached and tried for treason and if found guilty, endure the ultimate penalty for the heinous crime of treason laid down by our Founding Fathers.

Hannis Taylor continued his petition with a review of his forty years of study of the U.S. Constitution, and he told Congress that the attempt to reorganize the militia and the destruction of the express and explicit exemption of the militia from service outside of the United States "is the most indefensible and deadly assault ever made on the Constitution; indefensible because it has been "solemnly affirmed" by the various constitutional authorities he had cited earlier, whose work allowed none of the treasonous conduct of Pres. Wilson and Pres. Bush, not to mention Roosevelt, and the heinous pack of jackals gnawing away at our *personal right and 2nd Amendment right to keep and bear arms.*

Hannis Taylor also called the move "deadly, because if the militia, a body of troops strictly for home defense, can be transported to European battle fields in this war, it can be so transported in all wars that are yet to come... If such a revolution can be wrought solely by the fiat of an Executive, without a word of authorization, either from the American electorate or by the Congress, then surely our constitutional system based on the threefold division of power is at an end."

Hannis Taylor concluded his petition by appealing to the Congress to take action to stop the attack on the Constitution, and also asked the Congress, "Fourth, that the said joint committee be directed to ascertain and report whether there is now, or has been, a conspiracy between the leading newspapers of the United States, including some owned by foreigners in this country, to the end that the false foundationless statements should be circulated as to the nonexistence of the ancient and undoubted constitutional exemption in question, under a compact or agreement that no one be permitted to controvert or explain to the people the falsity of such statements..."

Would to God that we had men of the caliber, courage and fortitude of Hannis Taylor; willing to stand up to the scofflaws in the Congress and the White House and demand that they obey the Constitution which they swore an oath to uphold. Let them be reminded of the drastic penalty demanded by the Founding Fathers; for Wilson, Roosevelt, Bush and Clinton and all manner of men who refuse to obey the Constitution and the Bill of Rights, what ever may be their station in the public life of the United States of America.

To the people of the United States of America: "Enforce the penalty for treason without fear or favor, otherwise this nation shall surely perish." Let the scofflaws of the Constitution be impeached and removed from office.

CHAPTER 11

SOME ASPECTS OF THE COMMUNIST DOCTRINE OF GUN CONTROL AND WHY GUN CONTROL LAWS ARE UNCONSTITUTIONAL

Published below is a letter sent to an establishment newspaper touting the views of a government servant, an enemy of the 2nd Amendment, whose work is in direct contravention of the Dick Act, which we have just examined:

The Editor,
San Jose Mercury,
750 Rider Park Road
San Jose, CA 95190.

Dear Editor,

The letter you recently published by Stan Voyles, Deputy district attorney, Santa Clara County, "Second Amendment applies to states, not individuals" caused me much concern because it is so misleading and downright non-factual. The Annals of Congress, the Congressional Globe and the Congressional Records, give the correct position on the 2nd Amendment. I might add that without an in-depth study of these records for a minimum period of five years, one does not know the

United States Constitution and the Bill of Rights. Obviously, Mr. Voyles has not had the benefit of such an education. From the position taken by Mr. Voyles, I would presume that he attended a law school at which, like most, only a smattering of constitutional law is taught in one semester.

The Second Amendment to the United States Constitution is a personal right, the right to defend oneself, the oldest right known to mankind, and which, incidentally, dates back to Roman Law, on which much of our Constitution is based. As to the judiciary, they try to put their interpretations into it by twisting and violating the 9th Amendment, and most members of Congress, with a few notable exceptions, do not know the U.S. Constitution and Bill of Rights, other than to recite the articles and clauses. The late Senator Ervin was the only one who could confirm my list of personal rights, which rights can never be taken away through government action.

It seems highly likely that none of the present members of Congress, nor the judiciary, past (since the 1930s) and present, know anything about the Dick Act of 1902, and those federal prosecutors mentioned by Mr. Voyles, were all guilty of violating the Dick Act of 1902, the 2nd Amendment to the U.S. Constitution, and Article 1, Sec. 9, Part 3, of the U.S. Constitution.

The Federal Government is one of delegated powers and not original powers, and the primary powers of Congress are found in Article 1, Sec. 8, Clauses 1-18. Interfering with personal rights, among them the right to keep and bear arms is not found in the sole or delegated powers of the federal government, and incidentally, nor in the constitutions of the several States. Local, county, and any other legislative bodies are also bound by these restraints.

The secondary powers of the Senate are housekeeping powers and nowhere in the Constitution is the Congress authorized to tamper with personal rights of citizens nor with the 2nd Amendment right — and note it is a right, not a privilege, to keep and bear arms. If Mr. Voyles can show where in the Constitution it says that the right of citizens to keep and bear arms can be abridged by any government agency — local, county, State, or federal, local judges or magistrates — it would be very enlightening to say the least.

I don't know how Mr. Voyles can construe that the 2nd Amendment is addressed to States, and not to individuals. The very language of 2nd Amendment is addressed to We, the People (capitals intended), the sovereigns residing in the sovereign States: "The right of the PEOPLE..." The same language is used in the 4th Amendment. In fact the entire Bill of Rights is addressed to the people — citizens of the States, not to the federal government and the 10th Amendment makes the distinction between the people and the federal government even sharper: "The powers not delegated to the United States (singular) by the Constitution are reserved to the States (plural) respectively or to the People." (Capitals intended.)

St. George Tucker, one of the Founding Fathers, veteran of the War of Independence, professor of law at the College of William and Mary, a judge of the Virginia Court, and a champion of the entrenched 2nd Amendment rights of the people to keep and bear arms, made the issue crystal clear in his work, "Blackstone's Commentaries." (I have abbreviated the full title):

"This may be considered the palladium of liberty — The right (and again, note it is a right and not a privilege) of self-defense is the first law of nature: in most governments it has been the study of the rulers to keep this right within its narrowest limits possible...A well regulated militia being necessary for the security of a free state, the right of the PEOPLE to keep and bear arms shall not be abridged." In those days the words "well regulated" meant "well supplied."

Note that it says, first, the "right of the PEOPLE" and does not restrict that right to the militia only, and in any case, the militia is the whole people. An attack on the 2nd Amendment is an attack on the whole Constitution. Clauses and amendments cannot be isolated like the rascally Justice Douglas tried to do with the 1st Amendment, and as gun grabbers are also constantly attempting to do. In 1809 the great John Randolph said: "...the PEOPLE (not the States, not local government not the federal government) who will consent to remain unarmed while arms are put in the hands of a standing army governed by martial law are ripe for a master."

Randolph made it clear that the right to keep and bear arms is vested in the PEOPLE. What we have today, are courts, local boards, local and county governments, and their officers like Mr. Voyles, trying to insert clauses of their own making between the 1st and 9th Amendments, and this is very much the case with gun-grabbers who try to twist and squeeze the Constitution to fit their predilections, forbidden by the 9th Amendment. The unratified, unconstitutional, null and void, 14th Amendment attempted to rob the States of property rights and other

States rights, but the 14th, (even if it were a part of the Constitution, which it isn't) did not try to abridge the right of citizens to keep and bear arms, nor does it say that guns come under interstate commerce.

Chief Justice John Marshall, our third chief justice of the Supreme Court must be turning in his grave at the antics of local boards, counties, States and federal government attempts to abridge the right of We, the People to keep and bear arms. Nor can there be any restriction whatever imposed on *We, the People,* as to the amount and types of arms it is our right to keep and bear. I would like Mr. Voyles to point out where in the Constitution and Bill of Rights such restraints as to the number and types of guns each citizen may possess is written, or expressly implied? That would be quite an achievement, as it is simply not there!

The establishment press (and now Mr. Voyles) implies that the 2nd Amendment is only kept alive through the support of the National Rifle Association (N.R.A.) and that the 2nd Amendment is addressed to the States, not the people, but such a position is hopelessly wrong; the RIGHT to keep and bear arms is addressed to *We, the People,* as is the whole Constitution and the Bill of Rights, providentially drawn up by the Founding Fathers in this manner to prevent a tyrannical government enslaving us.

The right to keep and bear arms vested in We, the People, goes back to ancient Rome and existed in the thirteen colonies long before they came together to form the United States of America, and it is important to note that when the thirteen colonies came into the Union, they retained their States rights, and the personal rights of their citizens, one of which was the right to keep and bear arms, expressed in the Pennsylvania declaration of 1776, "... *The people* have the right to bear arms for the defense of themselves and the state" and of course, there was no N.R.A. in those days.

The Dick Act of 1902 absolutely forbids all forms of interference by government with the right of We, the People, to keep and bear arms. The 2nd Amendment right to keep and bear arms was won in heated debate by some of the greatest statesmen this nation has ever produced. One of them, Samuel Evans, a gun owner who believed in the right of citizens to keep and bear arms, and he expressed his concern that the right should never be abridged:

"...The Constitution shall never be construed to prevent the *people* of the United States who are peaceable citizens from keeping their arms." Note that "people" and "citizens" are interchangeable and mean the same thing. Other Founding Fathers who were no less staunch protectors of the right to keep and bear arms, vested in the people, included the following:

Patrick Henry: "Guard with a jealous attention the public liberty. Suspect every man who approaches that jewel. Unfortunately, nothing will preserve it but downright force. Whenever you give up that force, you are ruined. The great object is that *every man* be armed, everyone who is able may have a gun." Note that the singular, "MAN" is conclusive proof that it is an individual, personal, right.

John Adams: "Arms in the hands of *individual* citizens may be used at *individual* discretion...in private self-defense."

Thomas Jefferson: "No *free man* shall ever be debarred from the use of arms — The Constitution of most of our states (and of the United States) assert that all power is inherent in the *people,* that they may exercise it by themselves; that it is *their* right and duty to be at all times *armed...*"

Capital letters are intended throughout this letter to add emphasis not in the original.

George Mason: "I ask you, sir, what is the militia? It is the whole people except for a few public officials. To disarm the *people,* that is the best and most effective way to enslave them."

Zachariah Johnson: "The *people* are not to be deprived of their weapons. They are left in full possession of them..."

Tenche Cox: "...The unlimited power of the sword is not in the hands of either federal of state governments, but, where I trust in God it will ever remain, in the hands of the *people.*"

Fisher Ames: "The rights of conscience, of bearing arms, of changing governments are declared to be inherent in the *people.*

Alexander Hamilton: "The best we can hope for concerning the *people* is that they be properly armed."

Most State constitutions also spell out the right of citizens to keep and bear arms, and generally it has been accepted as such, other than by liberal courts like the Warren Burger Court, and Socialists like Civilleti and Katzenbach, that the right to keep and bear arms is always vested in the people, and not in the States or any government agency.

It is apparent from the statements by these attorneys general and from the hopelessly incorrect ruling of the Warren Burger court, that none of them have ever heard of the Dick Act of 1902, let alone studied it, or else, Burger, Civilleti and Katzenbach chose to deliberately violate the Dick Act. Whether out of ignorance or by design, these individuals should have been impeached and tried for treason for violating their oath to uphold the U.S. Constitution.

In addition, so-called unconstitutional gun control "laws;" the one in the 1930s, the one in 1968, and the 1993 so-called "Crime" bill, and the Brady bill, and the thousands of impertinent State "laws" and local ordinances implementing "gun control," are all null and void, and in violation of the Dick Act, the 2nd Amendment and Article 1, Section 9, Part 3, of the U.S. Constitution — "no bill of attainder or expost facto laws shall be passed." And remember, no legislative board, local, county, or State legislatures can purport to pass ordinances or laws that violate the Constitution of the United States and the Bill of Rights. All such legislative acts have got to conform with the supreme law of the land.

And Waco was a bill of attainder and expost facto violation, a 2nd Amendment violation, and the perpetrators ought to have been brought to justice and criminally charged for what they did to David Koresh and his people. What Attorney General Reno, the B.A.T.F. and the F.B.I. did at Waco, grossly violated constitutional restraints imposed upon the federal government by the Dick Act, and especially by Article 1, Sec. 9, Part 3 of the U.S. Constitution, and the 2nd Amendment. The American people have been denied these rights by a conspiracy of silence and by deliberate misrepresentation, or ignorance of these rights, such as occurs in the letter by Mr. Voyles.

Mr. Voyles tries to twist and squeeze the Constitution and Bill of Rights to make it seem as if the right to keep and bear arms is addressed to the militia. Let me remind Mr. Voyles that neither St. George Tucker, Thomas Paine, George Washington, James Madison, Noah Webster, Patrick Henry or Zachariah Johnson, said the right is vested in the militia, and in any case as George Mason said, "the militia consist of the WHOLE PEOPLE." Mr. Voyles did not say which militia he is talking about in his letter of March 9, 1997.

In 1982, the Subcommittee on the Constitution of the United States Senate Judiciary Committee, published "The Right To Keep And Bear Arms" and this report is mandatory reading for every person/citizen, every local board, local, state and federal government officer. An extract follows:

"The Second Amendment right to keep and bear arms, therefore, is a right of the individual citizen to privately possess and carry in a peaceful manner firearms and similar arms. Such an individual rights interpretation is in full accord with the history of the right to keep and bear arms previously discussed...It accurately reflects the majority of proposals that lead up to the Bill of Rights itself."

It is clear that freemen, persons, citizens, have the right to keep and bear arms, form a militia and for the militia to keep and bear arms also, the unorganized (unenrolled) militia being the largest: Pages 1391 - 1396; Appendix, Annals of Congress May 7, 1792 and the Dick Act of 1902. The very language of the Dick Act speaks of the "right of the people" and the 1st and 4th Amendments likewise, use the language "the right of the people."

Nor is it expressly implied or incidental to a power already in the Constitution, and the Bill of Rights, that the federal government, the Congress, the President, the several States, or any local municipality, town board, can abolish, usurp, infringe upon, or in any way, shape or form, alter or amend or abridge the right of citizens/people, freemen, militia, to keep and bear arms of whatever type or in any quantity they may deem necessary, for their protection, as guaranteed by the 2nd Amendment. The Right To Keep And Bear Arms report by the Senate Judiciary Committee makes this abundantly clear.

Mr. Voyles' assertion that the right to keep and bear arms is vested solely in the militia, springs from not knowing anything about the Dick Act of 1902. In this he is in good company as ninety eight percent of the Congress is also ignorant of the Dick Act. Certainly, the federal judiciary — federal judges and the Supreme Court — and especially Warren Burger, know nothing of it — nor does the A.B.A., nor Attorney General Reno, nor prosecutors at all levels of the court system in this country, and much less does President Clinton know the first thing about this vital legislation which gave a knock-out blow to all gun grabbers and violators of the 2nd Amendment.

The Dick Act passed by Congress on June 30, 1902, was written by Representative (General) Dick, and it is a very lengthy document from which I can only quote extracts in this letter. Known as the "Efficiency of the Militia Act HR 11654," the Dick Act makes all so-called "gun control" laws, the 1968 version, the Brady bill, Feinstein's "assault weapons" bill, the various Schumer bills, and the Lautenberg bill, null and void and of no force or effect, incumbent upon none. The Second Amendment combined with the Dick Act of 1902 also makes all B.A.T.F. regulations pertaining to guns without legal substance, archaic, unconstitutional, and incumbent upon none.

The Dick Act is the finest legislation protecting the 2nd Amendment rights of the citizens passed in this century. H.R. 11654 is one of the twin peaks upon which the Socialist ship "Gun Control" founders and sinks. The Dick Act confirms the existence of three types of militia; the regular Army; the Organized Militia — known as the National Guard — and the unorganized militia. It is found in the Congressional Record, House, pages 7706-7713, 321-352, 7594-7595, "Efficiency of the Militia" bill H.R. 11654:

"Be it enacted that the militia shall consist of every able-bodied male citizen, respective of States, Territories, and the District of Columbia and every able-bodied male of foreign birth who has declared his intention to become a citizen, who is more than 18 and less than 45 years of age, shall be divided into three classes; the organized militia, to be known as The National Guard of the State, Territory or District of Columbia, or by such other designations by the laws of the respective States or Territories, as may be given by the laws of the respective States or Territories, the *national voluntary* reserve as provided in this act, and the remainder to be known as the *reserve militia.*" Then, in answer to a question, Rep. Dick stated as follows:

"If the gentleman refers to the unenrolled militia as it is now termed, there would be 10,000,000 of them. Of the organized Militia, or the national Guard, 115,000."

How much clearer could it be that all men between the ages of 18 and 45 are the unenrolled (unorganized) militia with an absolute right to keep and bear arms under the 2nd Amendment to the U.S. Constitution. The revised militia act of 1902 (Dick Act) is further proof of what the Founding Fathers intended the law of the land to be. The number of unenrolled or unorganized militia would be a very large body of citizens today, approximately 45,000,000, and no Federal so-called gun control "laws" can deny the millions of citizens — by law the unenrolled (unorganized) militia — the right to keep and bear arms. Federal "law" abridging this right is 100 percent unconstitutional, and the same applies to State law, and laws passed by any other legislative body at whatever level.

And the citizens all come under the right to keep and bear arms as the Dick Act makes perfectly clear. The Militia Act and the revised Militia Act — the Dick Act, make it perfectly plain that they go together to give the citizen/people, the right to keep and bear arms for their own protection. For example, most States have wording similar to the Constitution of the State of Oregon:

"Article 1, Section 27, Right to bear arms — The *people* have the right to bear arms for the defense of themselves and the State, but the military shall be in subordination to the Civil power." I ask you, just where does it say that the right to bear arms is vested solely in the organized militia?

In the foregoing is revealed how shallow, ill-informed and vacuous are the courts in upholding any type of "gun control" so-called "legislation." In the first instance it is gross impertinence on the part of any local council, board, State legislature, and the Congress, to attempt to pass "laws" restricting the 2nd Amendment, as any such "law" is not in consonance with, or pursuant to, or incidental to another power expressly implied, something already in the Constitution.

Chief Justice John Marshall said that unless the power sought complies with the foregoing constitutional requirements, it is a prohibition of such a power (law, ordinance etc.) Therefore ALL so-called "gun laws" are nullities, and not laws at all, and incumbent upon none to observe. No ordinance or law can be based on a violation of the Constitution, and the Bill of Rights, and the Dick Act, and Art. 1, Sec. 9, Part 3 of the U.S. Constitution.

Neither local boards, State legislatures, the President, nor the Congress, nor the Supreme Court, can exceed the delegated powers of the federal government, nor can they add to or subtract one comma from the delegated powers of the federal government given by the Constitution and Bill of Rights, which powers were granted by We, the People. Any attempts to infringe on the right to bear arms vested in the people, is treason, sedition, appalling malfeasance, sophistry and mendacity, and should be treated as such.

To try and separate the right of We, the People from the 2nd Amendment and say that it is addressed solely to the States militia, is nothing but quackery, venal absurdity, puerile, degrading, ingenious mendacity, and nefarious double-speak. What Mr. Voyles and others of his beliefs try to do is separate the 2nd Amendment from the rest of the

Constitution and this cannot be done. The Constitution is a document of perfect equipoise; trying to isolate the 2nd Amendment from the rest of it is an attack on the whole Constitution.

The gun-grabbers and their favorite liberal judges make a big mistake by intermingling State law with federal law. All "gun laws" upheld by courts of one stripe or another, were either based on unconstitutional proclamations, a.k.a., "executive orders" (not empowered by the Constitution as only a king can issue a proclamation) or deliberate violations of the Constitution and the Bill of Rights, and the Dick Act, and Art. 1, Sec. 9, Part 3 of the U.S. Constitution. In all cases, such ordinances, "laws" or anti-gun "laws" passed by the Congress are in violation of the U.S. Constitution and the Bill of Rights as they go beyond the pale and the ken of the Constitution and are nullities and are ultra vires.

Chief Justice John Marshall stated that when a legislative body (including a town or city council) goes outside the pale and the ken of the Constitution, its directives, ordinances, rules, regulations that purport to abridge the right of citizens to keep and bear arms, are null and void and no law at all, being mere hypotheses heaped upon hypotheses. Local governments cannot pass ordinances that violate the 2nd Amendment rights of the people, nor any other amendment dealing with personal rights and, as I said before, the right to keep and bear arms is a personal right dating back to the Magna Carta.

According to Mr. Voyles, attorneys general Civilleti, Katzenbach and others claimed that "for over 200 years the federal courts have unanimously determined that the second Amendment concerns only the arming of the people in service to an organized state militia." This is sophistry at its worst, and Mr. Voyles has a duty to cite some of "two hundred years of unanimous cases." It is true that a handful of liberal lawyers, Socialist judges, and civil servants, tried to twist and squeeze the Constitution and Bill of Rights to fit their predilections, forbidden by the 9th Amendment, but a reading of the Dick Act, if for no other reason, makes such verdicts one hundred percent wrong and a violation of the U.S. Constitution, for which they should have been impeached.

One of the worst violations of the 2nd Amendment was carried out by a judge in the notorious, unconstitutional, Morton Grove case.

No wonder Thomas Jefferson said, "To consider the judges as the ultimate arbiters of all constitutional questions is a very dangerous doctrine indeed, and one which would place us under the despotism of an oligarchy."

As for Supreme Court rulings favoring so-called gun control laws, since 1933 the court has been dominated by Socialists, the majority of whom have sought consistently to legislate, and several of them, among them Warren Burger, lacked judicial restraint, making them unfit to be judges. Unconstitutional judicial legislating by the Supreme Court under color of "interpreting" the Constitution resulted in serious erosions of the Second, Fourth, Fifth, Ninth, and Tenth amendments to the United States Constitution and the Bill of Rights.

Even the radical Northern Republicans in their violent hatred of the South in the aftermath of the Civil War, as expressed in the third section of the fraudulent 14th Amendment, never attempted to take guns away from the citizens of the secessionist States. Presumably, with "200 years of unanimous decisions etc." Mr. Voyles can point to a few court rulings during the period 1860-1900, a period in our history when the Supreme Court was not ruled by Socialists, to prove his "200 years" contention? Hopefully, he will do so.

Mr. Voyles ought to know that depriving citizens of their 2nd Amendment rights is a bill of attainder, forbidden in Article 1, Sec. 9, Part 3 of the U.S. Constitution. If he does not, then a reading of the landmark case, Cummings vs. State of Missouri, which was a bill of attainder case, is strongly recommended. A bill of attainder is where a legislative act inflicts punishment without a judicial trial. So-called gun control laws are bills of pains and penalties, in some cases inflicted by the federal government and in other cases by States, and also by local boards or municipalities. Judges who uphold bill of attainder pains and penalties violations or expost facto prohibitions specified in Art. 1 Sec.9, Part 3 of U.S. Constitution, are no more fit to hold office than to fly to the moon. Boards, commissions, State legislatures and the Congress are all deemed to be legislative bodies. They all violate the same constitutional prohibitions when they purport to pass so-called gun control "laws" or "ordinances."

All so-called gun control "laws" are bills of attainder, pains and penalties, expost facto violations and unconstitutional. Congress cannot change the constitutional rights of citizens to keep and bear arms except by way of a constitutional amendment properly ratified by the required number of States. The Dick Act of 1902 forbids local boards, town councils, county boards, States or the Congress to deny the millions of citizens who make up the unorganized (unenrolled) militia, their personal right to keep and bear arms of any type and in any quantity they may deem fit for their protection.

Constant interference by the F.B.I., the B.A.T.F., and other law enforcement agencies with the rights of the citizens of the unorganized (unenrolled) militia is a violation of the 2nd Amendment and the Dick Act. The truth about the unorganized (unenrolled) militia has been hidden from We, the People, while the news media — the corrupt press, and the Federal government, constantly tries to impress on the minds of the people that somehow, it is unlawful for the unorganized (unenrolled) militia even to exist, and that they can be infiltrated, spied on and molested at will.

"This has got to be exposed as a gross violation of the unorganized (unenrolled) militia's 2nd Amendment rights and their personal rights in violation of the Dick Act of 1902, a law which these agencies are supposed to uphold. No law enforcement agency at any level has the right to interfere with the unorganized (unenrolled) militia which has an absolute right to exist and be armed, guaranteed by the 2nd Amendment and the Dick Act of 1902."

There is considerable evidence to support the contention that the right to keep and bear arms is a personal right, and it is found in the *Duke Law Journal* Volume 43, No.6 43, Duke L.J. 1236 (1994) by William van Alstyne, Professor of Law at Duke University. Only a few extracts of this valuable contribution to 2nd Amendment rights can be printed here, owing to space limitations:

"In startling contrast, during this time, however, the Second Amendment has generated almost no useful body of law. Indeed, it is substantially accurate to say that the useful case law of the Second Amendment, even in 1994, is mostly missing in action. In its place, what we have is roughly of the same scanty and utterly underdeveloped nature as was characteristic of the equally scanty and equally underdeveloped case law (such as it was then) of the First Amendment in 1904...In short, what was true of the First Amendment as of 1904, remains true of the Second Amendment even now..."

In my opinion this is because the mounting attacks on the 2nd Amendment are of recent vintage. Even during the evil of the Reconstruction legislation, the North never attempted to dispossess the South of its right to keep and bear arms To continue with the opinion of Professor William Van Alstyne:

"...The most one can divine from the Supreme Court's scanty decisions... is that such right to keep and bear arms as may be secured by this amendment may extend to such 'Arms' as would be serviceable within the militia (but not otherwise so — a sawed off shotgun may not qualify, though presumably by this test — the heavy automatic rifles assuredly would. (See United State 445 U.S. 55,65n.8 1980)...Robertson vs. Baldwin, 165 U.S. 275-282 (1897), referring to 'the right of the people to keep and bear Arms as a personal right.'"

"There are a few 19th century decisions, which have never been revisited by the Supreme Court merely mimicked others of the same era in holding that NONE of the rights enumerated in the Bill of Rights were made applicable by the 14th Amendment to the states — see 'Presser vs. Illinois, 116 U.S. 252, 265, (1886) (citing U.S. vs. Cruickshank, 92 U.S. 524,553 (1875)...'"

"The reference to a 'well regulated Militia' is in the first and last instance a reference to the ordinary citizenry. It is not at all a reference to regular armed soldiers as members of some standing army. And quite obviously, neither is it a reference merely to the state or to the local police. The very assumption of the clause, moreover, is that ordinary citizens (rather than merely soldiers, or merely the police), may themselves possess arms, for it is from these ordinary citizens who as citizens have a right to keep and bear arms (as the second clause provides) that such well regulated militia as a state may provide for, is itself to be drawn."

"Indeed, it is more than merely an assumption however, precisely because, 'the right of the people to keep and bear Arms' is itself stipulated in the second clause. It is *this right* that is expressly identified as *the right* that is not to be ('shall not be') infringed. The right is made the express guarantee of the clause. There is thus no room left for a claim that, despite this language, the amendment actually means to reserve to Congress some power to contradict its very terms, (e.g. that 'the Congress may if it thinks proper, forbid to the people to keep and bear arms to such extent as Congress sees fit to do...')"

On the one hand we have the Communists in the Legislature and the Clinton administration trying to disarm We, the People, and tax and interfere with what types of weapons we are allowed to carry under our 2nd Amendment rights, and on the other hand, we have the landmark case, De Shaney vs. Winnebago County Dept. of Social Services, 489 U.S. 189 (1989) that there is no constitutional obligation upon govern-

ment to protect every person from force or violence (and also no obligation or liability for failing to come to any person so threatened.)

Yet Blackstone's Commentaries says clearly that the right of self
defense is the oldest right known to mankind. That being the case, as it
most assuredly is, how does Government propose that citizens exercise
their right to self defense — which the 2nd Amendment *specifically*
defines as a personal right, since Government says it is not obliged to do
so? The very notion that government, having backed away from an
obligation to defend its citizens, can then go and fine and even imprison
the same citizens who by the use of arms, ward off the attackers, or guarantees their right to self protection? Where do the liberals get such an
unconstitutional idea from, and why should citizens obey such restrictions on the 2nd Amendment, which the Constitution says clearly, *shall*
not be infringed?

The 2nd Amendment was most certainly written for two or more
reasons:

1). It was to give the citizen the absolute personal right to keep and
bear arms for protection.

2). It was written to arm the citizens in a militia that would be the
protection of We, the People against some future, tyrannical government. The clause concerning the Militia was *not* written to limit ownership of arms to the Militia of the States. The clause was inserted *solely*
to show that the framers did not trust a standing Army and preferred to
have a Militia defense force. Both of these goals are crucial to the maintenance of liberty, and Thomas Cooley so stated.

In the light of the foregoing, it can now be seen just how unconstitutional was the federal government's actions at Waco and Ruby Ridge,
and what is even more frightening, is that the guilty in these violations
of a bill of attainder and expost facto laws, remain unpunished at the
time this work goes to print. In the case of those who were directly
responsible for these serious violations, a few have been placed on paid
leave; no other charges having been brought against those responsible
for the murders at Waco and Ruby Ridge, and there the matters rest. It
is indeed a most fearful state of affairs and indicative of just how far a
tyrannical central government has advanced. We, the People, might well
have to fight to get our country back.

CHAPTER 12

A DECLARATION OF WAR IS CONSTITUTIONALLY MANDATED

I n ordering U.S. military forces to Bosnia, President Clinton, ripped up, trashed, violated, trampled under the feet of the Constitutional Anarchists, the U.S. Constitution, thereby creating a constitutional crisis of the gravest magnitude. Clinton thought it his right to assume the power of a king. Dole sold his soul to the Council on Foreign Relations (CFR) for personal aggrandizement and gain by backing Clinton's unconstitutional power grab, which he must surely have known was an unconstitutional act?

The problem with the American people is that the present generation is so vague about what is at stake; their priceless heritage is being destroyed before their very eyes, and yet the majority of Americans don't see this at all. The American people, thanks to the perfidious conduct of their political leaders, do not regard Clinton's Bosnia adventure as a constitutional crisis of enormous magnitude.

Never have the United States (plural) been as threatened as they are now by the Clinton power grab. What is happening is a constitutional crisis that will lead to bigger and more frequent usurpation of powers by the Executive Branch, until, William Jefferson Clinton "will stand in the place where kings stood" and the U.S. Constitution is consigned to the trash can of history.

The United States has *one* law — the U.S. Constitution. (Common law was retained by the States, mentioned in Article VII of the Bill of Rights when they came into the Union.) There is no such thing as law by implication, it has to be *expressly* implied, but Pres. Clinton says he can commit this nation to war (disguised as a "peace-keeping operation") on his sole authority, because past presidents have taken a similar power. There is no law from the Constitution and the Bill of Rights solely by implication as Clinton suggests; it has to be *expressly* implied, otherwise the Constitution becomes a blank piece of paper, to use Thomas Jefferson's scathing indictment of such would-be kings.

As a Socialist, we expect such conduct from Clinton, but Dole professed to be a conservative, and so, is perhaps even more to blame than the President. Dole epitomizes Gen. George Washington's observation that political parties are "baneful." Clinton and Dole are contributing to the overthrow of the Republic by sending the military to Bosnia without the prescribed declaration of war first being issued by the Congress.

The previously-mentioned Federal Government agencies like the BATF, the FBI, the Department of Education, the National Security Agency, not being expressly implied in the U.S. Constitution, Article 1, Section 8, Clauses 1-18, renders them unconstitutional and without force of law. These entities and many more "government agencies" violate the 10th Amendment to the U.S. Constitution, the police powers of education, health and police protection. These powers reside in the States and were not surrendered to the Federal Government at the time of the signing of the Constitution.

Referring to pages 899-907, Congressional Globe, Feb 1869, and particularly to page 903, we find the following:

"That the United States will guarantee every state in the Union a republican form of government, and Congress is empowered to enforce this guarantee. The definition of republican government was solemnly announced by our fathers, first, in that great battle cry which preceded the Revolution, 'taxation without representation is tyranny' and secondly, in the Great Declaration at the birth of the Republic, that all men are equal in rights and that the government stands on the consent of the governed. A republic is where taxation and representation go hand in hand, where all are equal in rights and no man is excluded from participation of government..."

The governed has not given their consent to Clinton's power-grab expressed in sending troops to Bosnia in defiance of the Constitution. Clinton and Dole are guilty of taxation by false representation, as is Senator Feinstein, who told her constituents — 15 to 1 against Clinton's power grab — that she knows what is best and they must trust her! Only a person as totally ignorant of the Constitution as Feinstein is, would have made such an astounding statement, which comes straight out of the Communist Manifesto of 1848.

Although I have no way of proving it, I would say that neither Clinton, Dole, or Mrs. Feinstein has ever read — let alone studied — the Appendix of "Blackstone's Commentaries With Notes of Reference to the Constitution and Laws of the Federal Government of the United States and of the Commonwealth of Virginia." St. George Tucker, the author, fought in the American Revolution and taught law at the College of William and Mary, and was a judge of the Virginia Court. Had Clinton and Dole read page 349 of the Appendix they would have discovered the restrictions imposed on the president:

"These circumstances but too well justify the remark, that if a single executive do not exhibit all the features of a monarchy at first, like infant Hercules, it only requires time to mature its strength, to evince the extent of its powers."

It does not take much study to conclude that infant Hercules Clinton has now reached full maturity with the sending of troops to Bosnia and the Gulf, and unless he is curbed by the application of the Constitution, greater and more frequent grabs of legislative powers, and acts of tyranny, lie just ahead of this nation. On page 329 of the above, we find the following restrictions applied to the president:

"The first shall be commander in chief of the army and navy of the United States and of the militia of the several States, *when called into the service of the United States.* A power similar to that of a king of England, and of the stadtholder of Holland, before the revolution; yet qualified by more restrictions, which I believe, were not to be found in either of these governments. As, first; He cannot make rules for the regulation and government of the Army and the Navy himself, but must be governed according to regulations established by Congress." In short, none of the former presidents had any war powers, and neither does Clinton.

"...A third and infinitely more important check...as long as elections continue as frequent as the present, is that no appropriations for support of an army can be made for longer than two years, the period for which congress is chosen — this puts the power of the people at the end of the period."

"Fourthly; the Militia of the several States, though subject to his command when called into service *by the authority of Congress and must be governed by law; the States....*"

Herein lies the final authority exercised by the House and Senate — they have to give their consent by law to the President sending the military abroad. And consent has to be in the *proper form* of a declaration of war, an explanation of which comes later. But there is a restriction on the President calling out the Militia of the States; he can do so *only* for three reasons 1) to repel an invasion 2) to uphold laws 3) in the case of insurrection

Just because past presidents — notably Truman and Bush — violated their oath to uphold and defend the Constitution, *falsely* calling themselves commander in chief when they had zero authority to do so, this did not set a precedent for Clinton to follow. As St. George Tucker said, there has always been a tendency for the executive to try and take more powers, but the leash is there for the Congress to apply. Clinton should have been jerked up short by a congressional choke chain, but, unfortunately for the American people, Dole was holding the leash and he didn't do it because his controllers in the CFR told him to allow Clinton all the slack he needed to get American troops into the Bosnian and Gulf conflicts.

Only a very few members of the House and Senate have an understanding of what the war powers of the president are. They have no clear idea what the words "when actually called into service by the Congress" mean: The president *does not* assume the title of commander in chief of the armed forces simply by being elected to the office. If this were so, then the president would have the power of a king, but the words of condition in Article 11, Section 2, Part 1 of the U.S. Constitution "when *actually* called into service" are there to restrain him from acting like a king.

A careful reading of the foregoing leaves a clear picture: the president is *not* automatically the commander in chief upon being elected to office. The word "actual" forbids him to stand in the place where kings stood. A king has command of the armed forces and does not need the permission of the legislature to act. The president of the United States, on the other hand, *absolutely* requires Congressional permission *before* sending our troops anywhere.

I must repeat: Until the Congress confers the title of commander in chief upon him, the President is *not* the commander in chief. Conferring the title implies a *future action,* not a *past action,* which it would be if he, the President, automatically became the commander in chief upon being elected. Only Congress can confer the title, "commander in chief" upon the president and this can *only* be conferred after a constitutional declaration of war has been made by Congress.

Show me one place in the delegated powers of the executive where it says that the President has war powers. There is nothing in the delegated powers of Congress (Art. 1, Section 8, Clauses 1-18) that allows for such a false and fraudulent position to be taken by the President. Article 11, Section 2, part 1 of the U.S. Constitution states that the only duties the President has are *military* duties, when called into actual service; he has no role in planning or choosing reasons for taking America to war.

Only the House and Senate can plan a war or order military action in support of it, to be taken. If and when this is done by the House and Senate, then the House and Senate tell the President what he can and cannot do with our military forces; where they can be sent and for what purposes. Before that action by the joint session of Congress, he, the President, has zero power to take action such as sending troops to Bosnia, Haiti etc.

Yet, the several States had to come up with an estimated $200 million dollars in taxation to fund the unconstitutional power grab by Clinton and seconded by Dole, which is what experts say the Bosnia adventure will initially cost the people of the several States. The Democrat Party should openly declare itself the Communist party of the USA. It is a *war party.* Clinton is a Democrat whose Democrat predecessors dragged the people of the several States into World Wars I and II, Korea, Vietnam, and now Bosnia.

The war powers of the Congress and the President were thoroughly debated at the time the Mexican War engineered by Woodrow Wilson, acting on behalf of American oil interests, and was again, thoroughly debated in 1917 and 1918. A study of pages 7878- 7885, Oct. 6, 1917, Congressional Record, is what our legislators need to make, and some of our conservative talk-show hosts and guests would also benefit from a study these pages and avoid making the mistake of calling Clinton the commander in chief, as Michael Reagan did recently. This is misleading and confusing for those who look to Mr. Reagan for guidance.

Mr. Clinton can only become the commander in chief when called into actual service after a joint session of the Congress makes a constitutional declaration of war, after which Congress confers the title on him. Whenever I am an invited guest on talk show radio, I always ask the host if he can explain what a constitutional declaration of war means and what it involves? Thus far, not a single one of them was been able to answer this question correctly. Even a Columbia Law School professor who called in to challenge me on some constitutional matters when I was a guest on a radio talk show in New York, could not come up with the correct answers.

There is a reason for this. The declaration of war involves a five-step process and is probably the most complicated part of the Constitution. Congress has always been secretive about the process which goes back to Henry Clay, who was the most informed Senator on what comprises a joint session of the House and Senate in a constitutional declaration of war.

Congressional Record, House, July 21, 1888, pages 6635-6653, has an excellent definition of limited or partial wars. Our Founding Fathers knew a thing or two about wars and the zeal of the executive to seize power and wage war whenever the opportunity presented itself — which is why they hedged about with restrictions the president's powers.

The constitutional way for sending U.S. forces to fight a war overseas, would have been for the House and Senate to declare that they, not the President, were about to send troops to Bosnia for a year (Clinton's mythical time-table.) The House and Senate would then pass the necessary joint resolution and confer the title of commander in chief upon Clinton for 12 months. During this time the war powers of the President would be strictly limited to military matters. At the end of the 12 months the House and Senate would order the troops to return home and Clinton's title of commander in chief would fall away.

Clinton is the epitome of what James Madison warned the American people to be wary of:

"A standing military force with an overgrown Executive will not long be the safe companion to liberty. The means of defense against a foreign danger have always been the instrument of tyranny at home. Among the Romans it was a standing maxim to excite war whenever a revolt was apprehended. Throughout Europe the armies kept up the pretense of defending, having enslaved the people."

Isn't there a revolt going on against the Democrat Party and its

President? It is fairly obvious that there is a growing revolt against a failed President and his failed policies. To nullify the anger, Clinton excited talk of war in the Roman manner and now wants the people whom he will enslave by his Socialist policies to support his military adventure in Bosnia, and latterly, in a revived version of the private war of George Bush against Iraq. The American people would do well to rub their eyes and see just how they have been hoodwinked over so-called presidential powers to send troops to Bosnia, and the Middle East and take note that in violating his oath of office, Clinton was ably backed up by Sen. Dole.

We suggest that the American people read what the great Pomeroy had to say on presidential powers, which can be found in "Introduction to Constitutional Law" where Pomeroy states:

"The organic law nowhere prescribes, or limits the causes for which hostilities may be waged against a foreign country. The causes of war it leaves to the discretion and judgment of the legislature."

Clearly, this means that Clinton has no authority to involve the U.S. in a military adventure in Bosnia and the Middle East; and Pomeroy makes it clear this has naught to do with the old saw "support the troops in the field." In other words Clinton had zero authority to come to conclusions about the cause of war in Bosnia and the Middle East nor to make preparations to wage war, nor to send troops abroad for that purpose. All of these factors are the sole prerogative of the legislature, which also has the sole authority to fund the war.

In usurping these powers, Clinton, supported by Dole, violated his oath of office through *legislating,* which the executive is forbidden to do. This, if allowed to stand, gives Clinton the powers of a king and opens wide the door to tyranny at home and abroad. Congress created the Executive and the Judicial departments of government, and our Founding Father's experiences with King George III would not have allowed the Executive too much power and the same holds good for the Judicial department.

THE PRESIDENT AND SEN. DOLE ACTED IN IGNORANCE
OF THE CONSTITUTION

As an example of the above, hours after been advised of a so-called "non-binding" resolution by the Senate that he seek "approval of the Senate" (neither of these terms are in the Constitution) before sending

United States armed forces to Haiti, President Clinton made the following, remarkable statement:

"I would welcome the support of the Congress and I hope that I will have it. Like my predecessors of both parties, I have not agreed that I am constitutionally mandated to get it. I think we have done all that we need to do...." This unbelievable public admission that he does not know the Constitution he swore to uphold, displays for all to see the lack of real knowledge the President and the leaders of Congress have about the war-making powers of the President.

Clinton made his asinine statement after the United Nations agreed to mount an invasion of Haiti, hiding behind the U.N. for his authority. This in itself is a violation of the U.S. Constitution as we do not belong to the U.N. As Senator Sam Ervin once said: "There is no way under the noon-day sun that we could have joined the United Nations." The Constitution was framed precisely to prevent under-the-table deals being struck by the President, such as the underhand deals involving bribery and corruption made under-the-table by Bush in order to promote the illegal Gulf War.

Because this gross violation of the Constitution — sending all three branches of the services to Bosnia without a declaration of war — was allowed to pass without a challenge, every future president will feel free to involve the United States in every war the RIIA and the CFR which the U.N. believes should be fought for their interests. In spite of what the Socialists — Communists in the House and Senate may say, the President is duty-bound by the Constitution to obtain a properly drawn-up formal declaration of war from the Congress before he can rush the nation into war. A proper declaration of war is *mandatory* and not *voluntary*. Yes, the Founding Fathers did indeed write the Constitution to bind the hands of the Executive.

For the edification of the constitutional anarchists, the following is a properly drawn up declaration of war *mandated* by the Constitution, which President Clinton (and all future presidents) must obtain from the House and Senate, before taking our nation to war:

1. The House and Senate have to pass separate resolutions declaring that a state of belligerency exists between the United States and the belligerent nation. To pass such a resolution could take a few weeks or a few months. The Founding Fathers did not want some would-be king in the White House stampeding the nation into war.

2. The House and Senate must each pass a separate resolution that a

state of war exists between the United States and the belligerent nation which is a notice to the American people that the Nation is about to go to war. The word, "belligerent" must be mentioned. There can be no war without a state of belligerency existing. (Did Serbia or Iraq exhibit any belligerency toward the United States?)

3. The House and Senate would each pass separate resolutions informing the military that the nation is at war with the belligerent nation.

4. Then, the House and Senate would decide whether the war against the belligerent nation would be a perfect war, or an imperfect war. If an imperfect war (a limited war), then only one branch of the military could be engaged: If a perfect war (unlimited war), then all branches of the military services could be involved. (The Spanish American War, WWI and WWII are examples of properly drawn up declarations of war by the Congress, which ought to be studied by patriots who want to know more about these things.)

5. Then, the House and Senate would decide if the United States is engaged in a public war. In a public war, every man, woman and child in the United States is at war with every man, woman and child of the belligerent nation. Properly debated, such resolutions could take months to pass, which was what the Founding Fathers intended as a cooling-off period.

The so-called "police" actions constitute *imperfect* wars and as such they would still require a properly drawn up declaration by the Congress, giving the President temporary and limited permission as commander in chief in a military action against the belligerent nation or nations. The resolution could take the following form, or something like it:

"Resolved by the House and Senate of the United States of America in Congress assembled that a state of belligerency exists between (the particular nation) and the United States. The President is now given the title of commander in chief and is directed to authorize limited military action as a military officer to dispatch (the number of troops and their equipment) to the belligerent nation."

"The President will have this limited power of commander in chief for forty five days after which time he is to return all servicemen, together with at least 90 percent of their equipment to the United States. The House and the Senate reserves the right to make the policy in (the belligerent nation) or on any unconstitutional usurpation of power on the part of the President, the U.S. Constitution and the Bill of Rights being the law of the land."

Article II, Section 2 is very clear: The President is not automatically the commander in chief, nor can he become the commander in chief because the United Nations (U.N.) passes a resolution to make war on a nation. The U.N. has *zero* authority to declare war, for that constitutes meddling in the affairs of nations, and Vattel's "Law of Nations" does not recognize such interference in the affairs of sovereign nations. A United States declaration of war cannot be intertwined with, or be made a part of on the same document as a U.N. declaration of war, or a so-called "authorization" to commit U.S. forces to any type of military action. If such a thing were to happen it would violate the U.S. Constitution because it would admit tacitly, that the power of the United Nations to declare war, is greater than that of the House and Senate to declare war independently of the U.N., a position which would be 100 percent unconstitutional.

In the study of the debates about the United States joining the defunct League of Nations, we find that the very same issues came up then, as have come up with the U.N. The reason why the conspiracy to get the United States to join the League of Nations was defeated, was because the Senators who took the trouble to read the document, (something they were not allowed to do in the three-day so-called U.N. debate), saw that if the measure was passed by the Senate, it would give the League of Nations superior powers to declare war over and above the House and Senate's powers to declare war.

The U.S. Constitution would then have become subservient to the League of Nations Treaty. But the senators saw correctly that for this to happen, a constitutional amendment would have to be passed, setting the League of Nation's war powers above those of the U.S. Constitution. This, the Senators quite properly refused to allow. The same rules apply to the U.N. today, and we are not a member of the U.N. because constitutionally, we never joined it.

It is worth repeating: A declaration of war by the United States cannot be intertwined or intermingled or even be in the same document as a declaration of war by the U.N. To do so would make the U. N. an equal partner in international law with the United States, which is not only absurd, but 100 percent unconstitutional. Our international law (foreign policy) is taken from Vattel's "Law of Nations," the "Bible" used by the Founding Fathers. The U.N. takes its foreign policy from the Communist Manifesto of 1848.

This is why the Gulf of Tonkin Resolution which led to the Vietnam War was fatally flawed; it was entwined with a U.N. resolution. Inasmuch as the Gulf of Tonkin Resolution was prepared by the State Department and not the Congress, it was a doubly flawed document. Judge Joseph Story really knew the Constitution. In his book, "Constitution of the United States" (Book III) Page 412, we have the following fine explanation:

"A power to declare war is a power to make and carry out war. It is not a mere power to make known an existing thing, but to give life and effect to the thing itself...The true doctrine has been expressed in the Supreme Court: If from the imperfection of human language there should be any serious doubts respecting the extent of any given power, the objects, for which it was given, especially when those objects are expressed in the instrument itself, should have great influence in its construction."

As for what Mr. Clinton did in Haiti and again, when he rushed our armed forces to Bosnia, and latterly, to the Middle East, he may have thought that he had authority, but he did not have any authority. And even if he decided to go ahead on his own, as he almost admitted, Congress still had to fund the war, and Congress should have refused to do so, because of its unconstitutionality. Congress was incited to do so by passions built up about the wrongdoings of the Bosnian leaders (in the manner of George Bush against Saddam Hussein) which is why a proper declaration of war is mandated, so that passions can first have time to cool.

Instead of following the Constitution, we have Clinton doing his best to stir up passions and hatreds and inciting the armed forces to do the same. In 1991 — and it seems that Clinton based his assumption on this — the lame reasons for such an assumption of war powers by Clinton, were advanced by Mark Lowenthal, Senior Specialist in U.S. Foreign Policy at the State Department:

"...Several times in U.S. history, Congress has voted authorization for the President to use force without actually declaring war. The most well known was the Gulf of Tonkin Resolution (P.L 88-408.)" Other "precedents" cited by Lowenthal in this memorandum are Algerian

Cruisers 1815, Venezuela 1890, and Paraguay 1858, the Cuban Resolution 1962, Berlin Resolution, and this appeared in the Congressional Record, House, January 12, 1991, pages 448-449: "Memorandum on Past Congressional Authorization for the Use of Force, Congressional Research Service, Library of Congress, Washington D.C., Jan. 10, 1991."

Mr. Lowenthal may have unwittingly made a 100 percent false statement here, because like so many "experts," he never studied the Annals of Congress, the Congressional Globes and Congressional Records. The Algerian Cruisers, 1819, was a three-year war with the Barbary Pirates. It was done on a declaration of war as the Supreme Court stated, as was the three year naval war with France. Both were conducted on declaration of war by the Congress as *imperfect* wars.

Whether wars be perfect or imperfect, like the examples cited by Lowenthal, the House and Senate must pass a joint resolution that a public war exists between our nation and the other nation or nations. The joint session of Congress must say that a state of *belligerency* exists between that nation, and the United States. Without a statement by the House and Senate that a state of belligerency exists, there can be no declaration of war.

Glaringly absent from the Gulf of Tonkin Resolution was the mandatory House and Senate resolutions that a state of belligerency, and therefore, a state of war, existed between the United States and Vietnam and North Korea, without which nothing could be constitutionally done to pursue the war. The Spanish American War was a correct model of a declaration of war as it said that a state of belligerency existed *before* the declaration of war was passed by the House and Senate.

This may sound complicated, but that is how the Founding Fathers meant it to be. They made a cooling-off period mandatory, before actual war was declared. Further excellent reading on the subject can found in the Congressional Record, House, July 21, 1888, pages 6635 - 6653, Court of Claims, French Spoilations, Opinions of the Court delivered May 17, 1886. This was a ruling by Judge John Davis who far surpassed in stature in his understanding of the Constitution, any of the current justices of the Supreme Court.

It is made clear in the above-mentioned pages that the United States cannot refer to any other nation as "the enemy" until such times as a declaration of war has been passed by the House and Senate. The House and

Senate fully intended the naval war with France to be a limited or imperfect war, but it progressed to an unlimited war. Lowenthal was wrong to try and confuse the issue.

Thus, it becomes clear that the U.S. has no right to be taking part in the boycott of Iraq nor propping up the corrupt Al Sabah regime in "Kuwait" — that artificial entity created upon land stolen from Iraq through British force of arms, — nor do we rightly occupy Haiti and Panama. There is not one single word in the U.S. Constitution that says that Clinton, acting on his own, can rush troops to Bosnia; nor is there anything which would have allowed Clinton to send our military to Haiti, nor to protect the corrupt dictators of the Al Sabah regime in Kuwait. Much less is there any provision in the Constitution that would have allowed George Bush to kidnap Gen. Noriega of Panama and shanghai him to Florida.

The steps to be taken by Congress (House and Senate in a joint session) for a declaration of war were mandated by the Founding Fathers precisely to tie the hands of presidents, so that he cannot railroad the American people into war to satisfy some under-the-table deal about which the public knows nothing. It is right and proper to tie the president's hands, and it is meant to prevent unconstitutional wars being entered into by the Executive Branch of its own volition.

Confirmation of the foregoing is found in the Congressional Record, April 5, 1917, pages 319-326, which contain a perfect declaration of war against Germany as mandated by the Constitution. As much of a tricky tyrant as he was, Wilson knew that the Senate would not allow him to get America into WWI, without a proper declaration of war. This differs vastly from "approval by the Senate" for which there is no provision in the Constitution.

Further details about a constitutional declaration of war being necessary before the President can go charging off to war is found in pages 378 and 412, April 5, 1917 and in pages 7878-7885, Oct. 6, 1917. I strongly urge every American citizen to make himself or herself thoroughly familiar with what the Constitution has to say on this vital matter, by reading and studying the foregoing.

Page 7800 of the Congressional Record, October 6, 1917 is vitally important, because it quotes what Lincoln wrote to a friend concerning the constitutional limitation of war-making powers imposed on presidents:

"The provision of the Constitution giving war making powers to

Congress was dictated, as I understand it, by the following reasons: Kings had always been involving and impoverishing their people in wars, pretending, in not always, that the good of the people was the object. This our convention understood to be the most oppressive of all kingly oppressions, and resolved to so frame the Constitution that no man should hold the power of bringing this oppression upon us. But your view destroys the whole matter and places the President where kings have always stood."

An excellent statement in support of Lincoln's position was made by Rep De Fazio and is found in the Congressional Record, House, January 12, 1991, pages H402-H403:

"President Harry Truman introduced a large American military force into the Korean conflict without Congressional authorization whatsoever. His administration advanced the unheard of theory that the President, as commander in chief of the Armed Services of the United States, has full control over the use thereof... The framers (of the Constitution) sought to create an executive, not another king."

Now comes Clinton and he is of the opinion that he can act like a king in introducing a large United States army into Bosnia and the Middle East without a Congressional declaration of war.

St. George Tucker:

"...When under the odious name of ambition shall lead us to conquest, when a bold, though raw Militia shall be exchanged for a well-trained, well-disciplined and well appointed army; ready to take to the field at the nod of an ambitious president (Roosevelt, Bush, Clinton) and believe that the finger of heaven points to that course which his directs; then we may regard the day of our happiness as past, or hasting rapidly to its decline."

The Panama, Haiti and Iraq military adventures bear the stamp: "By the order of the Committee of 300 and for the benefit of the Rothschilds."

Henry Clay, undoubtedly the best constitutional scholar and authority on a constitutional declaration of war is quoted on page 7879, Congressional Record, Oct. 6, 1917, as follows:

"I conclude, therefore, Mr. President and fellow citizens with entire confidence, that Congress has the right, either of the beginning or during the prosecution of any war, to decide the objects at the beginning or during the prosecution of any war, to decide the objects and purposes for which it was proclaimed or for which it ought to continue. And I think it is the duty of the Congress by some deliberate and authentic act, to declare to what objects the present war shall be longer prosecuted."

"I suppose the President would not hesitate to regulate his conduct by the pronounced will of Congress to employ force and diplomatic power of the nation to execute his will. But if the President should decline or refuse to do so, and in an contempt of the supreme authority of Congress should persevere in waging war for other objects than those proclaimed by Congress, then it would be the imperative duty of that body to vindicate its authority by the most stringent and effectual and appropriate measures..."

"There can be no insuperable difficulty in Congress making such an authoritative declaration. Let it resolve simply, that the war shall or shall not be a war of conquest; and, if a war of conquest, what is to be conquered. Should a resolution pass disclaiming the President would conform to his constitutional duty..."

In other words, neither President Clinton nor any U.S. President can, on his own, rush the American people off to war against any nation, despite anything to the contrary declared by the Socialists — Communists in Congress (or those who have sold out to the CFR.) Nor can anything the President may say, alter the fact that a constitutional declaration of war is a mandatory prerequisite before any military action can be taken. And, if the President should be refused such a mandate, it is his duty to obey the Constitution. In short, President Clinton has no war powers of his own.

Pres. Clinton, having already dispatched the three branches of the armed services to Bosnia, and the Middle East, he, within 45 days of failing to secure a declaration of war from the Congress, was constitutionally-bound to have returned these forces — ALL OF THEM — to the United States. No amount of calling upon the nation to support the troops can erase the illegality of a continued flouting of the Constitution. Supporting the troops is not the primary issue at stake! Rather the primary issue at stake is whether he, the President, along with the Congress will obey the Constitution! On Page 7882 of the Congressional Record, October 6, 1917, we find the following:

"Constitutional Provisions involved (in declaration of war) — Section 8, Article 1 of the Constitution provides: The Congress shall have the power to lay and collect taxes, duties and imposts, and excise to pay the debts and provide the common defense and general welfare of the United States."

"It is clear, from the very first sentence that no war can be prosecuted without the consent of the Congress (and this has to be in the form of a properly expressed declaration of war.) There is NO power in the Constitution given to the Executive Branch to raise money for the purposes of making war. Only the Congress can do that. From this provision, (standing on its own,) it must follow without qualification that the duty of determining whether a war shall be prosecuted or not, whether the people's money shall be expended for the purposes of war or not, rests solely upon Congress, and with that power goes necessarily, the power to determine the purposes of the war, for if the Congress does not approve of the purpose of the war, it may refuse to lay the taxes upon the people to prosecute it..."

So where does Pres. Clinton get the idea that he can just rush our armed forces — or any part of them for that matter — to Bosnia and the Middle East at the behest of the upper-level parallel secret government — the CFR — without first having obtained, not "approval by the Senate" but, a constitutionally-correct and executed declaration of war by a joint session of the Congress.

To continue from the Congressional Record:

"Another reason for giving this (war making) power to the Congress was that the Congress, particularly the House of Representatives was assumed to be directly responsible to the people and would most nearly represent their views..."

The only power relating to war with which the Executive was trusted was that of acting commander and chief of the Army and Navy and of the Militia (subject to three restrictive limits in the case of the Militia) *when called into actual service, and not one minute before that.* This provision is found in Section 2, Article 11:

"The President shall be Commander in Chief of the Army and Navy of the United States and the militia of the several States when called into actual service of the United States."

In this is found the total sum and substance of the President's war powers. Whether the President agrees or not, he is constitutionally bound, first, to obtain a proper declaration of war from the Congress for military intervention in Bosnia or against any nation, now, and forever in the future. The Founding Fathers fully intended to hobble Presidents and tie their hands for the exact reasons stated in the Congressional Globes etc. To underline the point: the President has no war powers other than those enumerated in the foregoing, which was intended to clip the wings of high-fliers, whether Republicans like George Bush or Democrat (Communist) Party scofflaws like Mr. Clinton.

The President cannot enforce the laws of the United States in Iraq, Haiti, South Africa, Panama or Bosnia, or anywhere else. The matter was decided in the famous case, Milligan — 4 Wall — 2:

"The laws of the United States have no effect outside of the territory of the United States. Our Army in France or our Navy on the high seas may be engaged in worthy enterprises, but they are not enforcing the laws of the United States and the President derives his Constitutional obligations to enforce the laws of the country, no power to determine the cause of the present war..."

We do not need an amendment to the Constitution to stop the misrepresentation of the media about the alleged "commander in chief" status of President Clinton that are spread to hoodwink Americans into believing that Clinton can rush off to war at any time at the behest of the RIIA or the CFR, to act as a stooge for the international banker warlords. What war powers he has are already expressly implied in the Constitution and he, Pres. Clinton, has none other. This applies to all presidents of the U.S.A.

The venal, warped minds at work in the House and Senate, represented (unfortunately) by Boxer, Feinstein, Moynihan, Kennedy Jay Rockefeller and the chief House ignoramus of the Constitution, Charles Schumer, aided and abetted by Henry Hyde, will eventually destroy the Constitution if we let these legislators get away with every violation of the Constitution their venal minds can dredge up.

Moreover, besides those just mentioned, many other Representatives and Senators display ignorance about the President being the commander in chief of the armed services and they fall in line with the refrain, "his powers as commander in chief will be crippled if he is to wait for a constitutional declaration of war." The Founding Fathers were afraid of men like Bush and Clinton, that is why they worded their statements so carefully.

It states in the Constitution, in Article I, Section 8, Clause II: "To declare war and punish piracies..." It is expressly implied here that only the Congress can declare war and that the president is not commander in

chief except in time of war when the House and Senate in a joint resolution gives him the power of commander in chief to proceed against the
enemy. The term "commander in chief" was first used when the
Continental Congress called General George Washington into service at
the time of the American Revolution. Before that, Washington was not
the commander in chief of the armed services.

Neither Truman, Nixon, Reagan, Bush, and now Clinton, could have
been commander in chief of the nation's armed services, because during
their tenure in the White House, no constitutionally mandated and properly drawn up declaration of war was ever made. The Gulf of Tonkin
Resolution which started the Vietnam War was a hidden declaration of
war written up by the State Department, a usurpation of the separation
of powers between the three branches of government, and was thus, ultra
vires, since it did not emanate from the Congress nor was it drawn up by
the Congress.

It is already expressly implied in the U.S. Constitution that the president is not the commander in chief and he remains without this power
until it is granted to him by a joint session the House and Senate. Our
laws were taken directly from the Athenian legislature. To make the
Constitution of the United States last through the ages and to withstand
men like Roosevelt, Bush and Clinton, the Constitution was written so
these delegated powers were expressly implied.

The important thing to remember is that our Founding Fathers did
not desire a simplistic document. They wanted the Constitution to be
abstruse and complex. Simplistic constitutions (like the constitution of
the former USSR) allows plenty of leeway for tyrants. So if our
Constitution seems complex, it is meant to be that way.

Where in the Constitution is it stated or expressly implied that the
president is the commander in chief? It is just not there! During the time
that Socialist President Wilson was pushing the Nation into WWI, he
wanted ten additional powers not found in the Constitution. The House
and Senate thoroughly debated the matter and there are about 150 pages
of the Congressional Record which cover this debate. After diligent
study of these pages there is not found any power that would automatically make the President commander in chief of the armed forces, nor is
there any other place in the Constitution where it is so stated.

We know that at the time Vattel's "Law of Nations" was written,
Europe was controlled by absolute and non-absolute monarchies. Under

an absolute monarchy, the king or the prince could declare war. Many monarchs borrowed money to carry out their wars to the detriment of the people. Our Founding Fathers were determined not to give the power to make war to the President and that is why he never got this power and does not have this power to this very day.

The full information about the powers of kings and the president of the United States is all there in over 200 years of Annals of Congress, Congressional Globe and Congressional Record. Everywhere one looks in these journals one finds that over and over, it is expressly implied that the President is not the commander in chief save and except when that power is given to him by a joint resolution of the House and Senate, nor does he have the power to lay taxes (borrow money) like a king has.

For Clinton (and Bush before him) to say he is the commander in chief, and for this absurdity to be echoed by the news media and most members of the legislature, is a horrible error which some perpetuate in order to fool the American people. Of course matters went from bad to worse when Franklin Roosevelt was in the White House, engaging in an undeclared, unconstitutional war on German shipping, before the U.S. ever got into WWII.

Now, we have another deplorable situation where President Clinton exceeds his authority by sending our armed forces to Bosnia and the Middle East and conspires with the U.N. to this end. Where in the Constitution of the United States is he so empowered? The answer is, *"nowhere."* Sorry to disappoint those "moderate" and "progressive" *Socialists* who are striving to give legislative powers to the President in defiance of the Constitution, and those who defer to the CFR.

Senator Bayard had this to say back in 1884. Congressional Record, Senate March 17, 1884 pages 1962-1967:

"When ever for the few and simple powers to be sparingly administered, vested by the Constitution in the simple and severe government of a confederation of Republics (remember George Washington called the United States a Confederated Republic) there shall be substituted the powers and duties, excessive revenue, lavish expenditure, the corruption of a consolidated imperial republic, there will have struck the hour which announces its recipient disintegration — to be consumed through successive agonies of despotisms, oppression, war, separation, there will have struck the hours of our doom."

This is a very accurate portrayal of conditions in America as we enter the 21st century. The Founding Fathers knew the Executive was not be trusted with war-making powers, but had to be caged and kept under constraint, and not without good reason. They also knew that the central government would seek greater powers, that is why they gave the central government, strictly regulated and controlled powers, delegated by We, the People, to keep the howling monster caged forever.

Article 1, Section 9 of the Constitution of the United States denies, the President any war powers and gives them, instead to Congress to legislate on the constitutionally mandated declaration of war. As for the President, his powers are found in Section II of the U.S. Constitution, and he has none other. We can safely discount so-called "executive orders" as these are proclamations forbidden the Constitution. Only kings of England have the power to issue proclamations; the President of the United States, not being a king, does not.

In these days of a dizzying lurch toward Socialism, openly begun by the Franklin Roosevelt, the butcher of Hyde Park, it is important to know that all three branches of government are *not* coequal. The Continental Congress created the executive and judicial branches and Congress never intended them to be coequal. Congress (the legislature) has *superior* powers, especially through its control of the purse strings. Technically, Congress could close down the executive and the judiciary by simply refusing to fund them.

Unless President Clinton is constrained by the Constitution, he will continue to play with fire in Bosnia and the Middle East, which could very easily get out of hand and engulf all Europe in a war. If there is any leadership left in this country, now is the time for such leaders to come forward and demand that the President and likewise the House and Senate, obey the Constitution, and, if they refuse, then the necessary constitutional measures to force obedience to the Constitution, the only law, must to taken to correct the situation. The Constitution says that We, the People, are vested with the authority to remove from office those who violate the Constitution. Let us make sure that the Congress and the President abide by the Constitution or face the penalties for defiling the Constitution as mandated by the Founding Fathers.

CHAPTER 13

ABUSES OF THE CONSTITUTION BY THE FEDERAL GOVERNMENT

4TH AMENDMENT TRAMMELED, ROILED AND TRASHED
FIRST AMENDMENT DOES NOT PROHIBIT SCHOOL PRAYER
FEDERAL ELECTIONS
THE FLAG DEBATE

We have seen in Waco and Ruby Ridge the unmistakable evidence that the federal government and its octopus-like agencies have taken an open position to nullify the 4th Amendment rights of We, the People. There are scores of writers in this country, who are sounding a clarion call to the citizens to defend the Constitution, or face the prospect of losing it altogether. The enemy within our gates is engaging in low-intensity warfare tactics to dismantle the Constitution piece by piece, rather than try a head on assault on a target which is too strong for that.

My hundreds of warnings about what is going on with the irregular low-intensity warfare against the Constitution, reaches but a very small audience. This is due to the fact that in every facet of my work, I finance myself. There are no Rush Limbaugh-type sponsors in my background constantly and regularly funding my work.

What is needed is for a national institution of some kind or another to take up the cudgels against the one enemy of the Constitution we can readily identify, that being the federal government octopus. I will supply the Constitutional material that is so necessary to arm our people. But unless this national movement comes soon, we are going to see the United States go the way of ancient Greece and Rome, and that is not as far down the road as some might mistakenly imagine.

Every day, new attempts to destroy the 4th Amendment are being made by the federal government octopus. The latest monstrous assault on the right to privacy comes under the guise of fighting the proliferation of indoor growing of marijuana. Lest you think this is in a noble cause, let me remind you that history — and that includes the history of the United States — is replete with examples of tyrants seizing power under the pretext of doing good for the nation. War monger Bush and his relative, the late unlamented Franklin D. Roosevelt, were past masters in this deception. Don't forget Roosevelt gave us Pearl Harbor and Bush gave us the Gulf War, NAFTA, GATT, FinCen, all under pretexts of doing good for the nation and all 100 percent unconstitutional.

Our current warning to We, the People, concerns the virtually unrestrained use of thermal imagery to invade the privacy of the home. The use of this device should be outlawed under the 4th Amendment guarantee of privacy, whether for a noble cause or not. A noble cause does not in any way make right an unconstitutional act. There can be no exceptions to the Constitution and Bill of Rights.

The Agema 210 is invasive of citizen's rights to privacy. This hand-held thermal imager is very popular with police agencies all across the country, but particularly in California. Thermal imaging is a warrantless search and, as I said, is an invasion of the privacy of one's home. Another unconstitutional practice is getting National Guard helicopters to thermal image private property. Where does the federal government octopus think it gets this kind of "right?" When is the Republican Party going to put an end to it?

The hand-held Agema 210 thermal imager is a thoroughly unreliable device with a short range of only 200 feet or less, which means that the intruder has to come close to your house, dwelling, outbuildings. The government calls such an action, "non intrusive, passive!" The Agema 210 camera has vague calibrations and cannot take into account weather conditions nor sloppy work by its operator. All that it does is measure (inaccurately) relative heat intensities. Never mind being "non-intrusive," it is *intrusive*.

Now all your intrepid Agema 210 operator has to do is go to a magistrate to have a search warrant rubber-stamped. He does this by stating his credentials — that he is a "certified thermographer," meaning that he has attended a Justice Department training course, which is no more than a certificate of attendance. Unfortunately, too many of our magistrates, under the guise of acting for the benefit of the community, no matter that it trammels the Constitution, routinely rubber-stamp such warrants.

That sets the stage for the next step. Beware, you may be enjoying your jacuzzi or sauna when, without warning the door is kicked in by a variety of camo-clad, steel helmeted, flak jacketed, machine gun toting "federal agents" looking for your marijuana-growing hot house. This force arrives on your property because some neighbor who doesn't like you, or hates the fact that you have a nicer home or a better car, tells the police that "something is going on out there."

Yes, this happens many, many times each year. It is especially prevalent in rural or semi-rural areas, where the government has turned ordinary people into an army of snitchers. It was "neighbors" who told the government about Waco and Ruby Ridge and they will have no compunction on telling on you if it suits their purpose, or if they know a reward is possible. Just minding your own business and not troubling trouble lest it trouble you, is no longer a guarantee of your 4th Amendment rights.

Take the case of two campers in the Kings Range who had guns shoved in their faces by a horde of camo-flack jacketed steel helmeted men with their faces painted black. With a variety of weapons thrust into their ribs, the hapless pair saw their truck, camping equipment, *illegally* searched, as was their persons; 100 percent unconstitutional acts. Finding nothing the intrepid force got into their armored personnel carriers muttering something about "federal agents." How much longer are the American people going to put up with this sort of gross *misconduct?*

Hannah Nelson of the Pacific Justice Center says of thermal imaging: "It is a terrific recipe for spying on citizens in the supposed privacy of their homes. Have a hot tub and, the next thing, a thermal imager from some law enforcement agency will be off to the magistrate for a warrant." One bright note is that the Court of Appeals for the Ninth Circuit has ordered an evidentiary hearing on the use of thermal imagers. The net outcome will most probably be that the invasive tool will be declared legal, but with the proviso that thermal imaging be conducted only after a warrant has been secured and where the training and experience of the camera operator is not in question. This does not address 4th Amendment issues and one thing we must be clear about, "reliability and skill" will always be in question.

What we have here is a major Constitutional crisis building up over the invasion of our right to privacy through the use of thermal imagery. With such technology in the hands of law enforcement agencies, there is a potential for massive, endless abuse of the small fragments of our right to privacy that still remain. This is a national issue, which cannot, must not be ignored. We, the People of the several States have entered a period of unprecedented attack upon attack on the 2nd, 4th, 5th and 10th Amendments. Unless We, the People, are prepared to make the necessary sacrifices that will require us to stand up for the Constitution, then the end of our constitutional era is almost at hand.

EXAMPLES OF FINANCIAL IRREGULARITIES BY THE HOUSE & SENATE
CENTRALIZING COMMON LAW

There has been much misunderstanding over this law, which is a common law case, only applicable in the State where the criminal case occurred. Through its clients, the original State, decided voluntarily to bring Miranda before the Supreme Court. Having done so, the Miranda case of common law became binding only in that State and did not apply to all States. If the case is about the Constitution or about relations between the States, and a decision is handed down by the Supreme Court, then the decision is binding upon all of the States.

There is nothing in the Constitution that would allow the U.S. Supreme Court to force standardization in common law cases upon the States by the case as it does now. The Bill of Rights, Article VII forbids the standardization of common law of all of the States. The original 13 States kept their own common law intact when they entered the Union, and when the other States joined, they adopted the common law of one of the original 13 States into their State Constitution. The best place to look for the intent of Article VII of the Bill of Rights is in the Virginia Constitution at the time the Founding Fathers were drafting the Constitution.

Today we find legislators like Kennedy and the Trojan Horses in the Republican Party trying to standardize or "unify" the common law of the States, which the Founding Fathers forbad. Any so-called "U.S. Code" which purports to rewrite the common law of the several States with intent to standardize same, is null and void and of no effect whatsoever. The Founding Fathers feared a king or a dictator and that is why they wrote the Bill of Rights as they did. In short, they feared a centralized government and thought they had made sure it would never happen, but they never knew the cunning duplicity of men like Earl Warren or Edward Kennedy, whose life's work has been and still is to standardize the U.S. Code so that the central government can flout the 10th Amendment.

FREEDOM OF RELIGION

What the Supreme Court has been doing and is still doing, is taking advantage of the briefness (terseness) of the amendments in the Bill of Rights to flout the intent and circumvent the Constitution. In addition to the above examples, there is the so-called "freedom of religion" proviso of Article 1. The freedom of religion provision in this article was taken *directly* from the Virginia Constitution at the time the Founding Fathers were drafting the U.S. Constitution. The degenerate secular humanist Justice Earl Warren, being a lawyer, knew exactly what the Virginia Constitution had to say about the matter, but instead of using a scholarly approach, he used a secular humanist Communist approach and wrote part of the Communist Manifesto of 1848 into the law, in order to better promote atheism in our schools and destroy the family building block of this nation. Warren took advantage of the *brevity* of the Constitution in order to compromise and twist its meaning.

It was Warren's climactical decision that turned this nation into a Godless Nation, where we cannot even celebrate nationally, the birth and death of Christ. It was also his chance to wreck public schools, where discipline is now a dirty word and education gone to hell in a hand basket are the fruits of Warren's labors. The proliferation of drug usage among school children is the direct outcome of Warren's butchery of the Bill of Rights.

Warren knew very well that the Virginia State Constitution spells out that what is meant by freedom of religion is that no one religion shall have dominance over another. It was intended to keep the United States from having a State religion, as is the case in Denmark, for example. It was aimed primarily at the Church of England. The Founding Fathers did not want a national church with close ties to the central government.

THE FIRST AMENDMENT DOES NOT PROHIBIT SCHOOL PRAYERS

With his bill to restore voluntary prayer to the schools, Senator Helms touched upon one of the most detestable interferences of the Supreme Court-ACLU (or are they one and the same thing?) There is not one word, nor is it expressly implied, nor is it in consonance with or pursuant to the U.S. Constitution and the Bill of Rights, that would allow the courts to prohibit payers in our schools. And don't trot out the so-called "Separation of Church and State" the mythical "wall of separation" because elsewhere I have clearly undercut the metaphysical legerdemain of the fevered imaginations of the man who invented the phrase, Leo Pfeiffer.

What the Founding Fathers had in mind when they talked about freedom of religion was that they wanted to make sure that the Church of England did not become the official church of the government as it was in England; as Catholicism is the official religion of France and Italy and so on. That is all it meant.

If anyone can show where in the Constitution and the Bill of Rights it states that there is a "wall of separation" preventing prayer in schools then I would be happy to hear from them. Prayer in schools is a matter reserved to the States under the 10th Amendment and the central Government has no right to meddle in such issues, which should never have become an "issue" and probably would not have, but for the meddling of the ACLU. Earl Warren committed an abuse of the 9th Amendment when he read his predilections into the decision to ban prayer in schools.

One of the innumerable institutes which spring up like magic whenever there is an abuse of the Constitution — and they are almost always on the side of the Communists — is the Aspen Institute, that branch of British intelligence MI6 in the United States. Their paper, "Global Ideology, Humanist Studies and the Aspen Institute" says it all. The Communists are determined to keep prayer out of schools just as they are determined to remove Easter and Christmas from the calender of national holidays. Even former Communist countries like Hungary and Poland never did this.

It is abundantly clear that the Supreme Court went beyond the pale and the ken of the Constitution and the Bill of Rights when it banned prayers in schools. As Senator Helms said on page S722, "this decision brought with it a tidal wave of pornography, incest, illegitimacy, poverty, teenage suicide, AIDS, just to name a few." To which one could add, teenage marriages, drug addiction, rebellion against parents, violent teenage crime, an increase in the number of teenage gangs, teenage rape, disrespect for young girls and women, a staggering number of teenage abortions. The list is almost endless.

Today, we have a teenage population which is ready for anarchy, yet we have people like Mrs. Feinstein and Mrs. Boxer loudly proclaiming that they are horrified by crime and try to blame the rise in crime on guns. They should abandon their unconstitutional opposition to school prayer if they really want to see a big drop in the rate of teenage crime

As to the Government's belief that it can intervene in education in the States and interrupt a centuries old tradition of school prayer, I point to the comments of the Hon. James Jones of Arkansas found in the Congressional Record, Appendix, June 26, 1884:

"Aid to Common Schools, Views of General Jackson, Pres. Monroe and others: This long line of precedents and authorities, approved by, I believe all Presidents, and acted on continuously by the Government, is to my mind conclusive of two points; First, that the Government has a right and the constitutional power to pass this bill and to make appropriations and carry it into effect; and Second, that the Government cannot, even with the consent of the States, control the object for which the appropriation is made without a constitutional amendment, authorizing it; that this bill does not and could not convey directly or by any implication such power. For myself I follow the teachings and example of Jefferson, Madison, Calhoun, Andrew Jackson..."

And what are these teachings? They are that the Central Government cannot appropriate money for education in the States and then tell them how to spend it , nor can it say that such appropriations can be withheld if the States do things the Federal Government may not like — such as allowing prayer in schools. The States ought to call the carrot-and-stick bluff of the Federal Government. The old tale that the Federal Government can withhold subsidies if schools in the States allow prayers is just so much unconstitutional nonsense.

THE MCVEIGH TRIAL

If we were a nation willing to abide by the Constitution and the Bill of Rights, we would not have allowed the Federal Government to circumvent and trample on them in the McVeigh trial. We don't know as yet how much of a tight leash Judge Richard Matsch kept on the defense, but there is reason to believe it was to the point where his rulings favored the government's case. We may yet find out a great deal more if we are lucky, and I refer to my remarks in the WIR issue of April, 1997. Whatever else Judge Matsch is, he is certainly not one who obeys the U.S. Constitution and the Bill of Rights, more especially, Article III, Section 2, Part 2:

"The trial of all crimes, except in the case of impeachment shall be by jury and such trial be held in the State where the said crime shall have been committed."

This was stated in the WIR issue of May 1995: "In addition, one has to read Article III, Section 2 Part 2, in conjunction with the 10th Amendment..."

No exception to this law is permitted other than in the case of impeachment proceedings. There is no part of the Constitution that is written with such care as the foregoing and the 10th Amendment which jealously guards the right of the State's police powers and limits Congress as to what it can and cannot do when it comes to States rights guaranteed by the 10th Amendment. Moving the trial of McVeigh to Denver was patently unconstitutional and those who arranged this move should be impeached because of their actions. Judge Matsch had no con-stitutional authority to try the McVeigh case in Denver, and he was duty bound by his oath to uphold the Constitution and to refuse it. His was a clear breach of the Constitution in accommodating the government by putting expediency before the Constitution.

The Constitution must be obeyed at all times, regardless of the "merit" of the cause of action and we cannot twist and squeeze the Constitution to fit causes of action, just because we might favor them. Judges are expressly forbidden by the 9th Amendment to read their own predilections into matters before them. Strange indeed that any man call-ing himself a jurist dare in the climate of hysterical excitement of the McVeigh case, created by the media, disobey the U.S. Constitution. Moving the McVeigh trial to Denver by persons more ingenuous than loyal to the Constitution, was a flagrant violation of the Constitution.

The Constitution clearly lays out in Sec. 8, Art. 1, Clauses 1-18, the delegated powers given to Congress, which Congress cannot add to, or subtract from, and the right to move an accused person out of the State in which the crime was committed is not in the delegated powers, thus, in itself, it was an unconstitutional, and therefore, unlawful act.

Until the transcript of the McVeigh trial becomes available, we won't know whether justice was FULLY served. One man who believes that the whole truth did not come out at the trial, was State Rep. Charles Key from Oklahoma City, who filed a 758-page petition with close to 14,000 signatures of Oklahomans who want a new trial for McVeigh — in Oklahoma. Key avers that the Federal government has covered up evidence, and his petition drive gathered three times as many signatures than required for a grand jury to be convened, which happened on July 11, 1997. We can be certain that this important development will be censored by omission, by the media.

Key met strong resistance in his efforts to get a special House committee to investigate the bombing, which it turned down, after which an Oklahoma County judge denied his request for a county grand jury, ruling it would duplicate a federal investigation, a strange ruling indeed. But six-term Rep. Key was not dismayed and kept up a drumbeat until an appeals court overturned the ruling, which opened the way for Key's petition drive which he began in mid-April 1997.

In announcing the success of his petition drive, Key told the media that he didn't believe that the whole truth had come out about the bombing. "Federal prosecutors have only told half of the truth. We want all of the truth." Keys added that he believes that the federal government had prior knowledge of the truck bomb and is determined to get the grand jury to examine all possible suspects.

Another trained observer who harbors strong suspicions about the government's account of the Oklahoma City bombing, is noted British journalist and author, Ambrose Evans-Pritchard. A severe critic of President Clinton, Evans-Pritchard attacked the government's version in the London newspaper, "The Daily Telegraph" and the "Sunday Telegraph." The White House spin doctors were completely stunned when Evans-Pritchard's book, "The Secret Life of Bill Clinton" was published. The book's dust jacket says:

"Among the secrets Evans-Pritchard exposes:

* The Oklahoma City bombing as a government sting operation that flew out of control when the stingers were outstung. Evans-Pritchard tells the story that the FBI and the Justice Department don't want you to know."

How Much More Infringement of Rights Will We, The People, Continue to Tolerate?

In previous publications of mine (monographs and WIR) I focused attention on what is going on at Menwith Hill in England. Recent developments on both sides of the Atlantic show paranoia in the determined efforts to keep the work done at this British-U.S. SIGINT station at Menwith Hill absolutely secret. Menwith Hill is the location of the largest electronic surveillance-snooping joint effort of the British and United States Governments, in the world.

According to intelligence reports, Menwith was established to evade the laws of both countries which protect its citizens from unwarranted, warrantless electronic eavesdropping. Britain's defense secretary Malcolm Rifkind, told a British court that any public disclosures about what goes on at Menwith Hill will do "serious and unquantifiable damage."

Certain people who are concerned about protecting their right to privacy from intrusion by electronic snoopers claim that Menwith Hill is an National Security Agency (NSA) station which is rented to it by the British Government in defiance of British law, and that the NSA has no authority for keeping the public from trying to find out what is going on nor to keep the public off the base.

Menwith Hill in Yorkshire is an electronic eavesdropping SIGINT station which set up shop in 1966 and linked through satellite communications relaying stations which proceed from satellites fixed in position over the Equator. Reports I received put the number of U.S. NSA personnel at Menwith Hill at more than 1000 "interception specialists."

British Member of Parliament Max Madden, recently claimed that Menwith Hill is a switching station used to intercept private telephone calls in Britain and the United States, a practice forbidden by the laws of both countries and Madden says this goes on 24 hours a day. Switching stations long ago made obsolete a physical wire intercept on your telephone line. It can now be done by remote control from thousands of miles away. The days of voltage drop and clicking reels have long-since given way to silent, noiseless, undetectable, eavesdropping on a scale so massive as to be a menace to all free societies, everywhere.

LOSING OUR CONSTITUTIONAL RIGHTS

The problems facing our nation are rooted in the lack of knowledge of the Constitution and the Bill of Rights. We have far too much in the way of laws passed by the Congress without putting them to a test as to their constitutionality with the result that flagrant abuses of the

Constitution and the Bill of Rights are made "the law" on an almost daily basis. No law becomes law unless it has passed scrutiny as to its constitutionality. And about 70 percent of all laws passed since 1933 are unconstitutional because they failed to meet the stringent test as to their constitutionality. These so-called "laws" are null and void and must be eradicated as soon as possible.

What is the solution to the lawlessness sweeping over our nation? The solution lies in the hands of We, the People and we who have read the Annals of Congress, the Congressional Globes and the Congressional Records for a minimum period of five years, we know what has to be done. We must appoint State committees made up of competent people who have met the requirement of having knowledge of the Constitution and the Bill of Rights. These committees would study all laws passed since the 1900 and make recommendations to Congress that unconstitutional laws be annulled. The committees will compel the Congress to take the necessary action and free this nation of the Communist yoke around the necks of our people.

"FEDERAL" ELECTIONS

We hear people talking all the time about "Federal" elections, especially the jackals of the media who are prone to use this expression. The fact is that the Federal Government has no voters, and it can make none, so how then can it hold Federal elections? Congressional Record, Senate, June 27, 1879, pages 2388-2397, Senator Wallace:

"The Federal Government has no voters; it can make none; it can constitutionally control none...When it asserts the power to create and hold elections or to control the conduct of the voter on 'election day' or maintain equal 'suffrage' it tramples underfoot the very basis of the Federal System and seeks to build a consolidated government of democratic republic. This is plain purpose of the men in control of the Federal Government, and to this end, the teachings of leading republicans are now shaped. There are no national voters. Voters who vote for national representatives are qualified by State Constitutions and State laws and national citizenship is not required of a voter of the State by any provision of the Federal Government or in practice."

This makes the Federal Election Commission (FEC) one hundred percent unconstitutional and abuse of power by the Federal Government. It leaves the FEC outside of the Constitution, as dead as a dodo and about as able to do anything about elections as that extinct bird. In short the FEC is dead and null and void. The FEC cannot create a new class of national voters, because to do so would violate Article 1, Sec. IV Part 1 of the Constitution.

FLAG DEBATE

Led by Senator Diane Feinstein, the flag debate reached the height of absurdity and once again proved, if indeed it needed further proof, that only a handful of those in the Senate know what the United States Constitution and the Bill of Rights are about. Oh, they can recite the various articles and clauses, but when it comes to demonstrating an understanding the depth of profundity and the layer upon layer of complexities of the Constitution, they are weighed in the balance and found wanting.

Latterly, Sen. Feinstein has emerged as a committed enemy of the Constitution and the Bill of Rights. While carrying a concealed weapon, Feinstein goes about the country, railing about how terrible guns are. In the Senate, she grossly violated her oath of office and her pledge to uphold the Constitution, by making several attempts to abridge the 2nd Amendment, an act of treason. As I have so often said, our Founding Fathers regarded a violation of the oath of office as a heinous crime, and rightly so. The reason we are drowning in a cesspool of rotten "laws" is that the penalty for treason is not carried out. The penalty for treason is found in the Act of the First Congress, Sec 9.

Now comes Feinstein posing concern for the flag and she wants an amendment to the Bill of Rights to defend the flag from desecrators. If her wish were granted, it would be the first ever amendment to the Bill of Rights. I believe that Feinstein has a warped, ulterior motive, and that is, she wants to open the door to future proposed amendments to the Bill of Rights which would have the effect of nullifying much of it.

There is no need for a debate on the flag. Had the senators done their homework, they would have known this. There ought to be a provision in State law that would make it mandatory for any would-be senator or representative to first have to spend at least five years in the study of the Annals of Congress, the Congressional Globes and the Congressional Record, before they can represent We, the People, in Washington D.C.

Feinstein does not appear to be aware that the Constitution and the Bill of Rights cannot be compromised. To infringe a fundamental right to the Constitution, as happened with passage of the Brady bill and the so-called "assault weapons" ban, is an impossibility under our Constitution. Unless and until the 2nd Amendment is repealed, both these "laws" are ultra-vires and of no force or effect. Feinstein should have been impeached the minute she introduced her "assault weapons" bill.

Socialist Feinstein follows the Communist tradition of crafting words and phrases that are not in the Constitution and giving them an infallible meaning. A hammer used to kill someone is an "assault weapon." A knife used to kill someone is another "assault weapon." Carried to its logical absurdity, Feinstein should now designate different types of hammers and knives as "assault weapons" which should be banned.

The old ploy used in the Brady bill and the "assault weapons" bill, that they are anti-crime measures, dates back to the Communist Manifesto of 1848. Lenin, a staunch advocate of gun control, told his followers: "Only the Soviets can effectively arm the proletariat and disarm the bourgeoisie. Unless this is done, victory for Socialism is impossible."

So there we have it. Until the Socialists who infest the House and Senate can disarm We, the People, their goal of a One World Socialist Government for the United States cannot be realized. No one can doubt that Feinstein is one of the leading Socialists in the Senate, while in the House, that dubious distinction falls to Rep. Charles Schumer, an equally staunch advocate of compromising the Constitution, who demonstrates his abysmal ignorance of the Constitution almost every time he opens his mouth.

Yet, Schumer enjoys wide support in the Pentagon, and of course, the White House. The Omnibus Counter Terrorism Act of 1995 was largely drafted by the Pentagon, or at least its key portions were. There was absolutely no need for this bill; everything in it is already covered by the scores of existing sedition laws and especially, the Sedition Act of October 16, 1918. Much of the Pentagon-Schumer bill is a Bill of Attainder and expost facto violations, forbidden by the United States Constitution.

Show me a person holding office who advocates gun control and I will show you a would-be tyrant.

To get back to the debate on the U.S. Flag. In the first place, the flag does not come under the 1st Amendment, but under the War Powers of

Congress. I can find no mention of the flag in the 1st Amendment, nor is it expressly implied therein. The U.S. Constitution, does, in many other places express powers to protect the U.S. flag from desecration in public.

Protection of the U.S. flag is covered in the war powers of the Congress. Article 1, Section 8, Clause 13: "To provide a Navy." Here it is expressly implied that a Navy ship must have a U.S. flag under its protection. Clause II: "To declare war, grant letters of marque and reprisals and make rules concerning capture on land and water." It is expressly implied that the U.S. flag is a symbol of sovereignty of the nation, and therefore, has no connection with the 1st Amendment.

The U.S. flag accompanies our armed services to war to identify them from enemy forces, and to inspire them as a symbol of loyalty to uphold the sovereignty of the United States, and is also similarly held by our armed services in peacetime. It is expressly implied that the U.S. flag is under regulation in both war and peace.

Article 1, Section 8, Clause 15: "To provide for calling forth the militia to execute the laws of the Union etc." Here it is expressly implied that the U.S. flag is called out to "execute the laws, suppress insurrection and repel invasions."

The U.S. flag is protected under the provision of treason in Article III, Section 3, Part 1: "Treason against the United States shall consist only of levying war against them, or adhering to their enemies, giving them aid and comfort etc." Expressly implied in these words is the protection of the U.S. flag. When a person desecrates the U.S. flag in public where there are two or more witnesses, it is an overt act of treason, and they can be tried for treason. We don't need an amendment to the Bill of Rights — we already have the powers needed to deal with desecration of the U.S. flag.

Auxiliary powers of Congress contained in Article 1, Section 8, Clause 18, "To make all laws which shall be necessary and proper for carrying into execution the foregoing powers, and all powers vested in the Government of the United States, or in any department thereof." President Monroe called these the secondary powers of Congress and he defined Article 1, Section 8, as the primary powers.

The two words, "necessary" and "proper" protect the U.S. flag from desecration in the Congress and its war powers and it is "necessary" and "proper" for the House and Senate to protect the U.S. flag under its war powers. In addition, the U.S. flag is protected in its integrity and implied sovereignty under the war powers in our many scores of sedition laws. It is not generally known that the United States has many, many, sedition laws.

Sedition laws go back to the first or early session of Congress and they are Constitutional. Then there is the Sedition Act of 1918 (Oct. 16, 1918.) These laws were passed as Congress realized the dreadful danger to the United States arising from the hordes of Eastern European "refugees," who were, for the most part, virulent Communists, anarchists or Socialists coming to the United States with the intent and purpose of Socializing, then Communizing the country.

The Sedition Act of 1918 is a particularly efficacious law. Some of it can be found in the Congressional Record, Senate, Feb. 5, 1923, pages 3005-3027. The language of the act refers to "anarchists" but in reality, they were Communist terrorists, in deed and purpose, but, in political persuasion, they were Communists of the most virulent kind ever to set foot on these shores.

From Sec. 1 of the Sedition Act of October 16, 1918:

"That aliens who are anarchist aliens who believe in or advocate the overthrow by force or violence the government of the United States or of all forms of law: Aliens who advocate and teach the unlawful, destruction of property (and note an important point here, it does not say PUBLIC property, therefore it includes the destruction of the U.S. flag); aliens who are members of or affiliated with any organization that entertains a belief in, teaches, or advocates the overthrow by force by violence (aimed at Communists and their A.C.L.U. protectors) or violence of the Government of the United States or of all forms of law or that entertains or teaches disbelief in or opposition to all organized Government, or that advocates the duty, necessary, or propriety of the unlawful assaulting or killing of any officers, either of specific individuals or of officers generally of the government of the United States or of any of its organization, because of his or hers or their official character, or that advocate or teaches the unlawful destruction of property (and again it does not say *public* property, which will then include the U.S. flag), shall be excluded from admission to the U.S. etc."

Of course Comrade Earl Warren prostituted the Supreme Court by attempting to make it "lawful" for the anarchists-Communists to overthrow the Republic and in his endeavor he was ably assisted by Comrade William O.Douglas. Similarly, later judges tried to make it "legal" to

burn or otherwise destroy or desecrate the U.S. flag by predilections —
reading their own thoughts into the Constitution, forbidden by the 9th
Amendment. Justice Warren was particularly guilty of committing
heinous treason by taking treason cases out of the jurisdiction of State
courts where they rightfully belonged, thus in effect, making the United
States Constitution, "a blank piece of paper by construction" to quote
Thomas Jefferson.

Warren did the unspeakable; he used the 1st Amendment and blithe-
ly ignored the balance of the Constitution, a sure way to commit treason
and get away with it. This foul tactic was also the forte of Justice
William O. Douglas who virtually wrecked the Constitution through his
unprincipled tactics.

With regard to the U.S flag: As a rule of thumb, wherever one hears
the war powers of Congress recited, or reads about the war powers in the
Congressional Records, then one must realize that it is synonymous with
the protection, physically, and integrity of sovereignty, of the U.S. flag.
This is why when the flag is lowered on military establishments, it never
touches the ground and is folded in the shape of George Washington's
hat. One of the first visible signs of sovereignty of any nation is its flag.
Desecration of the U.S. flag is, therefore, desecration of our nation's
sovereignty, an act of treason, punishable under a host of sedition laws.
The bottom line is that we don't need Socialists like Feinstein and Boxer
meddling with the Bill of Rights out of supposed patriotism.

Is Feinstein trying to isolate the clauses of the Constitution and
rights under the Bill of Rights? I would suspect this is her intention.
Through the subterfuge of isolating the Articles of the Constitution,
Comrades Douglas and Warren rendered yeoman service to the
Socialists, anarchists and Communists in reading their own thoughts
into, and thereby subverting the Constitution. The cause of Socialism
was well served by Douglas and Warren, whose goal was the overthrow
of the Constitution. To attempt to isolate the various clauses of the
Constitution is to commit treason. There is no place in the Republic for
those who commit treason.

BIBLIOGRAPHIC REFERENCES FROM ANNALS OF CONGRESS, CONGRESSIONAL GLOBE AND CONGRESSIONAL RECORD

Please note that where actual Congressional sources are delineated they appear in the text. Otherwise references are used in a wide-ranging accurate manner as source material to add weight to statements on the Constitution and Bill of Rights. Therefore, the bibliography is not cross-referenced in the usual way as this would take at least 500 separate pages to accomplish. For this reason not all Congressional sources are listed below:

TREATIES/AGREEMENTS: U.N.: OTHERS

Pages 5981-5991	House.	Jun. 12, 1945
Pages 8008 8029	Senate.	Jul. 24 1945
Pages 8175-8191	Senate.	Jul. 28, 1945
Pages 16964-16974	Senate.	Nov. 26, 1945
Pages 12267-12288	Senate.	Dec. 18, 1945
Pages 6308-6312	House.	Jun. 14, 1898.
Pages 17943-17934	Senate.	Oct. 9 1975. Gulf of Tonkin Resolution
Pages 218-220	House.	Jan 19, 1977. On U.N.
Pages 5684-5687	Senate.	Sep. 22, 1919
Pages 447-449	Senate.	Jan 6, 1899
Pages 6586-6589	Senate.	Jul. 1, 1898
Pages 4046-4050	House.	Apr. 11, 1900. On treaties
Pages 4046-4050	House.	Apr. 11, 1900. On sovereignty
Pages 336-340	House.	Apr. 11, 1900. On Constitution
Pages 6751-6753	House.	Nov. 1, 1977. On U.N. "revolution"
Page 2891	House.	April 3, 1978. Panama Canal Fraud
Pages 5163-5168	Senate.	April 10, 1978. Panama Canal
Pages 225-247	Senate.	April 10, 1978. Panama Canal Swindle
Pages 250-273	Senate.	April 10, 1978. Panama Canal Payments
Pages 249-293	Senate.	April 10, 1978. Panama Canal Fraud
Pages 313-330	Senate.	April 10, 1978. Panama Canal Swindle
Pages E1145-1147	Senate.	April 10, 1978. Panama Canal Cost

Pages 118-120	Senate.	April 10, 1978. Vattel's Law of Nations, exposes Canal Treaty as a fraud
Pages 11717-11724	Senate.	Jul. 25, 1978 Abrogation
Pages 1300-1315	Senate.	Feb. 14, 1879 Constitutional law of Treaties
Pages 12267-12287	House.	Dec. 18, 1945. Exposes fake treaty
Pages 8008-8029	Senate.	Jul. 25, 1945
Pages 7998-8003	Senate.	Jul. 24, 1945. U.N. Charter
Pages 8175-8191	Senate.	Jul. 28, 1945. Charter ratified
Pages 1305-1306	Senate.	Feb. 14, 1879. Treaty only a law
Pages 7069-7079	House.	May 16, 1922. Treaty-making powers
Pages 2916-2920	Senate.	May 8, 1919. League of Nations
Pages 5678-5687	House.	Sep. 22, 1919. League of Nations

CIVIL RIGHTS DEBATES PRE AND POST CIVIL WAR

Pages 340-344	Dec. 9, 1873
Pages 945-950	Jan. 27, 1874
Pages 1249-1254	May 12, 1879. Senate. Judge Story
Pages 4138-4139	Apr. 18, 1896. Dartmouth College case
Pages 2932-2936	Apr. 2, 1890. Dartmouth College case
Pages 4153-4159	May 22, 1874. Dartmouth College Case
Pages 2932-2936	Apr. 2, 1890. On 13th, 14th, 15th Amendments
Pages 4782-4789	June 9, 1874. Senate. civil rights-Constitution
Pages 1791-1797	Feb. 26, 1875 civil rights-Constitution
Pages 2314-2318	Feb. 26, 1875.
Pages 113-117	Feb. 27, 1875.
Pages 4144-4153	May 22, 1874
Pages 256-159	Appendix Feb. 3, 1897.
Pages 103-105	Appendix Feb. 26, 1875. Senate.
Pages 1791-1797	Feb. 26, 1875.
Pages 103-105	Feb. 26, 1875. Senate.
Pages 373-385	Jan. 5, 1874. Lincoln's views on civil rights.
Pages 7973-7999	Aug. 27, 1888. Details Lincoln on civil rights and Negroes.
Pages 113-117	Feb. 27, 1875. House.
Pages 156-159	Feb. 3, 1875. House.
Pages 404-423	Jan. 6, 1874. House. Exposes unconstitutionality.

13th, 14th, 15th AMENDMENTS & RECONSTRUCTION

Pages 487-493	Jan. 18, 1882
Pages 2283-2285	Oct. 1893, House
Pages 288-291	Appendix Cong. Rec. March 3, 1919. House
Pages 1723-1727	Jan. 25, 1922. House Thaddeus Stevens
Pages 1162-1176	Apr. 4, 1865. South encouraged to secede
Pages 353-361	May 18, 19, 1870. Congr. Globe. On abuse by coercion, quotes coercion "as the means upon which modern Caesar's feed." "Equal protection" A fairy tale. Abused by Fed. courts.
Pages 2459-2468	May 8, 1866. Con. Globe Reconstruction — civil rights
Pages 2938-2944	Jun. 4, 1866. Con. Globe Secret committee wrote 14th Amnd.
Pages 62-66	Mar. 11, 1867. Con. Globe."Reorganization of rebel States."
Pages 279-284	Jan 4, 1867. Con. Globe. "Ours only country where treason made respectable and exempted from punishment."
Pages 108-111	Appndx. Cong. Globe Jan. 25, 1868. On Supreme Court.
Pages 110-117	Appndx. Cong. Globe. Feb. 5, 1868. First time term "Reconstruction" used.
Pages 8-12	Appndx. Cong. Globe Apr. 9, 1869. Amplifies significance of 3rd section of 14th Amendment which unless removed bars 14th from being ratified.
Pages 22-26	Cong. Globe Dec. 21, 1869. 13th, 14th and 15th amendments never ratified.

A CHRISTIAN NATION

Holy Trinity Church v. United States 1430US 471
Separation of Church & State not in Constitution. "To Build A Wall" by G. Ivers
Pages S4128 1132. pr. 5, 1979. Prayer in schools

LEADING PRINCIPLES OF CONSTITUTION

Pages 36-38	Oct. 20 1888 House. Appdx to Congr. Rec
Pages 7562-7566	Aug. 15,1888 Senate. Definition of treason
Pages 3374-3377	Jul. 31, 1911. Senate. History of U.S. Const
Pages 2314-2318	Feb. 26, 1897. Senate. General principles.

Pages 200-202   Jun. 13, 1913. House. Speeches Washington, Jefferson
Pages 681-700   Appendix Cong. Rec. House Jun. 30 and Jul. 2, 1899
                           Federal Election Law.
Pages 2315-2318   Oct. 9, 1893. House. Federal Elections.

CONGRESS HAS FIXED RULES OF WAR

Pages 8942-8950   Sept. 26, 1888. House. Defines Public wars etc.
Pages 1978-1980   Feb. 1897. Senate. Details on declaration of war
Pages 3773-3776   Apr. 13, 1898. Senate. Joint Declaration of War
Pages 8733-8737   Aug. 18, 1890. Senate. Polk talks about Public
                           and Private war and definition of declaration of
                           war and Constitution

Blackstone's Commentaries
Vattel's "Law of Nations"   } All say no authority for
"Twenty Years of Congress" J. Blaine   } suspending the
"Commentaries on the U.S. Constitution." Judge Story. } Constitution.

Pages 5405-5408   Apr. 22, 1918. War powers of the President.
Pages 319-412   April 5, 1917. House. Constitutional declaration
                           of War against Germany.
Pages 3994-3998   May 16, 1882. House. Declaration of War.
Pages 7878-7796   Oct. 6, 1917. Senate. On declaration of war, authority
                           of president.
Pages 6635-6654   Jul. 21 1888. House. Deals with limited and
                           unlimited wars, perfect and imperfect wars.
Pages 7786-7795   Oct. 4, 1917. On power to declare war.
Pages 2916-2920   Senate Jul. 21 1922: President is not the commander in
                           chief until "called into service by Congress."
Page 319   House Apr. 15, 1917. House of Representatives Rpt
                           No. 1. References other than Annals of Congr.
                           Congr. Globe. Congr. Recd.
Page 329   Appendix "Blackstone's Commentaries" which says
                           Pres. is not automatically commander in chief.
                           William Rawles. "A View of the Constitution."
Page 122, Vol. 4 Pt 7.   44th Session, 1876. John Marshall "Constitution
                           an instrument of grants and powers and inhibitions."
                           Defines treason.

CONSTITUTION GOLD-SILVER EXPOST FACTO LAWS, BILL OF
ATTAINDER, GENERAL WELFARE CLAUSE.

Pages 3554-3555	April 3, 1896. Senate. Record of what George Washington said about the Constitution.
Pages 1256-1259	Feb. 12, 1890. House. Constitutionality of House Rules.
Pages 3994-3998	May 16, 1883. House. All money for contracts in gold and silver.
Page 3989	May 8, 1884. House. Explains General Welfare Clause.
Pages 2817-2819	Jul. 18, 1919. Senate. League of Nations.
Pages 2916-2920	Jul. 21, 1919. Senate. U.S. cannot be a member of the League of Nations.
Pages 2109-2114	Jan. 27, 1919. Senate. U.S. could not join League.
Pages 1638-1641	Jan. 29, 1901. House. Meaning of "land" as in "law of the land", Magna Carta, explained.
Pages 6548-6561	Apr. 21, 1916. Senate. Contains speeches by James Monetary Control Act of 1980 signed by Pres. Carter. Monroe on the Constitution.
Pages 1198-1201	Feb. 16, 1882. Senate. Explains Bill of Attainder and expost facto laws.
Pages 332-338	Jun. 26, 1884. House. Constitutional problems with the idea of Federal aid to schools.
Pages 459-467	Dec. 17, 1921. On delegated powers.

COURTS AND CONGRESS

Pages 2132-2135	Feb. 15, 1936. Says courts can review Acts of Congress.
Pages 3837	Congressional Record Feb. 27, 1923. Discusses Chief Justice John Marshall Elliot's Debate Vol 3. Page 560. Congress can make exception to Supreme Court rulings. i.e. can over turn them.
Pages 85-89 Appndx	Cong. Globe Jan. 13 1868. Powers of Supreme Court. Jefferson describes it as an "oligarchy."
Pages 108-111 Appndx	Cong. Globe, Jan. 13,1868. Reconstruction and Supreme Court. 1884 Supreme Court declared civil rights act of 1875 unconstitutional. Invalidates civil rights act of 1965.
Pages 167-160	Cong. Globe Dec. 16, 1869. On restrictions Supreme Court to issue habeas corpus.
Pages E5287-E5289	Jun. 26, 1969. Unlawful behavior Justice Douglas.

CITIZENS AND CITIZEN'S RIGHTS
Vattel's "Law of Nations" pages 478-479. Explains constitutional meaning of citizenship. Prohibits "instant citizenship" of children of illegal aliens born on U.S. soil. Congressional Record, House, Pages 4257-4259. Says "subject to jurisdiction of U.S. government is key. Illegal aliens not subject to jurisdiction of U.S. government."

Dred Scott v. Hanford.
Howard 19, U.S. report. Civil rights citizenship.

Pages 1051-1062	Feb. 27 1866. Cong. Globe. About naturalization.
Pages 1083-1095	Apr. 18 1961. Rights of citizens.Who started Civil War. Democrats & Republicans settled old scores.

ABORTION
Vattel's Law of Nations prohibits abortion
Pages 12711-1217 Senate, Feb. 22 1979. Unconstitutional

9th AMENDMENT

Pages 2286-2296.	Feb. 26, 1900. Senate. Gives definition of 9th Amendment
Pages 2273-2297	Feb. 20, 1890 House

10th AMENDMENT

Pages 2273-2279	House, Judge Cooley. Feb. 15, 1883. Sen Calhoun. Congressional Globe Jan. 31, 1866. Fixes limits Fed. Govt.

2nd AMENDMENT AND PERSONAL RIGHT TO KEEP AND BEAR ARMS: GUN CONTROL

Pages 4914-4917	Sept. 8, 1976. House
Pages 4557-4762	Aug. 23, 1976. House
Pages 717-718	Feb. 8, 1976. House
Pages 8092-8094	Jul. 30, 1976. House
Pages 3846-3847	Jul. 16, 1975. House
Pages 20963-20965	Dec. 8, 1975. Senate
Page 5322	Oct. 8, 1975. House
Pages 6459-6460	Dec. 5, 1975. House. Tyranny, Federal Gun Control
Pages 1138-1140	Mar. 9, 1976. House
Pages 6650-6552	Oct. 25, 1977. House

Pages 5092-5094	Jun. 7, 1978. House. Vote against BATF gun control
Pages 3578-3589	May 28, 1978. Senate. Right settled by Const.
Pages E6650-E6657	Oct. 25, 1977. House. "Facts, Gun Control."
Pages H2713-2715	Apr. 1, 1976. House. "Police against registry."
Page H-7766	Jul. 22, 1976. House. "Crime not reduced by gun control."
Pages E3846-E3647	Jul. 16, 1975. House. "Right to bear arms."
Pages 4914-E4917	Sep. 8, 1976, Sen. "Right to bear arms."
Pages 7636-7638	Sep. 10, 1979, House. "BATF unconstitutional." Oregon State Const. Ar1. Sec. 27 Guarantees right bear arms.

DEFINITION OF REPUBLICAN FORM OF GOVERNMENT.

| Page 903 | Feb. 18, 1896 House. A good definition. |

FEDERAL RESERVE BOARD/BANKS
"Collected Speeches Louis T. McFadden."

Pages 4368-370	Feb. 23, 1923. House.
Pages 325-328	Mar. 25, 1923. Senate.
Pages 3422-3424	Jul. 3, 1919. Senate.
Pages 9287-9290	May 27, 1914. Senate. About panic of 1907.
Pages 1441-1454	Dec. 22, 1913. House. Rep. Lindbergh.
Pages 9284-9286	May 27, 1914. Senate.
Pages 5573-5576	Apr. 24, 1918. House.
Pages 5988-9009	Nov. 24, 1913. Senate.
Pages 744-752	Nov. 24, 1912. House.
Pages 1297-1302	Dec. 20, 1913. House.
Pages 7024-7028	Jul. 17, 1975. House.
Pages 6357-6360	Jun. 27, 1898. Senate.
Pages 744-752	Jan. 9, 1912. National Monetary Committee scope of duties.
Pages 4890-4894	Mar. 24, 1924. House. Role in Stock Mkt. Crash.
Pages 1441-1452	Dec. 1913. Debate limited to four hours.

"MONETARY CONTROL ACT OF 1980" SIGNED BY PRES. CARTER.

| Pages 1297-1302 | Dec. 20, 1913, House. |
| Pages 418-424 | Jan. 7, 1898. Senate. "Signal of danger." Law 12, USC. Fed. Res. exempted from taxation. |

Congressional Record, Appendix pages 33558-33559. Nov. 6, 1969.

COMMUNIST PENETRATION OF HOUSE AND SENATE: FRONTS USED.

Pages 12924-12951	Jul. 1, 1926. Senate. Details fraud of "Children's Bureau" pushed by Communist Florence Kelly. Also deals with Communist-front National Education Assoc.
Pages 12892-12895	Jul. 30, 1976. Creeping Socialism.
Pages 2820-2842	Feb. 8, 1917. Senate. Exposes Rockefeller's attempt to control education in America through General Education Board.
Pages 6852-6894	Nov. 26, 1974. House. Communist intrusion in so-called "coalition" governments.
Pages 9962-9967	May 31, 1924. Regulation of Child Labor covers Communist infiltration of "Women's movement" and "Children's Bureau."
Pages 991-992	Mar. 2, 1978. Lists Communist front operatives behind Canal giveaway.
Pages 3234-3236	House Jul. 3, 1945. Exposes Communist penetration of Womens Rights and proposers of the Equal Rights Amendment.
Page 15492	Sep. 10, 1978. Senate. Lists Communist backers ERA.
Pages 9971-9977	May 31, 1924. Hull House female Socialists.
Pages S3381 3388	Mar. 26, 1979. U.N. "Int.Year of the Child."

FOREIGN AID

Pages 3630-3645	Mar. 2, 1977. Senate.
Pages 407-431	Jan. 25, 1978. Senate IDC.
Pages H2017-H2036.	IDC and money wasted on foreign govts.

MILITIA AND NATIONAL GUARD

Pages 5283-5288	Apr. 1, 1916. Senate.
Pages 12949	Cong. Globe Feb. 14, 1867. Militia Civil war period.
Pages 80-87	Cong. Globe Dec. 15, 1868. Militia in Southern States.

EDUCATION

Pages 100-103	Cong. Globe May 29,1870. Discusses national disaster of poor education. The Hon S.N. Arnell.
Pages 9962-9977	May 31, 1924. Maternity & Infancy Act.

For other titles by Dr. John Coleman, call
(800) 729-4131

Conspirators' Hierarchy:
The Story of the Committee of 300
ISBN: 0-922356-57-2

Diplomacy By Deception
ISBN: 0-9640104-8-8

One World Order: Socialist Dictatorship
ISBN: 0-9640104-9-6

For other titles
call
800-729-4131